The Postcolonial Aura

The Postcolonial Aura

Third World Criticism in the Age of Global Capitalism

Arif Dirlik

WestviewPress

A Division of HarperCollins*Publishers*

Copyright © 1997 by Westview Press, A Member of the Perseus Books Group

Published in 1998 in the United States of America by Westview Press, 5500 Central Avenue, Boulder, Colorado 80301-2877, and in the United Kingdom by Westview Press, 12 Hid's Copse Road, Cumnor Hill, Oxford OX2 9JJ

Library of Congress Cataloging-in-Publication Data
Dirlik, Arif.
    The postcolonial aura : Third World criticism in the age of global
capitalism / Arif Dirlik.
        p.   cm.
    Includes bibliographical references and index.
    ISBN 0-8133-3249-4
    1. Developing countries—Historiography.   2. Culture—Study and
teaching.   I. Title.
D883.D57   1997
306—dc21   96-46800
                                                                          CIP

The paper used in this publication meets the requirements of the American National Standard for Permanence of Paper for Printed Library Materials Z39.48-1984.

10   9   8   7   6   5   4   3   2   1

Contents

Preface

The essays in this volume range in coverage from questions of cultural self-representation in China and problems in the construction of a Pacific region to more general problems of reconceptualizing global relationships in a way that is appropriate to contemporary circumstances. They are guided by two primary motivations. First is to evaluate critically contemporary reconceptualizations of the post–World War II mapping of global relations in terms of the Three Worlds idea; especially in the so-called postcolonial criticism that is currently fashionable. Second is to formulate alternative modes of analysis that recognize the radical transformations in global relations, while insisting on the necessity of recalling the political aspirations of earlier radical conceptualizations of global relations that were embedded in an urge to create alternative modernities, which are suppressed in much of a cultural criticism dominated by postmodernism and its "off-EuroAmerican" offshoot, postcolonialism. In the process, I seek to place the idea of postcoloniality in historical perspective, to bring into relief its intellectual and political implications, which resonate with the ideology of a transnational capitalism.

Against the repudiation in postcolonial criticism of global or translocal structures and metanarratives in the name of localized encounters and the politics of identity, I insist that attention to structural context, especially the context of a globalized capitalism, is necessary not just to grasp contemporary global relations, but the very phenomenon of postcolonial criticism, with its insistence on the autonomy of culture and the priority it gives to questions of ethnicity and culture over earlier concerns with class and gender. Postcolonial criticism is vague in compass; in current usage, "postcolonial critics" occupy a broad political spectrum, from Marxist-feminists such as Gayatri Spivak to Stuart Hall and Paul Gilroy, who seek to ground the politics of identity in the material circumstances of capitalism, to idealist constructionists such as Homi Bhabha, whose intellectual stances suggest but a leftish libertarianism. It may not be too surprising that the version of "postcolonial criticism" that has exerted the greatest influence in American universities is that which has foregrounded the politics of identity against questions of structure and totality, that finds in "hybridity," "heterogeneity," and "in-betweenness" (terms that Bhabha has done much to popularize) keys to the resolution of problems that plague contemporary societies.

Postcolonial criticism provides an example of how cultural criticism, through an inflation of its claims or an unbridled expansion of its scope, may dissipate its critical energies to end up in an uncritical, and narcissistic, celebration of its own novelty. Like its progenitor, postmodernism, postcolonialism has its intellectual origins in the poststructuralist revolt against the very real limitations of Eurocentric modernity (in both its liberal and Marxist versions), and has answered a very real critical need: not only in calling into question the obliviousness to the local of generalized notions of modernity, but also in calling attention to problems of a novel nature that have emerged with recent transformation in global political and social relations. The former includes, in addition to the homogenizing claims of modernity, its oppositional by-products that reify collective identities of one kind or another, with consequences that are often divisive, at times genocidal. The latter entails both the structural transformations that have attended the globalization of capitalism, and the related reconfiguration of post–World War II economic and political boundaries with the emergence of new social forces that find in the scrambling of reified identities outlets for expressing their own desires for liberation.

Postcolonial criticism has quickly spent its critical power, however, as its questioning of totalizing solutions has turned into exclusion from criticism of the historical and the structural contexts for the local, without reference to which criticism itself is deprived of critical self-consciousness and, as it celebrates itself, knowingly or unknowingly also celebrates the conditions that produced it. Whether postcolonial criticism has been appropriated by those who did not share its initial critical intentions is a moot question, as its methodological denial of structures and its methodological individualism have facilitated such appropriation.

Rather than a critique of earlier radicalisms from the inside as initially intended, postcolonialism in its unfolding has turned into a repudiation of the possibility of radical challenges to the existing system of social and political relations. Its preoccupation with local encounters and the politics of identity rules out a thoroughgoing critique of the structures of capitalism, or of other structurally shaped modes of exploitation and oppression, while also legitimizing arguments against collective identities that are necessary to struggles against domination and hegemony. Ironically, the call for attention to "difference" has ended up rendering "difference" itself into a metahistorical principle, making it nearly impossible to distinguish one kind of "difference" from another politically. The repudiation of teleology in postcolonial criticism (and postmodernism in general) has created intellectual spaces for the voicing of alternatives to a Eurocentric modernity, allowing significant speech to those silenced earlier, or disdained as castaways from history. On the other hand, the same postcolonialism is quick to undermine such alternatives by denying the possibility of authenticity of claims to collective identity. What theory giveth, theory taketh away, almost as soon as it has been given! At their most bizarre, so-called postcolonial critics have directed their condemnation against radicalisms past and present which, for their insistence on the importance of structures of power, have been charged with perpetuating "Eurocentrisms" or "colonialisms" that erase the subjectivities of the oppressed. The postcolonialist argument more often than not ends up in interpretations of the past and the present that differ little from earlier liberal interpretations, and as in those interpretations, at times end up blaming the victims of oppression for their own oppression, all in the name of affirming their subjectivities. It is not very surprising then that postcolonialism should have been favored with quick acceptance in the cultural institutions of capitalism.

The postcolonialist attacks on Eurocentrism, and especially the legacy of the Enlightenment, have ruffled feathers in those institutions, to be sure. Nevertheless, postcolonialism has been domesticated with relative ease (in a way, say, Marxism has not) into intra-elite conflicts within those institutions: between those who appreciate the utility of the postcolonialist argument under conditions of transnational capitalism, which can no longer be satisfied with Eurocentrism, and those who have refused to come to terms with recent transformations in global relations. The social and political solutions that have issued from the postcolonialist argument, namely arguments for multiculturalism and diversity against racial and patriarchal domination, resonate with the demands of a new social and political situation. At the same time, however, the postcolonialist focus on Eurocentrism to the exclusion of the structural connections between Eurocentric power and capitalism also provides an alibi against radical critiques of capitalism, shifting the debate over capitalism from the terrain of political economy to the terrain of culture. The postcolonialist fetishization of "difference," compelled by its logic to the level of the individual, moreover, delegitimizes collective oppositions that articulate significant differences at levels of collective experience that the postcolonialist argument rejects for their supposedly "homogenizing" or "essentializing" assumptions. In theoretically repudiating in the name of local subjectivities such historical phenomena as colonialism and imperialism (or nationalist oppositions to it), postcolonialism relegates to an ideological or cultural Eurocentrism the responsibility for past inequalities and oppressions, which shifts the ground from under movements that challenge the continued domination of the world by EuroAmerican corporate and political power, that nourish off not just memories of past inequalities, but their contemporary legacies. Add to this the fact that postcolonialism, for all its claims to representing what used to be called the Third World, issues from transnational intellectuals located in the centers of power; the threat they represent to Eurocentrism in terms of real power is minimal—indeed, postcolonialism has been described by some as a Eurocentrism that, through the agency of intellectuals that hail from non-EuroAmerican locations and their EuroAmerican groupies, marginalizes the concerns of those who continue to be victimized by EuroAmerican power, albeit through agencies that are much more difficult to identify because of their transnationality. As a poet friend, Russell Leong, remarked recently, "Multiculturalism = postcolonial Eurocentrism." The multiple ironies of the equation are worth pondering.

Similar ironies may be observed in the by-now ritualized attacks on the Enlightenment in the name of postcolonialism. That the European Enlightenment owed much to European expansion over the globe, and was ideologically complicit with European colonialism, is not particularly fresh news. Reductionist readings that suppress the complexities of the "Enlightenment," however, invent a straw target against which to dramatize the novelty of intellectual claims which, upon closer examination, are hardly novel, but replay post-Enlightenment liberal and libertarian themes, dressed up in the garb of postmodernist or postcolonialist jargon. "Forgotten" in the process is that the same Enlightenment was also the source of new critiques of oppression and exploitation in societies both in and outside of Europe. It produced not just conservative and liberal arguments for the conquest of the world, but also anarchism, Marxism, feminism, secularism and, dare I say, postcolonialism. To deny the Enlightenment is to deny the historicity of the very critiques directed against it.

If arguments against the Enlightenment, especially in EuroAmerican locations, gain a hearing today, I would like to suggest, it is because they are directed as much against radical criticisms of capitalism (such as Marxism) as they are against the continued ideological domination of the world by a capitalism of European origin. More to the point may be the attacks on Enlightenment rationalism which, oddly enough, is inconsistent not just with non-EuroAmerican ways of thinking, but also with the demands of contemporary capitalism, which require a malleability of the individual (as consumer or producer) to which an insistence on rationality stands as an obstacle. Here, too, postcolonialism, and postmodernism in general, resonate with a contemporary Global Capitalism. The postcolonialist (and postmodernist) insistence on the world as a social construct, against a representation of the world that recognizes to it a reality beyond human will and cognition, expresses a voluntarism that is very much synchronous with contemporary capitalism (Disney professes a similar epistemology). The libertarian political implications of such an epistemological stance likewise reflect, and legitimize, the contemporary political situation, at least in the United States. An epistemology that offers no means to distinguish different "differences," or even reality and fiction, opens the way to such social and political manipulation. It also invites its own bankruptcy, to which the recent *Social Text* scandal stands as eloquent testimonial.

The epistemology need not be blamed for the politics. Constructionism does provide crucial critical insights into the operations of power. It could be placed in the service of "imagining communities," rather than a tiresome and counterproductive preoccupation with "imagined communities." The question is why contemporary critical thinking dissipates its energies on the latter, rather than worrying about the former? Postcolonialism, similarly to postmodernism, has offered critical insights into a current ideological situation, but has been delimited also by its own complicity in this ideological situation. I suggest that there are good social reasons for this delimitation. One of the outstanding deficiencies in post-colonial criticism is its disavowal of class relations, which are incomprehensible without reference to the structural conditions of post colonialism, especially the conditions of Global Capitalism. Postcolonialism, if it is to be grasped critically, must be grasped both in terms of the relationship of Third World to First World societies, but also in terms of global class relationships under a transnational capitalism: as an expression of intra-class contradictions in a class situation that is no longer to be contained within national boundaries. Ethnicities, cultures, etc. may be grasped in different ways, and subjected to different evaluations; as they appear presently, they represent conflicting claims to empowerment within a transnational class. This class needs to be distinguished, nevertheless, by the common interests in a current structural situation that define them as a class and distance them from the social hinterlands for which they claim to speak.

Hence my insistence in the essays to follow on the necessity of attention to structural conditions, as well as to different modes of understanding ethnicity and culture, within the context of a changing capitalism. In a number of the essays, I offer alternative modes of analysis that I think account for a new global situation and a recognition of the intellectual demands of postcoloniality. There is a condition of postcoloniality, in the concrete historical sense of the end of formal economic and political colonialism, that does call for new ways of thinking about local and global relations; but these new ways of thinking, if they are to be critical, must retain a sense both of history and structure—the historical legacy of colonialism (as well as revolutionary struggles against it), and the structures of reconfigured relations of power under contemporary capitalism (which invoke new forms of collective resistance and opposition).

Above all, it is necessary to refocus attention on alternative ways of thinking out the problems of the present and the imagination of the future. I am not at all certain myself of posing "Luddites" against "ludics," but I offer the juxtaposition as one way of shocking cultural criticism out of its present complacency to recall once again the seriously critical (and political) impulses that lay at its origins.

It would be impossible here to name all the friends, colleagues, teachers and students who have over the years offered support by way of ideas, inspiration, institutional backing, or exemplary intellectual and moral integrity. I acknowledge below their contributions to individual essays. I am grateful to Harry Harootunian, Epifanio (Sonny) San Juan, Jr., and Rob Wilson for their support as colleagues and friends over the years; they also played an important part in the realization of the project in its concluding phase. Roxann Prazniak has been a constant presence over the years during which these pieces were written; I doubt very much that I would have mustered the courage to propose some of the political positions I advocate below were it not for her inspiration and support.

Arif Dirlik

Credits

"Culturalism as Hegemony Ideology and Liberating Practice," *Cultural Critique* 6 (Spring 1987): 13–50. Reprinted in Abdul JanMohamed and David Lloyd (eds.), *The Nature and Context of Minority Discourse* (New York: Oxford University Press, 1990). Reprinted by permission.

"The Postcolonial Aura: Third World Criticism in the Age of Global Capitalism," *Critical Inquiry* 20.2 (Winter 1994): 328–356. Copyright © 1994 by the University of Chicago. All rights reserved.

"The Global in the Local," in Rob Wilson and Wimal Dissayanake (eds.), *Global/Local: Cultural Production and the Transnational Imaginary* (Durham, NC: Duke University Press, 1996). Reprinted by permission.

"Three Worlds or One, or Many? The Reconfiguration of Global Relations Under Contemporary Capitalism," published originally in *Nature, Society, Thought* 7.1 (1995): 19–42. Reprinted by permission.

"The Past as Legacy and Project: Postcolonial Criticism in the Perspective of Indigenous Historicism" was first published in *American Indian Culture and Research Journal* 20.2 (1996). Reprinted by permission of the Regents of the University of California.

The Postcolonial Aura

1

Introduction: Postcoloniality and the Perspective of History

The essays below are contributions to the ongoing effort in contemporary cultural criticism to comprehend the reconfiguration of global relations under conditions of what might be described synoptically as global postmodernity. The essays examine from a diversity of perspectives problems in the new ideological formations, or the critiques of ideology, that have accompanied the economic, social, political and cultural remapping of the world, especially that part of the world that was encompassed earlier by the term Third World. An underlying premise of the essays, of which they may be viewed as demonstrations in a variety of locations, is the existence of a structural resonance between postmodernity as a historical condition generated by transformations in capitalism, and postmodernism as a way of speaking about that condition. Some of the essays trace this connection through an examination of ideological transformations in the Asia-Pacific region, which happens to be my area specialty, but is also important in its own right as a generator of postmodernity because of the crucial role it has come to play in the globalization of capitalism. The majority of the essays engage from this same perspective of a global capitalism the theoretical and ideological questions raised by contemporary reconceptualizations of global relations that are informed by a variety of postmodern perspectives; but especially the one offshoot of postmodernism that goes by the designation of postcolonialism.

In the preface to his collection of essays on postmodernism, Fredric Jameson writes that, "I would not want to have to decide whether the following chapters are inquiries into the nature of . . . 'postmodernist theory,' or mere examples of it."[1] In the indecision is an acknowledgment that in the process of subjecting postmodernism to critical scrutiny, his own Marxist theoretical stance has been infiltrated, disturbed and reconfigured by postmodernism, blurring the distinction between a Marxist discourse on postmodernism and an appropriation of Marxism into the discourse of postmodernity.

A consistent Marxist materialism may be an important contributing factor in the blurring of boundaries between the two discourses. Jameson's seminal contribution to the discussion of postmodernism was his grounding of postmodernism in the transformations of everyday life under Late Capitalism, as "the cultural logic" of the latter. The same procedure, however, confronts Marxism not just with the discourse of postmodernity, but with the material circumstances to which that discourse speaks, presenting theory with the necessity of accounting for historical circumstances, the novelty of which defies efforts to contain them within its received categories. If it is to be something other than a nostalgic escape into the past or a utopian avoidance of the present, the Marxist critique of postmodernism must also account for the radical transformations reshaping the world, and ways of speaking about it. A thoroughgoing materialism requires that the theory which informs the critique of postmodernism must itself undergo self-criticism and reconfiguration in the very process of its critical operations, assuming at least some features of postmodernism—provided that there is indeed some structural connection between postmodernism and its historical circumstances.

There is a similar confounding in the essays below of boundaries between postmodernism and Marxism in their enunciations or applications within Third World contexts. Marxism appears in the discussions as an indispensable theoretical resource for understanding the forces structuring "the condition of postmodernity," which is not to be divorced from the structural changes brought about by Global Capitalism. On the other hand, the very affirmation of postmodernism as an equally indispensable way of speaking about that condition calls into question the spatial and temporal premises of Marxism as a theory of modernity. It is important to sustain these seemingly contradictory stances, I think, in order to speak about the world in new ways, while avoiding ideological entrapment in its aura of novelty.

It is for this same reason that I retain the designation "Third World" in the title of the volume, as well as in some of the essays below. I argue in one essay below that the Third World may never have had any significance other than as a discursive category, and may be quite meaningless presently with the transformation of the conditions to which an earlier discourse referred ("Three Worlds or One, or Many? The Reconfiguration of Global Relations under Contemporary Capitalism"). It is important nevertheless to recall the idea of a Third World against the currently fashionable notion of the postcolonial, which is equally discursive, not because the idea of Three Worlds has any descriptive relevance presently but because there were political meanings embedded in the ideal of a Third World that may still be relevant, and that carry with them a perspective of the past on the present, with the critical possibilities that such a perspective affords. In an ideological situation where the future has been all but totally colonized by the ideology of capital, we can ill afford to overlook the critical perspectives afforded by past alternatives that have been suppressed by the history of capital. I take the recovery of these alternatives in memory to be not regressive, but rather as a means to keeping alive alternative visions of society that may yet open up the future in new ways.

This is a theme that appears in all the essays below, gaining in emphasis in the progression of the essays (which are presented here in the order in which they were originally written) which in their unfolding should provide some indication of my own gropings toward possible answers to questions raised by my critique of existing critical positions. I take history to be crucial to a critical hermeneutic that seeks to sustain contradictions between the present and the past, so as to keep open the possibilities they may offer by way of living in the world, without resorting to ideological or metaphysical resolutions that nourish off a distant and uncertain future. As contributions to cultural criticism, the discussions below share a common ground in a concern to affirm the centrality of history against a tendency to its marginalization in much of contemporary cultural criticism. It is not that cultural critics do not speak about history; indeed, they speak about it a great deal, but in ways that, for methodological reasons, preempt the possibility of serious confrontation between the present, the past and the future; the postmodernist "naturalization of the language paradigm," John O'Neill writes, "is the ideological counterpart to the dehistoricization and the depoliticization of the capitalist process."[2] Given my own disciplinary location, the effort to foreground history may be construed as an attempt to recover a disciplinary domain from the intrusions of cultural critics who happen to be for the most part literary historians and critics. It is not. I hope it is sufficiently clear from the discussions below that my critique of cultural criticism where it falls short of a sufficient recognition of questions of history and historicity is accompanied by a recognition of value to new ways of reading history that it has brought to the fore, to which, unfortunately, historians have been conspicuously oblivious. My concern is not with disciplinary delineations of history, but rather with history as epistemology, the marginalization of which deprives us of a crucial dimension to be accounted for in any serious consideration of human liberation.

It is history and historicity as they have been reworked under the sign of the postmodern that guides the analyses below. One of the fundamental contributions of postmodernism—indeed a defining feature of postmodernity—is the questioning of the teleology of the modern, and of other teleologies imbedded in economic, political and cultural narratives that have constituted the idea of the modern; so that it becomes possible once again to conceive the past not merely as a route to the present, but as a source of alternative historical trajectories that had to be suppressed so that the present could become a possibility. While this questioning has opened up new possibilities in understanding the past, and has been equally important in opening up the past as a reservoir of multiple political possibilities, it has not eliminated therefore the forces that constituted modernity historically which persist as a burden of the past over the present. While it has undermined the claims of modernity on historical consciousness, it has been less successful in accounting for the contradictory consequences of repudiating the modern, and even for the ways in which the modern continues to inform the postmodern. Above all, the multiplicity of historical trajectories that have resurfaced in historical consciousness with the dethroning of the modern, and as both generators and beneficiaries of the postmodern, present contradictions that point to novel political possibilities as well as new political dangers. At the precise moment when a "pathos of novelty" (in Hannah Arendt's words) makes the past seem irrelevant to the present, the proliferation of such contradictions calls for an accounting of those forces shaping the present which is no more immune than earlier ages to the burden of history. The recognition that what we call history may be no more than an aggregate of interactive and contradictory histories, in the multiplicity of choices it presents, may indeed have increased the burden of history by eliminating the familiar landmarks provided by earlier teleologies. No longer merely a route to the present that may be relegated to the past as soon as it has been traversed, history confronts us as a source of conflicting choices, with all the intellectual and political responsibilities implied by the ability to choose without the benefit of teleological legitimation. To make matters worse, the evidence of daily life and politics provides constant reminder that, however we may pretend otherwise, the same history limits choice by providing the conditions under which we may make those choices.

Before I proceed to elaborate on the different ways in which I deploy history in the essays to confront some of these problems and contradictions, it is necessary to emphasize that with one exception that addresses the question of the relationship between postmodernism and contemporary corporate power, the essays below are not concerned with general problems of postmodernism. Neither am I concerned with postmodernism in literature or the arts, where it may have the most concrete and precise meaning. The postmodernism that is of primary interest here is that which represents a new mapping of problems of economic, social, political and cultural development; the immediate referents are modernity and modernization, rather than modernism. This is the sense also in which I view the term "postcolonialism," which is the version of postmodernism that is of the greatest relevance in the essays below.

What I suggested above of cultural criticism may be said with equal validity of postcolonial criticism: that the same epistemological premises that account for its insights into history may be responsible also for fundamental problems in its representation of the past and its relationship to the present. It is necessary, before going on to discuss the problem of history in relationship to postcolonial criticism, to spell out what I understand by the epistemological claims of postcolonialism. Given the diffuseness and residual quality of much of the postcolonial argument, these claims may not apply equally to all those who would describe themselves as postcolonial critics; conversely, others may share in some of these premises without necessarily describing themselves as postcolonial critics. Suffice it to say that the summarization of the postcolonial position here is based primarily on the orientations of those postcolonial critics who have been most anxious to liberate cultural criticism from its subjection to historical narratives that presuppose structural contexts of one kind or another; and whose works eschew any significant incorporation of such larger narratives into the explanatory schemes that they employ. It is my impression that this version of postcolonial criticism has exerted enormous influence in redirecting cultural criticism away from earlier orientations, associated mostly with Marxism but also with feminism, although some feminists seem to have been able to appropriate it for their own problems. I will return in the conclusion to other postcolonial orientations which do not deny structural contexts but rather see in postcolonialist epistemology a corrective to an earlier preoccupation with structures, that is much closer to the position that informs these discussions.[3]

The Epistemology of Postcolonial Criticism

The affirmation of "difference" is basic to a postcolonial epistemology. Difference is important not just as a description of a situation, but more importantly because it shapes language, and therefore, the meaning of identity: every representation of the self carries upon it the trace of the "other." Identity, it follows, is never "essential," but the product of relationships. Whether informed by Bakhtin's dialogics or Derrida's "differance," difference and the negotiation of difference becomes crucial to the construction of identity and, by extension, of culture. The difference here, of course, is not a difference that divides but one that unites the self and the other in a mutual dependency.

Three aspects of this epistemological premise are worth emphasizing. First is that the production of meaning in linguistic encounters becomes a metaphor for all encounters, rendering the economy of discourse into a paradigm for all encounters, including the encounters of political economy. A subsidiary consequence of this metaphorization of social encounters seems to be a conviction that literary works suffice as evidence of what goes on in the world. Methodologically, one of the interesting byproducts of postcolonial criticism seems to be that there is little significant difference between the world and its representations in fiction. While I would not care to argue, as a professional historian, that historians do better than the producers of fiction in representations of the past, it is necessary still to raise the distinction as an epistemological problem. Contrary to the promise of a "new historicism," that wished to historicize literature, historical thinking over the last decade has been converted into a subfield of literature, with emphasis shifting from questions of evidence to questions of narrativization and representation, with consequences that undermine epistemologies in both literature and history.[4] The linguistic turn, if I may put it that way, has obviated the need to confront contrary evidence of great significance that may seem marginal from a perspective that is focused, parochially, on questions of narrative representation.

Secondly, and in a somewhat contrary direction, postcolonial criticism con-
ceptualizes such encounters in the language of the marketplace, with meanings
being negotiated as if the negotiators held equal power in the negotiations, each
side seeking maximum advantage. I will have something to say on the political
implications of these premises below. A third aspect, more immediately relevant
here, is the stress on the porosity of boundaries, which may account for the proliferation of the terminology of "border crossings" in the literature of cultural
criticism over the last decade. Boundaries that divide by essentialized notions of
self and the other must be rejected in favor of "border crossings" which underline
mutual dependency in the conceptualization of identity, which "enshrines syncretism and hybridity."[5] Hybridity and in-betweenness are signature words of
postcolonial criticism, along with heterogeneity, difference and multiplicity.

One of the fundamental consequences of these premises is that the most significant politics is the politics of identity, how identity is constructed at the level
of local encounters and according to local circumstances. Since the individual is
not a mere expression of "essentialized" group identity, but an active participant
in the formation of group identity in numerous localized encounters with others,
these encounters, rather than structures that may confine the "heterogeneity" of
the individual must provide the point of departure for analysis—as well as meaningful politics. Indeed, insistence on structures, or master narratives of any kind
(from capitalism to imperialism, from nationalism to revolution to ethnicity,
class, and gender) implies an essentialism that subordinates the local to imagined
and invented categories that reproduce the categories that hegemonic structures
of power have imposed upon the world. The persistence of hegemony is evident
in the suppression not just of the local politics of identity, but in the negation of
the subjectivity of the oppressed who have at their disposal means of resistance to
oppression that are not necessarily expressed at the level of politics, but in cultural appropriations that subvert hegemony. Political radicals, who insist on the
necessity of politics, including revolutionary politics, by implication, are part of
a structure of hegemony, because they perpetuate assumptions of structural
oppression that replicate assumptions of the dominant culture. Somewhere in the
course of the argument, it is necessary to point out, the debate over oppositional
politics becomes a debate over oppositional cultures, as if there is no need to distinguish the one from the other. What the abolition of this difference between
culture and politics means politically is revealing, as I will comment on later, of
the politics of postcoloniality.

The politics of identity, finally, has found favor with feminism, which has
enhanced significantly the popularity of postcolonial criticism. Third World
women and women of color in general have found in postcolonial criticism an
epistemology with which to counter universalized (and hegemonic) notions of
gender. This same epistemology could also be applied to class relations, although
that is considerably less common.[6] Postcolonial epistemology no doubt has contributed significantly to fine-tuning these concepts, and in turn has benefited

from the complexities they have introduced on matters of identity. On the other hand, it is important to note that such extensions of postcolonial epistemology have resulted in something of a confusion that disguises its historical specificity. The ritual invocations of the holy trinity of race-class-gender in these discussions mystify the increasingly privileged plaçe assumed by ethnicity and race in such analyses, due in part to a postcolonialist epistemology, the point of departure for which is not a generalized theory of identity formation in terms of social relationships (which is hardly original), but a very specific form of social relationships grounded in ethnic or racial relationships. It is an irony of postcolonial epistemology that, intended to combat ethnic, national and racial essentialisms, it should nevertheless foreground relationships informed by such essentialisms in cultural criticism at the cost of overshadowing those other relationships so that a preoccupation with ethnicity (however it is defined) becomes a sign of the postmodern; against the modernizationist assumption that it could be dissolved into class and even gender relations.

Postcolonial Criticism in the Perspective of History

The question of history appears in several guises in the discussions below which I would like to highlight here. I am concerned throughout with the relationship of history to a contemporary radical agenda; both in the critique of residual and emergent configurations of power, and in the consideration of radical political possibilities appropriate to the times.

As postcolonial criticism has emerged as the heir to earlier radical conceptualizations of global relations, examination of the historical circumstances of its emergence is crucial to an evaluation of its radical claims. The importance of the perspective of history in the spatial and temporal mapping of postcolonial criticism as a radical intellectual movement is the explicit subject of two of the essays below ("The Postcolonial Aura: Third World Criticism in the Age of Global Capitalism," and "Postcolonial or Postrevolutionary? The Problem of History in Postcolonial Criticism"). A more thorough historicization would require an internal mapping of postcolonial criticism, for subscription to an epistemology of postcolonialism does not necessarily imply an identical attitude toward other epistemologies (for example, Marxism), or, therefore, an identical political stance toward contemporary questions of power, which leads Paul Gilroy to speak of "the ethno-historical specificity of the discourse of cultural studies."[7] I will return to the importance of such a distinction in the concluding section of this introduction. Suffice it to say here that I am interested here not in an intellectual history of postcolonialism, which might be premature, but in the historical place of postcolonialism against earlier radical formulations of global relations.

It is difficult to say where postcolonialism belongs on a global map, since its proponents claim it to be applicable to all societies that have experienced colonialism, that range from the formerly colonial societies of Africa to the United

States (as a British colony in origin). The spatial uncertainty is itself an indication of the unsettling of boundaries. It is probably fair to say that the term presents itself as a substitute for what was called the Third World after World War II, and colonial/semi-colonial societies for the half century before that. Aijaz Ahmad has pointed out that in the early seventies, when the term "postcolonial" first appeared, it had concrete referents in societies that had liberated themselves recently from colonialism.[8] The scope of the term has been expanded considerably since then, but its claims need to be evaluated against that legacy. The postcolonial may be heir to an earlier terminology, but the radical way in which it breaks with the conceptualizations embedded in that terminology is evident in its extension to cover not only societies of the First World, but also in its claims to universal applicability globally.

The when and the where in the emergence of postcolonialism are somewhat easier to locate. The term in its current usage acquired popularity in the late 1980s, and rapidly catapulted to the forefront of cultural studies, making an impact not only across academic disciplines, but, through slogans such as "multiculturalism," in politics as well, especially the politics of academic institutions. The dynamic power moving the discourse of postcoloniality was the visible impact on cultural studies of intellectuals of Third World origin in First World institutions. The original location for it, in other words, was the First World, but a First World whose earlier distance from the Third World was abridged by the motions of intellectuals. Since then, it has also spread globally, even to unlikely locations such as postsocialist China.

The changes that made the motions of Third World intellectuals possible, and enabled them to acquire a hearing in First World institutions, point to the historical circumstances of the emergence of postcolonialism as a radical intellectual and political contender in contemporary thought and ideology. The emergence of postcolonialism to the forefront of consciousness has coincided over the last decade with the increasing visibility of the term "diaspora," which may well be the immediate social condition for a postcolonial consciousness. Diasporas have become a highly visible component of a global social landscape. Diasporic populations, however, contain a complex range of social groups, from political refugees to those driven to emigration out of economic necessity to highly educated and wealthy professionals who are cosmopolitan by education, outlook and their ability to function across cultural spaces. The participation of this last group in transnational motions of people has empowered diasporic populations in unprecedented ways. Transnational diasporic populations have scrambled national allegiances, and intensified ethnic and cultural encounters that cut across national boundaries, challenging earlier spatialities organized around nations with new spatialities in which such encounters play a formative part. They have called into question assumptions of homogeneous national cultures in both host societies (usually, but not necessarily, Eurocentric) and in societies of origin which deny authenticity to cultures of emigrants. Postcolonialism from this perspective appears as the ideology of articulate groups within diasporic populations who challenge earlier configurations of ethnicity and culture with a new consciousness that springs from their own conditions of existence. In the words of Edward Said, "liberation as an intellectual mission, born in the resistance and opposition to the confinements and ravages of imperialism, has now shifted from the settled, established and domesticated dynamics of culture to its unhoused, decentered, and exilic energies, whose incarnation today is the migrant, and whose consciouness is that of the intellectual and artist in exile, the political figure between domains, between forms, between homes, and between languages."[9]

Said's statement is reminiscent of what Georg Simmel wrote a century earlier of the "objectivity" of "the stranger"; that it "does not simply involve passivity and detachment; it is a particular structure composed of distance and nearness, indifference and involvement."[10] The important historical question is why, when the knowledge of the stranger, and the very features of his/her existence, were objects of suspicion and alienation in an earlier day, such knowledge can move to the forefront of consciousness in the contemporary world, especially the contemporary First World? Those signature words of postcolonial criticism, hybridity and in-betweenness, appear in postcolonial discourse as features of the modal personality, in contrast to the undesirable connotations they carried in an earlier day when, in the case of Asian-Americans, for example, they served as excuses for their exclusion from the United States. What is it that has changed?

Postcolonial criticism is suspicious of explanations based on structure on the grounds that such explanations erase local differences and encounters. This is possible when homogenizing structures are substituted for local differences, but it is not a necessity of structural explanations that are based on relationships, including the relationships between localized and global structures. I insist in the essays below that the new diasporic social formations, and the consciousness they generate, are not to be explained without reference to structural transformations in the global economy, which have empowered Third World societies in new ways. Thanks to these transformations, societies that earlier were marginal to a EuroAmerican capitalism, or were objects of exploitation to the latter, have emerged as key players in the global economy. Likewise, labor, including high-level intellectual labor, from these societies has become crucial to the operations of First World transnational corporations not merely in their operations abroad, but even at home—as with the high-level technological labor force that the U.S. computer and communications industries have come to depend upon. Hybridity and in-betweenness, once liabilities, have become assets that facilitate the transnational operations of global corporations. In the process, a Eurocentric conception of modernity has given way to a multicultural one, enabling the reassertion of Third World cultural formations that were suppressed earlier by Eurocentric ideologies.

While Eurocentrism is once again subject to challenge from alternative cultural positions, however, the reassertion of these cultural positions requires their articulation to the ideology of a globalized capitalism, which provides the totality within which local cultural encounters take place, and condition them without necessarily leading to homegenous consequences. In this sense, an excessive pre-occupation with Eurocentrism distracts attention from the more dynamic rela-tionship between local cultures and the cultural forces of a Global Capitalism. Also, while heterogeneity, hybridity, etc. at the local level may open up cultural boundaries to enable different groups to negotiate their differences, which is quite radical on the surface,[11] it is difficult to see where such opening up leads unless it also addresses the structural conditions set by the larger totality which conditions *all* the groups in question, whether they are based on class, gender, racial, religious or ethnic allegiances. In this perspective, while the postcolonialist argument addresses important questions at one level, it also distracts from the problems presented by a Global Capitalism, and even reinforces the ideology of the latter; the effort to accommodate in theory situations created by the dynam-ics of a contemporary capitalism in effect makes critique indistinguishable from the legitimation of these situations—unless critique incorporates questions of structure that go beyond the local. (In addition to the two essays on postcolonial criticism cited above, these problems are addressed at length in "The Global in the Local" and "The Postmodernization of Production and Its Organization: Flexible Production, Work and Culture," especially the latter.) My historicization of postcolonial criticism, it may be underlined here, is in terms of history con-ceived of structurally; the postcolonialist argument is in some ways much closer to a conventional historicism in its liberal, and even libertarian, versions.

A second way in which I deploy history below is in the critique of the histori-cal claims of the postcolonial argument which, contrary to its own professions, is totalizing itself in extending the postcolonial epistemology globally, and project-ing it back upon the past, without regard to structural differences between its own historical location and other histories, past and present. Postcolonialism's empha-sis on "difference" as an epistemological and methodological point of departure is enabling at the level of local differences. Without an account of structural con-ditions which are rejected as obstacles to grasping difference in its localized vari-ation, a radical insistence on difference results in the erasure of the significant dif-ferences in the meaning of difference at different locations, and an inability to recognize that not all differences are equally different. Hans Bertens has noted that postcolonialism, and postmodernism in general, in their insistence on dif-ference, seem to be incapable ironically of recognizing and accounting for "real" differences.[12]

The irony may be an irony of the times. The same global circumstances that generate postcoloniality would seem also to be marginalizing entire populations around the world, while also provoking among newly empowered Third World societies the reassertion of ethnicity, cultural nationalism and racism, with their claims to difference at levels quite at odds with the localized politics of identity that is the staple of postcolonial criticism; so much so that we seem to be living, and dealing with, two separate worlds, the world of cultural criticism and the world of newly reconfigured geopolitical essentialisms. While these two worlds may confront one another as mutually hostile ideological spaces, it is possible that they are both products of the same processes. In his *Postmodernism and Islam*, Akbar Ahmed writes that "ethno-religious revivalism is both cause and effect of postmodernism."[13] It is a cause because the resurfacing of native cultural formations following nearly a century of suppression under modernizing regimes challenges the Eurocentric assumptions that have hitherto guided development policies; effect because the decline of Eurocentrism with the reconfiguration of global power relations allows them to resurface. Postcolonial discourse and these reassertions of essentialized identities both foreground ethnicity, but with vastly different social, cultural and political implications (which is the "real" difference to which Bertens refers). Rather than confront this problem which is a challenge to any radical criticism of the world, postcolonial criticism cavalierly dismisses what it calls "essentialisms," and insists on flattening out global differences in the name of local differences, reducing to a localized empiricism spatial problems that call for a structural accounting. As I hinted above, in its own elevation of ethnicity in matters of cultural formation (as in the preoccupation with Eurocentrism and the response to it in ideas such as "multiculturalism"), postcolonial criticism may even be a significant ideological contributing factor to the contemporary saliency of ethnicity as an organizing principle of politics. The postcolonial idea of "difference" itself is quite vague in its reference. While postcolonialism formally rejects master narratives of culture represented by civilization or nation, postcolonial criticism in its language continues to speak in terms that equate nation, ethnicity and culture, rather than in terms of localized cultures and ethnicities. What sustains the claim to the politics of identity or the politics of location, ironically, is a methodological individualism that erases the ways in which the individual may be the embodiment of those master narratives in all their contradictoriness.[14]

The desocialized approach to difference in postcolonial criticism which homegenizes difference has its counterpart in the dehistoricization of difference on a temporal dimension, and the claiming for postcoloniality of the totality of modern history, if not all human history. From its origins as a description of post-independence colonial societies, postcolonialism has been inflated in meaning to describe the cultural condition of societies from the moment of their colonization, which coincides with the whole history of modernity, and also justifies, without regard to historical trajectory, the inclusion in the "postcolonial" of every society from Samoa to the United States. Moreover, since the interaction between human societies, and the phenomenon of colonialism, is not to be restricted to the modern period (except by reference to economic and political structures), there seems to be little reason to confine postcolonialism even to the modern period.

This is pretty much the implication of Frederick Buell's triumphalist celebration of postcolonial criticism in his recent *National Culture and the New Global System*.[15] In such projections upon the past, postcolonialism offers itself as a substitute not only to epistemologies grounded in distinctions between the colonizer and colonized, or in the Three Worlds idea, but also the revolutionary politics inspired by those epistemologies. Unlike these predecessors, which were carefully delineated in their historical scope, however, postcolonialism offers itself as a metanarrative that recognizes no historical boundaries. Ironically, even the point of departure for postcolonial criticism, Eurocentrism, loses its historical meaning in this perspective, as a postcolonial epistemology grounded in the "negotiation" or "dialogics" of meaning becomes coextensive with the history of modernity that is also the history of the European domination of the world that was to produce Eurocentrism (and capitalism, imperialism, socialism, nationalism, revolutions, Orientalism, etc.). The destructuring of the past is justified by those such as Buell by the necessity of restoring the agency and subjectivity in history of those who disappear beneath an emphasis on structural and structured oppressions, which is a straw target that one-dimensionally focuses on Eurocentric interpretations of modernity, and ignores the powerful expressions of agency and subjectivity in the struggles against it, as in revolutionary struggles, which were equally determinants of the history of modernity. On occasion it also issues in historical interpretations that differ little from earlier liberal interpretations in denying the importance of capitalism and colonialism in shaping the lives and the outlook of non-EuroAmerican peoples.[16]

Here, too, a methodological individualism is visible in shaping historical interpretation, but there is an additional aspect worth underlining. In two of the essays below ("There is More in the Rim than Meets the Eye: Thoughts on the 'Pacific Idea' and "Postcolonial or Postrevolutionary? The Problem of History in Postcolonial Criticism"), I raise the question of "forgetting" in these rereadings of the past. The Pacific historian Klaus Neumann observes of Papua New Guineans that these days they "do not appear overtly interested in being told about the horrors of colonialism, as such accounts potentially belittle today's descendants of yesterday's victims."[17] Similar shifts in attitude have been observed elsewhere, and may be related to the changes among minority populations in the U.S. from an emphasis on oppression to an emphasis on "role models" that appear as symbols of successful assimilation. While such a shift is perfectly understandable in existential terms, it needs to be noted nevertheless that it confounds individual success with the success of a whole group, ignoring systemic characteristics that might allow the success of individuals while the group as a whole continues to suffer from structural obstructions and disabilities. It also implies rewriting the history of oppression and the resistance to it in accordance with the needs of the successful among the oppressed, while erasing an earlier radical history that focused on the group and its liberation as a whole. Such new demands, which point to new class and gender divisions among oppressed groups, no doubt find a receptive outlet in postcolonialist epistemology, which in its metanarrativization represents the history of modernity as an ongoing process of negotiation and multiculturalism.

The third way in which I deploy history below is to counteract this new metanarrative by drawing attention to the different meanings to be attached to the relationship between power and cultural formation under different historical circumstances. Against a tendency in cultural criticism to conflate power and discourse, and to move the former into the reified realm of language and representation from its material expressions in everyday economic, social and political relationships, I argue for the necessity of a distinction between the two; not because I do not think that discourses are imbedded in and expressive of power relationships, but because the distinction restores the possibility of a dialectical understanding of the relationship. The essay, "Chinese History and the Question of Orientalism," argues that Orientalism as a representation of Asian societies was a product not just of a European imagination of Asia but of the historical interplay between European representations and Asian self-representations. If Orientalism served the purposes of European power, it was because of the power of Europeans who could utilize Orientalism to legitimize the literal and ideological conquest of Asia. Contemporary evidence of representations of Asia also indicates that if Orientalism has undergone a transformation, it is not because of a postcolonial dissolution of its premises, but because it is now Asians, in complicity with EuroAmericans, who promote Orientalist representations of Asia in what I describe as "self-Orientalization," to assert the new power of Asian societies within Global Capitalism.[18]

The necessity of such a distinction, if only on political common-sense grounds against a theoretical preoccupation with "essentialism" and "difference" is pursued further in a number of essays below which seek to distinguish hegemonic from counter-hegemonic employments of cultural identity.[19] Several essays refer to hegemonic constructions of regional and cultural formations that, while in some ways in opposition to Eurocentrism, nevertheless represent ideological formations that legitimize the operations of a globalized capitalism; it is my contention throughout these essays, in discussions of intellectuals as well as of their discourses, that the critique of Eurocentrism is no longer (if it ever was) sufficient as a critique of hegemony. Two other essays ("There Is More in the Rim than Meets the Eye: Thoughts on the Pacific Idea" and "The Past as Legacy and Project: History and the Construction of Identity") examine the mobilization of identity in opposition to such hegemonic constructions. Cultural essentialism, I argue in these essays, needs to be distinguished in terms of its relationship to structures of power. "There is More in the Rim Than Meets the Eye" describes the efforts of Pacific peoples to recover their own notions of spatiality and temporality against two centuries of EuroAmerican domination of the Pacific. "The Past as Legacy and Project" argues the same for indigenous peoples, contrasting their efforts at identity formation not just with hegemonic EuroAmerican erasures of their claims to their own spatialities and temporalities, but drawing further distinctions between various forms of identity formation in the present, especially cultural nationalism, ethnicity and indigenism.

Finally, I deploy history below to draw a distinction between culturalism with and without history, in defense of a historicist appreciation of culture and identity, against the spatial metaphors of hybridity and in-betweenness in postcolonial criticism. The perspective of the past on the present is most important here because of the distortion that earlier understandings of global relations have suffered as a result of reductionist readings that are informed, I suggest, by transformations in Third World politics. I have in mind here the critique in postcolonial criticism of earlier radical narratives fundamental to which is the allegation that these earlier narratives presupposed culturally homogeneous entities of one kind or another, which indicated also that they were unable to overcome the hegemonic constructions of the world imposed by a Eurocentric discourse. From a postcolonial perspective, narratives based on colonial/anticolonial oppositions or the Three Worlds idea are informed by binarisms that presuppose or promote essentialist notions of culture and identity, while nationalist narratives are dynamized by ethnic and cultural primordialism.

This may or not be the case, depending on specific historical circumstances. What is important is that these narratives, no less than postcolonial narratives, have been products of structural relationships, albeit located at different levels of political organization. Historically, it was not assumptions of homogenized cultures that produced binarisms or structural divisions of the world into the Three Worlds, but rather structures of hegemony and struggles against it that called forth the necessity of cultural homogenization; no less in the invention of Europe than in the case of the colonized or of Third World societies. Nationalism itself was a product of these same relations, that sought in primordialist homogenization of the nation the unity which was essential to ward off threats from the outside. This is not to deny that, in the process of delineating the inside from the outside, new internal hegemonies were created in the erasure of internal differences. As recent evidence reveals, homogenization was never total or complete; rather, the new political formations (conceived at whatever level) provided new sites of struggle among forces that were themselves products in their identities of the same political formations.

The search for identity along the divides of colonialism, Three Worlds, and nationalism has been interpreted in postcolonial criticism as a replication of the structuring of the world by a hegemonic Eurocentrism, and it no doubt was, which is especially evident in the idea of Three Worlds, that originated in European social science in the aftermath of World War II in a conceptual reordering of the world. But to recognize this is only to acknowledge a historical reality. There is a tendency these days to think that any acknowledgment of a European capitalist ordering of the world is entrapment in Eurocentrism, with a consequent denial of the subjectivity of the peoples who found their lives reordered by an outside hegemonic force. I argue, to the contrary, that this is merely a recognition of the historicity of modern identities, in the formation of which the European capitalist ordering of the world played a crucial part. If Eurocentrism is to be "unthought," the unthinking nevertheless has its points of departure in historical circumstances that are products of this history.[20]

As far as identity is concerned, it is no less an identity for being historical. To deny the historicity of identity is indeed to fall into some kind of essentialism, as in the language of hybridity or in-betweenness, which implies that there are essences that surround the borderlands. The assumption in earlier narratives that the struggle against colonial hegemony had to be conducted on grounds set by colonialism required neither a culturalist homogeneity nor the denial of agency; it merely took as its point of departure contemporary circumstances of power, and sought in the struggle against oppression the creation of new agencies and cultural identities. Anti-colonial struggles, or struggles conducted in the name of the Third World or national liberation, produced out of these historical circumstances alternative social and political visions that would enable transcending those circumstances, without falling back upon congealed cultural identities. Indeed, the necessity of struggle on two fronts (inside and outside) was to produce a radically historicist notion of culture. (This is the subject below of the two essays, "Culturalism as Hegemonic Ideology and Liberating Practice," and "The Past as Legacy and Project: History and the Construction of Identity".) In the words of Franz Fanon, whom postcolonial critics have sought to appropriate for their own denial of national cultures, in the process erasing the revolutionary nationalism that informed his thinking:

> A national culture is not a folklore, nor an abstract populism that believes it can discover a people's true nature. It is not made up of the inert dregs of gratuituous actions, that is to say actions which are less and less attached to the ever-present reality of the people. A national culture is the whole body of efforts made by a people in the sphere of thought to describe, justify and praise the action through which the people has created itself and keeps itself in existence. A national culture in underdeveloped countries should therefore take its place at the very heart of the struggle for freedom which these countries are carrying on.[21]

Whether in its anti-colonialist or Third World expression, or in the language of national liberation, radical struggles did not presuppose an essentialist primordialism, but rather viewed cultural identity as a project that was very much part of the struggle for liberation that it informed. That this is ignored in postcolonialist representations of these struggles raises the question of whether the objection is indeed to the essentialism of past conceptualizations of the world, or to the aims those struggles promoted, which have become undesirable from a contemporary perspective.

If those earlier assertions of cultural identity in liberation struggles seem inappropriate today, it is not because their aims were misguided, but because the alignment of the struggles along earlier divides has become irrelevant due to structural transformations in global relations. It makes little sense to speak of the Third World or anti-colonial struggles when the geography of the world economy has remapped the globe along entirely different boundaries. Even national boundaries are undergoing such a reworking, although it is quite premature presently to declare the nation a thing of the past. What is important to recall is not the nature of the struggles, but the visions of liberation that they produced, which sought in contemporary circumstances the production of alternative ways of living that would overcome both internal and external oppressions that had already become indistinguishable. Such radical visions are still urgently needed at a time when the reification of difference preempts the possibility of identities that may serve as the sources of new visions and struggles, while it also breeds new essentialisms that contribute to the proliferation of reactionary movements around the world. In a sense, the predicament of the contemporary world may be the predicament, in the words of Andrei Codrescu, of "the disappearance of the outside," which, having brought down the Berlin Wall, condemns us to wallow in the pleasures of "the Berlin mall."[22] Rather than erasing the memory of radical struggles of the past by converting the past itself into one big mall of identity transactions, it is necessary to recall it as an inventory of alternative modes of living out of which to construct new visions appropriate to the times.

Theory, History and Common Sense: Local Movements and Indigenism as Locations for a New Radicalism

A fundamental question raised by postcolonialism (and postmodernism in general) concerns the relationship between knowledge and everyday life: what kind of knowledge is appropriate to the purposes of the good life, by which I mean the rather modest goal of a life that is minimally subject to the ravages of exploitation and oppression.[23] Theory may unravel for us the nature of exploitation and oppression, but it does not in and of itself supply answers to that question; indeed, an overemphasis on theory which substitutes theory for life may deepen the problem it is intended to resolve. History may provide us with an inventory of possibilities, but it does not offer answers to the problem of choice except in its teleological versions (it matters little whether the teleology is that of capitalism, or of socialism as we have known it), the consequences of which already offer familiar lessons. The theorization of history, as the historicization of theory, may help us locate ourselves in space and time and provide some sense of what choices may be appropriate, but that is about all. In the end the choice is guided by a common sense appreciation of what is possible, and desirable. Common sense, of course, is not transparent, but must be theorized in its historicity; *it* is necessary, in turn, to tame the excesses of theory, or the despotism of the past.[24] Thus, common sense requires that, however complex identity may be in its heterogeneity or historicity, people, including postcolonial critics, act on an everyday basis with some fairly firm notions of identity; just as we do not, everytime we bite into a nectarine (invented by a Korean-American), worry about whether we are biting into an apple or a peach.[25] Common sense requires that we distinguish one type of identity formation from another in terms of their relationship to power. And common sense requires a recognition that everytime we interact with someone, the interaction carries on it the traces of the structures that encompass it, and the legacy of the history of all such interactions.

In the essay, "The Postmodernization of Production and Its Organization," I draw a distinction between postmodernism with or without capitalism, by which I mean that whether or not postmodernism fulfills its critical aspirations depends on its willingness to account for the structures of power of which it is both product and constituent, without which it merely degenerates into a celebration of the present, even to the extent of covering up contemporary modes of oppression and exploitation.[26] If I may paraphrase Georg Lukacs' description of Marxism as the "self-criticism" of the bourgeoisie, postmodernism is most plausible as an extension, and self-criticism, of modernity. Similarly, postcolonialism requires for the fulfillment of its critical aspirations an accounting of the global as a condition of the local, as well as an articulation of its own epistemology to the radical epistemologies of the past; without which it becomes a celebration of new global and social relations created by a globalized capitalism.

Let me illustrate this point with reference to "multiculturalism," which has been attached quite closely to a postcolonialist interpretation of relations between cultures. In the same essay on "The Postmodernization of Production," I trace at least one important source of multiculturalism to the concern of transnational corporations on how to deal with a "multicultural" work force, that preceded by the long academic concern with the question. And business has continued to be in the forefront of the current craze with globalism and multiculturalism. That does not make multiculturalism undesirable, but indicates the ways in which it is connected with the consolidation of current structures of power by admitting into it those who were formerly excluded but are now nearly impossible to keep out—both out of consideration of the needs of power, and because of social demands on it. In the end, however, multiculturalism does not point to a way out of existing structures of power, only to modifications within it.

Contrast that with what I will describe, inelegantly, as "multi-historicalism," which, unlike a multiculturalism that presupposes reified culturalisms, presupposes the historicity of cultures, and different historical trajectories out of different pasts, that provide "outsides" from which to view contemporary structures of power and the ideologies of history that legitimize them. Whatever we may think of something like "Afrocentrism," it is unwise nevertheless to ignore the questions it raises, fundamental to which is the recovery of histories that have been suppressed in the formation of a capitalist and Eurocentric modernity.[27] Multi-historicalism, in its very repudiation of a single historical trajectory in the past, also opens the way to thinking of the future in terms of alternative historical trajectories that defy the colonization of the future by current structures of power. To fulfill this radical possibility, however, multi-historicalism has to recognize the historicity of the cultural and social alternatives that it proposes rather than reify them; in other words, that a future historical trajectory to be constructed out of past legacy must be contingent in its liberatory possibilities on the reworking of past legacy by a contemporary consciousness, if only because no legacy of the past is free from its own particular modes of oppression and exploitation. It does not do simply to set other histories against a Eurocentric history, as if the latter were the only one marked by oppression and exploitation.

I propose below, in ways that may have some kinship with postmodernity and postcolonialism, that a contemporary radicalism must take local struggles as its point of departure, and that indigenism as one type of identity formation may provide an appropriate model for such struggles. Local struggles are already part of the global political landscape, and not for fortuituous reasons. As I argue in several of the essays below (especially in "The Global in the Local"), the very operations of capital that have dislocated earlier divisions of the world, including national boundaries, have created new contradictions that have brought problems of the local and the global to the forefront of political consciousness. Likewise, a contemporary radicalism must take as its point of departure these very same contradictions. But there is more to what I advocate than mere recognition of political realities.[28] The local is the site where action toward new community formations is the most plausible. This is also where indigenous ideals of social relationships and relationships to nature may have the most to offer; especially in their challenge to the voracious developmentalism of capitalism, which has also been assimilated to Marxism in its historical unfolding. As I explain below, what I have in mind is not indigenous ideals as they are reified in New Age consumptions of indigenism, but indigenous ideals as they have been reworked by a contemporary consciousness, where indigenism appears not merely as a reproduction of the past, but as a project to be realized.[29]

The difference of this idea of the local from that in postcolonial criticism should be evident in its insistence that, under the circumstances of a global capitalism, the local is impossible to conceive without reference to the global. It is also lodged in a different kind of knowledge; not that of the exile or the travelling theorist, but in local knowledge informed by and directed at local community formation. That does not make exilic knowledge irrelevant, since that knowledge itself speaks directly to contemporary historical circumstances, but regrounds it in the intermediation of social lives conceived locally[30]—an essential necessity, if local struggles are to have any chance of success against the seemingly insuperable forces of transnational structures of power.

Notes

1. Fredric Jameson, *Postmodernism, or, the Cultural Logic of Late Capitalism* (Durham, NC: Duke University Press, 1991), p.x.

2. John O'Neill, *The Poverty of Postmodernism* (London and New York: Routledge, 1995), p.18.

3. Since most of this argument is derivative of what is presented in greater detail in the essays that follow, I will not bother with documentation here except where I invoke sources that have come to my attention since the essays were written.

4. For "the rule of Literature" in contemporary postmodernism, see David Simpson's extensive argument in *The Academic Postmodern and the Rule of Literature: A Report on Half-Knowledge* (Chicago: The University of Chicago Press, 1995).

5. Frederick Buell, *National Culture and the New Global System* (Baltimore: The Johns Hopkins University Press, 1994), p.235.

6. There is, of course, no reason why the same epistemology should not be applied to relations between genders, or even between classes, say, the bourgeoisie and the proletariat. The latter, of course, would return us to Hegel's metaphor of master-slave relationships, not to speak of Prospero and Caliban, and back to the future by way of Eugene Genovese. In Chapter 9, I discuss the application of postmodernism to organizations, which provides an illustration of the use of this epistemology in class relations. It also illustrates how the same epistemology, without reference to structures of power relations, covers up hierarchies of power, and class oppression and exploitation.

7. Paul Gilroy, *The Black Atlantic: Modernity and Double Consciousness* (Cambridge, MA: Harvard University Press, 1994), p.5.

8. Aijaz Ahmad, "The Politics of Literary Postcoloniality," *Race and Class* 36.3 (1995):1–20.

9. Edward Said, *Culture and Imperialism* (New York: Vintage Books, 1994), p.332.

10. Georg Simmel, "The Stranger," in *The Sociology of Georg Simmel*, tr. and ed. with an introduction by Kurt H. Wolff (New York: The Free Press, 1950), pp.402–408.

11. An example of this line of reasoning is to be found in Lisa Lowe, "Heterogeneity, Hybridity, Multiplicity: Marking Asian American Differences," *Diaspora*, 1.1 (Spring 1991):24–44, which has been rather influential in some circles. I would like to add an elaboration here to my idea of totality. Totality does not imply a static homogeneity, as it is interpreted in some circles, but is subject itself to ongoing transformation due to the interaction of the forces it contains, which in turn structure the totality. The central relationship of capitalism, class relationship, must itself be understood in this dynamic sense. One of the products of Global Capitalism is emergent transnational classes which, for all their contradictions, must provide the frame of reference for analysis appropriate to the present. This is, of course, one of the factors that have rendered the division of First and Third Worlds irrelevant, because there is now a recognizable Third World capitalist class that participates in global rule. This is another phenomenon that is covered up by an excessive emphasis on Eurocentrism.

12. "In order to function—or even to survive—the politics of difference must exclude those who are *really* different, such as Iranian fundamentalists or staunch defenders of apartheid, that is, those who don't include themselves in their idea of difference, for whom it is only the others who are always different." Bertens, *The Idea of the Postmodern: A History* (London and New York: Routledge, 1995), pp.192–193.

13. Akbar S. Ahmed, *Postmodernism and Islam: Predicament and Promise* (London: Routledge, 1992), p.13.

14. Levine, Sober and Wright have explained "methodological individualism" as "the view that all social phenomena are best explained by the properties of the individuals who comprise the phenomena; or, equivalently, that any explanation involving macro-level,

social concepts should in principle be reduced to micro-level explanations involving only individuals and their properties," *New Left Review* 162 (March–April 1987):67–84. They further clarify their explanation by contrasting methodological individualism with atomism, radical holism and anti-reductionism. Unlike atomism, methodological individualism recognizes the importance of relationships, but at the individual level.

15. Frederick Buell, *National Culture and the New Global System* (Baltimore and London: The Johns Hopkins University Press, 1994).

16. For an important discussion of this problem, see Vinay Bahl, "Class Consciousness and Primordial Values in the Shaping of the Indian Working Class," *South Asia Bulletin*, vol. 13, no. 1 and 2 (1993):152–172. Bahl is especially critical of the work of Chakrabarty on the Indian working class for downplaying the importance of colonialism in shaping class politics, and ending up blaming the victims for their fate. For Chakrabarty's own reconsideration of his earlier position, and reaffirmation of the indispensability of capitalism as a framework of analysis, see Dipesh Chakrabarty, "Marx After Marxism: History, Subalternity and Difference," in Saree Makdisi, Cesare Cesarino and Rebecca E. Karl (eds.), *Marxism Beyond Marxism* (New York: Routledge, 1996), pp.55–70, especially p.62.

17. Klaus Neumann, "'In Order to Win Their Friendship': Renegotiating First Contact," *The Contemporary Pacific*, vol. 6 no. 1 (Spring 1994):111–145.

18. Already in 1980, in a review of Edward Said's *Orientalism*, Sadik Jalal al-'Azm noted this self-orientalization which he described as "Orientalism in reverse." See al-'Azm, "Orientalism and Orientalism in Reverse," *Khamsin* (1980):5–26.

19. A note is in order here on the question of hegemony, which too has been the subject of considerable manipulation in postcolonial criticism. In Antonio Gramsci's original formulation, hegemony was intended to supplement materialist with cultural analysis, not to substitute culture for material analysis (or even to suggest that they could be separated), which is the way in which the use of hegemony appears in much contemporary analysis. This has its counterpart in social relations in the use of the idea of subalternity. Gramsci, as a Marxist, was searching for ways out of subalternity, to enable the working class to achieve power. This, of course, appears presently as a celebration of subalternity, which may be fairly revealing of the obliviousness to (or maybe even mystification of) questions of power. For a discussion that sharply calls attention to these problems, see Teresa L. Ebert, "Ludic Feminism, the Body, Performance, and Labor: Bringing *Materialism* Back into Feminist Cultural Studies," *Cultural Critique* (Winter 1992–1993):5–50.

20. I owe "Unthinking Eurocentrism" to Ella Shohat and Robert Stam, *Unthinking Eurocentrism: Multiculturalism and the Media* (London and New York: Routledge, 1994).

21. Franz Fanon, *The Wretched of the Earth* (New York: Grove Press, 1968), p.188. In his "Critical Fanonism," *Critical Inquiry* 17 (Spring 1991):457–470, Henry Louis Gates, Jr., offers an interesting discussion of the different ways in which Fanon is interpreted these days. What is equally interesting is that Gates has little to say on the differences between past and present interpretations of Fanon, or the political implications of the conflicting interpretations of the present.

22. Andrei Codrescu, *The Disappearance of the Outside: A Manifesto for Escape* (Redding, MA: Addison-Wesley, 1990).

23. The question of course is not new, even if it needs to be rephrased in a radically different technological grammar, which is all the more reason for recalling past anwers to it. The classic formulation for an earlier period was that of Paulo Freire, *The Pedagogy of the*

Oppressed (New York: Continuum, 1993). Also pertinent are the many works of Ivan Illich, especially *Tools for Conviviality* (New York: Harper and Row, 1973) and *Deschooling Society* (New York: Harper and Row, 1971).

24. See John O'Neill, *The Poverty of Postmodernism*, Chapter 8, for a case for the necessity of articulating sociological theory to common sense experience, to create a theory that incorporates the voices of those that the theory speaks about.

25. Ulf Hannerz puts it nicely: "At times . . . the depictions of the postmodern age deserve some of its own incredulity. When it is claimed, for example, that identities become nothing but assemblages from whatever imagery is for the moment marketed through the media, then I wonder what kind of people the commentators on postmodernism know; I myself know hardly anybody of whom this would seem true." Hannerz, *Cultural Complexity* (New York: Columbia University Press, 1993), p.35.

26. This distinction corresponds in a different phraseology to Teresa Ebert's distinction between "ludic" and "resistance" postmodernism. Ebert, p.11.

27. There is reason to be critical of Afrocentrism, or any other "centrism," to the extent that it reifies the past. But this is not the usual reason for criticism. Even the most ardent critics of Afrocentrism, or indigenism, for that matter, might want to consider that while something like the sinocentric Confucian revival is taken seriously even when it is rejected, the general tendency is to dismiss ideologies of Afrocentrism or indigenism as myths that do not merit serious consideration. The Confucian revival is in keeping with conventions of Orientalism. It is also in keeping, more importantly, with the expectations of a capitalist teleology, since that revival has taken the form not of challenges to capitalism in the name of Confucian values, but an articulation of Confucian values (in highly reductionist interpretations) to capitalist development. Afrocentrism and indigenism, on the other hand, reassert values that are quite at odds with capitalist developmentalism. The response to them, even among so-called radicals, however, is also indicative of the persistence of residual ideologies of civilization: since Africans or Indians were not civilized, and continue to be haunted with political and economic weakness, any claims to history on their part must be mythical, while European, Chinese, East Indian, or Islamic (where relevant, as in Malaysia, for instance) claims, that are equally questionable, must be taken seriously—especially as they register impressive rates of economic development. This corresponds, in some ways, to a political skepticism that views any advocacy of the local as a throwback to romantic notions that go against history, rather than as an expression of contemporary structures of power, and the struggles against it. An example may be found in the work of David Simpson (cited above), which is quite perspicacious in its critique of academic postmodernism, but fails to distinguish the ways in which advocacies of the local, or the telling of stories, may carry different meanings in different historical contexts. One of the most fundamental problems of postcolonial "criticism" is to evaluate such differences critically, especially as it is appropriated in the First World academia.

28. How real these issues are may be gleaned from the initial response to Patrick Buchanan's right-wing populism in the current presidential campaign. Disingenuous Buchanan may be, but his message concerning the relationship between economic transnationalism and the plight of the working people struck a responsive chord among many. Equally revealing was the anxious response of the political and economic elite (regardless of party affiliation), with their references to Buchanan's armies of "pitchforked peasants." One commentator went so far as to describe Buchanan as a "leftwinger." See Clifford D. May, "Buchanan's Rise Undermines the Republican Revolution," *Rocky Moun-*

tain News, February 25, 1996, p.62A. For an alternative view, which recognizes the seriousness of the issues involved, see Thomas Friedman, "Balancing NAFTA and Neighborhood," *Rocky Mountain News*, April 13, 1996, p.44A.

29. I realize that this historicization of indigenism does violence to indigenous conceptions of time and space, which repudiate EuroAmerican notions of history. Thus, Vine DeLoria, Jr., writes of religion that the "dilemma over the nature of history occurs and will occur whenever a religion is divorced from space and made an exclusive agent of time." By contrast, "Indian tribes combine history and geography so that they have a 'sacred geography,' that is to say, every location within their homeland has a multitude of stories that recount the migrations, revelations, and particular historical incidents that cumulatively produced the tribe in its current condition." Vine DeLoria, Jr., *God Is Red: A Native View of Religion* (Golden, CO: Fulcrum Publishing, 1994), pp.121–122. Indigenism itself, however, has been reworked by the historical developments discussed here, so that there are also postmodern and postcolonial Indians. For examples, see Gerald Vizenor (ed.), *Narrative Chance: Postmodern Discourse on Native American Literature* (Norman and London: University of Oklahoma Press, 1993) and Gerald R. McMaster, "Border Zones: The 'Injunuity' of Aesthetic Tricks," *Cultural Studies* 9:1(1995):74–90. Nevertheless, in thinking of multi-historicalism as I suggest it here, one should include in it indigenous beliefs that repudiate history as epistemology.

30. This in some sense is implicit in those versions of diaspora that take diasporic populations not as off-ground floating ethnicities that can be homogenized culturally, but as networks of locally grounded peoples with a great deal of internal differentiation. I think it is this approach to the question of diaspora, as well as his meticulous attention both to historical specificity and structural context, that distinguishes the work of Paul Gilroy as a fruitful example of postcolonial criticism. See *The Black Atlantic*, op. cit.

2

Culturalism as Hegemonic Ideology and Liberating Practice

This discussion argues the radicalism of cultural activity against efforts to subsume the question of culture within other, seemingly more radical activities upon which individuals attempting to change the world have increasingly focused their attention. In a world where economic necessity and political crisis confront us daily, this argument may seem superfluous or even self-indulgent. This is especially the case where the question of culture relates to the non-Western world (the primary focus of this discussion) where millions of lives await the urgent resolution of practical problems for their very survival. Yet I will argue in the face of necessity that the realm of culture, as the realm of activity that is bound up with the most fundamental epistemological questions, demands priority of attention.

The radicalism of the issue of culture lies in the fact that culture affords us ways of seeing the world, and if the latter have any bearing on our efforts to change the world, then it is essential that we confront our ways of seeing. The idea of culture has developed historically in juxtaposition to the idea of reason. However, it is also the only basis upon which we may comprehend the world rationally (if reason is to have any bearing on the world of the living) and make it more reasonable. Culture, in other words, is also a way to comprehend the rational, not an abstract rationality divorced from the world of living people and set against the latter as its judge, but the rationality of the living. To avoid the question of culture is to avoid questions concerning the ways in which we see the world; it is to remain imprisoned, therefore, in a cultural unconscious, controlled by conditioned ways of seeing (even unto rationality), without the self-consciousness that must be the point of departure for all critical understanding and, by implication, for all radical activity.

To argue the radicalness of the question of culture is not to propound culturalism, that ideology which not only reduces everything to questions of culture, but has a reductionist conception of the latter as well. Thus the critique of culturalism as an ideology is a basic goal of this discussion. An authentically radical conception of culture forces our attention upon the contradictoriness of this concept itself. Culture is not only a way of seeing the world, but also a way of making and changing it. The first sense refers to the manner in which we usually understand and use the word, and it also signifies the cornerstone of culturalist ideology. It identifies for us entire peoples and eras in terms of the ways in which we think they see or·saw the world. It helps us place them vis-à-vis one another, usually with ourselves at the center of the world and at the end of time. It is, in short, a way of organizing the world, its time and space.

This first definition of culture, seemingly common-sensical, mystifies its second sense, of which it is logically and historically the product, but to which it bears a contradictory relationship. Having organized the world in terms of culture, it seems easier to think of people as the creation of culture, rather than the reverse. The activity which produces and reproduces culture appears merely as one of the many ways in which people act according to their culture.

This mystification is crucial to understanding the role culture has played as an instrument of hegemony in social and political relations. To demystify this usage, to reassert the sense of culture as activity, makes possible the re-presentation of cultural activity also as liberating practice. Though culture is not reducible to ideology, the question of culture is nevertheless ideological in a fundamental sense. And though it is not reducible to socio-political relations, neither can it be apprehended critically (rather than ideologically) outside of these relations. Culture is not a thing, to paraphrase E.P. Thompson, but a relationship. It is not merely an autonomous principle that is expressive of the totality constituted by these relationships, a totality that, once it has been constituted, appears as a seamless web of which culture is the architectonic principle, exterior to the socio-political relations and logically prior to them. Rendering culture as such an autonomous principle requires an ideological operation that mystifies the priority of the socio-political relationships that go into its production. A critical reading of culture, one that exposes it as an ideological operation crucial to the establishment of hegemony, requires that we view it not merely as an attribute of totalities but as an activity that is bound up with the operation of social relations, that expresses contradiction as much as it does cohesion. Culture is an activity in which the social relations that are possible but absent, because they have been displaced or rendered impossible (or "utopian") by existing social relations, are as fundamental as the relations whose existence it affirms.

This requires, above all, that we confront culture in terms of its most basic contradiction, that is, as both an autonomous and a dependent activity. The culturalist assertion of the autonomy of culture reduces all realms of social experience (from the economy to ideology) to the question of culture; cultural change then appears as the key to all other change. It is not possible to counter such reductionism effectively with a counter-reductionism that dissolves the question of culture into these other constituents of social life, including ideology. Such a reductionism does not confront, but bypasses, the question of culture because it does not address the fundamental issue of hegemony raised by the question of culture.

The discussion below examines some related problems. First is the question of culturalism. In an earlier essay, "Culture, Society and Revolution: A Critical Discussion of American Studies of Chinese Thought," I described it as a hegemonic ideology.[1] I feel, however, that the dilemmas presented by culturalism cannot be fully appreciated unless we view it simultaneously as a liberating possibility that contradicts its hegemonic practice. In order to elucidate the contradictory possibilities and practices offered by culturalism, I will analyze briefly the conditions under which it appears as liberating practice. To this end, I will discuss at some length two works, one from European history, the other by an Arab intellectual, that illustrate such practice: E.P. Thompson's *The Making of the English Working Class* and Abdallah Larouri's *The Crisis of the Arab Intellectual.* These works shed light on what has been called "culturalist Marxism" and what I have described in my essay on Chinese thought as a "social conception of culture."

Second, I would like to comment further on the question of culturalism as it has been viewed by Marxists, especially those from the Third World. Since culturalism as hegemonic ideology is central to bourgeois cultural assumptions, Marxism has been seen by many in the West and the non-West as the foremost ideological candidate in the struggle against culturalist hegemony. This, I think, has done more than anything else to underline the significance of Marxism as a cultural idea in contrast to its more economistic interpretation. Marxism, I will argue below, promises, but does not guarantee, to abolish the hegemonic practices associated with culturalism. Indeed, unless Marxism itself is examined critically from perspectives offered by culturalism, it may serve as a tool of hegemonic practice by mystifying hegemonic relations between and within societies.

Finally, since the idea of culturalism contains potentially contradictory possibilities of practice, to discuss it at the abstract level of ideas, without reference to its social context, is not only to engage in intellectual mystification, but is socially irresponsible as well. Accordingly, I will comment further in this discussion on the role of intellectuals, particularly those in academia, as producers of ideologies, a question to which I have referred in the introduction to my earlier essay. Culturalism, I have suggested in that article, represents not so much a professional paradigm as the absorption into the profession of a discourse that is broadly social (a discourse that antedates and shapes the profession). Nevertheless, academic intellectuals have played a significant part in articulating and legitimizing hegemonic culturalism which otherwise might have remained a diffuse social prejudice. This point is forcefully made by Edward Said in *Orientalism.* I would like to stress here that the discursive practices of intellectuals acquire further clarity when viewed within the broader social context of their alienation. Culturalism is ideological practice in a fundamental sense: it does not merely reflect the social practice of intellectuals—it helps define such practice. This, I believe, is difficult to understand outside of the alienation that intellectual activity has undergone, for intellectuals, whatever their formal ideological professions, have been absorbed into structures of domination that represent alienated social power. Any consideration of culturalism as a liberating possibility, therefore, must take into account these relationships. I may illustrate this briefly here by suggesting that even a Marxist or Third Worldist ideology may be hegemonic if it does not divorce itself from existing structures of alienated power.

Culturalism and Marxist Culturalism

I would like to start this discussion with a few remarks on the way I use the concept of "culturalism" in "Culture, Society and Revolution." The closest I come to defining it is as an "ensemble of intellectual orientations that crystallize methodologically around the reduction of social and historical questions to abstract questions of culture" and as "responsible," therefore, "not only for legitimizing hegemonic relations between societies, but also for mystifying hegemonic relations of exploitation and oppression within societies." The identifying characteristic of a culturalist intellectual orientation, I have suggested in the above article, is a "preoccupation with the cultural gap" that separates societies and that "results [in] . . . a preoccupation with culture as the central datum" in the study of thought in Third World societies. I have also stated that "in the study of cultures alien to our own, historicism and culturalism are but two sides of the same coin: it is a reaffirmation, in the midst of global history, of the separateness of the society we study."[2] History here appears as cultural interpretation, and the historian as cultural interpreter. The notion of "tradition" is essential to culturalism since it becomes a way to identify the Other. Historical explanation, therefore, assumes as its task the analysis of the confrontation between native tradition and the West which, viewed from the perspective of the historian, translates into a confrontation between Us and the Other. The hegemonic function of culturalism rests in the latter because this juxtaposition leaves to the Other but one choice: escape into tradition (and, therefore, the past) or absorption into the West (which is the present and the future)—not much of an alternative since culture, viewed as tradition, is little more than a congealed and therefore dead culture. The living belong to the West, native culture to the dead! The juxtaposition inevitably entails the "distancing" of the Other, if not into oblivion, then at best into the museum. Distancing in space is the most readily observable feature of culturalism, but, as Johannes Fabian argues in *Time and the Other*, it derives its hegemonic power from distancing in time, which is its inevitable accompaniment.[3]

Given the ways in which culture has been used to justify Western hegemony over the non-West, the concept of culture has become an embarrassment to the more radical students of these societies. Much of the reaction to the once popular (and still dominant in political practice) "modernization" approach to these societies, with its facile juxtaposition of the Modern (Western) against the Traditional (native), represents an effort to overcome the hegemonic implications of a Western logocentric view of the world. Not the least among these efforts are the various versions of "world-system" analysis which has found particular favor in recent years among radical students of non-Western societies. World-system analysis, which could with only slight unfairness be described as economism on a global scale, is inspired to a greater or lesser extent by Marxism and represents an essentially structuralist view of the world that in most uses bypasses the question of culture altogether.

These approaches, however admirable their intention and significant their undertaking, do not resolve the question of hegemony but bypass its most fundamental aspects. They may, indeed, become sources themselves of a new hegemony. An economism, whether of bourgeois or Marxist variety, that reduces the globe to a uniform cultural field upon which economic forces play out their fate, still distances the Other by portraying it as a plaything in the hands of economic forces. If we are to challenge hegemonic culturalism, we must make an effort to confront directly the questions that it raises, especially its epistemological underpinnings which exist independently of and prior to the question of culture itself.

The question of culture, moreover, has been of immense significance to non-Western radicals. Revolutionary socialists in the Third World have repeatedly stated "cultural revolution" to be one of their central goals, the other being an economic revolution to secure liberation from capitalist domination. Third World revolutions have done much to dramatize the importance of the question of culture in Marxism not only because cultural transformation has emerged as a central issue of revolution in social environments that lack the cultural preconditions for socialism as envisaged initially in Marxist theory, but even more so because of questions raised by the imperatives of economic development. In a world dominated by capitalism, economic revolution in itself has promised not liberation from capitalist hegemony but a more intense incorporation within its scope. An exclusive preoccupation with questions of economic development inevitably ushers in economism, the ideology of the bourgeoisie, which gains strength along with economic development since the latter produces social groups and classes that identify themselves primarily with an economic rationale of social change.

Culture, under the circumstances, has had to carry the burden for the realization of socialism. In the revolutionary tradition created in the course of the struggle for social and political liberation, Third World socialists have seen (or hoped to see) the makings of a new culture which is neither of the West nor of the past, in other words, which can be national without being parochial and cosmopolitan without being alien—a new culture, the making of which must accompany the making of a new world, but without which the latter cannot be conceived. Even where economism has taken over, socialist leadership has found it difficult to abandon the hope of creating a new culture that would be contemporary without being Western or capitalist; the question may be even more crucial in such cases since a new anti-capitalist culture is essential to counteract the bourgeois hegemony that economism must produce. Without revolutionary social transformation upon which a new culture of liberation must rest, such hope may only result in an eclecticism that represents not a new culture but the illusion of one; however, we have no reason to doubt the authenticity of the quest itself.

For Western intellectuals to deny the importance of the question of culture in the name of the higher truth of a scientistic economism, then, is at best arrogant; at worst, it aids in the establishment of a new kind of hegemony—bourgeois hegemony represented by economism. The rejection of culture as a question, on the grounds that it has served to hegemonize the non-Western world, not only reveals a limited appreciation of the possibilities offered by culture, but also perpetuates other, even more powerful, bourgeois assumptions about the world. We need not reject either the past of non-Western societies or their present peculiarities in order to challenge the premises of hegemonic culturalism. The point is to bring out the historical complexities of these societies (and to recognize the possibility of future diversity), not to perpetuate the image of them as undifferentiated cultural entities, this time so rendered in the name of economic truths. Challenges to culturalist hegemony that do not extend their criticism to this question perpetuate the most basic epistemological assumptions of such a hegemony.

The problem, therefore, is not whether the question of culture is a significant one, but rather how to conceive of a culture that may serve liberating rather than hegemonic purposes. Third World revolutionaries in their call for cultural revolution have suggested means, epistemological if not practical, for confronting this question. It is not likely that we will hear what they say, however, unless we take their questions seriously; indeed, it is more likely that we will be party to suppressing what they say, no matter how good our intentions. Before I discuss the critique of hegemony as it has appeared in the thinking of Third World intellectuals, I would like to examine the issue of hegemony as it has appeared in European Marxism. Debates within the latter, not involving issues of the Other, help enunciate clearly the epistemological questions raised by culturalism as hegemonic principle and liberating practice.

The question that arises here is whether or not we are justified in viewing culturalism merely as a feature of intellectual relations between the West and the Rest. I think not. Indeed, its presentation as an exclusive feature of this relationship not only imprisons the critique of culturalism itself in a culturalist discourse, but is socially and politically reactionary as well (all we need here is to remember that Western culturalism finds its counterpoint in native chauvinism!). Culturalism viewed as a global ideological phenomenon (not restricted to relations between the West and Others, but very much alive *within* Western societies themselves), on the other hand, brings into relief the problem of culture as it appears in the relationship between societies and makes possible a more thorough social critique of the hegemonic functions assumed by the concept of culture in the ideology of culturalism. This perspective also brings out with some clarity the possibilities implicit in culturalism as liberating practice, which contradicts its function as hegemonic principle. To elucidate this possibility, it is necessary to examine culturalism also as an attribute of relations between classes.

The question of culture has received considerable attention among Western Marxists in recent years, mainly in connection with problems presented by the debate over Marxist structuralism versus Marxist historicism. The nature of this question, as it pertains to historical work, may be illustrated through a brief discussion of E. P. Thompson's *The Making of the English Working Class,* a work that has exerted a seminal influence not only on Marxist thinking on culture in history, but on a whole generation of socio-historical writing. It has also provoked considerable controversy among Marxists over the question of agency versus structure in history, possibility the central question of Marxism in our day.

In an article entitled "Edward Thompson, Eugene Genovese, and Socialist Humanist History," Richard Johnson has pointed to *The Making of the English Working Class,* along with Genovese's *Roll Jordan Roll,* as outstanding examples of what he calls "culturalist Marxism." Johnson's use of the latter term in this context does not differ significantly from the way I have used it. Culturalism represents, according to Johnson, "A break away from . . . theoretical development and complex economism to an overriding concern with 'culture' and 'experience.'"[4] Thompson has rejected "absolutely" this suggestion that his work could be described as "culturalist."[5] As is typical of his various debates with his structuralist critics, Thompson's response to this is unduly defensive and intemperate; he is ready to throw out the baby with the bathwater. Culturalism in its non-Marxist sense has implications which must render the suggestion offensive to any Marxist since it implies an ideology of culture that sets it apart from and above the social relations on which any Marxist understanding of culture must rest. This, however, is not the point of Johnson's critique. It is indeed illuminating to view *The Making of the English Working Class* as a culturalist work *within* the context of Marxism, to juxtapose it to Marxist approaches that deny a significant, even semi-autonomous, role to culture in history. The two culturalisms share a common vocabulary, but they diverge radically in epistemology. The possibility of a Marxist culturalism brings into relief the epistemological foundations of hegemonic culturalism as a liberating practice (although this is not what Johnson does, because, essentially involved with structuralism, he misses the point about his own undertaking). In this, I think, lies the power of *The Making of the English Working Class.*

This Marxist culturalism, as its non-Marxist counterpart, is historicist, radically so. In Thompson's own eloquent words:

> But the fact is, again, the material took command of me, far more than I had ever expected. If you want a generalization I would have to say that the historian has got to be listening all the time. He should not set up a book or research project with a totally clear sense of exactly what he is going to be able to do. The material itself has got to speak through him. And I think this happens.[6]

This historicism has led culturalist Marxists to a suspicion of theory in favor of descriptive history. To quote Genovese this time:

> Many years of studying the astonishing effort of black people to live decently as human beings even in slavery has convinced me that no theoretical advance suggested in their experience could ever deserve as much attention as that demanded by their demonstration of the beauty and power of the human spirit under conditions of extreme oppression.[7]

Thompson's appreciation of theory, as he has stated repeatedly since *The Making of the English Working Class* in his debates with structuralist Marxists, is radically historicist. Theory to him, to quote Johnson, is merely "a moment in the historian's method." Thompson's approach to concepts is ruthlessly empirical. This is evident in his use of class, the central concept of his work, which has provoked considerable controversy. "Class," in Thompson's view, "is defined by men as they live their own history, and, in the end, this is its only definition."[8] Class is, we might add, what people do and how they think in "class ways."

Not surprisingly, tradition, too, plays a major part in this "culturalist Marxism." The first part of *The Making of the English Working Class* is devoted almost entirely to decoding the language of protest that is, as Thompson presents it, authentically an exclusively English. Particularly revealing in this respect is his apology to "Scottish and Welsh" readers in his preface: "I have neglected these histories, not out of chauvinism, but out of respect. It is because class is a cultural as much as an economic formation that I have been cautious as to generalizing beyond English experience."[9] The statement is reminiscent of the one used by some students of non-Western societies: to apply theory of Western origin to the analysis of non-Western societies is not only misleading but "imperialistic" as well!

Indeed, for the historian of China or of other non-Western societies, the conceptual apparatus that informs this "culturalist Marxism" is puzzlingly reminiscent of the one I have referred to as the source of culturalist hegemony in Western studies of non-Western thought and culture. Yet this is where the comparison stops. Both Thompson and Genovese are consciously anti-hegemonic in their intentions, Genovese more explicitly so since his work draws directly on Gramsci's critique of hegemony. And whatever we may think of the history/theory debate which their works have provoked (of which more later), none but the most ardent structuralist would deny that seemingly the same culturalism that appears as hegemonic principle in studies of non-Western societies manifests itself here as liberating practice.

This is not to suggest that culturalism appears as liberating practice within Western society and as hegemonic principle in relations between the West and the non-West, but to illustrate that culturalism in and of itself does not account for ideological hegemony. The parallel within the West to the hegemonic use of culture in studies of the Third World is to be found in the use of culture in establishing the ideological hegemony of one class over another. Here, too, culture has been utilized to distance the Other, if not in space (which is somewhat more problematic though by no means impossible) then at least in time, through the assertion of the ideological and cultural backwardness of the working classes, with similar hegemonic consequences, particularly in denying contemporary relevance to the culture of the Other. Culturalist hegemony is secured here by presenting the consequence of oppression, cultural impoverishment, as its cause, but above all by distancing the culture of the Other. Speaking of the emergence of the notion of the "masses" in nineteenth-century England, Raymond Williams writes:

> Masses are other people. . . . There are in fact no masses; there are only ways of seeing people as masses. In an urban industrial society there are many opportunities for such ways of seeing. The point is not to reiterate the objective conditions but to consider, personally and collectively, what these have done to our thinking. The fact is, surely, that a way of seeing other people which has become characteristic of our kind of society, has been capitalized for the purposes of political or cultural exploitation. What we see, neutrally, is other people, many others, people unknown to us. In practice, we mass them, and interpret them, according to some convenient formula. Within its terms, the formula will hold. Yet it is the formula, not the mass, which it is our real business to examine. It may help us to do this if we remember that we ourselves are all the time being massed by others. To the degree that we find the formula inadequate for ourselves, we can wish to extend to others the courtesy of acknowledging the unknown.[10]

What then accounts for the contradictory consequences that issue from what is seemingly the same approach to history in terms of conceptual premises about the past and the present? The immediate answers would seem to be the humanism of Marxist culturalists or their sympathies for the oppressed, which enable them to turn the tables on hegemonic culturalists. While this is true to some extent, it explains differences only on a superficial level. Humanism is not sufficient to bridge the distances established by hegemonic culturalism between or within societies. Indeed, humanism may simply result in a cultural relativism which, as Fabian has argued, does not overcome but confirms culturalist distancing. This is especially the case with cultural relativism within the context of relations between the West and the non-West and similarly with the notion of sympathy or even empathy for the oppressed. Sympathy neither precludes condescension, nor, at the least, a sense of the irrelevance of the Other, no matter how admired. Naipaul, in *A Bend in the River*, captures this problem in the figure of the Belgian priest Father Huysmans who, in love with Africa, views himself as the last witness to its dying civilization. This kind of sympathy that identifies with the Other and yet denies him "coevalness" (in Fabian's words) is essential, I think, to the "orientalizing" of the Other.

The differences, rather, must be sought in the fundamental epistemological divergence that underlies these seemingly identical conceptualizations of history. The liberating conclusions of Marxist culturalism as represented in the works of Thompson and Genovese (and to which Williams has made fundamental contributions) rest in going beyond expressions of sympathy for the working classes in order to counter their distancing in hegemonic culturalism. As Thompson has explained his goals:

> I am seeking to rescue the poor stockinger, the Luddite cropper, the "obsolete" hand-loom weaver, the "utopian" artisan, and even the deluded follower of Joanna Southcott from the enormous condescension of posterity. Their crafts and traditions may have been dying. Their hostility to the new industrialism may have been backward-looking. Their communitarian ideals may have been fantasies. Their insurrectionary conspiracies may have been foolhardy. But they lived through these times of acute social disturbance, and we do not. Their aspirations are valid in terms of their own experience.[11]

This activity of "rescuing," I would like to suggest, entails more than simply bringing the benighted into the light of history. Thompson seeks not merely to remind us of the English working class, but to re-present it as the defender of the most central values of English society. As he puts it in the concluding lines of his book:

> Yet the working people should not be seen only as the lost myriads of eternity. They had also nourished, for fifty years, and with incomparable fortitude, the Liberty Tree. We may thank them for these years of heroic culture.[12]

The working people, then, did not merely contribute to the making of English society—their activities were central to the establishment of its most basic values.

This "centering" of the working people (the Other, in this instance) is crucial to understanding the epistemological under-pinnings of Marxist culturalism as liberating practice. The centering of the working class must of necessity be accompanied by the "decentering" of the ruling, or the hegemonic, class, since the two groups by definition make contradictory claims upon history. Thompson's goal, ultimately, is to show that the struggles of the working class in England, rather than being expressive of cultural backwardness or political irrelevance, helped preserve and promote the democratic values which the ruling class claimed for itself but was ever ready to compromise. From this perspective, the heroes of hegemonic history (the putative creators of democratic political values) appear as obstacles to the practice of democracy or, at the very least, lose their centrality in the creation and perpetuation of those values. If this does not necessarily replace the hegemonic class with the working class at the center of history (I do not believe this is Thompson's intention), it at least denies to history a center, without which culturalist hegemony is deprived of its frame of reference.

The same may be said of Thompson's use of tradition, which differs fundamentally from the use of this concept in hegemonic culturalism, to which the notion of tradition is crucial. Thompson (as well as Genovese) has an activist conception of tradition, which is consonant with the fundamental activist epistemology that underlies his work as a whole. He approaches tradition not as a burden of the past upon the present, an inert legacy that shapes the consciousness of people with its own prerogatives, but as an activity in the production of a past that is rooted in the social struggles over hegemony. An irrefutable tradition that defines the center of history is crucial to ruling-class history, and so is the presentation of that tradition as something prior to everyday life. Contrarily, in Thompson's presentation, tradition does not shape social relations, rather it is produced and reproduces itself in the course of ongoing social activity. Traditions are unique (the past *does* make a difference for the present), but not the processes that produce traditions, for they are part and parcel of the structure of social conflict. The investigation of the language of protest in the English tradition is to Thompson both end and means: the language is important because it has shaped the way people have thought about social relations, but it must also be decoded in order to reveal the social conflict it signifies. The revelation of conflict, embedded in the very language of tradition, renders tradition problematic, raising immediate questions about its claims to centrality.

In raising questions about the center of history, Marxist culturalism appears as liberating practice. Hegemony requires a center, not only in space but also in time. The decentering of the hegemonic group, be it class or nation, deprives history of a center and the hegemonic group of its claims upon history. Culturalism that achieves this end points to a liberating possibility, if only as a possibility. This, I feel, is the intention, and the meaning, of Marxist culturalism.

This abolition of a center in the historical process is what Harootunian has in mind, I think, when he observes: "The social process has no center. . . . Instead, society is composed of multiple contradictions in relationships of overdetermination so as to create the potential for ideological conflict in the general effort to determine what is natural for groups and individuals."[13] What I would like to reflect on here is what this statement implies, not only for groups within history or society, but for historians and their relationship to history. Depriving history of a center, it seems to me, also deprives the historian of centrality. Without elaborating the implications of his observation, Johnson suggests that Althusser and the structuralists "intervene" in or "read" history; Thompson, on the other hand, "listens" while Genovese "tells." In the passage cited above, Thompson presents himself as the "mouthpiece" through which the people in history speak. Whether or not this is what he achieves is not as important a question here as his intention: to decenter the historians' discourse in order to make room at the center of history for its subjects whose "experiences" take precedence over the historian's discourse because they lived that history and the historian did not. The concession here, while fundamentally epistemological, is not merely so; it is a concession of the historian's hegemony over the past, the Other, as it were.

Historicism, Structuralism and Hegemony: The Alienation of Intellectuals and the Abstraction of Society

Such is the meaning of the historicism of culturalist Marxism; it explains why historicism appears here as a condition of culturalism as liberating practice. Ironically, structuralism may have provided a method that reveals the structuralist analysis of society as a hegemonic one. The use of categories or, more broadly, of abstractions, in history has emerged as the central issue around which the controversy between historicist and structuralist Marxists has revolved. I think it is naive to suppose that culturalist Marxism, because it is historicist, rejects the use of concepts and categories in social analysis. *The Making of the English Working Class* and *Roll Jordan Roll* take as their point of departure the concept of class, and they are fundamentally ideological in retaining this concept, especially so because their authors recognize the problematic nature of the concept. Still, there is an unbridgeable gap between Thompson and Genovese and their structuralist critics concerning the issue of concepts and theory in history (which makes efforts at conciliation rather naive). If I read these works correctly, what they reject are not concepts or theory, but the substitution of concepts or theory for lived experience: if the categories of the historian clash with the experiences of the historical subject, it is the former that must be abandoned in the name of the latter, and not the other way around. In other words, questions raised concerning abstract categories parallel at the level of epistemology questions raised concerning the historian's place vis-à-vis the historical subject: just as the historian is "decentered" in favor of the historical subject, so are the categories of the historian's discourse "decentered" in favor of the subject's experience. Hence Thompson's insistence that the category of class should not be employed to conceptualize people in history who did not think of themselves in terms of this category.

Thompson has done much better at caricaturizing Althusser's structuralism (as with his "orrery of errors" which identifies structuralism with its vulgarization) than at dealing with the issues raised by structuralism. At times, his attacks on theory seem to deny it any place in analysis, which is not only obscurantist, but places his own work in basic contradiction since his own analysis is structured by highly theoretical concepts. Nevertheless, his work, in the presence it provides to the subjects of history, dramatizes the absence in structuralist analysis of the historical subject, in spite of theoretical claims to the contrary.

The controversy over abstractions, therefore, is at the same time a controversy over hegemony. Thompson feels categories are a means for distancing the Other, and he discusses Althusser's use of them: "a category . . . finds its definition only within a highly theorized structural totality, which disallows the real *experiential* historical process of class formation."[14] If this sounds unfair to Althusser, we may recall the observation of Poulantzas that "social classes are not empirical groups of individuals. . . . The class membership of the various agents depends on the class places they occupy."[15] Agent here is a misnomer because it does not make much sense to speak of agents when people have been rendered into categories. The immediate issue here is that such categorization represents little more than a taxonomic distancing. I am not sure that Thompson himself has even suggested this directly, but the implication of his views is that categories, including that of class, are in themselves instruments of hegemony *if* they serve to distance the subjects of history from the historian; for surely "class" then becomes a counterpart (albeit viewed with sympathy by a Marxist) of Williams's "masses," a way of defining the Other whom we do not know, an who only exists in our mind as part of an internally undifferentiated totality.

The criticism of abstraction may, of course, be carried to the ridiculous and naive extreme of denying abstraction any part in understanding, which is the same as denying the latter any organization or direction. Indeed, the only consequence of rejecting abstractions may be acquiescence in tacit ideological premises which are present whether or not we wish to acknowledge them. This, obviously, does not characterize the thinking or the work of culturalist Marxists, but points to the difference between Marxist historicism, acutely aware of the ideological nature of historical discourses (within history or among historians), and an antitheoretical historicism with its pretensions to truth.

Culturalist Marxism points to an epistemological issue with crucial social significance: abstractions, substituted for living people, may become tools of hegemony regardless of the goodwill or the professions of sympathy for the cause of liberation on the part of their practitioners. Abstractions inevitably create an ideological and, therefore, social distance between subject and object since their very purpose is to objectify human agency in history. If knowledge is power, as Foucault suggests, abstractions are the instruments of power which the knowing subject employs to establish control over understanding and over the known. This is most evident in the claims to comprehend society scientifically (not to be confused with systematically) which, whatever their ideological point of departure, presuppose that human agency must be reconstituted in accordance with "scientific principles" as understood by the "social scientist." The consciousness of the comprehending subject, in other words, takes precedence over the consciousness of the historical agent and constitutes the latter as its object in accordance with its own discourse. This, it should be obvious, licenses the comprehending subject to speak in the name of its object and, in case of opposition between the two, justifies the suppression of the latter in the name of higher truths, be they scientific or otherwise.

The historian, as a matter of practice, participates in three discourses: a discourse with the subjects of history, a discourse among historians, and a discourse with his social environment. To the extent that the historian assumes the prerogatives of the knowing subject, discourse among historians takes precedence over discourse with the subjects of history, and the latter is constituted in accordance with the prerogatives of the former. The result is the alienation of the historical subject through the abstractions that express the historian's discourse.

This alienation is an unavoidable consequence of professionalism. Intellectuals have been described by Gouldner as "speech communities."[16] This is all the more the case with professional intellectuals whose activity requires, nay demands, the creation of a language that defines professional activity. The historian's alienation from the historical subject is, in other words, a consequence of participation in a profession: it is a social alienation. This is the social price paid for expertise.

This alienation, however, is social in another, more fundamental, sense. Professions may not be tools of hegemonic social classes, but neither do they operate in isolation from the discourse of their environment with its hegemonic assumptions about society and the world. The validity of the learning produced by professionals is judged according to its resonance with these assumptions of the broader social discourse. The question of the participation of intellectuals in hegemonic practices assumes particular seriousness since the latter appear in the guise of what Gramsci calls "organic intellectuals," who are recruited into the service of "alienated social power," which I use here to denote not merely the state, as Marx had in mind, but the whole complex of institutions of power within the environment established by the state ("ideological state apparatuses," in Althusser's terms)[17] or, to put it less academically, the establishment. To the extent that professionalism is a socially desirable goal, professions are part of this alienated establishment. The alienation of the historian from the historical subject, it follows, finds its counterpart in the alienation of the historian as a professional from his immediate social environment. Hegemony over the historical subject is but an extension into the past of the hegemonic relationship the historian bears to his society as part of the establishment.

To the extent that expertise rather than political affiliation determines membership in the establishment, I might add, the struggle over hegemony ceases to be expressed simply as a struggle between right, middle, and left, or between conservative, liberal, and socialist, but as a struggle between the establishment and those who are marginalized (hegemonized) by the establishment.

It is here, I think, that we find the social context for the struggle between culturalism as hegemonic principle and as liberating practice, between sociologism and historicism, between economism and humanism. Culturalist Marxism is the expression not so much of Marxism but of "decentered" intellectuals who have discovered in Marxist historicism a means to counter hegemony, past and present, by challenging the hegemonic practices of professional and therefore regnant assumptions of the dominant social discourse. None of this implies that culturalist Marxists are themselves immune to the social practices that they call into question. The challenge, nevertheless, is liberating in its rejection of a center to the historical and, therefore, social process.

The Third World Intellectual and Marxist Historicism

This is where Marxist culturalism has something of profound significance to tell us. Before we look at that, however, it will be helpful to distinguish the differences in the form that hegemonic culturalism takes in ideological relations between the West and the non-West from the form in which it appears in Western societies.

Simply stated, culturalist hegemony within the context of global relations is a "double-hegemony": it involves, in addition to the relationship between the West and the non-West, the hegemonic relations within non-Western societies. The interplay between these two creates a complexity over the question of hegemony that, while broadly recognized (at least since Lenin), continues to confound students of non-Western societies.

The question of hegemony between societies is perhaps the easiest to recognize because of its naked assumptions about Western centrality in the world. There are good reasons, moreover, not only intellectual but social, why Western students of non-Western societies should be well-prepared to recognize this form of hegemony. We all know that Western intrusion in the non-Western world displaces or "decenters" intellectuals in these societies who, as it were, learn to live in two cultural worlds without belonging in either one completely. This, to a lesser extent, also happens to intellectuals in the West who engage in the study of non-Western societies—Said's "orientalists." In our preoccupation with the hegemonic role these intellectuals play in relations between the West and the non-West, we fail to recognize sometimes that "orientalist" intellectuals are themselves "orientalized" by virtue of what they do because hegemonic culturalism, as it distances the non-Western world, also distances intellectually those who study it. We have all experienced at one time or another doubts on the part of our colleagues as to whether or not the work we are engaged in justifies complete integration into our disciplines! "Orientalists," in other words, have good reason to "decenter" Western hegemony and call an end to hegemonic relations between societies.

This does not in itself resolve the question of hegemony, however, but may itself serve as a cover for reactionary social attitudes, no matter how radical the claims. In order to be thorough, the critique of culturalist hegemony must be extended to the role culture plays as an instrument of hegemony *within* societies. As Third World Marxist critics of culturalist hegemony have long understood, this critique of internal hegemony is not only necessary if liberation from hegemony is to be total, extended beyond the elite to the people at large, but is also a precondition of cultural liberation of the society as a whole. Those Third World intellectuals who refuse to acknowledge this necessity and take recourse instead in the affirmation of a pre-Western tradition as a source of contemporary identity, or simply reject that tradition in favor of Westernism as an obstacle to development, only serve as grist for the mills of Western cultural hegemonism which finds confirmed in them its own tendency to view those societies as prisoners between the past and the West. To the extent that these intellectuals distance themselves from the present of their societies by taking refuge in the past or the West, they not only produce a hegemonic relationship between themselves and their societies, but facilitate the distancing of their societies in the hegemonic culturalism of the West.

This form of hegemony is somewhat more difficult to recognize. To the elitist "orientalist," it does not present itself as a problem, not only because it coincides with his own culturalist assumptions, but even more so because, given his hegemonic relationship to his own society, he does not recognize the question as a significant one. But there is also a more problematic radical "orientalism" that will allow the elite in Third World societies the kind of hegemonic behavior that it will not permit the elite in its own society. This kind of "orientalism," what we might call Third-Worldism, is in some ways more pernicious than the "orientalism" of the elites because it mystifies the question of hegemony in radical language. We often forget that the assumptions about other societies that go into the making of Western culturalist hegemony derive their plausibility from their coincidence with the assumptions held by chauvinistic nationalists about their own societies. The ruling classes in these societies, who uphold these assumptions, are not democratic by virtue of being a Third World ruling elite, but share in the social hegemonism of all ruling classes. Yet radical students of these societies have all too often been unwilling to criticize this kind of hegemony for fear of playing into the hands of Western imperialism.

In a discussion of this problem that is as cogent as it is honest and passionate, Abdallah Laroui in his *The Crisis of the Arab Intellectual* addresses the question of historical or cultural "retardation" that he believes must be part of non-Western intellectuals' confrontation with the West. The response to the intellectual crisis created by this sense of "retardation," Laroui argues, has been an uneasy eclecticism or an escape into tradition, which for Laroui, is not an abstract "thing" that "maintains itself by itself," but an ideological creation that "demands as much activity as progress." This activity, even if it provides the intellectual with some identity, only confirms retardation. Moreover, it is as alienating an activity as the escape into the West. In Laroui's words:

> Now there are two types of alienation: the one is visible and openly criticized, the other all the more insidious as it is denied on principle. Westernization indeed signifies an alienation, a way of becoming other, an avenue to self-division (though one's estimation of this transformation may be positive or negative, according to one's ideology). But there exists another form of alienation in modern Arab society, one that is prevalent but veiled: this is the exaggerated medievalization obtained through quasi-magical identification with the great period of classical Arabian culture.[18]

These two attitudes, "fundamentalist and liberal," Laroui suggests, "were opposed yet nonetheless complementary: liberalism was necessary but did not perforce imply a break with the past, traditionalism was tempting therapeutics but did not resolve urgent problems."[19]

Alienation, As Laroui sees it, is not an abstract question but simply implies distancing of intellectuals from the present of their societies. How Westernization leads to this result does not need belaboring. Of traditionalism Laroui says:

> For all objective observers, the true alienation is this loss of self in the absolutes of language, culture, and the saga of the past. The Arab intellectual blithely plunges into them, hoping thus to prove his perfect freedom and to express his deepest personality. Here, then, are found the inward chains binding him to a present he yet claims to repudiate. Historical consciousness alone will allow him to free himself of them. Then he will see reality perhaps for the first time. He will see that the absolutes he worships are alien to him, for they may be interiorized only through intellectual analysis and synthesis, that is, through voluntary effort—never through inward understanding and intuition.[20]

Laroui's own solution to the problem is to suggest a radical Marxist historicism that he believes will reconnect the intellectual with the present.

> The historicism we are leading up to, one that is in many respects instrumental is not the passive acceptance of any past whatsoever and above all not the acceptance of one's own national past; rather, it is the voluntary choice of realizing the unity of historical meaning by the reappropriation of a selective past. This choice is motivated by pragmatic considerations, perhaps by modesty, above all by nationalism in the most natural sense of the word; the will to gain the respect of others by the shortest possible route. In this perspective we see clearly that it is not the moderate liberal who is being realistic, for he chooses to believe in the improbable equality of nations. Rather, it is the radical nationalist who is the realist; provided that he affirms his existence, he cares little if he loses his essence (his authenticity).[21]

This paragraph is problematic on a number of grounds; what concerns me here, however, is the clear link that Laroui establishes between the intellectual and the present of his society through the epistemology of historicism, specifically Marxist historicism, which, moreover, is connected in his mind to revolutionary activity in the present. As he states in the very next paragraph: "Praxis therefore is historicism in action." And it should come as no surprise that all anti-historicism takes on an anti-praxis value. "An abstract universalism, expressing itself in economism, anthropology, or structuralism, knows nothing of involution and consequently takes no account of hegemony."[22]

I do not wish to read into Laroui's discussion issues that he does not address, not directly anyway. Nevertheless, in its advocacy of a radical historicism, as well as in the reasons it adduces for this advocacy, *The Crisis of the Arab Intellectual* has a direct bearing on questions raised by culturalism—both in its hegemonic and liberating practices. Laroui's idea of historicism draws heavily on Joseph Levenson's work on China, which I have depicted as an articulation of hegemonic culturalism,[23] but, on the other hand, his historicism is much closer in intention and implication to that of culturalist Marxists. The difference, I think, is the difference between historicism and Marxist historicism.

Levenson portrays the dilemma of Chinese intellectuals as a product of the necessity of choosing between the past and the West. His account of intellectual development in modern China is an account of the victory of its attraction to the West as opposed to its own ties to the past, which became increasingly emotional as the undeniable validity of Western ideas impressed itself upon the consciousness of Chinese intellectuals. Acceptance of the universality of Western values was accompanied by the inexorable historicization of Chinese values. The intellect/emotion bifurcation created by this confrontation was resolved by Marxism, which historicized Chinese values but salvaged their truth for the past (as the truth of a past mode of production), just as it legitimized acceptance of the West as the source of present truth while promising its eventual historicization (as the truth of an equally historical capitalism).

This dilemma is also the point of departure for Laroui, but it leads him in different directions. The fundamental difference is existential: Levenson is the American academic writing about the passing away of a culture he admired; Laroui is a Third World intellectual trying to rid his society of the hegemony of the past in order that the society itself may be salvaged. According to Levenson's analysis, he is indeed the object of the discourse striving to reassert himself as a subject of history. While Levenson sees the dilemma as a psychic one, that is, as the reintegration of the Chinese intellectual by overcoming the separation of value from history, Laroui sees it as a social problem: to reintegrate the intellectual within the society from which he has become alienated because he has identified himself with the past or the West. For Laroui, the confrontation between Arabs and the West is not merely an abstract confrontation between the ideas and values of civilizations removed from history, each with its own claims to truth, but a political and social confrontation as well: between oppressor societies and a society that has been "proletarianized" by the oppression. As he explains his idea of "New Nationalism":

> Where, in confrontation with Europe, the fundamentalist opposed a culture (Chinese, Indian, Islamic) and the liberal opposed a nation (Chinese, Turkish, Egyptian, Iranian), the revolutionary opposes a class—one that is often extended to include all that part of the human race exploited by the European bourgeoisie. One may refer to it as class nationalism that nevertheless retains many of the motifs of political and cultural nationalisms; hence the difficulties experienced by analysts who have attempted to define it. Revolutionary nationalism has three aspects: an exploited class, a dominated people, and a hard-pressed culture. The opposition to Europe also assumes a triple aspect.[24]

This is no longer the "Confucian China" of the Sinologist; it is the "proletarian" nation of revolutionary intellectuals (Li Dazhao, Sun Yat-sen, Mao Zedong come to mind immediately). If it does not bring the proletariat (or the oppressed

classes) into the forefront of history, it at least makes them into a central component of the national struggle—as a referent against which the fate of ideas and
values must be judged.

The idea of the "Proletarian nation," of course, still addresses only one aspect
of the problem of hegemony, that between nations, but it does open up the possibility of dealing with the other aspect, that within societies. Laroui is quite
aware (though this remains vague) that the ways in which Arab intellectuals have
sought to resolve the dilemma of cultural choice (through recourse to the past or
the West) has not only alienated them from the present of their societies, but also
serves to distance society and guarantee the hegemony of intellectuals. The goal
of cultural activity, therefore, must be to abolish this hegemony as well by reintegrating the intellectual within society. His, I think, is an idea of culture not significantly different from what I have called "a social concept of culture." For him,
culture is the culture of everyday life, "quotidian temporality," as he puts it.[25]

The difference of Laroui's historicism from Levenson's does not rest merely in
existential, but in ideological and epistemological, differences as well. It is ultimately a difference between historicism and Marxist historicism. To Levenson,
Marxism, too, is an abstraction, an instrument that helps Chinese intellectuals
rationalize their dilemma. For Laroui, Marxism is an epistemology that
promises understanding and resolution: its significance lies not in the intellectual activity that distances the past and renders it irrelevant to the present, but
in its relevance to praxis in the present. Marxism itself, moreover, must be
refracted through the native present: it is not merely a means to historicize the
native legacy; it itself must be historicized to serve the cause of present society.
The distinction between historicist and structuralist Marxism, which is of no
concern to Levenson since he distances Marxism as well, is of crucial significance to Laroui.

This distinction expresses an epistemological judgment that coincides with
that of what we have called culturalist Marxism. This is not surprising; Laroui's
intellectual forebears, as of culturalist Marxism in Europe, are Lukács and
Gramsci and, through them, Lenin. And as with European culturalist Marxism,
Laroui rejects the abstract in favor of the concrete. Abstractions are alienating;
they also serve as tools of hegemony, regardless of whether or not they are of the
liberal or the Marxist variety. In his preface, he says:

> Those who criticize historicism as a philosophy—I refer in particular to the French-
> man L. Althusser—are interested primarily in a rationale of understanding: they take
> as models the exact sciences, which presume an eternal present and a homogeneous
> milieu. A society that believes itself to be at the apogee of evolution and that strives
> to preserve the equilibrium it imagines it has attained will experience no difficulty in
> transposing such rationale to the social and human sciences. But a society that rejects
> its present, that lacks homogeneity, that feels itself to be different from those cultures
> that appear to be in the ascendant, will rediscover historicism as the theoretical jus-
> tification for its course of action, sometimes in the guise of Marxism.[26]

Laroui's rejection of abstraction is rejection not of conceptual abstraction per se; given the complexity of the problems he deals with, his own argument proceeds at a very high, even opaque, level of abstraction. Indeed, one could argue that this argument, carried within the context of a cosmopolitan intellectual discourse, is inaccessible to the society with whom he would reconnect the intellectual and thus perpetuates the alienation that he himself criticizes. Nevertheless, it is important to note that he is critical of the alienating discourse that makes the subjects of history into its objects and that seeks to concretize culture in order to bring it to the level of everyday life. "The future of a given ideology," he tells us, "is not assured unless it offers the possibility of concretizing the frustrated hopes of a community."[27] Beneath all the opaqueness of his presentation, this is the message of his historicism.

The statement, "praxis is historicism in action," offers the key, I think, to understanding the coincidence in Laroui's analysis of an anti-abstractionist (not anti-theoretical) historicism and an empirical notion of culture with a dialectic of the present. It is through praxis that the basic contradiction in society is discovered or defined. Revolutionary political praxis does not confront culture as an external and therefore, abstract force, but only as a contradiction immanent in the structure of the social present. While theory may be crucial in disclosing this structure, moreover, theory (with its abstractions) is but a "moment" in the practice of politics, in the identification of political possibilities; for political praxis, if it is to avoid alienation, must comprehend society not abstractly but concretely, in terms of the empirical alignment of social forces. Political analysis, as Gramsci was well aware, parallels historical analysis; the difference between the two lies not in the method but in the object of analysis: politics is but practical history.

Laroui's activist epistemology finds in historicism the means to comprehend the present as a dialectical moment, a moment that is structured by the contradictory "inter-presence" of the native past and the West and that holds forth in the resolution of this contradiction the possibility of a future culture that is neither of the past nor of the West. Historicism for Laroui is not merely a heuristic device, but acquiescence in a globalized (or "totalized," in Lukács's sense) historical consciousness that the decentering of intellectuals forces upon them, provided that they are willing to recognize themselves for what they are (regardless of their constant and alienating efforts to escape it)—the alienated products of this contradiction. This recognition presupposes a sense of history as an open-ended possibility, without a center to the historical process (Laroui is highly critical of evolutionism of whatever ideological persuasion), and of culture as an open-ended activity, without any central design, in which human agency creates the future out of the ingredients of the present, without any goals save the creation of a culture that is at once local and universal, without any centrality assigned to either. Laroui's historicism, nevertheless, is empirical without being empiricist and cosmopolitan without being relativist. It is a Marxist historicism in which the future is informed by the dialectic of the present. Future culture, which is to take form in the course of human activity, is the product neither of arbitrary eclecticism nor of abstract intellectual design, but of social praxis that seeks to eliminate the alienation of the intellectual and, with it, the existing structure of hegemony by abolishing the cultural distancing of the intellectual from his social present. The contradiction in culture, in other words, may be resolved only through social transformation since the problem of culture, as the expression of the problems of alienation and hegemony, is also a social problem. The resolution of one points the way to the resolution of the other, as a new society points to a new culture (or vice versa).

The dialectic of the present is ever present as the point of departure in the cultural thinking of Third World radical socialists who have stressed "cultural revolution" as a central project of socialist revolution. Unlike the hegemonic use of culture in culturalist ideology, where it appears as alienated (because determinative of the present as an external force), this radical conceptualization of culture resists alienation by positing the present as the focus of cultural activity. In the words of Mariategui, the Peruvian Marxist: "Peru's past interests us to the extent [that] it can explain Peru's present. Constructive generations think of the past as an origin, never as a program."[28] The words are echoed in Kwameh Nkrumah's philosophical declaration, *Consciencism:* "Consciencism is that philosophical standpoint which, taking its start from the present content of the African conscience, indicates the way in which progress is forged out of conflict in that conscience."[29]

While this resistance to the alienation of culture is motivated at least in part by a desire to deny the hegemonic claims of the ruling classes, the "keepers" of tradition, by challenging the contemporary relevance of the inherited culture upon which such claims are based, it does not follow that the inherited culture of the oppressed, substituted for that of the ruling classes, is sufficient source for the creation of a new culture. A romantic escape into popular culture, that of the oppressed, is another way of distancing the present, of which the past is a living part but which is not, therefore, identical with the past. As Franz Fanon puts it:

> A national culture is not a folklore, nor an abstract populism that believes it can discover the people's true nature. It is not made up of the inert dregs of gratuitous actions, that is to say actions which are less and less attached to the ever-present reality of the people. A national culture is the whole body of efforts made by a people in the sphere of thought to describe, justify and praise the action through which the people has created itself and keeps itself in existence. A national culture in underdeveloped countries should therefore take its place at the very heart of the struggle for freedom which these countries are carrying on.[30]

The insistence on the present as a new beginning implies more than a simple recognition that the present, defined by a historically unprecedented contradiction, contains the past only as a dialectical moment. It signifies not simply a denial of the hegemony of the past over the present, but a denial of the culturalist hegemony of the West which, in portraying the native present as a prisoner of the native past, parochializes not simply the native culture of the past but its very present. A present-oriented historicism, therefore, is not simply consistent with the cosmopolitan intention of radical socialism, but a very condition of the assertion by the Other of his "coevalness." The reaffirmation of the present as the only realm of cultural activity, in other words, is the assertion by the Other of his right to recognition as a subject of history. In a world where the native has been denied in ideology the very cosmopolitanism which has been forced upon him in reality, this reaffirmation of the present is the ultimate recognition of existence, radically opposite to the illusory search for an authenticity outside of that reality. This radical, present-oriented historicism is a pre-condition for the creation of an authentically cosmopolitan (Laroui prefers "universalistic") culture, a cosmopolitanism that is not defined in terms of the hegemonic culture of the West, but one that incorporates the native present (and the past) in the creation of a culture in which all are universal because all are equally parochial.

This activity of creating a new culture out of the dialectics of the present finally provides the means for transforming the intellectual from a plaything in the hands of the past or the West into an agent of cultural (that is to say social and political) change. Basic to radical socialism, with its cultural revolutionary intention, is the recognition that culture has at least a semi-autonomous role in revolutionary change: while the creation of a new culture must take as its point of departure the drastic overturning of existing social relations, the new culture thus created serves as the source of, or promotes, further social change. Revolution, in other words, is conceived here as a dialectical process where culture and society are structurally interrelated but are also autonomous moments of the dialectic. This presentation of the revolutionary process as a dialectic between culture and society presupposes a conception of revolution in which human activity plays a central role, where the revolutionary is at once the product and the subject of history. Mao Zedong in China had his counterpart in Che Guevara in Cuba who once stated that "the revolution is made by man, but man must forge his revolutionary spirit day by day."[31] While this brings the human agent into the center of the social process, it does not do so without profound ambiguity. While the revolutionary as subject of history has a sense of his direction, the latter provides no more than a tentative guideline, for ultimately the direction of revolution must emerge in the course of the struggle that *is* the revolution, just as its culture must be forged out of the relationship between the revolutionary and the revolutionized. In other words, the revolutionary, too, must be "listening" all the time and must not merely impose his abstractions upon the revolutionary process, which would merely involve the projection of his own alienation onto the latter. While the revolutionary is in the process of leading, in other words, his leadership must be defined in terms of the dialectic between the revolutionary consciousness and the consciousness of the social present with which he must integrate himself if the revolution is to issue in a new culture of liberation. This dialectic, too, has no center, and it is only to the extent that revolutionaries resist the temptation to establish such a center that revolution appears as a liberating possibility.

Culture, Hegemony and Liberation

Culturalism as hegemonic ideology mystifies the hegemonic role that culture plays in relationships between and within societies. A hegemonic culturalism abstracts culture from its social and political context in order to present it as an autochthonous attribute of entire groups and peoples that is exterior to, and independent of, social relationships. Culture, thus abstracted, is alienated from the social present, and is made into a timeless attribute of peoples that determines the character of the relationships into which they enter with others. It serves as a principle for organizing time and space, with the culture of the self at the center of space and the apogee of time. Abstraction is the epistemological starting point of culturalism as hegemonic ideology.

What makes culturalism truly hegemonic rather than nakedly oppressive (a distinction that we owe to Gramsci) is the participation of the hegemonized in this abstraction. Orientalism is inconceivable without "self-orientalization." Laroui's argument provides us with a cogent critique of the participation of Third World intellectuals in this kind of abstraction which alienates them from their social present. Laroui owes a great deal for this insight to Joseph Levenson's work on China, which powerfully argues the defensive nature of this abstraction for Chinese intellectuals confronted with the West. What Laroui brings out, from his Marxist perspective, is that this abstraction is not merely defensive; it also serves the purposes of class hegemony within Third World societies.

The task of culturalism as liberating practice is defined by opposition to this practice of abstraction. What needs to be challenged in the opposition to culturalist hegemony is not the validity or relevance of the notion of culture, but the abstractionist epistemology that renders culture into an alien force ruling over living people. Whether or not culturalism is an entirely appropriate term for describing this oppositional activity is problematic. Obviously, as liberating practice it challenges the very basis of the understanding of culture in the ideology of hegemonic culturalism by concretizing it within the realm of social relations. It is a Marxist culturalism, in other words, whose understanding of culture is fundamentally different from that of culturalist ideology.

What justifies the usage, nevertheless, is a need to insist on the necessity of recognition of some autonomy, even priority, to the question of culture in any meaningful liberating practice. This is especially necessary in the case of Marxism which is vulnerable to a tendency toward an abstractionist epistemology that is contradictory to its liberating intention: Marxism, too, can (and has) become hegemonic by serving to distance the Other through its reduction of people to abstract categories. What we have described as culturalist Marxism (after Johnson) restores concreteness to social analysis by pointing to the particularity that not only recognizes the burden of history but, through that, the subjectivity of the historical agent that rests upon the particularity of social experience. This culturalist Marxism resists economistic reductionism by recognizing culture as a semi-autonomous realm: not merely a superstructural element or the organic expression of a totality, but an active element in history that exists in a dialectical relationship to other constituent elements of society that is at once a relationship of unity and contradiction. This is the meaning of culturalism *within* the context of Marxism.

In both of the texts discussed in detail above, this view of culture results in an activist epistemology, one that finds in praxis, rather than in theoretical speculation, the source of non-hegemonic understanding. This, it needs to be stressed, is not an epistemology the goal of which is to discover abstract truths, but an epistemology with an intention, one that seeks to overcome the alienation that is implicit in the notion of truth conceived abstractly. An epistemology that takes praxis as its point of departure calls attention to all knowable truth as historical truth. In the case of Thompson, this activist epistemology takes the form of recognizing the priority of the experiences of those who lived and made history. Laroui expresses it in his affirmation of existence over an alienating (because abstract) search for authenticity or essence. In any case, both authors discover in historicism the method of this epistemology.

This historicism, as with all Marxist historicism, is a post-theoretical, that is to say, a poststructuralist historicism; it takes for granted the prior existence of a theoretical epistemology which is implicit in the concepts that guide its historical analysis. As with all historicism, it represents history as a narrative, but unlike anti-theoretical historicism, with its pretensions to capturing the unadorned truth of history in narrative, the narratives of this historicism are cast around concepts, are intended, indeed, to demonstrate the realization of the concept in history. Its opposition to structuralism rests in its assimilation of theory to history, rather than the other way around as is the case with structuralism.

This is a historicism, in other words, that does not reject theory, but seeks to transcend its positivistic use, which, in its efforts to introduce the language of science into the study of society, not only results in an ideological reductionism, but also militates against an activist epistemology. The most significant concepts of social analysis, concepts that bear upon questions of political power (class, state, nation, democracy, socialism), are irreducible into abstractions without being rendered ideological. Abstractions are ideological not only because they represent "strategies of containment" in the definition of meaning, but because these strategies play a crucial role in the struggle for hegemony by suppressing alternative meanings that challenge hegemony. Concepts reduced to abstractions, moreover, lose their temporality, and hence their ability to explain and to guide change. An authentically critical practice must take as a central task of social analysis the examination of the very concepts that make social analysis possible. Only then is it possible to reveal the interrelationship of concepts and thus expose the ideological reductionism that must accompany any abstraction of the concept from these relationships. Only in this fashion, furthermore, is it possible to retain the concrete in the abstract, because the phenomena of life that concepts represent exist in the concrete not as isolated phenomena but as relationships. To deny the admission into analysis the clutter of social relations may salvage for analysis the elegance of simplicity, but only at the cost of irrelevance or, worse, the ideological mystification of social relations. This is where historicism appears crucial. For to assert the priority of the concrete in abstraction is to assert the historicity of the conceptual, and historical concepts may be comprehended only historically. This is what Frederic Jameson has in mind when he writes in a different context:

> This very antithesis [theory vs. interpretive practice] marks out the double standard and the formal dilemma of all cultural study today . . . an uneasy struggle for priority between models and history, between theoretical speculation and textual analysis, in which the former seeks to transform the latter into so many mere examples, adduced to support its abstract propositions, while the latter continues insistently to imply that the theory itself was just so much methodological scaffolding, which can readily be dismantled once the serious business of practical criticism is under way. These two tendencies—theory and literary history—have so often in Western academic thought been felt to be rigorously incompatible that it is worth reminding the reader, in conclusion, of the existence of a third position which transcends both. That position is, of course, *Marxism, which, in the form of the dialectic, affirms a primacy of theory which is at one and the same time a recognition of the primacy of History itself.* (emphasis mine)[32]

What are the conclusions that may be drawn from the coincidences between culturalist Marxism and Marxist historicism as presented by Laroui? Most striking is the coincidence of historicism as an activist epistemology with the "decentering" of the intellectual. The Third World intellectual, subject to the challenge of cultural domination by the West, experiences this "decentering" as a condition of existence. Traditionalism or Westernism may offer to some the promise of bringing the intellectual back to the center of intellectual and political life. Indeed, from a Western perspective, this effort is the easiest to comprehend since it fits in easily with the assumptions about the world of culturalist hegemony. These routes, nevertheless, alienate the intellectual from the present of his society, decenter him, in other words, vis-à-vis the present. It may bring power to intellectuals, but it does not bring them escape from culturalist hegemony (or, for that matter, political and social hegemony).

It follows that culturalism as liberating practice must resist this abstraction of culture and the intellectual. Hence the insistence on the necessity of reintegration of the intellectual within a present social reality that exists apart from a frozen tradition or a reified West and that is the object of hegemonic practice (as the location of "backwardness"). To recover that reality, nay to center it, is to decenter the hegemonic claims of the past or the West.

Historicism, in other words, rejects structure in the name of agency and restores the human subject to history. The decentered intellectual would appear in this discourse as a condition of liberating practice. Hegemonic culturalism (not to say a hegemonic political science) has long pointed to the alienation of intellectuals as a source of revolutionary activity. This is stating the obvious. The more important question, usually ignored, is from what are these intellectuals alienated. To that we may venture a simple answer: alienated social power that feeds upon those whom it hegemonizes.

By way of conclusion, I would like to return to a question that I raised earlier in this discussion: the status of Third Worldism as viewed from the perspective of culturalism as liberating practice. In recent years, a Third-Worldist establishment has come into being. Though still not universally recognized and highly vulnerable, this establishment raises new questions about the issues that I have discussed here. This establishment has found an institutional basis in various organizations of an international nature. It is strong in academia, where it has made its influence felt intellectually in the spread of challenges to older Western-centered "modernizationism" in the form of dependency theory and various versions of world-system analysis. Intellectually, it has made a significant impact in challenging a Western-centered view of the world through its advocacy of a global perspective.

This emergent establishment, if we may call it that, represents a radical alliance of the decentered intellectuals of both Western and non-Western societies. The challenge to Western cultural hegemonism may take the form here of a cultural-political relativism (with liberals); among radical Third-Worldists, it may on occasion be carried so far as to reverse the assumptions of earlier hegemonism; that is, non-Western societies may be held up as examples for the emulation of Western societies.

This development is a very significant one in terms of the hegemonic relations between Western and non-Western societies. Conservatives as usual have been quick to recognize the threat, as witnessed by recent attacks on UNESCO (the international cultural organization par excellence), as well as in the reaffirmation of the necessity of instilling in education a sense of the "Western tradition."

While its challenge to the power of a Western-centered leadership is quite evident, however, the relationship of this emergent Third-Worldist establishment to non-Western societies is highly problematic. To the extent that intellectuals of the Third World become part of such an establishment, with its own language and its own organizationally defined goals, they too are alienated from the constituencies in whose name they speak. That this establishment is predominantly economistic in its orientation is a case in point. While its appreciation of the world is global, moreover, it conceives of the globe in highly abstract structuralist terms. In this establishment, Third World intellectuals themselves produce an alienating ideology that distances them from their own societies, to which they of necessity come to bear a hegemonic relationship. Indeed, appearances to the contrary, it may be suggested that their participation in this establishment has contributed to the increasingly monolithic reality that oppression has come to assume in recent years: radical opposition to hegemony has been undercut by the incorporation of opposition into a new hegemonic structure of power. Ideologically, this is expressed in the abandonment of cultural opposition (or "cultural revolution") in favor of a supposedly more pragmatic economistic ideology.

What is at issue here is not the confounding of ideological identity, but the identification of what constitutes a liberating practice, which points to epistemological questions that cut across ideological divides. That Marxists should be participants in hegemonic practices is not surprising (nor is it a new phenomenon). Though ideological Marxism pretends to the contrary, Marxists are subject to the same ideological proposition that they apply to others: "it is not the consciousness of man that determines his social being, on the contrary, it is his social being that determines his consciousness." Marxism loses its critical edge and appears ideological to the extent that Marxists suppress the applicability of this proposition to themselves—or to the categories of Marxism. The assignment of a privileged position to the knowing subject over the subjects of history is paralleled at the level of thought by the privileging of theory over history. Whatever precision is thereby acquired, the gains are more than offset by the suppression of the temporality of categories that is the result of this disjuncture between history and theory, which alienates categories from their historical subject. The consequences are not merely intellectual but profoundly social: it renders Marxists into controllers of the hegemony and Marxism into a hegemonic ideology.

The question of culture derives its significance for liberating practice from the questions it raises concerning the historicity of theory or of a theoretical grasp of the world. Recalling culture in its double meaning, both as a "way of seeing" and as a way of making the world, returns the historical subject (or agent) to his dialectical temporality which, Jameson has suggested, decenters him from his privileged position in history. The dialectic, conceived in its "quotidian temporality" as the praxis which intermediates abstract design and social existence rather than as an excuse for an abstract evolutionism, offers the possibility of reintegrating the present and the future, theory and history, category and social subject but, above all, the knowing subject and the subject of history; in other words, there is the possibility of a truly liberating practice which can exist *only* as a possibility and which must take as its premise the denial of a center to the social process and of a predestined direction to history.

This is the reasoning that, I think, underlies the advocacy of cultural revolution in radical Marxist thinking in the Third World which, even more so than its counterpart in the West, has long recognized the insufficiency of economism as a condition of socialism or even as a basis for challenging capitalist hegemony. This radicalism has rested in the urge to reconnect the intellectual with the social present not just to counter hegemonic alienation, but to create a new global culture that must be neither of the West nor of the past. The basic premise of this reasoning is that culturalist hegemony can be overcome only by the creation of a new culture that is at once universal and particular. Such a culture must be forged out of the ingredients of present society, for any other alternative must of necessity reintroduce alienation into the cultural process. In all cases, we find a coincidence of an activist epistemology (an anti-abstractionist historicism) with revolutionary practice. And, finally, common to all is the perception that true cosmopolitanism may be achieved only by moving from the particular to the universal (the latter is taken for granted) and not by imposing universals of whatever kind upon the particular.

This cultural revolutionary ideal appears more and more as an illusory utopianism in a world where necessity (economic *and* political) calls forth economism. It does not help either that the idea of cultural revolution has in practice created its own problems because its proponents have been unable to live up to the critical premises of their own reasoning. Nevertheless, we must continue to listen to their voices, if only as a constant reminder of the need to counter the mystification of the problem of liberation by self-professed radical alternatives which, out of cynicism or self-delusion, promise liberation but offer new forms of hegemony instead. To do otherwise would be no less than resignation to a profound fatalism that closes off all doors to the possibility of human liberation even as a vision.

Notes

Earlier versions of this paper were presented in a seminar at the Department of Far Eastern Languages and Civilizations at the University of Chicago in February 1985 and the conference on "The Nature and Context of Minority Discourse" at the University of California, Berkeley, May 22–25, 1986. I would like to thank participants in both events for their valuable input.

1. Arif Dirlik, "Culture, Society and Revolution: A Critical Discussion of American Studies of Chinese Thought," *Working Papers in Asian/Pacific Studies* 1 (Durham: Asian/Pacific Studies Institute, Duke University, 1985).

2. Ibid., pp.40, 44, 54, 55–56.

3. Johannes Fabian, *Time and the Other: How Anthropology Makes Its Object* (New York: Columbia University Press, 1983); see especially Chapter 1.

4. Richard Johnson, "Edward Thompson, Eugene Genovese, and Socialist Humanist History," *History Workshop* 6 (Autumn 1978):81.

5. E. P. Thompson, "Politics of Theory," in *People's History and Socialist Theory,* ed. R. Samuel (London: Routledge & Kegan Paul, 1981), pp.396–408.

6. Interview with E. P. Thompson, quoted in Johnson, "Edward Thompson, Eugene Genovese, and Socialist Humanist History," p.84.

7. Eugene Genovese, *Roll Jordan Roll: The World the Slaves Made* (New York: Pantheon Books, 1974), p.xvi.

8. E. P. Thompson, "Eighteenth-Century English Society: Class Struggle Without Class?" *Social History* 3.2 (May 1978):146.

9. E. P. Thompson, *The Making of the English Working Class* (New York: Vintage Books, 1963), p.13.

10. Raymond Williams, *Culture and Society, 1780–1950* (London: Penguin Books, 1968), p.289.

11. Thompson, *The Making of the English Working Class,* pp.12–13.

12. Ibid., p.832.

13. Harry Harootunian, "Ideology as Conflict," in *Conflict in Modern Japanese History: The Neglected Tradition,* T. Najita and V. Koschmann, eds. (Princeton: Princeton University Press, 1982), p.29.

14. Thompson, "Eighteenth-Century English Society," p.148.

15. Nicos Poulantzas, *Classes in Contemporary Capitalism* (London: New Left Books, 1975), p.17.

16. See Alvin Gouldner, *The Future of Intellectuals and the Rise of the New Class* (New York: Continuum Books, 1979).

17. Louis Althusser, "Ideology and Ideological State Apparatuses," in *Lenin and Philosophy and Other Essays,* trans. Ben Brewster (New York: Monthly Review Press, 1971).

18. Abdallah Laroui, *The Crisis of the Arab Intellectual: Traditionalism or Historicism?* (Berkeley: Univ. of California Press, 1976), p.156.

19. Ibid., p.121.

20Ibid., pp.156–157.

21. Ibid., pp.99–100.

22. Ibid., p.100.

23. Joseph Levenson, *Confucian China and Its Modern Fate,* 3 vols. (Berkeley: University of California Press, 1958–1965). For further discussion, see Dirlik, op. cit.

24. Laroui, *The Crisis of the Arab Intellectual,* pp.121–122.

25. Ibid., p.70.

26. Ibid., p.x.

27. Ibid., p.108.

28. José Carlos Mariategui, *Seven Interpretative Essays on Peruvian Reality* (Austin: University of Texas Press, 1971), p.274.

29. Kwameh Nkrumah, *Consciencism: Philosophy and Ideology for Decolonization and Development with Particular Reference to the African Revolution* (London: Heineman, 1964), p.79.

30. Franz Fanon, *The Wretched of the Earth* (New York: Grove Press, 1968), p.188.

31. Ernesto Che Guevara, *Socialism and Man* (New York: Pathfinder Press, 1978), p.21.

32. Fredric Jameson, *The Political Unconscious: Narrative as a Socially Symbolic Act* (Ithaca: Cornell Univ. Press, 1982), pp.13–14.

3

The Postcolonial Aura:
Third World Criticism in the Age
of Global Capitalism

"When exactly . . . does the 'postcolonial' begin?" queries Ella Shohat in a discussion of the subject.[1] Misreading the question deliberately, I will supply here an answer that is only partially facetious: "When Third World intellectuals have arrived in First World academe."

My goal in the discussion below is to review the term "postcolonial," and the various intellectual/cultural positions associated with it, within the context of contemporary transformations in global relationships, and the reconsiderations these transformations call for of problems of domination and hegemony, as well as of received critical practices. "Postcolonial" is the most recent entrant to achieve prominent visibility in the ranks of those "post" marked words (seminal among them, postmodernism) that serve as signposts in(to) contemporary cultural criticism. Unlike other "post" marked words, "postcolonial" claims as its special provenance the terrain that in an earlier day used to go by the name of "Third World" and is intended, therefore, to achieve an authentic globalization of cultural discourses: by the extension globally of the intellectual concerns and orientations originating at the central sites of EuroAmerican cultural criticism; and by the introduction into the latter of voices and subjectivities from the margins of earlier political and/or ideological colonialism, which now demand a hearing at those very sites at the center. The goal, indeed, is no less than the abolition of all distinctions between center and periphery, and all other "binarisms" that are allegedly a legacy of colonial(ist) ways of thinking, and to reveal societies globally in their complex heterogeneity and contingency. While intellectuals who hail from one part of that terrain, India, have played a conspicuously prominent role in its formulation and dissemination, the appeals of "postcoloniality" would seem to cut across national, regional, and even political boundaries, which on the surface at least would seem to substantiate its claims to globalism.

My answer to Shohat's question is only partially facetious because the popularity that the term "postcolonial" has achieved in the last few years has less to do with its rigorousness as a concept, or the new vistas it has opened up for critical inquiry, than it does with the increased visibility as intellectual pacesetters in cultural criticism of academic intellectuals of Third World origin. I suggest below that most of the critical themes of which postcolonial criticism claims to be the fountainhead predated in their emergence the appearance, or at least the popular currency, of the term "postcolonial" and, therefore, owe little to it for inspiration. Whether or not there was a "postcolonial consciousness" before it was so termed, that might have played a part in the production of those themes, is a question to which I will return below. As far as it is possible to tell from the literature, however, it was only from the mid-1980s that the label "postcolonial" was attached to those themes with increasing frequency, and that in conjunction with the use of the label to describe academic intellectuals of Third World origin, the so-called postcolonial intellectuals, who themselves seemed to acquire an academic respectability they did not have before.[2] A description of a diffuse group of intellectuals, of their concerns and orientations, was to turn by the end of the decade into a description of a global condition, in which sense it has acquired the status of a new orthodoxy both in cultural criticism and in academic programs. Shohat's question above refers to this global condition; given the ambiguity imbedded in the term "postcolonial," to redirect her question to the emergence of "postcolonial intellectuals" seems to be justifiable in order to put the horse back in front of the cart. It is intended also to underline the First World origins (and situation) of the term.

My answer is also facetious, however, because the ascendancy in First World academia of intellectuals of Third World origin, in pointing to the role they have played in the propagation of "postcolonial" as a critical orientation, begs the question of why they and their intellectual concerns and orientations have been accorded the respectability that they have. The themes that are now claimed for "postcolonial criticism," both in what they repudiate of the past and in what they affirm for the present, I venture to suggest, resonate with concerns and orientations that have their origins in a new world situation that has also become part of consciousness globally over the last decade. I am referring here to that world situation created by transformations within the capitalist world economy, by the emergence of what has been described variously as Global Capitalism, Flexible Production, Late Capitalism, etc., that has "disorganized" earlier conceptualizations of global relations, especially relations comprehended earlier by such binarisms as colonizer/colonized, First/Third Worlds, or the "West and the Rest," in all of which, furthermore, the nation-state as the unit of political organization globally was taken for granted. It is no reflection on the abilities of "postcolonial critics" to suggest that they, and the critical orientations that they represent, have acquired respectability to the extent that they have answered to the conceptual needs of the social, political and cultural problems thrown up by this new world situation.

It is, however, a reflection on the ideology of postcolonialism that except for a rare nod in this direction,[3] postcolonial critics have been largely silent on the relationship of the idea of postcolonialism to its context in contemporary capitalism; indeed, they have suppressed the necessity of considering such a possible relationship by repudiating a "foundational" role to capitalism in history.

A consideration of this relationship is my primary goal in the discussion below. I argue, first, that there is a parallel between the ascendancy in cultural criticism of the idea of postcoloniality and an emergent consciousness of Global Capitalism in the 1980s and, secondly, that the appeals of the critical themes in "postcolonial criticism" have much to do with their resonance with the conceptual needs presented by transformations in global relationships due to changes within the capitalist world economy. This also explains, I think, why a concept that is intended to achieve a radical revision in our comprehension of the world should appear to be complicitous in "the consecration of hegemony," as Shohat has put it.[4] If postcolonial as concept has not necessarily served as a fountainhead for the criticism of ideology in earlier ways of viewing global relationships, it has nevertheless helped concentrate under one term what had been earlier diffuse criticisms. At the same time, however, postcolonial criticism has been silent about its own status as a possible ideological effect of a new world situation "after colonialism." Postcolonial as a description of intellectuals of Third World origin needs to be distinguished, I suggest below, from postcolonial as a description of this world situation. In this latter usage, the term mystifies both politically and methodologically a situation that represents not the abolition but the reconfiguration of earlier forms of domination. The complicity of "postcolonial" in hegemony lies in postcolonialism's diversion of attention from contemporary problems of social, political and cultural domination, and its obfuscation of its own relationship to what is but a condition of its emergence: a Global Capitalism which, however fragmented in appearance, serves nevertheless as the structuring principle of global relations.

Postcolonial Intellectuals and Postcolonial Criticism

The term "postcolonial" in its various usages carries a multiplicity of meanings which need to be distinguished for analytical purposes. Three uses of the term seem to me to be especially prominent (and significant): (a) as a literal description of conditions in formerly colonial societies, in which case the term has concrete referents, as in "postcolonial societies" or "postcolonial intellectuals." It should be noted, however, that colonies here include both those encompassed earlier in a Third World, and settler colonies usually associated with the First World, such as Canada and Australia, (b) as a description of a global condition after the period of colonialism, in which case the usage is somewhat more abstract and less concrete in reference, comparable in its vagueness to the earlier term, Third World, for which it is intended as a substitute, (c) as a description of a discourse on the above conditions that is informed by the epistemological and psychic orientations that are products of those conditions.

Even at its most concrete, the term "postcolonial" is not transparent in meaning as each meaning is overdetermined by the others. Postcolonial intellectuals
are clearly the producers of a postcolonial discourse, but who exactly are the postcolonial intellectuals? Here the contrast between "postcolonial" and its predeces-
sor term, Third World, may be revealing. The term Third World, postcolonial
critics insist, was quite vague in encompassing within one uniform category
vastly heterogeneous historical circumstances; and in locking in fixed positions,
structurally if not geographically, societies and populations whose locations
shifted with changing global relationships. While this objection is quite valid, the
fixing of societal locations misleadingly or not permitted the identification of,
say, Third World intellectuals with the concreteness of places of origin. Postcolonial does not permit such identification. I wondered above whether or not there
might not have been a postcolonial consciousness even before it was so labelled;
by which I mean the consciousness which postcolonial intellectuals claim as a
hallmark of postcoloniality. The answer is, probably there was, although it was
invisible as it was subsumed under the category Third World. Now that postcoloniality has been released from the fixity of Third World location, the identity of
the postcolonial is no longer structural but discursive. "Postcolonial" in this perspective represents an attempt to regroup intellectuals of uncertain location
under the banner of "postcolonial discourse." Intellectuals in the flesh may be the
producers of the themes that constitute postcolonial discourse, but it is participation in the discourse that defines them as "postcolonial intellectuals" nevertheless. Hence it is important to delineate the discourse so as to identify postcolonial
intellectuals themselves.

Gyan Prakash frames concisely a question that, I think, provides the point of
departure for postcolonial discourse: how does the Third World write "its own
history?"[5] Like other postcolonial critics, such as Gayatri Spivak, he finds the
answer to his question in the model of historical writing provided by the work on
Indian history of the *Subaltern Studies* group,[6] which also provides, although it
does not exhaust, the major themes in postcolonial discourse.

These themes are enunciated cogently in a recent essay by Prakash which, to
my knowledge, offers the most condensed exposition of postcolonialism currently available. Prakash's introduction to his essay is worth quoting at some
length:

> One of the distinct effects of the recent emergence of postcolonial criticism has been
> to force a radical re-thinking and re-formulation of forms of knowledge and social
> identities authored and authorized by colonialism and western domination. For this
> reason, it has also created a ferment in the field of knowledge. This is not to say that
> colonialism and its legacies remained unquestioned until recently: nationalism and
> marxism come immediately to mind as powerful challenges to colonialism. But both
> of these operated with master-narratives that put Europe at its center. [*sic*] Thus,
> when nationalism, reversing Orientalist thought, attributed agency and history to the
> subjected nation, it also staked a claim to the order of Reason and Progress instituted

by colonialism; and when marxists pilloried colonialism, their criticism was framed by a universalist mode-of-production narrative. Recent postcolonial criticism, on the other hand, seeks to undo the Eurocentrism produced by the institution of the west's trajectory, its appropriation of the other as History. It does so, however, with the acute realization that postcoloniality is not born and nurtured in a panoptic distance from history. The postcolonial exists as an aftermath, and after—after being worked over by colonialism.

Criticism formed in the enunciation of discourses of domination occupies a space that is neither inside nor outside the history of western domination but in a tangential relation to it. This is what Homi Bhabha calls an in-between, hybrid position of practice and negotiation, or what Gayatri Chakravorty Spivak terms catachresis; "reversing, displacing, and seizing the apparatus of value-coding."[7]

To elaborate on these themes: (a) postcolonial criticism repudiates all master-narratives and, since the most powerful current master-narratives are Eurocentric, as the products of a post-Enlightenment European constitution of history, takes the criticism of Eurocentrism as its central task. (b) Foremost among these master-narratives to be repudiated is the narrative of modernization, both in its bourgeois and its Marxist incarnations. Bourgeois modernization ("developmentalism") represents the renovation and redeployment of "colonial modernity . . . as economic development."[8] Marxism, while it rejects bourgeois modernization, nevertheless perpetuates the teleological assumptions of the latter by framing inquiry by a narrative of modes of production in which postcolonial history appears as a transition (or an aborted transition) to capitalism.[9] The repudiation of the narrative of modes of production, it needs to be added, does not mean the repudiation of Marxism as postcolonial criticism acknowledges a strong Marxist inspiration.[10] (c) Needless to say, Orientalism, in its constitution of the colony as Europe's Other, in which the Other is reduced to an essence without history, must be repudiated. But so must nationalism which, while challenging Orientalism, has perpetuated the essentialism of Orientalism (by affirming a national essence in history), as well as its procedures of representation.[11] (d) The repudiation of master-narratives is necessary to dispose of the hegemonic Eurocentric assumptions built into those master-narratives which have been employed in the past to frame Third World histories. It is necessary also to resist all spatial homogenization and temporal teleology. This requires the repudiation of all "foundational" historical writing. According to Prakash, a foundational view is one that assumes "that history is ultimately founded in and representable through some identity—individual, class, or structure—which resists further decomposition into heterogeneity."[12] The most significant conclusion to follow from the repudiation of "foundational" historiography is the rejection of capitalism as a "foundational category" on the grounds that "we cannot thematize Indian history in terms of the development of capitalism and simultaneously contest capitalism's homogenization of the contemporary world."[13] (Obviously, given the logic of the argument, any Third World country could be substituted here for India.) (e) "Postfoundational history," in its repudiation of essence and structure, and a simultaneous affirmation of heterogeneity, also repudiates any "fixing" of the "Third World subject" and, therefore, of the Third World as a category: "the rejection of those modes of thinking which configure the Third World in such irreducible essences as religiosity, underdevelopment, poverty, nationhood, non-Westernness . . . unsettles the calm presence that the essentialist categories—east and west, First World and Third World—inhabit in our thought. This disruption makes it possible to treat the Third World as a variety of shifting positions which have been discursively articulated in history. Viewed in this manner, the Orientalist, nationalist, Marxist and other historiographies become visible as discursive attempts to constitute their objects of knowledge, that is, the Third World. As a result, rather than appearing as a fixed and essential object, the Third World emerges as a series of historical positions, including those that enunciate essentialisms."[14] It might be noteworthy here that with the repudiation of capitalism and structure as "foundational categories," there is no mention in the above statement of a capitalist structuring of the world, however heterogeneous and "discrepant" the histories within it, as a constituting moment of history. (f) Finally, postfoundational history approaches "Third World identities as relational rather than essential."[15] Postfoundational history (which is also postcolonial history) shifts attention from "national origin" to "subject position." The consequence is that "the formation of Third World positions suggests engagement rather than insularity. It is difficult to overlook that all the Third World voices identified in this essay speak within and to discourses familiar to the 'West' instead of originating from some autonomous essence, which does not warrant the conclusion that the Third World historiography has always been enslaved, but that the careful maintenance and policing of East-West boundaries has never succeeded in stopping the flows across and against boundaries and that the self-other opposition has never quite been able to order all differences into binary opposites. The Third World, far from being confined to its assigned space, has penetrated the inner sanctum of the First World in the process of being 'Third-Worlded'—arousing, inciting, and affiliating with the subordinated others in the First World. It has reached across boundaries and barriers to connect with the minority voices in the First World: socialists, radicals, feminists, minorities."[16] To underline the affirmations in the above statement, which are quite representative of the postcolonial stance on contemporary global relations (and of its claims to transcending earlier conceptualizations of the world): (1) attention needs to be shifted from national origin to subject position; hence a "politics of location" takes precedence over politics informed by fixed categories (in this case the nation, but quite obviously referring also to categories such as Third World and class, among others), (2) while First/Third World positions may not be interchangeable, they are nevertheless quite fluid, which implies a necessity of qualifying, if not repudiating, binary oppositions in the articulation of their relationship, (3) hence local interactions take priority over global structures in the shaping of these relationships; which implies that they are best comprehended historically in their heterogeneity than structurally in their "fixity," (4) these conclusions follow from the "hybridness" or "in-betweenness" of the postcolonial subject which is not to be contained within fixed categories or binary oppositions, (5) since "postcolonial" criticism has focused on the postcolonial" subject to the exclusion of an account of the world outside of the subject, the global condition implied by postcoloniality appears at best as a projection onto the world of "postcolonial" subjectivity and epistemology; a discursive constitution of the world, in other words, in accordance with the constitution of the "postcolonial" subject, much as it had been constituted earlier by the epistemologies that are the object of "postcolonial" criticism.

If postcolonial criticism as discourse is any guide to identifying postcolonial intellectuals, the literal sense of "postcolonial" is its least significant aspect, if not altogether misleading. Viewed in terms of the themes that I have outlined above, on the one hand, "postcolonial" is broadly inclusive; as intellectual concerns these themes are by no means the monopoly of postcolonial criticism, and one does not have to be post*colonial* in any strict sense of the term to share in them, for which the most eloquent evidence is that they were already central to cultural discussions before they were so labelled. Crucial premises of postcolonial criticism, such as the repudiation of post-Enlightenment metanarratives, were enunciated first in poststructuralist thinking, and in the various postmodernisms that it has informed.[17] Taking the term literally as post*colonial*, some practitioners of postcolonial criticism describe as postcolonial societies such as the United States and Australia which started off as settler colonies—regardless of their status as First World societies, and colonizers themselves of their indigenous populations (to be fair, the latter could also be said of many Third World societies). According to Ashcroft, Griffiths and Tiffin, three enthusiastic proponents of the postcolonial idea, postcolonial covers

> all the cultures affected by the imperial process from the moment of colonization to the present day ... so the literatures of African countries, Australia, Bangladesh, Canada, Caribbean countries, India, Malaysia, Malta, New Zealand, Pakistan, Singapore, South Pacific Island countries, and Sri Lanka are all postcolonial literatures. The literature of the USA should also be placed in this category. Perhaps because of its current position of power, and the neocolonizing role it has played, its postcolonial nature has not been generally recognized. But its relationship with the metropolitan centre as it evolved over the last two centuries has been paradigmatic for postcolonial literatures everywhere. What each of these literatures has in common beyond their special and distinctive characteristics is that they emerged in their present form out of the experience of colonization and asserted themselves by foregrounding the tension with the imperial power, and by emphasizing their differences from the assumptions of the imperial centre. It is this which makes them distinctly postcolonial.[18]

At the same time, the themes of postcolonial criticism have been outstanding themes in the cultural discourses of Third World societies which were never, strictly speaking, colonies, and/or conducted successful revolutions against EuroAmerican domination, such as China.

There are no clear temporal boundaries either to the use of the term, because the themes it encompasses are as old as the history of colonialism; to use the example of China again, such themes as the status of native history vis-à-vis EuroAmerican conceptualizations of history, national identity and its contested nature, national historical trajectory in the context of global modernization, and even questions of subjectivity created by a sense of "in-betweenness," are as old as the history of the Chinese encounter with the EuroAmerican West.[19] One might go so far as to suggest that if a crisis in historical consciousness, with all its implications for national and individual identity, is a basic theme of postcoloniality, then the First World itself is postcolonial. To the extent that the EuroAmerican self-image was shaped by the experience of colonizing the world (since the constitution of the Other is at once also the constitution of the Self), the end of colonialism presents the colonizer as much as the colonized with a problem of identity. The crisis created by the commemoration of the five-hundredth anniversary of Columbus' adventure comes to mind immediately. Indeed, some postcolonial critics have gone so far as to claim for postcoloniality all of modern history, substituting postcoloniality as a condition for everything from imperialism to revolution. Again to quote Ashcroft, Griffiths and Tiffin,

> European imperialism took various forms in different times and places and proceeded both through conscious planning and contingent occurrences. As a result of this complex development something occurred for which the *plan* of imperial expansion had not bargained: the immensely prestigious and powerful imperial culture found itself appropriated in projects of counter-colonial resistance which drew upon the many indigenous local and hybrid *processes* of self-determination to defy, erode and sometimes supplant the prodigious power of imperial cultural knowledge. Postcolonial literatures are a result of this interaction between imperial culture and the complex of indigenous cultural practices. As a consequence, postcolonial theory has existed for a long time before that particular name was used to describe it. Once colonised peoples had cause to reflect on and express the tension which ensued from this problematic and contested, but eventually vibrant and powerful mixture of imperial language and local experience, postcolonial 'theory' came into being.[20]

Never mind the awkward statements about "theory" in this passage. What is important is that "postcolonialism" is coextensive with "colonialism," which not only confounds what we might mean by these terms, but also abolishes any possibility of drawing distinctions between the present and the past, or the indigenous oppressed and the oppressor settlers. If postcoloniality is a set of discursive attributes, moreover, there is no reason why in its extension to the past we should stop with the beginnings of modernity. Indeed, a recent work has carried this logic to its conclusion, claiming for postcoloniality all of human history, since "hybridity" and "in-betweenness" have been characteristics of cultural formation throughout![21]

On the other hand, the term "postcolonial," understood in terms of its discursive thematics, excludes from its scope most of those who inhabit post*colonial* societies, or hail from them. It does not account for the attractions of modernization and nationalism to vast numbers in Third World populations, let alone those marginalized by national incorporation in the global economy. Prakash seems to acknowledge this when he observes that, "outside the First World, in India itself, the power of western discourses operates through its authorization and deployment by the nation-state—the ideologies of modernization and instrumental science are so deeply sedimented in the national body politic that they neither manifest themselves nor function exclusively as forms of imperial power."[22] It excludes the many ethnic groups in post*colonial* societies (among others) who, obviously unaware of their "hybridity," go on massacring one another. It also excludes radical postcolonials, who continue to claim that their societies are still colonized, and believe that the assertion of integrated identities and subjectivities are essential to their ability to struggle against colonialism. Of particular note are indigenous radical activists who refuse to go along with the postcolonial repudiation of "essentialized" identities. When faced with this kind of challenge, some postcolonial critics are quick to forget their claims to openness and playfulness, as in the following statement by a Canadian "postcolonial critic," Diana Brydon:

> While postcolonial theorists embrace hybridity and heterogeneity as the characteristic postcolonial mode, some native writers in Canada resist what they see as a violating appropriation to insist on their ownership of their stories and their exclusive claim to an authenticity that should not be ventriloquized or parodied. When directed against the Western canon, postmodernist techniques of intertextuality, parody and literary borrowing may appear radical or even potentially revolutionary. When directed against native myths and stories, these same techniques would seem to repeat the imperialist history of plunder and theft. . . . Although I can sympathize with such arguments as tactical strategies in insisting on self-definition and resisting appropriation, even tactically they prove self-defeating because they depend on a view of cultural authenticity that condemns them to a continued marginality and an eventual death. . . . Ironically, such tactics encourage native peoples to isolate themselves from contemporary life and full citizenhood.[23]

In other words, be hybrid or die! Brydon's attitude is also revealing of the tendency of most postcolonials to take for granted the present economic and political organization of the world.

The problem of the relationship between postcoloniality and power is not restricted to its manifestations in the response to postcoloniality of people, such as the indigenous peoples of Australia or the Americas, about whose continued oppression there is little question. Intellectuals in India ask Spivak to explain "questions that arise out of the way you perceive yourself ('The postcolonial diasporic Indian who seeks to decolonize the mind'), and the way you constitute us (for convenience, 'native' intellectuals)," to which Spivak's answer is: "your description of how I constituted you does not seem quite correct. I thought I constituted you, equally with the diasporic Indian, as the postcolonial intellectual!" The interrogators are not quite convinced: "Perhaps the relationship of distance and proximity between you and us is that what we write and teach has political and other actual consequences for us that are in a sense different from the consequences, or lack of consequences, for you." They express doubts in another sense as well: "What are the theories or explanations, the narratives of affiliation and disaffiliation that you bring to the politically contaminated and ambivalent function of the non-resident Indian (NRI) who comes back to India, however temporarily, upon the wings of progress?"[24] As phrased by Prakash, it is not clear that even the work of the *Subaltern Studies* collective, which serves as the inspiration of so much of the thematics of "postcoloniality," may be included under "postcolonial." I have no wish to impose an unwarranted uniformity on *Subaltern Studies* writers, but it seems to be that their more radical ideas, chief among them the idea of class, are somewhat watered down in the course of their re-presentation in the enunciation of "postcolonial criticism."[25] It is also misleading in my opinion to mention in the same breath as "postcolonial critics," intellectuals as widely different politically as Edward Said, Aijaz Ahmad, Homi Bhabha, Gyan Prakash (and even Gayatri Spivak and Lata Mani). In a literal sense, they may all share in "postcoloniality," and some of its themes. Said's situation as a Palestinian intellectual does not permit him to cross the borders of Israel with the ease that his "in-betweenness" might suggest (which also raises the question for postcoloniality of what borders are at issue). Aijaz Ahmad, vehemently critical of the Three Worlds concept, nevertheless grounds his critique within the operations of capital, which is quite different from the denial of a "foundational" status to capitalism in the understanding of postcoloniality by Prakash.[26] Spivak and Mani, while quite cognizant of the different roles in different contexts that "in-betweenness" imposes upon them,[27] nevertheless ground their politics firmly in feminism (and, in the case of Spivak, Marxism).

Finally, examining the notion of "postcoloniality" in a different geographical context, Africa, Kwame A. Appiah points to another pitfall in the literal use of postcoloniality as post*colonial*, this time a temporal one. Appiah shares in the understanding of postcolonial as postmodernization, post–Third World and postnationalist, and points out that while the first generation of African writers after the end of colonialism were nationalists, the second generation has rejected nationalism.[28] In a recent discussion (a response to the controversy provoked by his criticism of postcolonial Sub-Saharan Africa), Achille Mbembe hints at an answer as to why this should be the case when he states that "the younger generation of Africans have no direct or immediate experience" of colonization, whatever role it may have played as a "foundational" event in African history.[29] "Postcolonial," in other words, is applicable not to all of the post*colonial* period, but only to that period after colonialism when a "forgetting" of its memories has begun to set in, among other things.

What, then, may be the value of a term that includes so much beyond and excludes so much of its own postulated premise, the colonial? What it leaves us with is what I have already hinted at: postcolonial, rather than a description of anything, is a discourse that seeks to constitute the world in the self-image of intellectuals who view themselves (or have come to view themselves) as postcolonial intellectuals; to recall my initial statement above, Third World intellectuals who have arrived in First World academe, whose preoccupation with postcoloniality is an expression not so much of agony over identity, as it often appears, but of newfound power. Two further questions need to be addressed before I elaborate further on this proposition; one concerns the role intellectuals from India have played in the enunciation of postcolonial discourse, the other concerns the language of this discourse.

Spivak comments (in passing) in an interview that, "in India, people who can think of the three-worlds explanation are totally pissed off by not being recognised as the centre of the non-aligned nations, rather than a 'Third World' country."[30] This state of being "pissed off" at categorization as just another Third World country is not restricted to Indian intellectuals (and others in India), but could be found in any Third World country (my country of origin, Turkey, and the country I study, China, come to mind immediately), which speaks to the sorry state of Third World consciousness, if there is one. It is also impossible to say whether or not Indian intellectuals being "pissed off" at such categorization has anything to do with the themes that appear in postcolonial discourse, in particular the repudiation of Third World as a category. Nevertheless, intellectuals from India, as I noted above, have been prominent in identifying themselves as "postcolonial intellectuals," as well as in the enunciation of postcolonial criticism. There is nothing wrong with this, of course, except in a certain confusion that has been introduced into the discourse between what are but specific problems in Indian historiography and general problems of a global condition described as "postcolonial," and the projection globally of subjectivities that are (on the basis of the disagreements among Indian intellectuals to which I alluded above) representative only of very few among intellectuals in India. Most of the generalizations that appear in the discourse of postolonial intellectuals from India may appear novel in the historiography of India but are not novel "discoveries" from broader perspectives. It is no reflection on the historical writing of *Subaltern Studies* historians that their qualifications of class in Indian history, their views on the nation as contested category, and their injunction that the history of capitalism must be understood not just as a triumphal march of a homogenizing capital but also in terms of the resistance to it at both the national and the local level, that rendered its consequences quite fractured and heterogeneous, however well taken, do not represent earth shattering conceptual innovations; as Said notes in his preface to *Selected Subaltern Studies* (see n. 6), these approaches represent the application in Indian historiography of trends in historical writing that were quite widespread by the 1970s, under the impact especially of social historians such as E. P. Thompson, Eric Hobsbawm, and a whole host of others. All this indicates is that historians of India were participants in the transformations in historical thinking in all areas; transformations in which Third World sensibilities were just one among a number of factors, that also included new ways of thinking about Marxism, the entry into history of feminism, and poststructuralism. To be sure, I think it very important that Third World sensibilities must be brought into play repeatedly in order to counteract a tendency toward cultural imperialism of First World thinkers and historians, who extend the meaning of concepts of First World derivation globally without giving a second thought to the social differences that must qualify those concepts historically and contextually, but this is no reason to inflate a "postcolonial" sensibility, especially one that is itself bound by national and local experiences, indefinitely. And yet such a tendency (for which *Subaltern Studies* writers may themselves not be responsible at all) is plainly visible in the exposition of postcoloniality by someone like Prakash who, writing of Indian historiography in one sentence, projects his observations globally in the very next one.

These observations are not intended to single out postcolonial intellectuals from India, which not only would be misleading about Indian intellectuals in general, but also about postcolonial intellectuals in general; the appeals of postcoloniality are not restricted to intellectuals of any one national origin, and the problems to which I pointed above are problems of a general nature, born out of a contradiction between an insistence on heterogeneity, difference and historicity, and a tendency to generalize from the local to the global, all the while denying that there are global forces at work which may condition the local in the first place. What my observations point to is a new assertiveness on the part of Third World intellectuals that makes this procedure possible. Another example may be found among Chinese intellectuals, in the so-called Confucian revival in recent years. The latter obviously do not describe themselves as "postcolonial," for their point of departure is the newfound power of Chinese societies within global capitalism which, if anything, shows in their efforts to suppress memories of an earlier day when China, too, suffered from EuroAmerican hegemony (though not colonialism). In their case the effort takes the form of articulating to the values of capitalism a "Confucianism" that in an earlier day was deemed to be inconsistent with capitalist modernization; so that Confucianism has been rendered into a prime mover of capitalist development, which has also found quite a sympathetic ear among First World ideologues who now look to a Confucian ethic to relieve the crisis of capitalism.[31] While quite different from "postcoloniality" in its urge to become part of a hegemonic ideology of capitalism, however, it shares with the latter a counterhegemonic self-assertiveness on the part of another group of for-

merly Third World intellectuals. And it may not be a coincidence that Chinese
intellectuals in First World academia have played a major part in the enunciation
of this Confucian revival, although it is by no means restricted to them.

A somewhat different but parallel observation could be made with regard to
the appeals of postcoloniality to intellectuals from settler colonies. A changing
global situation in recent years has transformed earlier identifications with
EuroAmerica in these societies to new kinds of regional affinities; most clearly in
the case of Australia seeking to remake itself as an "Asian" society, but also in
Canada which seeks to become part of a new Asia-Pacific economy. While it
would be erroneous to say that settlers earlier did not have an awareness of being
colonized, or lacked all identification with the Third World (Canada versus the
United States, for example), it is also misleading to erase memories of racist
exclusion and oppression practiced by the settlers themselves toward non-White
immigrants, or the indigenous populations. It is difficult to escape the observation, in light of what I have written above, that in these societies "postcoloniality"
serves to erase such memories; on the one hand to identify more explicitly than
earlier with Third World victims of colonialism and, on the other hand, to counteract indigenous demands for authenticity—and, even more radically, for land
and political sovereignty.

The second question that needs to be considered concerns the language of
postcolonial discourse, which is the language of First World poststructuralism, as
postcolonial critics readily concede themselves, although they do not dwell too
long on its implications. Prakash's statement (which I quoted above) that, "all the
Third World voices identified in this essay, speak within and to discourses familiar to the 'West'" acknowledges this problem, but goes on to conceal its implications in his conclusion that all this proves is that "the maintenance and policing
of East-West boundaries has never succeeded in stopping the flows across and
against boundaries,".as if the flows in the two directions have been equal in their
potency. This is important not just for the inequalities disguised by assertions of
flows, hybridity, etc. More importantly, I think, it enables us to place temporally
a postcoloniality that otherwise may stretch across the entire history of colonialism. Here, once again, a comparison with China may be instructive, this time over
the issue of Marxism. Postcolonial critics insist that they are Marxists, but Marxists who reject the "nineteenth century heritage" of Marxism, with its universalistic pretensions that ignored historical differences.[32] This is a problem that Chinese Marxist revolutionaries faced and addressed in the 1930s: how to articulate
Marxism to Chinese conditions (and vice versa). Their answer was that Marxism
must be translated into a Chinese vernacular, not just in a national but, more
importantly, in a local sense: the language of the peasantry. The result was what
is commonly called "the Sinification of Marxism," embodied in Mao Zedong
Thought, so-called.[33] In the approach to a similar problem of postcolonial critics,
the translation takes the form not of translation into a national (as that is
rejected) or local (which is affirmed) vernacular, but the form of a rephrasing of

Marxism in the language of poststructuralism, where Marxism is "decon-structed," "decentered," etc. In other words, a critique that starts off with a repu-diation of the universalistic pretensions of Marxist language ends up not with its dispersion into local vernaculars, but with a return to another First World lan-guage with universalistic epistemological pretensions. It enables us, at least, to locate postcolonial criticism in the contemporary First World.

This is not a particularly telling point. Postcolonial critics recognize that the "critical gaze" their studies "direct at the archeology of knowledge enshrined in the west arise from the fact that most of them are being written in the First World academy."[34] Rather, in drawing attention to the language of postcolonial discourse, I seek to "deconstruct" the professions of "hybridity" and "in-betweenness" of postcolonial intellectuals. The hybridity that postcolonial criticism refers to is uni-formly a hybridity between the post*colonial* and the First World; never, to my knowledge, between one post*colonial* intellectual and another. But hybridity and in-betweenness do not serve very revealing purposes in the former case either. While postcolonial criticism quite validly points to the "over-determined" nature of concepts and subjectivities (and I am quite sure that the postcolonial subjectiv-ity is overdetermined, while less sure that it is "more" over-determined than any other), it conveniently ignores the part location in ideological and institutional structures gives direction to the resolution of contradictions presented by hybrid-ity—and the consequences of location in generating vast differences in power.[35] If the language of postcolonial discourse is any guide to its ideological direction, in this case the contradictions presented by hybridity would seem to be given direc-tion by the location of postcolonial intellectuals in the academic institutions of the First World. However much postcolonial intellectuals may insist on hybridity, and the transposability of locations, it is also necessary to insist that not all positions are equal in power; as Spivak's interrogators in India seem to recognize in their ref-erence to the "wings of progress" that brought her to India. To insist on hybridity against one's own language, it seems to me, is to disguise not only ideological loca-tion, but also the differences of power that go with different locations. Postcolonial intellectuals, in their First World institutional location, are ensconced in positions of power not only vis-à-vis the "native" intellectuals back at home, but also vis-à-vis their First World neighbors here. My neighbors in Farmville, VA, are no match in power for the highly paid, highly prestigious postcolonial intellectuals at Columbia, Duke, Princeton or UC–Santa Cruz; some of them might even be will-ing to swap positions with the latter, and take the anguish that comes with hybrid-ity so long as it brings with it the power and the prestige it seems to command.[36]

"Postcoloniality," Appiah writes, "has become . . . a condition of pessimism,"[37] and there is much to be pessimistic about the world situation of which postcolo-niality is an expression. This is not the message of "postcolonialism," however, as it acquires respectability and gains admission in United States academic institu-tions. While this discourse shares in the same themes as postcolonial discourses everywhere, it rearranges these themes into a celebration of the end of colonialism, as if the only tasks left for the present were to abolish the ideological and cultural legacy of colonialism; which sounds convincing only to the extent that, with its gaze fixed on the past, it avoids confrontation of the present. The current global condition appears in the discourse only as a projection of the subjectivities and epistemologies of First World intellectuals of Third World origin; which is another way of saying that the discourse constitutes the world in the self-image of these intellectuals: which makes it an expression not of powerlessness, but of newfound power. Postcolonial intellectuals have "arrived" in the First World Academy not just because they have broken new intellectual ground (although they *have* rephrased older themes), but because intellectual orientations that earlier were regarded as marginal or subversive have acquired a new respectability. Postcoloniality, it has been noted, has found favor even among academic conservatives who prefer it to less tractable vocabulary that insists on keeping in the foreground contemporary problems of political division and oppression.[38]

"Postcoloniality" has been the subject already of some telling criticism. Critics have noted that, in spite of its insistence on historicity and difference, "postcoloniality" mimics in its deployment the "ahistorical and universalizing" tendencies in colonialist thinking.[39] "If the theory promises a decentering of history in hybridity, syncretism, multidimensional time, and so forth," Anne McClintock writes, "the *singularity* of the term effects a re-centering of global history around the single rubric of European time. Colonialism returns at the moment of its disappearance."[40] In a world situation in which severe inequalities persist in older colonial forms or in their neocolonial reconfigurations, moreover, "the unified temporality of 'postcoloniality' risks reproducing the colonial discourse of an allochronic other, living in another time, still lagging behind us, the genuine postcolonials."[41] The spatial homogenization that accompanies a "unified temporality" not only fails to discriminate between vastly different social and political situations but also, to the extent that it "fails to discriminate between the diverse modalities of hybridity," may end up in "the consecration of hegemony."[42] Divorced from such discrimination, and without a sense of totality, O'Hanlon and Washbrook observe, "postcoloniality" also ends up mimicking methodologically the colonialist epistemology that it sets out to repudiate: "the solutions it offers—methodological individualism, the depoliticising insulation of social from material domains, a view of social relations that is in practice extremely voluntaristic, the refusal of any kind of programmatic politics—do not seem to us radical, subversive or emancipatory. They are on the contrary conservative and implicitly authoritarian, as they were indeed when recommended more overtly in the heyday of Britain's own imperial power."[43] "Postcolonialism's" repudiation of structure and totality in the name of history, ironically, ends up not in an affirmation of historicity, but in a self-referential "universalising historicism" that reintroduces an unexamined totality by the back door by projecting globally what are but local experiences. The problem here may be the problem of all historicism without a sense of structure, a web of translocal relationships without which it is impossible in the first place to determine what is different, heterogeneous and local. In his critique of "essentializing" procedures (of India, of the Third World), Prakash offers as a substitute an understanding of these categories in terms of "relationships," but does not elaborate on what these relationships might be. The critique of an "essentialist" fixing of the Third World is not novel; Karl Pletsch's eloquent critique of "Three Worlds" theory (without the aid of "postcoloniality"), published a decade ago, enunciated clearly the problem of ideological essentializing in modernization "theory."[44] Neither is Prakash's conceptual "innovation," relationships. Pletsch himself pointed to the importance of global relationships to understanding problems of development (as well as the conceptual underpinnings of modernization theory); and an understanding of modern global history in terms of relationships, needless to say, is the crucial thesis of "world-system analysis."

The difference between the latter and Prakash's "postfoundational" understanding of "relationships" rests on his rejection of foundational categories, chief among them capitalism. What O'Hanlon and Washbrook say on this issue is worth quoting at some length because of its relevance to the argument here:

> What his [Prakash's] position leaves quite obscure is what this category of "capitalist modernity" occupies for him. If our strategy should be to "refuse" it in favour of marginal histories, of multiple and heterogeneous identities, this suggests that capitalist modernity is nothing more than a potentially disposable fiction, held in place simply by our acceptance of its cognitive categories and values. Indeed, Prakash is particularly disparaging of Marxist and social historians' concern with capitalism as a "system" of political economy and coercive instrumentalities. Yet in other moments Prakash tells us that history's proper task is to challenge precisely this "homogenization of the world by contemporary capitalism." If this is so, and there is indeed a graspable logic to the way in which modern capitalism has spread itself globally, how are we to go about the central task of comprehending this logic in the terms that Prakash suggests?[45]

Prakash's answer to his critics simply evades the issues raised in this passage (while coming close to acknowledging a central role to capitalism) because to recognize them would make his "postfoundational" history untenable.[46] The political consequences of "postcolonialist" repudiation of the totality implied by metanarratives have been drawn out by Fernando Coronil in his observation that the opposition to metanarratives produces disjointed mini-narratives, which reinforce dominant worldviews; reacting against determinisms, it presents free-floating events; refusing to fix identity in structural categories, it essentializes identity through difference; resisting the location of power in structures or institutions, it diffuses it throughout society and ultimately dissolves it."[47] It also relieves this "self-defined minority of subaltern critics," O'Hanlon and Washbrook note, of the necessity of "doing what they constantly demand of others, which is to historicise the conditions of their own emergence as authoritative voices—conditions which could hardly be described without reference of some kind to material and class relations."[48]

Finally, the postcolonial repudiation of the Third World is intimately linked with the repudiation as "foundational categories" of capitalism, and the capitalist structuring of the modern world. Once again, "essentialism" serves as a straw man, diverting attention from radical conceptualizations of the Third World, which are not essentialist but relational, as in world-system approaches. The latter comprehends the Third World as a structural position within a capitalist world order; a position that changes with changing structural relationships, rather than "fixing" it ahistorically, as Prakash would have it. To be sure, world-system analysis is as discursive in its location of the Third World as one based on modernization; but, as I have argued above, so is "postcolonialist" analysis. The question then becomes a question of the ability of competing discourses to account for historical changes in global relationships, and the oppositional practices to which they point. I will say more on the former below. As for oppositional practices, "postcoloniality" by its very logic permits little beyond local struggles and, without reference to structure or totality, directionless ones at that. For all its contradictions, Shohat writes, "'Third World' usefully evokes structural commonalities of struggles. The invocation of the 'Third World' implies a belief that the shared history of neocolonialism and internal racism form sufficient common ground for alliances among . . . diverse peoples. If one does not believe or envision such commonalities, then indeed the term 'Third World' should be discarded."[49]

The denial to capitalism of "foundational" status is also revealing of a culturalism in the postcolonialist argument that has important ideological consequences. This involves the issue of Eurocentrism. Without capitalism as the foundation for European power and the motive force of its globalization, Eurocentrism would have been just another ethnocentrism (comparable to any other ethnocentrism from the Chinese and the Indian to the most trivial tribal solipsism). An exclusive focus on Eurocentrism as a cultural or ideological problem, that blurs the power relationships that dynamized it and endowed it with hegemonic persuasiveness, fails to explain why this particular ethnocentrism was able to define modern global history, and itself as the universal aspiration and end of that history, in contrast to the regionalism or localism of other ethnocentrisms. By throwing the cover of culture over material relationships, as if the one had little to do with the other, such a focus diverts the task of criticism from the criticism of capitalism to the criticism of Eurocentric ideology, which helps disguise its own ideological limitation but also, ironically, provides an alibi for inequality, exploitation and oppression in their modern guises under capitalist relationships. I will say more below on the contemporary circumstances of capitalism that enable such a separation of capitalism from Eurocentrism (the deterritorialization of capital under Global Capitalism). Suffice it to note here that the postcolonialist argument projects upon the past the same mystification of the relationship between power and culture that is characteristic of the ideology of Global Capitalism—of which it is a product.

These criticisms, however vehement on occasion, do not necessarily indicate that "postcolonialism's" critics deny to it all value; indeed, critics such as Coronil, McClintock and Shohat explicitly acknowledge some value to the issues raised by "postcolonialism" and postcolonial intellectuals. There is no denying, indeed, that "postcolonialism" is expressive of a current crisis in the conceptualization of the world, not just a crisis in the ideology of linear progress, but a crisis in the modes of comprehending the world associated with such concepts as the "Third World" and the "nation-state." Nor is it to be denied that as the global situation has become blurred with the disappearance of socialist states, and the emergence of important differences economically and politically among so-called Third World societies, as well as the diasporic motions of populations across national and regional boundaries, fragmentation of the global into the local has emerged into the foreground of historical and political consciousness. Crossing national, cultural, class, gender and ethnic boundaries, moreover, with its promise of a genuine cosmopolitanism, is appealing in its own right.

Within the institutional site of the First World academy, fragmentation of earlier metanarratives appears benign (except to hidebound conservatives) for its promise of more democratic, multicultural and cosmopolitan epistemologies. In the world outside the academy, however, it shows in murderous ethnic conflict, continued inequality between societies, classes and genders, and the absence of oppositional possibilities which, always lacking in coherence, are rendered even more impotent than earlier by the fetishization of difference, fragmentation, etc.

The predicament to which this gap points is rendered more serious in the confounding of ideological metanarratives with actualities of power; to mistake fragmentation in one realm with fragmentation in the other, ignoring the possibility that ideological fragmentation may represent not the dissolution of power but rather its further concentration. It is necessary, to account for this possibility, to retain a sense of structure and totality in the confrontation of fragmentation and locality; the alternative to which may be complicity in the consolidation of hegemony in the very process of questioning it. "Postcoloniality," while it represents an effort at adjusting to a changing global situation, for the same reason appears as an exemplary illustration of this predicament. Critics have hinted at its possible relationship to a new situation in the capitalist transformation of the world without examining this relationship at length. I would like to look at this relationship more closely.

Global Capitalism and the Condition of Postcoloniality

David Harvey and Fredric Jameson, among others, perceive a relationship between postmodernism and a new phase in the development of capitalism that has been described variously as Late Capitalism, Flexible Production or Accumulation, Disorganized Capitalism, or Global Capitalism.[50] As a progeny of postmodernism, I would like to suggest here, postcolonialism too is expressive of the "logic" of this phase of capitalism, this time on Third World terrain.

Fundamental to the structure of the new Global Capitalism (the term I prefer) is what Frobel and others have described as "a new international division of labor": in other words, the transnationalization of production where, through subcontracting, the process of production (of the same commodity even) is globalized.[51] The international division of labor in production may not be entirely novel; but new technologies have expanded the spatial extension of production, as well as its speed, to an unprecedented level. These same technologies have endowed capital and production with unprecedented mobility, so that the location of production seems to be in a constant state of change, seeking for maximum advantage for capital against labor, as well as to avoid social and political interference (hence, flexible production). For these reasons, analysts of capitalism perceive in Global Capitalism a qualitative difference from similar practices earlier—and a new phase of capitalism.

Second is the "decentering" of capitalism nationally. In other words, it is increasingly difficult to point to any nation or region as the center of global capitalism. More than one analyst (in a position of power) has found an analogue to the emerging organization of production in the northern European "Hanseatic League" of the early modern period, that is the period before the emergence of nation-states (one of them describing it as a "high-tech Hanseatic League"); in other words, a network of urban formations, without a clearly definable center, whose links to one another are far stronger than their relationships to their immediate hinterlands.[52]

The medium linking this network together, thirdly, is the transnational corporation, which has taken over from national markets as the locus of economic activity; not just as a passive medium for the transmission of capital, commodities and production, but as a determinant of the transmission, and its direction. While the analogy with the Hanseatic League suggest decentralization, in other words, production is heavily concentrated behind this facade in the corporation. One articulate spokesman for the new economic order suggests that the share of decisionmaking for production between the corporation and the market is roughly 70 to 30 percent.[53] With power lodged in transnational corporations, which by definition transcend nations in organization and/or loyalty, the power of the nation-state to regulate the economy internally is constricted, while global regulation (and defense) of the economic order emerges as a major task. This is manifested not only in the proliferation of global organizations, but also in efforts to organize extranational regional organizations to give coherence to the functioning of the economy.[54]

Fourthly, the transnationalization of production is the source at once of unprecedented unity globally, and of unprecedented fragmentation (in the history of capitalism). The homogenization of the globe economically, socially and culturally is such that Marx's predictions of the nineteenth century, premature for his time, finally seem to be on the point of vindication. At the same time, however, there is a parallel process of fragmentation at work; globally, in the disappearing of a center to capitalism, and locally, in the fragmentation of the production process into subnational regions and localities. As supranational regional organizations, such as the European Economic Community, Pacific Basin Economic Community, and the North American Free Trade Zone (to mention some that have been realized or are the objects of intense organizational activity) manifest this fragmentation at the global level, localities within the same nation competing with one another to place themselves in the pathways of transnational capital represent it at the most basic local level. Nations, themselves, it is arguable, represented attempts historically to contain fragmentation, but under attack from the outside (transnational organization) and the inside (subnational economic regions and localities), it is not quite clear how this new fragmentation is to be contained.[55]

A fifth important (perhaps the most important) consequence of the transnationalization of capital may be that for the first time in the history of capitalism, the capitalist mode of production appears as an authentically global abstraction, divorced from its historically specific origins in Europe. In other words, the narrative of capitalism is no longer a narrative of the history of Europe; so that, for the first time, non-European capitalist societies make their own claims on the history of capitalism. Corresponding to economic fragmentation, in other words, is cultural fragmentation or, to put it in its positive guide, "multiculturalism." The most dramatic instance of this new cultural situation may be the effort over the last decade to appropriate capitalism for the so-called Confucian values of East Asian societies, which is a reversal of a long-standing conviction (in Europe and East Asia) that Confucianism was historically an obstacle to capitalism. I think it is arguable that the apparent end of Eurocentrism is an illusion, because capitalist culture as it has taken shape has Eurocentrism built into the very structure of its narrative, which may explain why even as Europe and the United States lose their domination of the capitalist world economy, culturally European and American values retain their domination. It is noteworthy that what makes something like the East Asian Confucian revival plausible is not its offer of alternative values to those of EuroAmerican origin, but its articulation of native culture into a capitalist narrative. Having said this, it is important to reiterate nevertheless that the question of world culture has become much more complex than in earlier phases of capitalism.

The fragmentation of space, and its consequences for Eurocentrism, also imply a fragmentation of the temporality of capitalism: the challenge to Eurocentrism, in other words, means that it is possible to conceive of the future in ways other than those of EuroAmerican political and social models. Here, once again, it is difficult to distinguish reality from illusion, but the complexity is undeniable.

Finally, the transnationalization of production calls into question earlier divisions of the world into First, Second and Third Worlds. The Second World, the world of socialism, is for all practical purposes, of the past. But the new global configuration also calls into question the distinctions between the First and Third Worlds. Parts of the earlier Third World are today on the pathways of transnational capital, and belong in the "developed" sector of the world economy. Likewise, parts of the First World marginalized in the new global economy are hardly distinguishable in way of life from what used to be viewed as Third World characteristics. It may not be fortuitous that the North-South distinction has gradually taken over from the earlier division of the globe into the three worlds—so long as we remember that the references of North and South are not merely to concrete geographic locations, but metaphorical references: North denoting the pathways of transnational capital, and, South, the marginalized populations of the world, regardless of their location (which is where "postcoloniality" comes in!).

Ideologues of Global Capital have described this condition as "Global Regionalism" or "Global Localism," adding quickly, however, that "Global Localism" is 70 percent global and only 30 percent local.[56] They have also appropriated for capital the radical ecological slogan, "Think globally, act locally."[57]

The situation created by Global Capitalism helps explain certain phenomena that have become apparent over the past two to three decades, but especially since the eighties: global motions of peoples (and, therefore, cultures), the weakening of boundaries (among societies, as well as among social categories), the replications in societies internally of inequalities and discrepancies once associated with colonial differences, simultaneous homogenization and fragmentation within and across societies, the interpenetration of the global and the local, and the disorganization of a world conceived in terms of "three worlds" or nation-states. Some of these phenomena have also contributed to an appearance of equalization of differences within and across societies, as well as of democratization within and between societies. What is ironic is that the managers of this world situation themselves concede the concentration of power in their (or their organizations') hands; as well as their manipulation of peoples, boundaries and cultures to appropriate the local for the global, to admit different cultures into the realm of capital only to break them down and to remake them in accordance with the requirements of production and consumption, and even to reconstitute subjectivities across national boundaries to create producers and consumers more responsive to the operations of capital. Those who do not respond, or the "basket-cases" which are not essential to those operations—four-fifths of the global population by their count—need not be colonized; they are simply marginalized. What the new "flexible production" has made possible is that it is no longer necessary to utilize explicit coercion against labor, at home or abroad (in colonies); those peoples or places that are not responsive to the needs (or demands) of capital, or are too far gone to respond "efficiently," simply find themselves out of its pathways. And it is easier even than in the heyday of colonialism or modernization theory to say convincingly: "it is their own fault."

If I may now return to Shohat's question with which I began this essay—"When exactly ... does the 'postcolonial' begin?"—and give it a less facetious answer consistent with his intention, the answer is: "with the emergence of Global Capitalism," not in the sense of an exact coincidence in time, but in the sense that the one is a condition for the other.

There is little that is remarkable about this conclusion, which is but an extension to postcolonialism of the relationship Harvey and Jameson have established between postmodernism and developments within capitalism. If postcolonialism is a progeny of postmodernism, then these developments within capitalism are also directly or indirectly pertinent to understanding postcolonialism. Postcolonial critics readily concede the debt they owe to postmodernist, poststructuralist thinking; indeed, their most original contribution would seem to lie in their rephrasing of older problems in the study of the Third World in the language of poststructuralism. What is remarkable, therefore, is not my conclusion here but that a consideration of the relationship between "postcolonialism" and Global Capitalism should be absent from the writings of postcolonial intellectuals; all the more remarkable because this relationship is arguably less abstract and more direct than any relationship between Global Capitalism and postmodernism, as it pertains not just to cultural/epistemological but to social and political formations.

"Postcoloniality" represents a response to a genuine need: the need to overcome a crisis of understanding produced by the inability of old categories to account for the world. The metanarrative of progress that underlies two centuries of thinking first in Europe and then globally with the expansion of Europe is in deep crisis; not just out of a loss of faith in progress or its disintegrative effects in actuality, but more importantly because over the last decade in particular our sense of time has been jumbled up: as conservatism has become "revolutionary" ("the Reagan Revolution") while revolutionaries have turned first into conservatives and then into reactionaries (as in formerly socialist countries such as the Soviet Union and China); as religious millenarianisms long thought to be castaways from Enlightenment have made a comeback into politics, sometimes allied to high-tech revolutions, as in the United States; and as fascism has been reborn out of the ashes of Communist regimes. The crisis of "progress" has brought in its wake a crisis of modernization, more in its Marxist than its bourgeois guise, and called into question the structure of the world as conceived by modernizationists and radicals alike in the decades after World War II: "the Three Worlds." The Three Worlds as fixed in social theory (bourgeois or Marxist) geographically or structurally are indeed no longer tenable, as the globe has become as jumbled up spatially as the ideology of progress is temporally: with the appearance of Third Worlds in the First World, and First Worlds in the Third; with the diasporas of people that have relocated the Self there and the Other here, and the consequent confounding of borders and boundaries; and with the culture flows that have been at once homogenizing and heterogenizing, where some groups share in a common global culture regardless of location even as they are alienated from the culture of their "hinterlands," and others are driven back into cultural legacies long thought to be residual, to take refuge in cultural havens that are as far apart from one another as at the origins of modernity—even though they may be watching the same TV shows.

Politically speaking, the Second and the Third Worlds have been the major casualties of this crisis. The Second World, the world of socialist states, is already, to put it bluntly, "history." What has happened to the Third World (the immediate subject of "postcoloniality") may be less apparent but no less significant. We may note here that the two major crises of the early nineties that are global in implication are the crises occasioned by Iraq's invasion of Kuwait and the current situation in Somalia. In the Gulf crisis, a Third World country appeared as the imperialist culprit against (a socially and politically reactionary but economically powerful) neighbor, and had to be driven back by the combined armies of the First, Second and the Third Worlds, led by an imperial power now turned into a paradigm of righteousness. The "invasion" (I borrow the word from a TV report) of Somalia, if anything, is more revealing: if in the case of the Gulf crisis one "Third" World country had to be saved from another, in Somalia we have a Third World country that has to be saved from itself. The Third World, viewed by radicals only two decades ago as a hope for the future, now has to be saved from itself. The crisis could not get much deeper.

"Postcoloniality" addresses this situation of crisis that eludes understanding in terms of older conceptualizations,[58] which may explain why it should have created immediate "ferment" in intellectual circles. But this still begs the question of "why now?" and why it has taken the intellectual direction it has. After all, there is more than one conceptual way out of a crisis, and we must inquire why this particular way has acquired immediate popularity—in First World institutions. To put it bluntly, "postcoloniality" is designed to *avoid* making sense of the current crisis and, in the process, to cover up the origins of postcolonial intellectuals in a Global Capitalism of which they are not so much victims as beneficiaries.

"Postcoloniality" resonates with the problems thrown up by Global Capitalism. As the crisis of the Third World has become inescapably apparent during the decade of the eighties, so have the effects of Global Capitalism: the Reagan (and Thatcher) Revolution was not so much a revolution heralding a new beginning as a revolution aimed at reorganizing the globe politically so as to give free reign to a Global Capitalism straining against the harness of political restrictions that limited its motions. The overthrow of socialist states was one part of the program. Another part was taming the Third World; if necessary by invasion, preferably by encirclement: economically, or by "Patriot" missiles. But these are at best options of the last resort. By far the best option is control from the inside: through the creation of classes amenable to incorporation into or alliance with global capital.

I use "control" here advisedly; under conditions of Global Capitalism, control is not to be imposed, it has to be negotiated. Transnational capital is no longer just EuroAmerican; and neither is modernity just EuroAmerican modernity. The complicated social and cultural composition of transnational capitalism makes it difficult to sustain a simple equation between capitalist modernity and Eurocentric (and patriarchal) cultural values and political forms. Others who have achieved success within the capitalist world system demand a voice for their values within the culture of transnational capital; the East Asian Confucian revival to which I referred above is exemplary of the phenomenon. Eurocentrism, as the very condition for the emergence of these alternative voices, retains its cultural hegemony; but it is more evident than ever before that, in order for this hegemony to be sustained, its boundaries must be rendered more porous than earlier, to absorb in its realm alternative cultural possibilities which might otherwise serve as sources of destructive oppositions—the mutual "bashing" between Japan and the United States in recent years, which revives racist and Orientalist vocabulary, attests to the dangers of conflict among the very ranks of transnational capital. And who knows, in the end, what values are most functional to the needs of a changing "capital"? Commentator after commentator has remarked in recent years that the "communitarian" values of "Confucianism" may be more suitable to a contemporary managerial capitalism than the individualistic values of an entrepreneurial capitalism of an earlier day. What is clear is that Global Capitalism is (and must be) much more fluid culturally than a Eurocentric capitalism.

This is also the condition of "postcoloniality," and the cultural moves associated with it. Obscurantist conservatives, anxious to explain away cultural problems by substituting the machinations of subversives for systemic analysis, attribute the cultural problems that became apparent in the eighties (most recently, multiculturalism) to the invasion of academic institutions (and politics in general) by Marxists, feminists, ethnics, etc. What they ignore is the possible relationship between the Reagan economic revolution and these cultural developments; in other words, the cultural requirements of transnational corporations which, in their very globalism, can no longer afford the cultural parochialism of an earlier day. Focusing on "Liberal Arts" institutions, they overlook conveniently how much headway "multiculturalism" has made in business schools and among the managers of transnational corporations, who are eager all of a sudden to learn about the secrets in "oriental" philosophies of East Asian economic success, who cannibalize cultures all over the world in order better to market their commodities, and who have become aware all of a sudden of a need to "internationalize" academic institutions (which often takes the form not of promoting scholarship in a conventional sense but rather the form of "importing" and "exporting" students and faculty). While in an earlier day it might have been Marxist and feminist radicals, with the aid of the few ethnics, who spearheaded multiculturalism, by now the initiative has passed into the hands of "enlightened" administrators and trustees who are quite aware of the "manpower" needs of the new economic situation. Much less than a conflict between conservatives and radicals (although that, too, is there obviously), the conflict shapes up now as a conflict between an older elite (and a small business threatened from the inside and the outside) and the elite vanguard of international business. *The Harvard Business Review* is one of the foremost, and earliest (in the United States) advocates of transnational-ism—and multiculturalism.

The Reaganites may have been misled by visions of many Dinesh D'Souzas, which were not forthcoming. Their failure to grasp the social and political conse-quences of the economic victory for transnationalism they had engineered became apparent during the 1992 elections when, against the calls from right-wingers for a return to such "native" American values as Eurocentrism, patriar-chalism, and racism, George Bush often looked befuddled; possibly because he grasped much better than right-wingers such as Pat Buchanan the dilemmas pre-sented by the victory of transnationalism over all its competitors in the Second and Third Worlds. The result has been the victory of high-tech yuppies, much better attuned to the new world situation, and aware of the difficulties it presents. It is no coincidence that Robert Reich, frequent contributor to *The Harvard Busi-ness Review*, keen analyst of developments within the capitalist world economy, and an advocate of the "borderless economy," should have been a close confidant of President Clinton.

This is, I think, also the context for the emergence of "postcoloniality," and its rapid success in academic institutions as a substitute for earlier conceptualiza-tions of the world. "Postcoloniality," in the particular direction it has taken as a discourse, also resonates with the problems of the contemporary world. It addresses issues that, while they may have been issues all along in global studies, are now rephrased in such a way that they are in tune with issues in Global Cap-italism: Eurocentrism and its relationship to capitalism; the kind of modernity that is relevant to a postmodern/postsocialist/post–Third World situation; the place of the nation in development; the relationship between the local and the global; the place of borders and boundaries in a world where capital, production and peoples are in constant motion; the status of structures in a world that more than ever seems to be without recognizable structure; interpenetrations and reversals between the different "worlds"; borderlands subjectivities and episte-mologies ("hybridity"); homogeneity vs. heterogeneity; and so forth.

"Postcoloniality," however, is also appealing because it disguises the power rela-tions that shape a seemingly shapeless world, and contributes to a conceptualiza-tion of that world that, while functional to the consolidation of hegemony, is also subversive of possibilities of resistance. "Postcolonial critics" have engaged in valid criticism of past forms of ideological hegemony, but have had little to say about its contemporary figurations. Indeed, in their simultaneous repudiation of structure and affirmation of the local in problems of oppression and liberation, they have mystified the ways in which totalizing structures persist in the midst of apparent disintegration and fluidity. They have rendered into problems of sub-jectivity and epistemology concrete and material problems of the everyday world. While capital in its motions continues to structure the world, the refusal to capi-tal of "foundational" status renders impossible that "cognitive mapping," which must be the point of departure for any practice of resistance, while any cognitive mapping there is remains in the domain of those who manage the capitalist world economy.[59] Indeed, in the projection of the current state of conceptual "disorganization" upon the colonial past, "postcolonial critics" have also deprived colonialism of any but local logic, so that the historical legacy of colonialism (in an Iraq, or a Somalia, or, for that matter, any Third World society) appears irrelevant to the present; which shifts the burden of persistent problems on to the victims themselves.

"Postcoloniality," Appiah writes, "is the condition of what we might ungenerously call a *comprador* intelligentsia"[60] (emphasis in the original). I think this is missing the point because the world-situation that justified the term "comprador" no longer exists. I would suggest, rather, that "postcoloniality" is the condition of the intelligentsia of Global Capitalism. I think Ahmad is closer to the mark when he states, with characteristic bluntness, that "postcoloniality is . . . like most things, a matter of class."[61] While the statement is not entirely fair in ignoring that postcoloniality also has its appeals to many among the oppressed who would rather forget memories of past oppression in order be able to live in the present,[62] it is an uncompromising reminder nevertheless of the continued importance, albeit reconfigured on a global basis, of class relations in understanding contemporary cultural developments.

The question, then, is not whether or not this global intelligentsia can (or should) return to national loyalties but whether or not, in recognition of its own class position in Global Capitalism, it can generate a thoroughgoing criticism of its own ideology, and formulate practices of resistance against the system of which it is a product.

Notes

My being (more or less) one of the Third World intellectuals in First World academe does not privilege the criticism of postcolonial intellectuals that I offer below, but it does call for some comment. It is not clear to me how important the views I discuss (or the intellectuals who promote them) are in their impact on contemporary intellectual life. "Postcolonial" has been entering the vocabulary of academic programs in recent years, and over the last two years there have been a number of conferences/symposia inspired by this vocabulary ("Postcolonialism," "after Orientalism," etc.), as well as special issues devoted to the subject in periodicals such as *Social Text* and *Public Culture*. Given the small number of intellectuals directly concerned with "postcoloniality," and the diffuseness in their use of the term, it might make more sense to study the reception of the term. What makes it important to study it as a concept, I argue below, is that the ideas associated with postcoloniality are significant and widespread as concerns, even if they predate in their emergence the appearance of the term "postcolonial" itself. It is not the importance of these ideas that I question, in other words, but their appropriation for "postcoloniality." Otherwise, there is a "Third World" sensibility and mode of perception that has become increasingly visible in cultural discussions over the last decade. I myself share in the concerns (and even some of the viewpoints) of "postcolonial intellectuals," though from a somewhat different perspective than those who describe themselves as such; most recently in my *After the Revolution: Waking to Global Capitalism* (Hanover, NH: The University of New England Press for Wesleyan University Press, 1994).

For their assistance with sources/comments, I would like to thank the following, while relieving them of any complicity in my views: Harry Harootunian, Roxann Prazniak, Rob Wilson and Zhang Xudong. The present essay is a slightly revised version (to take account of recent literature) of an essay that was published first in *Critical Inquiry*, 20:2 (Winter 1994):328–356. Since the essay was first published, I have had occasion to discuss the ideas in it in seminars at Duke University, the University of California–Santa Cruz, the University of Hawaii, Washington University at St. Louis, and the Humanities Institute at Stony Brook. It would be impossible to name the participants in these various seminars. My gratitude to them all.

1. Ella Shohat, "Notes on the 'Post-Colonial,'" *Social Text* 31/32 (1992):99–113.

2. In 1985, Gayatri Spivak insisted in an interview that she did not belong to the "top level of the United States Academy" because she taught in the South and the Southwest whereas "the cultural elite in the United States inhabit the Northeastern seaboard or the West coast." See Gayatri Chakravorty Spivak, *The Post-Colonial Critic: Interviews, Strategies, Dialogues*, Sarah Harasym (ed.) (New York and London: Routledge, 1990), p.114. Since then Professor Spivak has moved to the "Northeastern seaboard," although the move has not spared her, she tells me, the difficulties that a Third World woman of color, and a radical one at that, faces in such institutions.

3. Ibid., passim. See also Arjun Appadurai, "Global Ethnoscapes: Notes and Queries for a Transnational Anthropology," in Richard G. Fox (ed.), *Recapturing Anthropology: Working in the Present* (Santa Fe, N.M.: School of American Research Press, 1991), pp.191–210. Aijaz Ahmad, who I do not include among the "postcolonial critics" here, does an excellent job of relating the problems of "postcoloniality" to contemporary capitalism, if only in passing and somewhat differently from what I undertake below. See his "Jameson's Rhetoric of Otherness and the 'National Allegory,'" *Social Text* 17 (Fall 1987):3–25 and the more recent *In Theory: Classes, Nations, Literatures* (London: Verso Books, 1992).

4. Shohat, p.103.

5. Gyan Prakash, "Writing Post-Orientalist Histories of the Third World: Perspectives from Indian Historiography," *Comparative Studies in Society and History* 32.2 (1990):383–408.

6. Ibid., p.399. See also Gayatri Chakravorty Spivak, "Subaltern Studies: Deconstructing Historiography," in Ranajit Guha and Gayatri Chakravorty Spivak (eds.), *Selected Subaltern Studies* (New York: Oxford University Press, 1988), pp.3–32.

7. Gyan Prakash, "Postcolonial Criticism and Indian Historiography," *Social Text* 31/32, pp.8–19. I use Prakash's discussions of "postcoloniality" as my point of departure here because he has made the most systematic attempts at accounting for the concept and also because his discussions bring to the fore the implications of the concept for historical understanding. As this statement reveals, Prakash himself draws heavily for inspiration on the characteristics of "postcolonial" consciousness delineated by others, especially Homi Bhabha who has been responsible for the prominence in discussions of postcoloniality of the vocabulary of "hybridity," etc. Bhabha's work, however, is responsible for more than the vocabulary of "postcolonialism," as he has proven himself to be something of a master of political mystification and theoretical obfuscation, of a reduction of social and political problems to psychological ones, and of the substitution of poststructuralist

linguistic manipulation for historical and social explanation—which show up in much of postcolonial writings, but rarely with the same virtuosity (and incomprehensibleness) that he brings to it. For some of his more influential writings, see "Of Mimicry and Man: The Ambivalence of Colonial Discourse," *October* 28 (1984):125–133; "The Comment to Theory," in Jim Pines and Paul Willemen (eds.), *Questions of Third World Cinema* (London: BFI Publishing, 1989), pp.111–132; "The Other Question: Difference, Discrimination and the Discourse of Colonialism," in F. Barker, P. Hulme, M. Iversen and D. Loxley (eds.), *Literature, Politics and Theory* (London and New York: Methuen, 1986), pp.148–172; his essays in Homi Bhabha (ed.), *Nation and Narration* (London and New York: Routledge, 1990), and, most recently, *The Location of Culture* (London and New York: Routledge, 1994). Bhabha may be exemplary of the Third World intellectual who has been completely reworked by the language of First World cultural criticism. This is not to deny, to rephrase what I said above, his enormous linguistic talents, which may be inseparable from his conviction in the priority of language, his conversion of material problems into metaphorical ones, and his apparent concern for aesthetic playfulness over clarity in his writing.

8. Prakash, "Post-Orientalist Histories," p.393.

9. Ibid., p.395. See also Dipesh Chakrabarty, "Post-Coloniality and the Artifice of History: Who Speaks for 'Indian' Pasts?" *Representations* 37 (Winter 1992):1–26.

10. Prakash, "Postcolonial Criticism," pp.14–15. See also Spivak, *The Post-Colonial Critic*, passim. As the term "subaltern" would indicate, Antonio Gramsci's inspiration is readily visible in the works of subaltern historians.

11. Prakash, "Post-Orientalist Histories," pp.390–391.

12. Ibid., p.397.

13. Prakash, "Postcolonial Criticism," p.13.

14. Prakash, "Post-Orientalist Histories," p.13.

15. Ibid., p.399.

16. Ibid., p.403.

17. Indeed, Lyotard has "defined" postmodern as "incredulity toward metanarratives." Jean-Francois Lyotard, *The Postmodern Condition: A Report on Knowledge* (Minneapolis: University of Minnesota Press, 1984), p.xxiv.

18. Bill Ashcroft, Gareth Griffiths and Helen Tiffin, *The Empire Writes Back: Theory and Practice in Post-Colonial Literatures* (London: Routledge, 1989), p.2. Note that in this instance, the postcolonial concerns itself with literature, although the implications obviously go beyond the literary realm, which is characteristic of much of these discussions. Also, in case the reader might wonder why Latin American literatures—which may be more "paradigmatic" than any—are not included in the list, it is noteworthy that in the writings of Australian and Canadian postcolonials, "postcolonial" more often than not is associated with the former Commonwealth countries, rather than with the Third World in general—and this in spite of immense differences economically and politically between countries comprising the Commonwealth. This is indicated by Stephen Slemon, "Unsettling the Empire: Resistance Theory for the Second World," in Ashcroft, Griffiths and Tiffin (eds.), *the post-colonial studies reader* (London and New York: Routledge, 1995), pp.104–110. Reprinted in abridged form from *World Literature Written in English*, 30:2 (1990).

19. For discussions of similar problems in Chinese historiography, see Joseph Levenson, *Confucian China and Its Modern Fate* (Berkeley: University of California Press, 1968); Rey

Chow, *Woman and Chinese Modernity* (Minneapolis: University of Minnesota Press, 1991); Arif Dirlik, *Revolution and History: Origins of Marxist Historiography in China, 1919–1937* (Berkeley: University of California Press, 1978); and Arif Dirlik, "The Globalization of Marxist Historical Discourse and the Problem of Hegemony in Marxism," *Journal of Third World Studies* 4.1 (Spring 1987):151–164.

20. Ashcroft, Griffiths and Tiffin (eds.), *the post-colonial studies reader*, p.1.

21. Frederick Buell, *National Culture and the New Global System* (Baltimore and London: The Johns Hopkins University Press, 1994).

22. Prakash, "Postcolonial Criticism," p.10.

23. Diana Brydon, "The White Inuit Speaks: Contamination as Literary Strategy," in *the post-colonial studies reader*:136–142. Originally published in Ian Adam and Helen Tiffin(eds.), *Past the Last Post: Theorizing Post-Colonialism and Post-Modernism* (New York: Harvester Wheatsheaf, 1991). Similar warnings toward Australian aboriginal claims to "authenticity," although phrased much more gently, are to be found in *The Empire Writes Back* and in Gareth Griffiths, "The Myth of Authenticity," in Chris Tiffin and Alan Lawson (eds.), *De-Scribing Empire: Post-Colonialism and Textuality* (London and New York: Routledge, 1994), pp.70–85.

24. Spivak, *The Post-Colonial Critic*, pp.67–68.

25. This is at any rate a question that needs to be clarified. It seems to me that Prakash's denial of "foundational" status to class goes beyond what is but a *historicization* of class in the work of *subaltern* historians, in the same way that, say, E. P. Thompson historicizes the concept in *The Making of the English Working Class*. For a note on the question of class, see Dipesh Chakrabarty, "Invitation to a Dialogue," *Subaltern Studies*, 4 (1985). The procedure of generalization may also play a part in the deradicalization of subaltern ideas by removing them from their specific historiographical context, where they *do* play an innovative, radical role. For instance, the qualification of the role of colonialism in Indian history is intended by these historians to bring to the fore the mystifications of the past in nationalist histories, which is a radical act. Made into a general principle of "postcolonialism," this qualification turns into a downplaying of colonialism in history. For an acknowledgment of doubt concerning the "success" attributed to subaltern historiography, see Chakrabarty, "Postcoloniality and the Artifice of History," op. cit.

26. Note not just the ideas but the tone in the following statement by Ahmad: "But one could start with a radically different premise, namely the proposition that we live not in three worlds but in one; that this world includes the experience of colonialism and imperialism on both sides of Jameson's global divide . . . that societies in formations of backward capitalism are as much constituted by the division of classes as are societies in the advanced capitalist countries; that socialism is not restricted to something called the second world but is simply the name of a resistance that saturates the globe today, as capitalism, itself does; that the different parts of the capitalist system are to be known not in terms of binary opposition but as a contradictory unity, with differences, yes, but also with profound overlaps." "Jameson's Rhetoric of Otherness and the 'National Allegory,'" p.9.

27. Spivak, "Can the Subaltern Speak?" in Cary Nelson and Lawrence Grossberg (eds.), *Marxism and the Interpretation of Culture* (Urbana and Chicago: University of Illinois Press, 1988), pp.271–313; Lata Mani, "Multiple Mediations: Feminist Scholarship in the Age of Multinational Reception," in James Clifford and Vivek Dhareshwar (eds.), *Travelling Theories Travelling Theorists* (Santa Cruz: Center for Cultural Theory, 1989), pp.1–23.

28. Kwame A. Appiah, "Is the Post- in Postmodernism the Post- in Postcolonial?" *Critical Inquiry* 17 (Winter 1991):336–357.

29. Achille Mbembe, "Prosaics of Servitude and Authoritarian Civilities," *Public Culture* 5.1 (Fall 1992):123–145.

30. Spivak, *The Post-Colonial Critic*, p.91.

31. For a sampling of essays, see Joseph P.L. Jiang, *Confucianism and Modernization: A Symposium* (Taipei: Freedom Council, 1987). Scholars such as Tu Wei-ming and Yu Ying-shih have played a major part in efforts to revive Confucianism; while the quasi-fascist regime of Singapore (especially under Lee Kuan Yew) has been a major promoter of the idea.

32. Prakash, "Postcolonial Criticism," pp.14–15.

33. For a discussion of this problem in detail, see Arif Dirlik, "Mao Zedong and 'Chinese Marxism,'" *Encyclopedia of Asian Philosophy* (London: Routledge).

34. Prakash, "Postcolonial Criticism," p.10.

35. Althusser recognized this problem with specific reference to Mao Zedong thought. See "Contradiction and Overdetermination," in Louis Althusser, *For Marx*, trans. Ben Brewster (New York: Vintage Books, 1970), pp.87–128. For the "molding" of ideology, see "Ideology and Ideological State Apparatuses," in Louis Althusser, *Lenin and Philosophy*, trans. Ben Brewster (New York: Monthly Review Press, 1971), pp.127–186. Lata Mani gives a good (personal) account of the contextual formation of ideology in her "Multiple Mediations." The risk in contextual ideological formation, of course, is the transformation of what is a problem into what is a celebration: game playing. This is evident throughout in Spivak's "playfulness" in *The Post-Colonial Critic* as well as in, say, James Clifford's approach to the question of ethnography and culture. For a brief example of the latter, among Clifford's many works, see "Notes on Theory and Travel," *Travelling Theories Travelling Theorists*, pp.177–188. My objection here is not to the importance of immediate context in ideology formation (and the variability and transposability of roles it implies) but to the mystification of such emphasis on the local of the larger contexts that differentiate power relations, and suggest more stable and directed positions. No matter how much the ethnographer may strive to change places with the native, in the end the ethnographer returns to the First World academy and the native back to the "wilds." This is the problem with "postcoloniality," and is evident in the tendency of so much "postcolonial criticism" to start off with a sociology of power relationships only to take refuge in aesthetic phraseology.

36. Conversely, absence from powerful institutions may lead to silence. This is an explanation that Nicholas Thomas has offered for the obliviousness of postcolonial criticism to the problem of indigenous peoples who, to the extent that they are present in the academy, are only marginally so. See Thomas, *Colonialism's Culture: Anthropology, Travel and Government* (Princeton, N.J.: Princeton University Press, 1994), p.172.

37. Appiah, "Is the Post- in Postmodernism the Post- in Postcolonial?," p.353.

38. See the example Shohat gives of his experiences at CUNY. "Notes on the 'Post-Colonial,'" p.99.

39. Ibid.

40. Anne McClintock, "The Angel of Progress: Pitfalls of the Term 'Post-Colonialism,'" *Social Text* 31/32:84–98. Recall the statement I quoted above from Diana Brydon.

41. Shohat, "Notes on the 'Post-Colonial,'" p.104.

42. Ibid., p.110.

43. Rosalind O'Hanlon and David Washbrook, "After Orientalism: Culture, Criticism, and Politics in the Third World," *Comparative Studies in Society and History* 34:1 (January 1992):141–167.

44. Karl Pletsch, "The Three Worlds, or the Division of Social Scientific Labor, Circa 1950–1975," *Comparative Studies in Society and History* 23:4 (1981).

45. O'Hanlon and Washbrook, "After Orientalism," p.147.

46. Spivak, "Postcolonial Criticism," pp.13–14.

47. Fernando Coronil, "Can Postcoloniality be Decolonized? Imperial Banality and Postcolonial Power," *Public Culture* 5:1 (Fall 1992):89–108.

48. O'Hanlon and Washbrook, "After Orientalism," pp.165–166.

49. Shohat, "Notes on the 'Post-Colonial,'" p.111.

50. David Harvey, *The Condition of Postmodernity* (Cambridge, MA: Basil Blackwell, 1989) and Fredric Jameson, "Postmodernism, or the Cultural Logic of Late Capitalism," *New Left Review* 146 (July/August 1984).

51. F. Frobel, J. Heinrichs and O. Kreye, *The New International Division of Labor* (Cambridge, MA: Cambridge University Press, 1980). "Disorganized Capitalism" comes from Claus Offe, *Disorganized Capitalism* (Cambridge, MA: The MIT Press, 1985), while "Global Capitalism" is the term used by Robert J.S. Ross and Kent C. Trachte, *Global Capitalism: The New Leviathan* (Albany, N.Y.: State University of New York Press, 1990). Other noteworthy books on the subject are Leslie Sklair, *Sociology of the Global System* (Baltimore: The Johns Hopkins University Press, 1991), which spells out the implications for the Third World of Global Capitalism; and, especially in light of what I say below of the new presidency of the United States, Robert Reich, *The Work of Nations* (New York: Alfred A. Knopf, 1991). Reich's book incorporates his contributions to *The Harvard Business Review* with such suggestive titles (in the present context) as "Who is Us?" and "Who is Them?" For "subcontracting," see Gary Gereffi, "Global Sourcing and Regional Divisions of Labor in the Pacific Rim," in Arif Dirlik (ed.), *What Is in a Rim? Critical Perspectives on the Asia-Pacific Idea* (Boulder, CO: Westview Press).

52. Riccardo Petrella, "World City-States of the Future," *New Perspectives Quarterly* (Fall 1991):59–64. See also "A New Hanseatic League?" *The New York Times*, February 23, 1992, p.E3.

53. Kenichi Ohmae, "Beyond Friction to Fact: The Borderless Economy," *New Perspectives Quarterly* (Spring 1990):20–21.

54. While I stress transnational corporations here, it is important to note that the functioning of corporations is made possible by a whole gamut of transnational organizations, from state-led ones, such as the World Bank and IMF, to what might be described as organizations of a global "civil society," from NGOs to professional associations. Taking note of these organizations also serves as a reminder that, in spite of the appearance of decentralization and the dispersion of power, the powerful of the First World, through their immense concentration of wealth as well as the influence they exert on these organizations, continue to dominate the world, albeit at a greater distance (especially in terms of social and public responsibility) from their own societies.

55. This phenomenon is addressed in most of the works cited above; see n.47.

56. Ohmae, op. cit. See also James Gardner, "Global Regionalism," *New Perspectives Quarterly* (Winter 1992):58–59.

57. "The Logic of Global Business: An Interview with ABB's Percy Barnevik," *The Harvard Business Review* (March–April 1991), pp.90–105.

58. See Achille Mbembe, "The Banality of Power and the Aesthetics of Vulgarity," *Public Culture* 4.2 (Spring 1992):1–30, and the discussion his essay provoked in *Public Culture* 5.1 (Fall 1992).

59. For "cognitive mapping," see Fredric Jameson, "Cognitive Mapping," in Nelson and Gossberg, *Marxism and the Interpretation of Culture*, pp.347–357. Jameson has been a forceful advocate of the necessity of retaining a sense of totality and structure to a socialist politics. His own totalization of the global structure has come under severe criticism (see Ahmad, above). I should stress here that it is not necessary to agree with his particular mode of totalization to recognize the validity of his argument.

60. Appiah, "Is the Post- in Postmodernism the Post- in Postcolonial?" p.348.

61. Aijaz Ahmad, "The Politics of Literary Postcoloniality," *Race and Class* 36.3(1995):1–20. See also Benita Parry, "Signs of Our Times: Discussion of Homi Bhabha's *The Location of Culture*," *Third Text* 28/29 (Autumn/Winter 1994):3–24.

62. This is an aspect of postcoloniality, and of its appeals, that clearly calls for greater attention. A historian of the Pacific, Klaus Neumann, writes that "these days Papua New Guineans . . . do not appear overtly interested in being told about the horrors of colonialism, as such accounts potentially belittle today's descendants of yesterday's victims," in "'In Order to Win Their Friendship': Renegotiating First Contact," *The Contemporary Pacific*, 6.1 (1994):110–145. Likewise, Deirdre Jordan notes the complaints of adult aboriginal students in Australia about emphasis on white oppression, "which seems designed to call forth in them responses of hostility and racism and which, they believe, causes a crisis of identity." "Aboriginal Identity: Uses of the Past, Problems for the Future?" in Jeremy R. Beckett (ed.), *Past and Present: The Construction of Aboriginality* (Canberra: Aboriginal Studies Press, 1994):109–119. There are others, needless to say, who would suppress memories of the past for reasons of self-interest.

4

The Global in the Local

About ten years ago, a movie called *Local Hero* (directed by Bill Forsyth) appeared on the screens of artsier movie theaters in the United States. The movie narrated the study of a friendly confrontation between a global oil company located in Houston, Texas, and a small town on the Scottish coast, which the corporation plans to buy out and to raze so that it may build a complex for its North Sea oil operations. The corporation seeks to bargain the townspeople out of their property—since, we are told, they are not mere Third World people who may simply be pushed out of the way. The locals, though excited by the promise of unimagined wealth, not only prove to be crafty negotiators, but in the end manage to humanize the initially very urban young company executive sent there to do the negotiating, as well as the tough but spacy owner of the company (played beautifully by Burt Lancaster), both of whom end up falling in love with the place and its inhabitants. The film ends with the CEO scrapping the planned oil complex in favor of building a research laboratory where refineries and docks were to have been. The locals win, the town wins, the environment wins, and the corporation is happy—except for the young executive who is shipped back mercilessly to Houston, and the jungle of urban life and global corporate operations, with only memories of what might have been.

The film in its execution conveyed all the warmth of its message, but what seemed most remarkable about it at the time was its romantic nostalgia for the concretely (and, therefore, humanely) local against the abstractly (and, therefore, dehumanizingly) global. In hindsight it seems romantic still, but somewhat less nostalgic. We know that the humanization of one corporate CEO does not add up to the humanization of capital, and are even more aware than before that the salvaging of one local community from the ravages of capital does not stop the onslaught of capital on community. We have learned, if anything, that to save one community it may be necessary to destroy another.

What makes *Local Hero* seem less nostalgic is the emergence in the intervening decade of a concern with the local as the site of resistance to capital, and the location for imagining alternative possibilities for the future. Romantic the movie may have been, but within the context of what was to follow, its nostalgia for the local community appears as something more than a mere fabulation of a past irrevocably lost; as a nostalgia that becomes an active ingredient in the formation of a contemporary discourse on the local which has rescued "fabulation" itself from the opprobrium of a more "realistic" time to render it into a principle for the reconstruction of the local.¹ It would seem by the early nineties that local movements, or movements to save and reconstruct local societies, have emerged as the primary (if not the only) expressions of resistance to domination: from the tree-hugging women of the Chipko movement in Northern India to the women workers of the maquiladora industries of the United States–Mexican border, from indigenous people's movements seeking secession from colonialist states to the western Kansas counties which wish to secede from Kansas and the United States because they feel abused by their governments, local movements have emerged as a pervasive phenomenon of the contemporary world.² These movements find resonance in radical social theory in the increasing frequency with which the term "local" appears in considerations of the present and the future of society globally. In this theorizing the "local" retains the concrete associations of the local community—as in *Local Hero*—but more as reference than as specific description (or prescription); the meaning (the very scope) of the local is subject otherwise to negotiation in accordance with those considerations.

I reflect on the "local" below as a site both of promise and predicament. My primary concern is with the local as site of promise, and the social and ideological changes globally that have dynamized a radical re-thinking of the local over the last decade. I am interested especially in the relationship between the emergence of a Global Capitalism and the emergence of concern with the local as a site of resistance and liberation. Consideration of this relationship is crucial, it seems to me, to distinguishing a "critical localism" from localism as an ideological articulation of capitalism in its current phase. Throughout, however, I try also to remain cognizant of the local as a site of predicament. In its promise of liberation, localism may also serve to disguise oppression and parochialism. It is indeed ironic that the local should emerge as a site of promise at a historical moment when localism of the most conventional kind has reemerged as the source of genocidal conflict around the world. The latter, too, must surely enter any consideration of the local as site of resistance to and liberation from oppression. In either case, the local that is at issue here is not the "local" in any conventional or traditional sense, but a very contemporary "local" that serves as a site for the working out of the most fundamental contradictions of the age.

Rethinking the Local

It is too early, presently, to sort out the factors that have contributed to the ascendancy of a concern with the local over the last decade, and any such undertaking must of necessity be highly speculative. What the "local" implies in different contexts is highly uncertain. Suffice it to say here that a concern for the local seems to appear in the foreground in connection with certain social movements (chief among them ecological, women's, ethnic and indigenous people's movements) and the intellectual repudiation of past ideologies (chief among them, for the sake of brevity here, the intellectual developments associated with, or that have gone into the making of, "postmodernism").

Why there should be a connection between the repudiation of past ideologies and the reemergence of the local as a concern is not very mysterious. Localism as an orientation in either a "traditional" or a modern sense has never disappeared, but rather has been suppressed or, at best, marginalized in various ideologies of modernity. Localism does not speak of an incurable social disease that must sooner or later bring about its natural demise; and there is nothing about it that is inherently undesirable. What makes it seem so is a historical consciousness that identifies civilization and progress with political, social and cultural homogenization, and justifies the suppression of the local in the name of the general and the universal. Modernist teleology has gone the farthest of all in stamping upon the local its derogatory image: as enclaves of backwardness left out of progress, as the realm of rural stagnation against the dynamism of the urban, industrial civilization of capitalism, as the realm of particularistic culture against universal scientific rationality and, perhaps most importantly, as the obstacle to full realization of that political form of modernity, the nation-state.[3]

This teleology has been resisted not only in the name of "traditional" localism that sought to preserve received forms of local society, but by radical critics of modernity as well. Anti-modernism rendered the local into a refuge from the ravages of modernity. Socialists, while not resisting modernity *per se*, have sought to localize modernity so as to render it more manageable—beginning with the social experiments of the utopian socialists, and culminating in Peter Kropotkin's plans for "industrial villages" as the foundation for anarchist society.[4] Karl Marx and Friedrich Engels, who rejected "utopian" in favor of "scientific" socialism nevertheless saw in "abolishing the contrast between town and country" one of the keys to resolving the problems of capitalist society, which had brought this contrast "to its extreme point."[5] Third World revolutions in the twentieth century would perpetuate these concerns for local society; especially those revolutions which, compelled by force of circumstances to pursue agrarian strategies of revolution, had to face local societies and their participation in revolution as a condition of revolutionary success. In these cases, ironically, local society would also emerge as a source of national identity, against the cosmopolitanism of urban centers drawn increasingly into the global culture of capitalism.[6]

The teleology of modernity, nevertheless, was to emerge victorious in the twentieth century over earlier socialist doubts about its consequences. The concern for the local persisted in the thinking of agrarian utopians and anarchists, but they, too, were to be marginalized for their insistence on the continued relevance of the local.[7] In the immediate decades after World War II, the modernizationist repudiation of the local prevailed in both bourgeois and Marxist social science.

It is not surprising, therefore, that the local should appear in contemporary discourse hand-in-hand with the repudiation of modernist teleology, the rejection as ideology of the "metanarratives" which have framed the history of modernization, whether capitalist or socialist. "Postmodernism," which has been described as "incredulity toward metanarratives," provides a convenient if loose term for characterizing the various challenges to modernist teleology, not because those who do so think of themselves as "postmodernists," but because every such challenge in its own way contributes to the making of a postmodern consciousness. Be that as it may, the repudiation of modernist teleology implies that there is nothing natural or inherently desirable about modernization (in capitalist or socialist form), and that the narrative of modernization is a narrative of compelling into modernity those who did not necessarily wish to be modern. This critique, too, is not necessarily novel, but long has been fundamental to the radical criticism of capitalism; from Marx and Engels to Kropotkin, radicals in the nineteenth century rejected the "naturalness" of capitalist development and pointed to coercion as key to the global success of capitalism. Marx, however, viewed it as a progressive development whereas Kropotkin viewed complicity in development (with specific reference to the nation-state) as the consequence of "brainwashing thanks to . . . education deformed and vitiated by the state, and our state prejudices"—which may be one reason among others that anarchism has made something of a comeback among radicals in recent years as Marxism has suffered for its association with modernization.[8]

The repudiation of the metanarrative of modernization, and its redirection of attention to coercion over teleology in development, have had two immediate consequences. First, it rescues from invisibility those who were earlier viewed as castaways from history, whose social and cultural forms of existence appear in the narrative of modernization at best as irrelevancies, at worst as minor obstacles to be extinguished on the way to development. Having refused to die a natural death, but instead come into self-awareness as victims of coercion, they demand now not just restoration of *their* history, further splintering the already cracked facade of modernity. The demand is almost inevitably accompanied by a reassertion of the local against the universalistic claims of modernism.[9]

The repudiation of the metanarrative of modernization, secondly, has allowed greater visibility to "local narratives." Rather than an inexorable march of global conquest from its origins in Europe, the history of modernization appears now as a temporal succession of spatially dispersed local encounters, to which the local objects of progress made their own contributions through resistance or complicity, contributing in significant ways to the formation of modernity, as well as to its contradictions. Also questioned in this view are the claims of nationalism which, a product itself of modernization, has sought to homogenize the societies it has claimed for itself, suppressing further such local encounters, and the "heterogeneity" they imply.[10]

Were it simply an ideological phenomenon, the postmodern repudiation of the metanarrative of modernity could be dismissed as a momentary loss of faith in modernity, another instance of those chronic failures of nerve that seem to attend moments of crisis in development, especially on occasions of transition, that will go away as soon as the transition has been completed and the crisis resolved. If so, this new round of anti-modernism might be at best a passive enabling condition that allows us to hear previously inaudible voices, that will be muted again as soon as the business of development is once again under way, with capitalism having disposed of the competition that for nearly a century shaped and "distorted" its development.

It is possible that the disillusionment with capitalism, accompanied by a loss of faith in socialism that gathered force in the 1980s to reach its culmination in the fall of socialist states in 1989, has played a fundamental part in the resurgence of an anti-modernism that has redirected the attention of radicals to local solutions to problems of development. It is more than possible, as I will argue below, that rather than signal the death of developmentalism, this new round of anti-modernism has something to do with a new phase in the development of capitalism. What is not so certain is that the concerns expressed by this anti-modernism will go away once the crisis of transition has been overcome, because these concerns are not merely ideological but the very products of the ecological, social and political consequences of development. They are responses to a real crisis created by developments within capitalism, and the whole project of modernity, and solutions to the crisis (as in the past) will have to be factored into considerations of further development. Above all, however, what is likely to give these concerns lasting power is that they express the demands not just of the powerless victims of development, although that is significant enough, but of formerly powerless groups who have acquired new power by virtue of the process of development itself, who now seek to redefine it in accordance with their own interests and perceptions.

It is neither necessary nor possible to recapitulate here what these groups are, except in the broadest terms to indicate the ways in which their emergence from invisibility and silence contributed to the questioning of metanarratives of development. Primary within the United States are the emergence into politics of Afro-Americans and women in the 1960s, followed (and due to the stimulus they provided) by other ethnic and indigenous people's movements. Globally, Third World revolutions (especially in China, followed by Vietnam) played a major part in questioning earlier (capitalist *and* socialist) models of development, but even more important in the long run have been the emergence from the 1970s of successful instances of capitalist development in the Third World which, having achieved success, proceeded to question the assumptions of Eurocentric models of development, countering the latter with models of development that claimed inspiration in native cultural and ideological norms; I have in mind here the cultural claims of East Asian societies.

I will say more about the latter in the next section in connection with the emergence of a Global Capitalism. A few words are necessary here concerning the various "people's movements" in the United States (and elsewhere in the First World), which called into question not just the claims of capitalist society, but received notions of socialism as well. Most obvious is the questioning by women, ethnic, racial, and indigenous peoples of the socialist claims to the centrality of class as the fundamental problem of capitalist society. The result was not only a more thorough examination of social categories in political organization, but also a greater awareness of the political manipulation of social categories; the imposition on social complexity of reductionist interpretations of categories, in other words, to rationalize ideological rule in the name of the groups so represented. The response to categorical reductionism was to assert the historicity and contextuality of social categories, which was to find expression in the works of E. P. Thompson, E. Genovese and J. Scott, and the "new social history" their works inspired.[11] What is important here is that new consciousness of the historicity of social categories drew attention to the local culture of the people in social movements against earlier emphases on a one-to-one relationship between social existence and ideology.

Even before the crisis of socialism became evident in the 1980s, and postmodernism became a household word, in other words, developments in social movements and in the relationships between the "Three Worlds" called into question the spatial and temporal teleology of development, as well as the conceptual teleology that had characterized earlier radical thinking. On the other hand, it is necessary to note that whatever the material circumstances that rendered "postmodernism" intelligible and plausible, it was the generation that came of age with these developments that was to play the crucial part in its articulation. The concern for the local (whether literally local, or in reference to the "local" needs of social groups) gathered force simultaneously with the repudiation of teleology. I can do no more than suggest here that an ecological consciousness, which has done much to reassert the primacy of the local (as the most viable location for living in harmony with nature), was a product of the same circumstances, and obviously bore some relationship to the shift in social and political consciousness.

Development as maldevelopment; adjustment to nature against the urge to conquer it; the porosity of borderlands against the rigidity of political forms, in particular the nation-state; heterogeneity over homogeneity; overdetermination against categorically defined subjectivities; ideology as culture, and culture as daily negotiation; enlightenment as hegemony; "local knowledge" against universal scientific rationality; native sensibilities and spiritualities as a supplement to, if not a substitute for, reason; oral against written culture; political movements as "politics of difference" and "politics of location." The list could go on.

It enumerates elements of a postmodern consciousness that serve as enabling conditions for a contemporary localism, but also produce it. The consciousness itself is an articulation not of powerlessness, but of newfound power among social groups who demand recognition of their social existence and consciousness against a modernity that had denied them a historical and, therefore, a political presence. Governor John D. Waihee III of Hawaii, referring to the Hawaiian sovereignty movement, acknowledged recently that what seems possible today would have been unimaginable only two decades ago.[12]

The suspicion of Enlightenment metanarratives for their denial of difference makes for a suspicion of all metanarratives which suppress or overlook differences, allows for localized consciousness, and points to the local as the site for working out "alternative public spheres" and alternative social formations.[13] This is the promise held out by the local. The local, however, also indicates fragmentation and, given the issues of power involved, political and cultural manipulation as well. This is the predicament. That traces of earlier forms of exploitation and oppression persist in the local, albeit in forms worked over by modernity, aggravates the predicament.

This predicament becomes more apparent when we view the problem of the local from the perspective of the global: the local as object of the operations of capital, which provides the broadest context for inquiry into the sources and consequences of contemporary localism. The emergence of the concern for the local over the last two decades has accompanied a significant transformation within capitalism with far-reaching economic, political, social and cultural consequences. This transformation, and its implications for the local, need to be considered in any evaluation of the local as source of promise and predicament.

"Global Localism"

David Harvey and Fredric Jameson, among others, have perceived a relationship between postmodernism and a new phase in the development of capitalism that has been described as Late Capitalism, Flexible Production or Accumulation, Disorganized Capitalism, or Global Capitalism.[14] Global Capitalism represents a further deterritorialization, abstraction and concentration of capital. In a fundamental sense, Global Capitalism represents an unprecedented penetration of local society globally by the economy and culture of capital; so that the local understood in a "traditional" sense may be less relevant than ever. It is ironic then that capital itself should justify its operations increasingly in the language of the local. The irony allows us to see the local in all its contradictoriness.

Fundamental to the structure of the new Global Capitalism (the term I prefer) is what Frobel and others have described as "a new international division of labor": in other words, the transnationalization of production where, through subcontracting, the process of production (of the same commodity even) is globalized.[15] The international division of labor in production may not be entirely novel; but new technologies have expanded the spatial extension of production, as well as its speed, to an unprecedented level. These same technologies have endowed capital and production with unprecedented mobility, so that the location of production seems to be in a constant state of change, seeking for maximum advantage for capital against labor, as well as to avoid social and political interference (hence, flexible production). For these reasons, analysts of capitalism perceive in Global Capitalism a qualitative difference from similar practices earlier—and a new phase of capitalism.

Second is the "decentering" of capitalism nationally. In other words, it is increasingly difficult to point to any nation or region as the center of global capitalism. More than one analyst (in a position of power) has found an analogue to the emerging organization of production in the northern European "Hanseatic League" of the early modern period, that is the period before the emergence of nation-states (one of them describing it as a "high-tech Hanseatic League"); in other words, a network of urban formations, without a clearly definable center, whose links to one another are far stronger than their relationships to their immediate hinterlands.[16]

The medium linking this network together, thirdly, is the transnational corporation, which has taken over from national markets as the locus of economic activity; not just as a passive medium for the transmission of capital, commodities and production, but as a determinant of the transmission, and its direction. While the analogy with the Hanseatic League suggests decentralization, in other words, production is heavily concentrated behind this facade in the corporation. One articulate spokesman for the new economic order suggests that the share of decisionmaking for production between the corporation and the market is roughly 70 to 30 percent.[17] With power lodged in transnational corporations, which by definition transcend nations in organization and/or loyalty, the power of the nation-state to regulate the economy internally is constricted, while global regulation (and defense) of the economic order emerges as a major task. This is manifested not only in the proliferation of global organizations, but also in efforts to organize extranational regional organizations to give coherence to the functioning of the economy.

Fourthly, the transnationalization of production is the source at once of unprecedented unity globally, and of unprecedented fragmentation (in the history of capitalism). The homogenization of the globe economically, socially and culturally is such that Marx's predictions of the nineteenth century, premature for his time, finally seem to be on the point of vindication. At the same time, however, there is a parallel process of fragmentation at work; globally in the disappearing of a center to capitalism, and locally, in the fragmentation of the production process into subnational regions and localities. As supranational regional organizations such as the European Economic Community, Pacific Basic Economic Community and the North American Free Trade Zone (to mention some that have been realized or are the objects of intense organizational activity) manifest this fragmentation at the global level, localities within the same nation competing with one another to place themselves in the pathways of transnational capital represent it at the most basic local level. Nations, themselves, it is arguable, represented attempts historically to contain fragmentation, but under attack from the outside (transnational organization) and the inside (subnational economic regions and localities), it is not quite clear how this new fragmentation is to be contained.[18]

A fifth important (perhaps the most important) consequence of the transnationalization of capital may be that for the first time in the history of capitalism, the capitalist mode of production appears as an authentically global abstraction, divorced from its historically specific origins in Europe. In other words, the narrative of capitalism is no longer a narrative of the history of Europe; so that, for the first time, non-European capitalist societies make their own claims on the history of capitalism. Corresponding to economic fragmentation, in other words, is cultural fragmentation or, to put it in its positive guise, "multiculturalism." The most dramatic instance of this new cultural situation may be the effort over the last decade to appropriate capitalism for the so-called Confucian values of East Asian societies, which is a reversal of a long-standing conviction (in Europe and East Asia) that Confucianism was historically an obstacle to capitalism. I think it is arguable that the apparent end of Eurocentrism is an illusion, because capitalist culture as it has taken shape has Eurocentrism built into the very structure of its narrative, which may explain why even as Europe and the United States lose their domination of the capitalist world economy, culturally European and American values retain their domination. It is noteworthy that what makes something like the East Asian Confucian revival plausible is not its offer of alternative values to those of EuroAmerican origin, but its articulation of native culture into a capitalist narrative. Having said this, it is important to reiterate nevertheless that the question of world culture has become much more complex than in earlier phases of capitalism.

The fragmentation of space, and its consequences for Eurocentrism, also imply a fragmentation of the temporality of capitalism: the challenge to Eurocentrism, in other words, means that it is possible to conceive of the future in ways other than those of EuroAmerican political and social models. Here, once again, it is difficult to distinguish reality from illusion, but the complexity is undeniable.

Finally, the transnationalization of production calls into question earlier divisions of the world into First, Second and Third Worlds. The Second World, the world of socialism, is for all practical purposes, of the past. But the new global configuration also calls into question the distinctions between the First and Third Worlds. Parts of the earlier Third World are today on the pathways of transnational capital, and belong in the "developed" sector of the world economy. Likewise, parts of the First World marginalized in the new global economy are hardly distinguishable in way of life from what used to be viewed as Third World characteristics. It may not be fortuitous that the North-South distinction has gradually taken over from the earlier division of the globe into the three worlds—so long as we remember that the references of North and South are not merely to concrete geographic locations, but metaphorical references: North denoting the pathways of transnational capital, and, South, the marginalized populations of the world, regardless of their actual location.

Ideologues of global capital have described this condition as "Global Regionalism" or "Global Localism," adding quickly, however, that "Global Localism" is 70 percent global and only 30 percent local.[19] They have also appropriated for capital the radical ecological slogan, "Think globally, act locally."[20] The terms capture cogently the simultaneous homogenization and fragmentation that is at work in the world economy. Production and economic activity (hence, "economic development") become localized in regions below the nation, while their management requires supranational supervision and coordination. In other words, the new pathways for the development of capital cut across national boundaries and intrude on national economic sovereignty, which renders irrelevant the notion of a national market or a national economic unit, and undermines national sovereignty from within by fragmenting the national economy.[21] Similarly, the necessity of supranational coordination transforms the functions of the nation-state from without, incorporating it within larger regional or global economic units.

The situation created by Global Capitalism helps explain certain phenomena that have become apparent over the past two to three decades, but especially since the eighties: global motions of peoples (and, therefore, cultures), the weakening of boundaries (among societies, as well as among social categories), the replication in societies internally of inequalities and discrepancies once associated with colonial differences, simultaneous homogenization and fragmentation within and across societies, the interpenetration of the global and the local (which shows culturally in a simultaneous cosmopolitanism and localism of which the most cogent expression may be "multiculturalism"), and the disorganization of a world conceived in terms of "three worlds" or nation-states. Some of these phenomena have also contributed to an appearance of equalization of differences within and across societies, as well as of democratization within and between societies. What is ironic is that the managers of this world situation themselves concede the concentration of power in their (or their organizations') hands; as well as their manipulation of peoples, boundaries and cultures to appropriate the local for the global, to admit different cultures into the realm of capital only to break them down and to remake them in accordance with the requirements of production and consumption, and even to reconstitute subjectivities across national boundaries to create producers and consumers more responsive to the operations of capital. Those who do not respond, or the "basket-cases" which are not essential to those operations—four-fifths of the global population by their count—need not be colonized; they are simply marginalized. What the new "flexible production" has made possible is that it is no longer necessary to utilize explicit coercion against labor, at home or abroad (in colonies); those peoples or places that are not responsive to the needs (or demands) of capital, or are too far gone to respond "efficiently," simply find themselves out of its pathways.

Much of what I have described above as the conditions for the production of contemporary localism (a postmodern consciousness, embedded in new forms of empowerment) appears in this perspective as a product of the operations of Global Capitalism. It should also be apparent from the above that the local is of concern presently not only to those who view it as a site of liberation struggles, but, with an even greater sense of immediacy, to managers of global capital as well as to those responsible for the economic welfare of their communities. I will take up the latter in the next section. The concern for the local on the part of capital, and what the operations of capital may imply for the local, is apparent in the following analysis by an advocate of "guerrilla marketing."

> 1984 is here, the problem is how to manage it. The answer we propose, gentlemen, is guerrilla marketing. Just as the guerrilla fighter must know the terrain of the struggle in order to control it, so it is with the multinational corporation of today. Our terrain is the world. Our ends can be accomplished with the extension of techniques already in the process of development. The world market is now being computer micromapped into consumer zones according to residual cultural factors (i.e. idioms, local traditions, religious affiliations, political ideologies, folk mores, traditional sexual roles, etc.), dominant cultural factors (i.e. typologies of life-styles based on consumption patterns: television ratings, musical tastes, fashions, motion picture and concert attendance, home video rentals, magazine subscriptions, home computer software selection, shopping mall participation, etc.), and emergent cultural factors (i.e. interactive and participatory video, mobile micromalls equipped with holography and super conductivity, computer interfacing with consumers, robotic services, etc.). The emergent marketing terrain which must be our primary concern can only be covered totally if the 304 geographical consumption zones already computer mapped (the horizontal) can be cross referenced not only with the relatively homogeneous "conscious" needs of the macroconsumer units, but also with the heterogeneous multiplicity of "unconscious" needs of the microconsumer (the vertical). This latter mapping process has so far readily yielded to computer solution through the identification and classification of a maximum of 507 microconsumption types per macroconsumption unit. Through an extension of this mapping, even the most autonomous and unconventional desires may be reconstructed for the benefit of market extension and control. Emergent marketing strategies must move further beyond the commodity itself and toward the commodity as image, following marketing contingencies all the way down. And here, precisely, is the task of guerrilla marketing: to go all the way with the images we create and strike where there is indecision (flowing from constructed situations without determinant outcomes just like the guerrilla fighter). For the multinational of today profits are necessary but not sufficient conditions for growth which our whole history shows to be equivalent to survival. We remain dependent on market control and extension. But now this requires more than the control of production and consumption—to grow we must sell a total image. Like guerrilla fighters, we must win hearts and minds. This task can be accom-

plished by constructing and reconstructing them all the way down in what can only be viewed as an endless process.[22]

Cleansed of its computer vocabulary, this text would read very much like one of those local analyses upon which guerrilla revolutionaries have based strategy.[23] But the resemblance does not stop there. As with guerrilla struggle, where the requirements of a fluid strategy called forth a need for organizational flexibility in order to deal with diverse circumstances without abandoning long-term organizational goals, the imperatives of guerrilla marketing, too, have resulted in a reconceptualization of the transnational corporation as an organization. "Global localism" implies, organizationally, that the corporation domesticate itself in various localities without forgetting its global aims and organization. This has created for companies organizational problems that resemble closely those of a centralized Communist Party engaged in guerrilla warfare. The CEO of one such company, who chooses to describe his company as "multidomestic" rather than multi- or transnational, describes the organizational problems his company faces much as Mao Zedong used to describe problems facing the Communist Party of China.

> ABB (Asea Brown Boveri) is an organization with three internal contradictions. We want to be global and local, big and small, radically decentralized with centralized reports and control. If we resolve those contradictions, we create real organizational advantage.[24]

The radical slogan of an earlier day, "Think globally, act locally," has been assimilated by transnational corporations with far greater success than in any radical strategy. The recognition of the local in marketing strategy, however, does not mean any serious recognition of the autonomy of the local, but is intended to recognize the features of the local so as to incorporate localities into the imperatives of the global. The "domestication" of the corporation into local society serves only to further mystify the location of power, which rests not in the locality but in the global headquarters of the company which coordinates the activities of its local branches. To recall what I cited above from Kenichi Ohmae, "global localism" is "seventy percent global and thirty percent local." The guiding vision of the contemporary transnational corporation is to homogenize the world under its guidance. The same CEO writes:

> Are we above governments? No. We answer to governments. We obey the laws in every country in which we operate, and we don't make the laws. However, we do change relations *between* countries. We function as a lubricant for worldwide economic integration. (emphasis in the original)[25]

Some lubricant, that "changes" the relations it facilitates! It points to a crucial point, nevertheless. The transnational corporations of the day, much like radical guerrillas, do not just respond to circumstances, but create the conditions for their success. To achieve this end, however, they must first grasp social, political and cultural relations in their full complexity. The goal of analysis itself is not social need but the teleology of the organization, although that teleology must be articulated to local languages in order to acquire legitimacy transnationally.

From the perspective of Global Capitalism, the local is a site not of liberation but manipulation; stated differently, it is a site the inhabitants of which must be liberated from themselves (stripped of their identity) to be homogenized into the global culture of capital (their identities reconstructed accordingly). Ironically, even as it seeks to homogenize populations globally, consuming their cultures, Global Capitalism enhances awareness of the local, pointing to it also as the site of resistance to capital.

This is nevertheless the predicament of the local. A preoccupation with the local that leaves the global outside its line of vision is vulnerable to manipulation at the hands of global capital which of necessity commands a more comprehensive vision of a global totality. Differences of interest and power on the site of the local, which are essential to its reconstruction along non-traditional, democratic, lines, render the local all the more vulnerable to such manipulation as capital plays on these differences, and the advocates of different visions and interests seek to play capital against one another.[26] The local in the process becomes the site upon which the multifaceted contradictions of contemporary society play out, where critique turns into ideology and ideology into critique, depending upon its location at any one fleeting moment.

Considerations on the Local as Site of Resistance

In the first section above, I suggested that the postmodern repudiation of Enlightenment metanarratives and the teleology of modernity has allowed the reemergence of the local as a site of resistance and the struggle for liberation.[27] It is the struggle for historical and political presence of groups suppressed or marginalized by modernization, I argued further, that has dynamized this postmodern consciousness and has produced the contemporary notion of the local, which must be distinguished from "traditional" localism if only because such struggles are themselves informed by the modernity that they reject. This is the local as it has been worked over by modernity. It finds expression presently in the so-called "politics of difference," that presupposes local differences (literally, or metaphorically, with reference to social groups) both as a point of departure and as a goal of liberation.

My discussion of Global Capitalism is intended to support this thesis, while introducing into the consideration of the local as a contemporary phenomenon what I take to be a crucial dimension that is missing from most postmodernist discussions of the subject. Postmodernist repudiation of metanarratives and teleology has made also for a suspicion of universalizing "foundational" explanatory themes, in particular Marxist ideas of totality and class. Totalities do not go away because they have been repudiated. Global Capitalism, both in its disorganizing of earlier structures and the reconfiguration of global relations (including class relations, now more global than ever), points to just such a totality that produces, and provides the context for, the contemporary phenomenon of the local. To the extent that it refuses to recognize this context, the idea of the local is prey to the manipulations of capital, and its ideology of "Global Localism." I have argued elsewhere that to the extent that postmodern criticism fails to account for the totality that is its context, its ideological criticism becomes indistinguishable from an ideological legitimation of the social forms that are the creation of Global Capitalism.[28] It is crucial, therefore, that postmodern cultural criticism reconnect with actual movements of resistance to capital that continue to be informed by practices of resistance that are coeval with the history of capitalism. Postmodernism needs the connection to restore a sense of the structures of oppression and inequality, to check its slide into political irrelevance upon the slippery slopes of a fluid narcissism. The latter needs postmodernism for its articulation of the pitfalls to liberation that are implicit in teleological notions of change, and conceptual teleologies that bind in reductionist categories a social existence and conscious that is shifting, complex and contradictory; that, rather than look at the process of the struggle for liberation as the source of alternative futures, seek to contain with predetermined visions of the future a process that needs to be an open-ended process of multiple social negotiations.

The intrusion of Global Capitalism into local societies has been accompanied by a proliferation of local movements of resistance in recent years in which women's and ecological movements are particularly prominent. These movements already show a keen appreciation of the relationship of local to global struggles, as well as a sharp sensitivity to the complexities of movement building that is indicative of a contemporary consciousness. An example is provided in the following statement by Rachael Kamel, a union activist connected with the American Friends Service Committee. Having described the plight of workers (mostly women) in the United States, the Mexican maquiladoras, and the Philippines, as they are played off against one another by transnationals, and suggested several ways of coordinating resistance, Kamel writes:

> Each of the projects we have described may seem tiny, especially when contrasted to the size and power of transnational corporations. Yet each is also a small step toward building a movement that could bring together hundreds of local grassroots campaigns, within the United States and internationally.
>
> At this writing, the idea of a broad-based, multinational movement to tackle the problems of the global factory is still a vision. What we have tried to document in this guide is that the global factory is composed of thousands of concrete local situations—and that each of us, whatever setting we live and work in, can take small, accessible actions to confront our specific situations.
>
> *By understanding that every local story is part of a global "big picture," we can open up space for dialog [sic] and sharing of experiences—especially across barriers of lan-*

guage, nationality, gender, race and class. And as that process of communication moves toward networking and coalition-building, the vision of a multinational movement can become a reality. (emphasis mine)[29]

Note that Kamel describes corporations as "transnational," while using the older term "multinational" to describe resistance movements. Also noteworthy is the complexity of the situations she describes. Kamel deems essential to the success of local organizing four constituencies: labor unions, community groups, religious institutions, and local government.[30] These constituencies must be brought together, and still leave open spaces for dialogue among the groups she enumerates in the statement above. Hardly a proponent of postmodern consciousness could wish for greater complexity and contradiction!

The affirmation of the local and, therefore, of diversity thus defined, is not without its own problems, as activists such as Kamel and Vandana Shiva are well aware. One such problem is the celebration of premodern pasts which, in the name of resistance to the modern and the rationalist homogenization of the world, results in a localism or a "Third-Worldism" that is willing to overlook past oppressions out of a preoccupation with capitalist or Eurocentric oppression, that in the name of the recovery of spirituality affirms past religiosities that were themselves excuses for class and patriarchal inequalities. One consequence of Global Capitalism is that there are no longer any local societies that have not been worked over already by capital and modernity; insistence on local "purity" may well serve as excuses for a reactionary revival of older forms of oppression, as women in particular have been quick to point out in India and among the indigenous people's movements in North America.[31] The local is valuable as a site for resistance to the global, but only to the extent that it also serves as the site of negotiation to abolish inequality and oppression inherited from the past, which is a condition of any promise it may have for the future. It is neither possible nor desirable to dismiss the awareness that is the product of modernity as just another trick of Eurocentrism.

What this points to is a "critical localism" which, even as it subjects the present to the critical evaluation from past perspectives, retains in the evaluation of the past the critical perspectives afforded by modernity. Excluded from this localism are romantic nostalgia for communities past, hegemonic nationalist yearnings of a new kind (as with the so-called Confucian revival in east Asia), or historicism that would imprison the present in the past. An example of the latter are well-intentioned but misguided efforts in China scholarship recently to assert a "China-centered" view of history; well-intentioned because these efforts seek to rescue Chinese history from its subjection to the hegemony of EuroAmerican teleologies and concepts; misguided because the effort is accompanied by assertions that the Chinese themselves are incapable of doing this because they have been tainted by Western concepts and, therefore, lost touch with their own past.

Such efforts, which deny to the Chinese contemporaneity while giving born-again EuroAmericans the privilege of interpreting China's past for the Chinese, are reminiscent of nineteenth century Europeans who, claiming historicalness for themselves while denying it to others, appropriated the meaning of history for the whole world, especially the Third World.[32] At the other extreme is that ethnocentrism in the critique of hegemony, which falls into affirmations of pre-Western ethnicities and spiritualities, without accounting for the problem of oppression in general, which has not been the monopoly of the West or of capitalism, even though it may have been carried to unprecedented levels in the modern world in the denial of alternative modes of existence. The dilemmas faced by struggles against EuroAmericans and capitalist oppression, I believe, should not be evaded by sweeping under the rug premodern forms of oppression. As a first cut, it is necessary to distinguish stateless communities (or those communities where state organization and local community coincided, such as tribal organizations around the world),[33] and communities which provided excuses for far-flung state organizations, as in the case of premodern empires to be found in China, India and the Ottoman Empire. The former are easier to sympathize with, the latter much less so, as the affirmation of premodern pasts in their case, however anti-hegemonic in terms of their relationship to the West, barely disguises national chauvinisms of a new kind—as in the case of the Confucian revival, for instance, which is not unrelated to assertions of a "Greater Chinese" economic region. These two positions are quite different in their sources and implications; and it is important to distinguish EuroAmericans speaking for Third World pasts from those of Third World peoples speaking for their pasts in efforts to rescue their identities from "death by assimilation" (in the words of writer Frank Chin). Nevertheless, both positions are problematic; it is not only silly to deny the undeniable—that economic and cultural conjunctures for the past century have defined the conditions of existence for non-European or American peoples—but also socially (distinct from politically) reactionary to ignore past forms of oppression of various dimensions that have been brought to the forefront of historical consciousness by these conjunctures. It is the continued existence of such forms of oppression, compounded and overdetermined now by new forms of oppression, that makes Marxist and gender analyses in particular as relevant as ever to critical understanding.

The local as I use it here has meaning only inasmuch as it is a product of the conjuncture of structures located in the same temporality but with different spatialities, which is what gives rise to the problem of spatiality and, therefore, of the local, in the first place. The conjunctural situation also defines the culture of the local, which is stripped of its reification by daily confrontation between different cultures, and appears instead in the nakedness of its everyday practice. Unlike under conditions of isolation and stability, where culture appears timeless in its daily reproduction (if such is ever entirely the case), the conjunctural situation reveals cultural activity as an activity in production and ceaseless reconstruction.

That culture is thus constructed does not imply that the present is, therefore, immune to the burden of the past; only that the burden itself is restructured in the course of present activity. Neither does it mean that the past is unimportant; it only underlines the claims of the present, of the living, on the past, rather than the other way around. Culture is no less cultural for being subject to change through the "practice of everyday life" (the term is Michel deCertau's), of which it is as much source as product. It is the prevalence of cultural conjuncture as a condition of life globally that has brought forth the sharp consciousness of culture as an ongoing construction of everyday practice; which has been illuminated in the works of Pierre Bourdieu and Marshall Sahlins, who have argued out the implications for culture and history of conjunctions between past and present, between different social and cultural structures (which prolematize the relationship between different presents, as well as between the present and the past), and even between structure and event, especially where the event is of an unprecedented nature such as the contacts of non-European peoples with Europeans.[34]

The immediate question here is what this ongoing construction of culture implies in terms of the resistance of the local to the global. Ashis Nandy has written that:

> When two cultures of unequal secular power enter into a dialogue, a new hierarchy inevitably emerges, unless the dialogue creates a shared space for each participant's distinctive, unstated theory of the other cultures or, in its absence, each participant's general theory of culture. The concept of cultural relativism, expressed in the popular anthropological view that each culture must be studied in terms of its own categories, is limited because it stops short of insisting that every culture must recognize the way it is construed by other cultures. It is easy to leave other cultures to their own devices in the name of cultural relativism, particularly if the visions of the future of these other cultures have already been cannibalized by the worldview of one's own. It is less easy to live with an alien culture's estimate of oneself, to integrate it within one's selfhood and to live with that self-induced inner tension. It is even more difficult to live with the inner dialogue within one's own culture which is triggered off by the dialogue with other cultures because, then, the carefully built cultural defences against disturbing dialogues—and against the threatening insights emerging from the dialogues—begin to crumble.[35]

Nandy's view of cultural dialogue has been inspired by the approach to culture of Mohandas Gandhi, who, Richard Fox tells us in his recent illuminating study of Gandhi, believed that "cultures change through collective experiments,"[36] experiments that had the present for their point of departure, but opened up to diverse pasts in their pursuit of "truth." The local, I would like to suggest here, is the site for such experimentation. The "experimentation," however, has to be global in compass. Resistance that seeks to reaffirm some "authentic" local culture, in ignoring the conjunctures that produced it, is condemned to failure; if only because the so-called authentic local culture is daily disorganized by the global forces (e.g., guerrilla marketeers) that seek to reconstitute it, to assimilate it to the global homogenization that it seeks.

This is the second problem with the local as a strategic concept of resistance, which is even more serious: the assimilation of the local into the global, so that different localities become pawns in the hands of global capital in its guerrilla warfare against societies globally. This may, indeed, be the most serious challenge facing resistance/liberation movements in our day: how to deal with global companies which, at the least sign of interference with their activities (be those labor demands or efforts to restrict the harm they inflict on local societies and ecologies), threaten to pick up and move to new localities, which new technologies enable them to do; more accurately, which is a major goal of the development of new technologies? How does resistance deal with a General Motors, which holds entire communities and cities in suspense in shutting down production plants, waiting to see the outcome of communities competing with one another in offering better and sweeter deals to the corporation to keep it in their respective communities to save jobs—and the livelihood of the entire community? Local resistance under the circumstances, if it is to be meaningful at all, must be translocal both in consciousness and action; a big "if," and possibly cause for a widespread sense of futility globally. The dilemma is heightened by the fact that local consciousness, which is necessary as the basis for resistance, contradicts the translocal activity and consciousness that is a necessity of successful resistance. If this contradiction is overcome, the very fragmentation of the globe by capital may be turned to an advantage of resistance movements: the demand for the authentically local against its exploitation as a means to assimilation may "overload" global capitalism, driving it to fragmentation.[37]

Apart from the part it may play in resistance to Global Capitalism, how the local may serve as a building block for the future is a question to which Henry Giroux has provided a suggestive answer. Giroux's "border pedagogy" is derivative of postmodern/postcolonial "politics of difference," but dissatisfied with the affirmation of difference as an end in itself, which he rightly perceives to be subversive of meaningful politics, he seeks ways to formulate new kinds of "unity in diversity" that may serve as grounds for "nontotalizing politics."[38] "Nontotalizing politics" must attend "to the partial, specific, contexts of differentiated communities and forms of power," not "to ignore larger theoretical and relational narratives," but to "embrace the local and the global."[39] Especially important is his idea of "formative narratives" which cogently expresses the considerations I have suggested above:

> The postmodern attack on totality and foundationalism is not without its drawbacks. While it rightly focuses on the importance of local narratives and rejects the notion that truth precedes the notion of representation, it also runs the risk of blurring the distinction between master narratives that are monocausal and formative narratives, that provide the basis for historically and relationally placing different groups or local narratives within some common project. To draw out this point further, it is difficult

to imagine any politics of difference as a form of radical social theory if it doesn't offer a formative narrative capable of analyzing difference within rather than against unity.[40]

I stated above that the meaning of the local in contemporary discussions is uncertain, and have refrained throughout from burdening it with a definition that might have constricted analysis. Giroux's statement indicates why it is necessary *not* to define the contemporary idea of the local too strictly. The local in this statement (local narratives) retains its concrete associations spatially, but the boundaries of the local need to be kept open (or porous) if the local is to serve as a critical concept. The contemporary local is itself a site of invention and construction, that must be defined in the process of working out social contradictions—in the process of constructing "formative" narratives—for the simple reason that the local in the present is ultimately the site for the global.

Notes

1. Subramani, *South Pacific Literature: From Myth to Fabulation* (Suva: University of the South Pacific, 1985), for a case for fabulation.

2. For the movements referred to, see Vandana Shiva, *Staying Alive* (London: ZED Books, Ltd., 1988); Rachael Kamel, *The Global Factory: Analysis and Action for a New Economic Era* (American Friends Service Committee, 1990); Maivan Lam, *The Age of Association: The Indigenous Assertion of Self-Determination at the United Nations.* Unpublished ms., cited with the author's permission.

3. For extended discussions of this problem, see Peter A. Kropotkin, "The State: Its Historical Role," in P. Kropotkin, *Selected Writings on Anarchism and Revolution,* ed. with an introduction by Martin A. Miller, pp.211–264 (Cambridge, MA: The MIT Press, 1975); and Raymond Williams, *The Country and the City* (New York: Oxford University Press, 1973).

4. Leo Loubere, *Utopian Socialism: Its History Since 1800* (Cambridge, MA: Schenkman Publishing Company, 1974), and Peter Kropotkin, *Fields, Factories and Workshops of Tomorrow,* introduced and edited by Colin Ward (New York: Harper & Row, 1974).

5. As Raymond Williams notes, it was to be forgotten in the twentieth century that Marx and Engels placed a great deal of emphasis on abolishing the division of labor between town and country. Item 9 of the program for socialism in the *Communist Manifesto* reads: "Combination of agriculture with manufacturing industries; gradual abolition of the distinction between town and country, by a more equable distribution of the population over the country." Karl Marx and Friedrich Engels, "Manifesto of the Communist Party," in Robert C. Tucker (ed.), *The Marx-Engels Reader* (New York: W.W. Norton & Co., 1972), p.352.

6. See Arif Dirlik, *Anarchism in the Chinese Revolution* (Berkeley: University of California Press, 1991), and Arif Dirlik, "Mao Zedong and 'Chinese Marxism,'" in *Encyclopedia of Asian Philosophy* (London: Routledge), for further discussion.

7. I have in mind here such thinker-activists as Ivan Illich and Murray Bookchin, who have consistently upheld the significance of the local and the "vernacular." Among their

many works, see Ivan Illich, *Shadow Work* (Salem, N.H.: Marion Boyars, Inc., 1981), and Murray Bookchin, *Post Scarcity Anarchism* (Palo Alto, CA: Ramparts Press, 1971).

8. Kropotkin, "The State," p.252.

9. For a cogent statement, see Russell Means, "The Same Old Song," in Ward Churchill (ed.), *Marxism and Native Americans* (Boston: South End Press, n.d.), pp.19–33. The implications for our understanding of the state of the restoration of local, stateless societies into history (left out of history by virtue of their statelessness) is the theme of Pierre Clastres's *Society Against the State,* tr. Robert Hurley in collaboration with Abe Stein (New York: Zone Books, 1987). Writes Clastres: "It is said that the history of peoples who have a history is the history of class struggle. It might be said, with at least as much truthfulness, that the history of peoples without history is the history of their struggle against the state" (p.218).

10. Partha Chatterjee, in *Nationalist Thought and the Colonial World—A Derivative Discourse* (London: ZED Books, 1986), discusses this problem at length.

11. For a further discussion of this problem, with reference to the work of E.P. Thompson and Eugene Genovese, see Arif Dirlik, "Culturalism as Hegemonic Ideology and Liberating Practice," *Cultural Critique* (Spring 1987):13–50. For the ways in which such problems appeared in contemporary movements, which stimulated this new awareness, see Frances Fox Piven and Richard A. Cloward, *Poor People's Movements: Why They Succeed, How They Fail* (New York: Random House, 1977). For a work that brings together postmodernity and the legacy of such social movements and relates them explicitly to the problem of the local, see Henry Giroux, *Border Crossings: Cultural Workers and the Politics of Education* (New York and London: Routledge, 1992). A distinguished pedagogue, Giroux describes himself as "a critical populist," heir to the legacies "of the IWW, Bill Haywood, C. Wright Mills, Martin Luther King, and Michael Harrington. In other words, people who speak to people in a language that dignifies their history and experience" (p.13).

12. "A Century After Queen's Overthrow, Talk of Sovereignty Shakes Hawaii," *The New York Times,* November 8, 1992, "National Report."

13. Giroux, *Border Crossings,* pp.21–22.

14. David Harvey, *The Condition of Postmodernity* (Cambridge, MA: Basil Blackwell, 1989), and Fredric Jameson, "Postmodernism, or, the Cultural Logic of Late Capitalism," *New Left Review* 146 (July/August 1984).

15. See p.82, n.51.

16. See p. 82, n.52.

17. See p. 82, n.53.

18. See p. 82, n.55.

19. See p. 82, n.56.

20. "The Logic of Global Business: An Interview with ABB's Percy Barnevik," *The Harvard Business Review* (March–April 1991):90–105.

21. This is the basic argument of Reich, *The Work of Nations.*

22. From a conference on marketing held at the Research Triangle Park, North Carolina, February 27, 1987. Quoted in Rick Roderick, "The Antinomy of Post-Modern Bourgeois Thought," paper presented at the Marxism and Society seminar, Duke University, March 1987, with the author's permission.

23. See, for example, Mao Zedong's meticulous "mapping" of local Chinese social relations and structure in his *Report from Xunwu,* tr. with an introduction and notes by Roger R. Thompson (Stanford: Stanford University Press, 1990). The implications of the report

are drawn out by Roxann Prazniak in her review essay, "The Art of Folk Revolution," in *Peasant Studies* 17:3 (Spring 1990):295–306.

24. "The Logic of Global Business,"*The Harvard Business Review,* p.95.

25. Ibid., p.105.

26. For a fascinating discussion involving Hawaii, see Jeff Tobin, "Cultural Construction and Native Nationalism: Report from the Hawaiian Front," in Arif Dirlik and Rob Wilson (eds.), *Asia/Pacific as Space of Cultural Production* (special issue of *boundary 2* [Spring 1994]).

27. This is what Michel Foucault referred to as the "insurrection of subjugated knowledges" in "Two Lectures," in Foucault, *Power/Knowledge: Selected Interviews and Other Writings, 1972–1977,* ed. Colin Gordon (New York: Pantheon Books, 1980), pp.78–108.

28. See Chapter 3.

29. Kamel, *Global Factory,* p.75.

30. Ibid., p.26.

31. Meera Nanda, "Is Modern Science a Western Patriarchal Myth? A Critique of the Populist Orthodoxy," *South Asia Bulletin,* vol. 11, no. 1 and 2 (1991):32–61.

32. For a seminal and influential work to argue this position, see Paul Cohen, *Discovering History in China* (N.Y.: Columbia University Press, 1984).

33. For an excellent account of indigenous people's movements and their relationship to existing states, see Lam, *The Age of Association.*

34. See Pierre Bourdieu, *The Logic of Practice* (Stanford, CA: Stanford University Press, 1990), for a recent discussion of his views, and Marshall Sahlins, *Islands of History* (Chicago: University of Chicago Press, 1985).

35. Ashis Nandy, *Traditions, Tyranny and Utopias: Essays in the Politics of Awareness* (Delhi: Oxford University Press, 1987), pp.16–19.

36. Richard G. Fox, *Gandhian Utopia: Experiments with Culture* (Boston: Beacon Press, 1989), p.26.

37. This notion of "overloading the system" as a means of resistance I owe to Wallerstein. "Development: Lodestar or Illusion?" in Immanuel Wallerstein, *Unthinking Social Science: The Limits of Nineteenth Century Paradigms* (London: Polity Press, 1991), p.124. What I have in mind here may be illustrated by an episode from South Pacific culture. In his analysis of oral traditions in the South Pacific, Subramani observes that South Pacific writers have, "in some instances, rediscovered their oral literatures by reading translations of them by European researchers." The goal of European researchers in undertaking this kind of activity around the globe, at least initially, was to understand the natives to better control, convert or assimilate them. With a new cultural consciousness that aims at liberation, these same "researchers" now serve the cause of liberation, and the assertion of local identity against assimilation. Subramani, *South Pacific Literature: From Myth to Fabulation* (Suva: University of the South Pacific, 1985), p.32.

38. Giroux, *Border Crossings,* p.79. For "unity in diversity," see Yuji Ichioka, "'Unity Within Diversity': Louis Adamic and Japanese Americans," *Working Papers* in Asian/Pacific Studies, no. 1 (1987).

39. Giroux, *Border Crossings,* p.79.

40. Ibid., p.54.

5

Chinese History and the Question of Orientalism

I consider below some questions raised by Orientalism as concept and practice. These questions have their origins in Edward Said's *Orientalism*, published in 1978, which has had a lasting impact on Third World cultural studies in Europe and the United States.[1] Provocative as Said's book was in its critique of Orientalism as practice, its larger significance rests on Said's relentless demonstration of the intersection of historical interpretation, culture and politics in EuroAmerican studies of Asia. I will argue, contrary to critics of Said, that questions raised by this intersection are still very much relevant to problems of historical interpretation of Asia in general, and China in particular. On the other hand, I will suggest also that contemporary historiographical evidence calls for a recasting of the relationship between history, culture and politics in a configuration that is significantly different than Said's conceptualization of it in *Orientalism*. On the basis of this reconfigured understanding of Orientalism, I will reflect by way of conclusion on the possibilities of escaping the burden of Orientalism in historical studies. As Orientalism as concept refers to the "Orient" as a whole, I should add, in illustrating my arguments I will draw on evidence from the career of Orientalism not just in the historiography of China but other histories as well. Finally, I am concerned here not with specific historiographical questions, but questions that are best characterized as metahistorical.

Orientalism

To summarize very briefly, in Said's own words,

> Orientalism . . . refers to several overlapping domains: first, the changing historical and cultural relationship between Europe and Asia, a relationship with a 4000-year-old history; second, the scientific discipline in the west according to which, beginning in the early nineteenth century, one specialized in the study of various Oriental cultures and traditions; and, third, the ideological suppositions, images and fantasies about a currently important and politically urgent region of the world called the Ori-

ent. The relatively common denominator between these three aspects of Orientalism is the line separating Occident from Orient and this, I have argued, is less a fact of nature than it is a fact of human production, which I have called imaginative geography. This is, however, neither to say that the division between Orient and Occident is unchanging nor is it to say that it is simply fictional.[2]

Said's study was concerned almost exclusively with the second and the third aspects of Orientalism as it related to Western Asia, and drew upon the work of prominent English and French Orientalists to argue his thesis. A central aspect of the work was to represent contemporary area studies as a linear descendant of the Orientalist tradition in EuroAmerica. Two guiding assumptions of the argument are worth spelling out.

First, "one of the legacies of Orientalism, and indeed one of its epistemological foundations, is historicism, that is, the view . . . that if humankind has a history it is produced by men and women, and can be understood historically as, at each given period, epoch or moment, possessing a complex, but coherent unity." Said described this notion of historicism more precisely as a "universalizing historicism," that placed different histories conceived as "coherent unities" on a temporal scale.[3] Spatial differences were thereby rendered into temporal differences, and different societies placed at different locations in a progressive temporality in which EuroAmerica stood at the epitome of progress: "As primitivity, as the age-old antetype of Europe, as a fecund night out of which European rationality developed, the Orient's actuality receded inexorably into a kind of paradigmatic fossilization."[4]

Orientalist epistemology as it emerges from Said's analysis is also clearly culturalist, by which I mean a representation of societies in terms of essentialized cultural characteristics, more often than not enunciated in foundational texts. Culturalist essentialism is homogenizing both spatially and temporally. Spatially, it ignores differences within individual societies, and, in the case of Orientalism, differences between Asian societies, which are endowed with common characteristics that mark them as "Oriental." It is homogenizing temporally in substituting a cultural essence that defies time for culture as lived experience that is subject to temporal production and reproduction. Culturalism, in other words, nourishes off a de-socialized and de-historicized conceptualization of culture (as "organically and internally coherent, bound together by a spirit, genius, *Klima*, or national idea,"[5] which is the sense in which it appears in eighteenth-century European historicism, and also informs Said's use of "historicism") that suppresses relations both between and within societies in the production of culture as ongoing historical activity (which is informed by an alternative sense of historicism). Such culturalism is important to understanding why, in Orientalism, so-called Oriental societies may appear at once as objects of admiration for their civilizational achievements, but also relegated to the past as fossilized relics because, with culture substituted for history, they have no "real" historicity and, as Johannes Fabian puts it in a different context, no real contemporaneity, since their presents are but simple reproductions of their pasts.[6]

This epistemology, secondly, is bound up with questions of EuroAmerican power over the Orient. In *Orientalism*, Said singles out four preconditions without which Orientalism "could not have occurred": European expansion which brought Europeans into contact with other societies; the confrontation with other histories this contact necessitated, which culminated in comparative history; "sympathetic identification," which for some offered the only access to the panoply of alien cultures, "each permeated by an inimical creative spirit" (this, informed by, and informing, eighteenth-century historicism); and, finally, "the impulse to classify nature and man into types," and to bring order into the profuse variety of experience that could no longer be contained in inherited conceptions of the world.[7] Expansion, we may observe, was the point of departure for the new epistemologies for re-ordering the world. Orientalism was an integral consequence of this process.

Orientalism, as part of this epistemological reordering of the world, is not a mere intellectual instrument of imperialism, it *is* "intellectual imperialism." For Said, Orientalism is a "discourse" in the sense that Michel Foucault used that term: "Orientalism can be discussed and analyzed as the corporate institution for dealing with the Orient—dealing with it by making statements about it, authorizing views of it, describing it, by teaching it, settling it, ruling over it; in short, Orientalism as a Western style for dominating, restructuring, and having authority over the Orient."[8] It is important to underline here that, while Said is quite aware of the complex relationship between power and Orientalism, he is adamant that Orientalism does not merely serve or represent power, but is itself "a *distribution* of geopolitical awareness into aesthetic, scholarly, economic, sociological, historical, and philological texts"[9]—in other words, Orientalism as discourse is an epistemology of power. As such, it is integral to a modern EuroAmerican cultural consciousness (and unconsciousness).

It is noteworthy that Said sets out to study in *Orientalism* this dimension of modern EuroAmerican culture, rather than the "Oriental" societies represented in it. In fact, one of his basic goals is to demonstrate how such representations of the Orient have silenced the "Orientals," and undercut their ability to represent themselves. His argument on Orientalism, however, might not have been as compelling had he stopped here. *Orientalism* concludes not with condemnation or closure, but with a further set of questions: "How does one *represent* other cultures? What is *another* culture? Is the notion of a distinct culture (or race, or religion, or civilization) a useful one, or does it always get involved either in self-congratulation (when one discusses one's own) or hostility and aggression (when one discusses the "other")?"[10]

Power, specifically EuroAmerican political power, is key to the argument Said presents on Orientalism, and configures the relationship between politics, culture and history that structures his conceptualization of Orientalism. Following the logic of the argument, we might expect a power shift in global relations to reconfigure that relationship, in which case Orientalism may be consigned to the past as a manifestation of one specific period in EuroAmerican relationship to the world. This is indeed one contemporary verdict on Orientalism (not to speak of those who deny it altogether, past or present).

I would like to suggest here a contrary position: that far from being a phenomenon of the past, Orientalism, and the culturalist epistemology that nourished it, are very much alive in the present, but not necessarily where Said located it, and in a reconfigured relationship between politics, culture and history. The nature of this relationship is such, moreover, that it raises certain fundamental questions about Said's conceptualization of Orientalism, its location and structure. One question that is of particular interest is: is Orientalism an autonomous product of EuroAmerican development, which is then projected upon the "Orient," or is it rather the product of an unfolding relationship between EuroAmericans and Asians, that required the complicity of the latter in endowing it with plausibility; to mimic what E.P. Thompson said of classes, is Orientalism a thing or a relationship? Let me offer some observations on contemporary self-representations before I return to this question, and what it might tell us about the historical meaning of Orientalism.

"The Orientalism of the Orientals"[11]

Said's argument in *Orientalism* may be open to criticism from a variety of perspectives, and it has received its share of criticism, especially from "Orientalists." Whatever may be the merit or lack thereof of these criticisms, the central argument of the book is in my opinion indisputable: Orientalism was an integral part (at once as constituent and product) of a Eurocentric conceptualization of the world that was fully articulated in the course of the nineteenth century, that placed Europe at the center and pinnacle of development, and ordered the globe spatially and temporally in accordance with the criteria of European development. Non-European societies were characterized in this reordering of the world not by what they had but by what they lacked; in other words, the lack of one or more of those characteristics that accounted for European development. Rather than provide contemporary alternatives to European development, they were perceived predominantly to be located at some rung or other of the ladder of development that Europe already had left behind. They provided Europeans with glimpses not of alternative presents, but of a past stage of European development, what has been described as "a theory of our contemporary ancestors."[12] The development of this new view of the world went hand in hand with the progress of European colonization and domination of the world.

While we may have come a long way since the nineteenth century, it is hardly arguable that Eurocentrism is already a thing of the past. Post–World War II modernization "theory," still fundamental to our views of the world, continues to bear upon it strong traces of Eurocentrism. The difference is that it is now a surplus of history rather than a historical lack that defines the state of "premodern" non-European societies; what we call "tradition." It is the burden of the past in one form or another, that marks a society as traditional, which impedes its ascent to modernity. In spite of radical challenges, including challenges from intellectuals from non-European societies, that modernity and tradition, or development and underdevelopment, may be different aspects of the same historical process, the conceptual isolation of the one from the other (of a developed "inside" from an undeveloped "outside") persists not just in the popular consciousness but in intellectual work as well. The "inside" now has come to include some non-European societies, which has created some problems for earlier versions of the modernization explanation, but arguably has contributed further to enhancing the power of the idea of modernization itself.[13] The question I would like to raise here is whether Orientalism was just the autonomous creation of Europeans, or whether it presupposed in its emergence the complicity of "Orientals." This is what I had in mind when I referred to Orientalism above as possibly a "relationship." In *Orientalism* Said raises a number of questions which he does not pursue. These questions, brought to the surface, call for a number of qualifications with regard to the location, production and consequences of Orientalism that are, I think, fundamental to understanding Orientalism, and its place in modernity.

Said's *Orientalism*, as he is quick to acknowledge, is a study in EuroAmerican thought, and it has little to say on the question of how intellectuals and others in Asian societies may have contributed to the emergence of Orientalism as practice and concept. And even if Orientalism was a product of a European intellectual space, how did "Oriental" intellectuals respond to it, or receive it? Were the "Orientals" indeed as silent, or incapable of representing themselves, as Said's study suggests? How does "Orientalism," and the whole question of a modern consciousness appear when we bring the "Orientals" into the picture, not as silent objects of a European discourse, but as active participants in its emergence? What bearing would such a reconstructed picture of Orientalism have on the question of the relationship between Orientalism and power? While Said is quite right in arguing that Orientalism nourishes off an inside/outside (or Occident/Orient) distinction, moreover, is it possible that in the long run the consequence of Orientalism is to call such a distinction into question?

First, the Orientalists. Said notes that Orientalism, by its very epistemological assumptions, called for "sympathetic identification" as a means to grasping an alien culture. I take this to imply that in the very process of understanding an alien culture, the Orientalist needs in some measure to be "Orientalized," if you like, which brings the Orientalist closer to the Other while distancing him/her from the society of the Self. If only as specialist or expert, the Orientalist comes not just to speak about but also *for* the Other. In a recent work on Chinese modernization, the editor Kurt Werner Radtke, presumably speaking for the contributors to the volume, writes that "the contributors, all intellectuals and China specialists, have in the course of their lives been affected by the process of sinifica-tion."[14] There is nothing peculiar about this except that, while we have no diffi-culty thinking of "Westernized Chinese," which is the subject of much scholarly attention, we do not often think of the "Sinified Westerner." If we do, the distinc-tions between self and other, or subject and object, crucial to the analysis of Ori-entalism, become blurred though not necessarily abolished, as I will argue below. Suffice it to say here that examples of "Orientalized Westerners" abound from the origins of Orientalism to the present: from the Jesuits in China to Lawrence of Arabia, who sought to live as Chinese or Arabs; from William "Oriental" Jones, the founder of British Orientalism, to the "sinified" contributors to Radtke's vol-ume.[15] Their "Orientalization" was what qualified the Orientalists to speak for the Orient. To the extent that they were "Orientalized," however, they themselves assumed some of the exoticism of the Orient, which on occasion marginalized them, and even rendered them suspect ideologically at home. The latter inevitably raises questions concerning the relationship between Orientalism and power.

Such suspicion may be a consequence of the fact that however "condescend-ing" they may have been in their "veneration" of "Oriental" cultures (in Raymond Schwab's words), Orientalists have been responsible also for introducing elements of Asian cultures into their societies, for their use of the "Orient" in self-criticism, as well as the critique of EuroAmerican modernity. French and German Orien-talists of the early nineteenth century called for an "Oriental Renaissance," which would make the "Orient" (understood in terms of India, instead of Greece and Rome) into the basis of a new departure in European history.[16] The use of the "Orient" in self-criticism is almost a discourse within a discourse of Orientalism, from Montesquieu's *Persian Letters* and Oliver Goldsmith's *Citizen of the World* in the eighteenth century to Andre Malraux's, *The Temptation of the West* and radi-cal U.S. intellectuals' critiques of the U.S. in the twentieth.[17]

Most revealingly, Orientalism, itself a product of Eurocentrism, may even find service in the critique of Eurocentrism. A recent example of this is the notion of a "China-centered history" proposed by Paul Cohen and John Schrecker.[18] "China-centered history" as conceived by these authors is in keeping with the epistemo-logical procedures of Orientalism, especially in drawing a clear methodological line between Chinese and other histories, and arguing that Chinese history may be understood only in terms that are internal to it. Schrecker's *The Chinese Revolution in Historical Perspective* illustrates the approach by attempting to understand Chi-nese history over a three-thousand-year period in terms of the two Chinese con-cepts of *fengjian* and *junxian*. What is interesting about "China-centered history," however, is the authors' explicit positioning of themselves against Eurocentric his-tories of China. I will have more to say about this approach later.

Finally, as with the Oriental Renaissance, Orientalism could serve as a critique of European modernity, and a means to redirecting it. Such was the case with the Theosophical movement in the middle of the nineteenth century, which attracted the likes of Lafcadio Hearn in the United States.[19] Whatever these uses of the "Orient" may say about Orientalism, they suggest also that Orientalism played a transformative part in EuroAmerica.

A similar complexity attends the relationship of the Orientalist to the "Orient." There is considerable evidence also that those in Asian societies did not necessarily perceive the Orientalist as a vanguard of EuroAmerican power; to the extent that the Orientalist was "Orientalized," s/he could find acceptance in the society of the Other. The Jesuits are the classic example. In case they seem to belong to another age, we might adduce contemporary examples. In his recent proposal of a "Cultural China," Tu Wei-ming includes non-Chinese China specialists in the outer realm of his notion of a "Cultural China," the inner two realms consisting respectively of Chinese in China and Chinese overseas.[20] As if echoing his sentiments, *Sinorama* magazine in Taiwan published in 1991 a volume (compiled from earlier publications in the magazine), entitled *When West Meets East—International Sinology and Sinologists.*[21] Published in Chinese and English, the volume offers accounts of Sinologists, all European with the exception of John King Fairbank, in order to, in the words of the publisher Yuming Shaw, see China through the eyes of others and "better appreciate ourselves."[22] While the editors are by no means unaware of the connection between sinology and "trade and imperialism" (p.29), the volume is on the whole quite laudatory of the part foreign sinology ("culture's other half") has played in globalizing Chinese civilization.

Second, and even more complex, is the question of "the Orientalism of the Orientals," of which the *Sinorama* collection is emblematic. While the Occident/Orient distinction, and Orientalism as concept and practice, are of European origin, and the term Orientalism has been used almost exclusively to describe the attitudes of Europeans toward Asian societies, I would like to suggest here that the usage needs to be extended to Asian views of Asia, to account for tendencies to self-Orientalization which would become an integral part of the history of Orientalism. We tend to view the EuroAmerican impact on Asian societies primarily as an impact of "Western" ideas and institutions on Asia. To the extent that Orientalism had become a part of "Western" ideas by the early nineteenth century, the "Western" impact included also the impact on Asian societies of European ideas of the Orient. How EuroAmerican images of Asia may have been incorporated into the self-images of Asians in the process may in the end be inseparable from the impact of "Western" ideas per se. One fundamental consequence of recognizing this possibility is to call into question the notion of Asian "traditions" which may turn out, upon closer examination, to be "invented traditions," the products rather than the preconditions of contact between Asians and Europeans, that may owe more to Orientalist perceptions of Asia than the self-perceptions of Asians at the point of contact.

One of the most fascinating examples of what I have in mind here was the so-called Bengal Renaissance, the rediscovery of Hindu traditions in the nineteenth century by Bengali intellectuals. British Orientalism was to play the crucial part in the Bengal Renaissance by both authoring translations of and authorizing the rejuvenated study of ancient Hindu texts, which kindled the interest in these texts of Bengali intellectuals. In the process, a Hindu tradition was invented in the course of the nineteenth century in which Orientalist interpretations of India played a significant part. Schwab's description of these textual interchanges is worth quoting at some length because of its relevance to the argument here:

> Europe's knowledge of the Upanishads through Anquetil [-Duperron, Abraham Hyacinthe] has as its origins a Hindu unitarian attempt. ... In 1665 the Mughal Prince of Delhi, Muhammad Dara Shikoh . . . wanted to compare the sacred books of all peoples in order to attain and adopt the ultimate truth. . . . Not satisfied with that and having heard of the Vedas, he summoned the ascetics of Banaras to instruct him in Brahmanical doctrine. For this occasion he ordered a remarkable version of the Upanishads made in Persian, the lingua franca of Asia at that time. It is this text that, in the following century, found its way to Anquetil through the efforts of Gentil and that Anquetil retranslated between 1776 and 1796, first into French and then into Latin, and published in 1801–2. As good historical fortune would have it, the same pundit-scholar who had been Dara's principal translator also became Bernier's most valuable instructor, and Bernier . . . brought a separate manuscript of the *Oupnek'hat* to France . . . the work that Dara had initiated impressed an important adept: it was this text which a century and half later fell into the hands of Rammohun Roy, and which he, in turn, translated and annotated in local dialects and English. It must be said that shortly after his birth the example of such parallels had been established by William Jones, who himself had become a student of Brahmans Radhakanta Sarman and Sarvoru Trivedi: the Hindus were moved by Jones' sincere desire to know their true beliefs. They soon became the pupils of their disciples, whose processes they adopted, beginning with the printing press, an instrument whose diffusion always rendered a critical spirit inevitable within a short time.[23]

The most famous product of the Bengal Renaissance would be Rabindranath Tagore, who in the early twentieth century was to emerge as a "missionary" of a Pan-Asian civilization, distinguished from the "materialist" West by its spiritual-ity. But it was not merely the tradition of the Bengal Renaissance that played a formative part in Tagore's thinking. He was also influenced deeply around the turn of the century by Okakura Kakuzo (himself a student in Tokyo University of Ernest Fenollosa), by the Theosophist Margaret Noble from Ireland (who helped Okakura with his influential book, *The Ideals of the East*), and, as I noted above, by *Letters from John Chinaman*. Tagore, in turn, was to assume the role of a "missionary" of Asian civilization in Japan and China, where he exerted at least some influence on intellectuals such as Zhang Junmai and Liang Shuming, themselves involved in efforts to rejuvenate Chinese and Eastern cultures.[24] In the end, however, Tagore's messages of Pan-Asianism and Asian spirituality were received more favorably in Europe and the United States, where they had origi-nated in the first place, than in China or Japan (or, for that matter, India), all caught up in the contemporary concerns of national formation.

There are obvious differences between the Indian and Chinese encounters with Europeans, but similar processes are observable in the latter case as well. Unlike in India where the Brahmanical texts were rescued from esoteric obscurity by British Orientalists, and made into the source of Indian Civilization, Confucianism in China was state orthodoxy, and when Jesuits formulated their representations of China as a Confucian state, they no doubt had the benefit of drawing on the self-image of the bureaucratic elite. Nevertheless, the Jesuit "invention of Confucianism," as Lionel Jensen has described it, had the effect of codifying Confucianism as an emblem of Chinese society not just for EuroAmericans, but also for twentieth century Chinese who drew not only on Chinese but also EuroAmerican scholarship in their own evaluations of China's past.[25] Benjamin Elman has suggested Jesuit influence in the emergence of textual criticism, which was to have a significant intellectual and political consequence in the interpretation of Confucianism during the Qing.[26] Where there seems to be little doubt concerning the Jesuit impact on the Chinese self-image is in the mapping of the world, of China, and of China's place in the world. Witek credits Matteo Ricci with coining the term, Yaxiya, among others, which "presented to the Chinese . . . a unified conception of the world."[27] In a "ten-year project," Jesuits produced for the Kangxi Emperor the first comprehensive map of China. The Kangxi Emperor, according to Theodore Foss, was anxious to know "the extent of the empire," and especially to see a map of the Great Wall, a desire which was nurtured by a Jesuit advisor. The Emperor's desire for control over his territories coincided in the project with the Jesuits' wish to fathom the extent of the realm that could be opened up to Christianity to produce the first map of China as a whole; in the process, local knowledges (Chinese maps of localities) were transformed into a map of the whole realm that became available to Chinese at the same time as to the Europeans, and through the agency of the latter.[28] Arthur Waldron has provided us with a fascinating account of how "the myth of the Great Wall," invented by the Jesuits, would come to play a central part in Chinese nationalist consciousness at a later time.[29]

It is in the twentieth century, however, that EuroAmerican Orientalist perceptions and methods become a visible component in the formulation of the Chinese self-image, and Chinese perceptions of the past. The process was facilitated by the emergence of nationalism. Nationalism, once it has emerged, tends to project itself over both space and time; homogenizing all differences across the territory occupied by the nation, and projecting itself back in time to some mythical origin to erase the different temporalities of the past, so that all history becomes a history of national emergence. In the process, some trait or traits become emblematic of the nation, while others that are inconsistent with the national self-image are swept aside as foreign intrusions. In this metonymic reductionism, nationalism shares much in common with the culturalist procedures of Orientalism, now at the scale of the nation.[30]

The EuroAmerican assault on imperial China both provoked the emergence of Chinese nationalism and, ironically, provided it with images of the Chinese past that could be incorporated in a new national identity.[31] While different political strands in Chinese nationalism focused on different aspects of the past, and evaluated the historical legacy differently, metonymic reductionism has been apparent in the identification of China among liberals and conservatives with Confucianism, despotism, bureaucratism, familism, or even racial characteristics, all of them traceable to Orientalist representations, or an unchanging "feudal" or "Asiatic" society, in a Marxist version of Orientalism.[32] What was common to all was a rewriting of Chinese history with images, concepts and standards drawn from a contemporary consciousness of which "Western" ideas, including the "imaginative geography" of Orientalism, were an integral component. This consciousness was formed now not just by the circulation of EuroAmericans in China, as in the case of the Jesuits, but by the circulation of Chinese abroad.

This latter situation also has implied that the origins of our images of China's past have become increasingly blurred. A fascinating example is provided by the career of John King Fairbank, who has been held responsible for both the virtues and the woes of U.S. China scholarship. Fairbank's case is doubly interesting because he himself rejected European-style Orientalism, and played a major part in launching U.S. China scholarship in the direction of Modern Chinese studies. A younger generation of scholars has accused Fairbank of promoting a Eurocentric "impact-response" view, which rendered Chinese into passive objects of Western impact. To be sure, Fairbank did place a great deal of emphasis on the ways in which Chinese tradition (perceived largely in terms of bureaucratic despotism) held China back; so that only the Western impact could provide the dynamic force of change in modern Chinese history. But how different were Fairbank's premises from those expressed in the following lines by a prominent Chinese intellectual, in explanation of China's modern fate?

First, we were lacking in science. In the competition between individuals or nations, what ultimately determines success or failure is the level of knowledge. The contest between scientific and non-scientific knowledge is similar to the contest between the automobile and the rickshaw. The basis of Western science was already established at the time of the Jia Qing and Dao Guang Emperors, when our ancestors were still writing eight-legged essays, and discussing YinYang and the Five Elements. Secondly, by the middle of the eighteenth century, the West was already using machinery to produce wealth and conduct war, whereas our industry, agriculture, transportation and military affairs followed the models of the Tang and the Song. Thirdly, the political visage of the West during the Middle Ages closely resembled that of the Spring-Autumn Period, while following the Renaissance it was more like that of the Warring States period. In the conflict for supremacy among the powers, Westerners cultivated a strong patriotism, and a deep national spirit. We on the other hand were stuck corpse-like in familism *(jiazu guannian)* and localism *(jiaxiang guannian)*. So in the early years of the nineteenth century, though Western nations were small, their unity gave them a foundation of steel; our nation was big, but it was but a pan of sand, without power. In sum, by the nineteenth century, the Western world already enjoyed the so-called modern culture, while the Eastern world was still mired in the Middle Ages.[33]

The above is from the introduction to Jiang Tingfu's *Outline of Modern Chinese History*. Jiang Tingfu had received his Ph.D. in diplomatic history from Columbia University, before he went back to China to establish the field of modern Chinese diplomatic history in Qinghua University. It was there that in the 1930s John King Fairbank as a graduate student worked with Jiang Tingfu. In pointing to the strong parallelisms between Fairbank's and Jiang's views of modern China I do not wish to imply that Fairbank's views were shaped by Jiang's; if anything unites their views, it is a common origin in liberal interpretations of Chinese history. But the parallelisms do suggest the confounding of the origins in Europe or China of such views. By the twentieth century in particular, Orientalist conceptions had no distinct spatial origin.[34]

This circulation of ideas is more than ever the condition of our understanding of China, which has led some to the conclusion that Orientalism is no longer a problem. What I would like to propose instead is that what has changed is the power relationship between China and EuroAmerica, rather than the abolition of Orientalism. On the contrary, the very transformation of power may have culminated in the reification of Orientalism at the level of a global ideology. Orientalism, which earlier articulated a distancing of Asian societies from the EuroAmerican, now appears in the articulation of differences within a global modernity as Asian societies emerge as dynamic participants in a Global Capitalism.[35] In this contemporary guise, Orientalism provides the site for contention between the conflicting ideological loyalties of an elite that is no longer identifiable easily as Eastern or Western, Chinese or non-Chinese.

The foremost example of this may be the appearance of "cultural nationalisms" in East and South Asia in the midst of the so-called globalization of Asian societies.[36] One aspect of this cultural nationalism, especially pertinent to Chinese societies, is the so-called Confucian revival. I have discussed this at length elsewhere; so I will summarize it very briefly here.[37] While the discussion of Confucianism among China scholars and Chinese intellectuals has never stopped, the intensive discussions of the 1980s do indeed mark this most recent phase as a "revival." The discussion this time involves not just China specialists or Chinese intellectuals, but state leaders, businessmen, sociologists (such as Peter Berger) and futurologists (such as Herman Kahn). While in the past there has been a tendency to relegate Confucianism to the past, as an obstacle to modernization, this time around Confucianism is reaffirmed as a positive force in capitalist modernization, relevant not only to the experience of Chinese societies but to East Asian societies in general, and perhaps globally. Theoretically speaking, in its reversal of Max Weber's judgment on Confucianism, the "new Confucianism" seeks to refute Orientalist evaluations of Confucianism. There is, however, no challenge to Weber's formulations on modernization per se: what Weber portrayed as inimical to the development of capitalism in China (Confucian values of harmony, familism, patrimonialism) is now reaffirmed as being eminently functional to capitalist development, at least in its present stage. Otherwise, the conceptualization of Confucianism is quite reminiscent of earlier Orientalist conceptions of Confucianism as a de-socialized and de-historicized metonym for Chinese society; one advocate states that although Confucianism has a complex history, it may be used "loosely" as being "synonymous with Chinese culture."[38] Confucianism, moreover, has been "deterritorialized" from its Chinese sources to be rendered into a characteristic of East and Southeast Asian societies in general. Tu Wei-ming, whose name has been most closely associated with the Confucian revival, seeks to make Confucianism into a global philosophy (parallelling Christianity in Europe) that may be transplanted anywhere—from the U.S. to Africa. His efforts are quite reminiscent of the missionizing Pan-Asianism of Rabindranath Tagore; and, as with Tagore, they ignore that the term "Confucian societies" disguises national appropriations of what may or may not be a common legacy of East Asian societies. But he is not alone in the undertaking. In recent years, political figures such as Lee Kuan Yew of Singapore and Prime Minister Mahathir of Malaysia have joined in a new chorus of "Asianism" against the West—in the case of the latter, obviously, it is Islam rather than Confucianism, that is the point of departure. This, too, is consistent with earlier Pan-Asianism, where different Pan-Asianists projected upon Asia the different "characteristics" of their various national societies. Finally, these intellectual trends are clearly products of a contemporary circulation of intellectuals and ideas; Confucian revivalists, including Tu Wei-ming, readily cite Herman Kahn and Peter Berger as the "Western" authorities who have legitimized the "new Confucianism." On the other hand, the assertion of "Asian cultural differences" by Lee Kuan Yew of Singapore, Mahathir Mohamad of Malaysia and the People's Republic of China leadership, especially over issues of democracy and human rights, resonates with prevalent anti-Eurocentric sentiments in Europe and the United States.

In a different vein, one Chinese intellectual in a recent work has explicitly reaffirmed the positivity of "Orientalism" against Said's arguments. In her recently published *Occidentalism: Theory of Counter-Discourse in Post-Mao China*, Chen Xiaomei goes so far as to charge Said with a new kind of neocolonialism.[39] The "Occidentalism" in Chen's title refers to Chinese reification of the "Occident," much like the Orientalist "reifications" of the "Orient." Occidentalism is very much a mirror image of Orientalism and, in Chen's usage, includes Orientalism as a premise; the TV series "He Shang" which is her point of departure obviously combines "Occidentalism" where the West is concerned with "Orientalism" in its depictions of China. Chen, however, seeks to refute the connection Said establishes between Orientalism and Eurocentric power, arguing that such representations carry different significations in different contexts. In the case of "Occidentalism" (or Orientalism, for that matter), she draws a distinction in the Chinese context between official Occidentalism, that uses representations of the West to justify political repression at home, and anti-official Occidentalism, exemplified by "He Shang" that serves as legitimation for resistance against oppression. The issue is not Orientalism, in other words, the issue is the implication for power of Orientalism in different social and political contexts.

Finally, I will mention as an instance of Orientalism something that is very much bound with global exchanges, and has received some critical attention among Chinese intellectuals: the reification of Chinese culture into a commodity, mainly in the cause of global tourism. Yang Congrong, from whose essay I have derived the title for this section, has pointed to the commodification of Chinese culture in theme parks, tourist brochures, etc., that represents an "Orientalism of Oriental societies." In this case, culture is totally deterritorialized, and placed in global tourist circuits, which now endow it with signification. The theme park is emblematic of the reification of culture in its spatialization of cultural artifacts, which derive their meaning from their positioning in the theme park, rather than their locations in the complex geographical and social entity that we know as China. And the theme park comes to serve as a substitute for China, as in the Chinese state TV advertisement that "you can see all of the four-thousand-year old culture of China in half an hour in the Chinese culture theme park in Guangzhou." In this case, government and business collude in perpetuating a distinction between east and west, so as to make an "exoticized" east more saleable to a tourist industry to which east-west distinctions offer one more commodity for sale to consumers who are no longer identifiable clearly as "eastern" or "western."[40]

Orientalism Reconsidered

Orientalism emerged historically in accompaniment to Eurocentrism.[41] The consequence of Eurocentrism historically was to erase the part that non-Europe had played in European development in the course of centuries of interaction, and, on the contrary, to distance other histories from the European. The emergence of Eurocentrism also coincided historically with the establishment of EuroAmerican domination and colonialization of the world. Eurocentrism served the cause of colonialism by representing the world outside of Europe as "empty," at least culturally speaking, or backward,[42] defined in terms of "lack," and hence in need of European intervention. Europe had everything to give to the world; what it received in return were images of its own past—and the rightful material returns from its civilizing activity.

The "Orientalization" of Asian societies not only erased the part they had played in "the making of Europe," but also the spatial and temporal complexities of these societies. The question of representation raised in Said's *Orientalism* is not the correctness or erroneousness of Orientalist representation, but the metonymic reductionism that led to the portrayal of these societies in terms of some cultural trait or other, that homogenized differences within individual societies, and froze them in history. Where the representation was extended to Asia as a whole, metonymic reductionism took the form of projecting upon Asia as a whole the characteristics of the particular society of the individual Orientalist's acquaintance.

However individual Orientalists may have responded to Asia, moreover, Orientalism as *discourse* implied also a power relationship: Europeans, placed at the pinnacle of progress, were in a better position than the natives themselves to know what Asians were about, since they had the advantage of a more prodigious (and panoptical) historical hindsight. I noted above that Orientalists did not just speak about Asia, they also spoke for Asia. While this points to perturbations within Orientalism, it also raises the question of power: power to speak for the Other. The Oriental may speak about the past, of which s/he is an embodiment, but not about the present, in which s/he is not a genuine participant; especially the critical Oriental, who appears as a degeneration of the ideal type to the extent that s/he has learned to speak in the language of the present. Advocates of a "China-centered history" to whom I have referred above have suggested that contemporary Chinese, who have been touched by "Western" ideas and methods (especially Marxism, it seems), have lost touch with their own past, and are at a disadvantage, therefore, in providing a truly China-centered history.

Where Orientalism as articulated by Said is wanting, I think, is in ignoring the "Oriental's" participation in the unfolding of the discourse on the Orient, which raises some questions both about the location of the discourse and, therefore, its implications for power. I have suggested above that Orientalism, regardless of its ties to Eurocentrism both in origin and in its history, in some basic ways required the participation of "Orientals" for its legitimation. And in its practice, Orientalism from the beginning took shape as an exchange of images and representations, corresponding to the circulation of intellectuals and others, first the circulation of Europeans in Asia, but increasingly with a counter-circulation of Asians in Europe and the United States.

Rather than view Orientalism as an autochtonous product of a European modernity, therefore, it makes some sense to view it as a product of those "contact zones" in which Europeans encountered non-Europeans, where a European modernity produced and was also challenged by alternative modernities as the Others in their turn entered the discourse on modernity. I borrow the term "contact zone" from Mary Louis Pratt, who has described it as "the space of colonial encounters, the space in which peoples geographically and historically separated come into contact with each other and establish ongoing relations, usually involving conditions of coercion, radical inequality, and intractable conflict."[43] But the contact zone is not merely a zone of domination, it is also a zone of exchange, even if it is unequal exchange, which Pratt describes as "transculturation," whereby "subordinated or marginal groups select and invent from materials transmitted to them by a dominant or metropolitan culture. While subjugated peoples cannot readily control what emanates from the dominant culture, they do determine to various extents what they absorb into their own, and what they use it for.[44] We may note also that, in the contact zone, in the process of the very effort to communicate with the dominated, the dominant or the metropolitan culture goes through a language change, if to a lesser extent than the dominated.

The idea (and the reality) of the contact zone enable the explanation of some of the contradictions in Orientalism that I have described above. The contact zone is a zone of domination, because it does not abolish the structures of power of which it is an expression, and to which it serves as a zone of mediation. But the contact zone also implies a distance, a distance from the society of the Self, as well as of the Other. The Orientalist, I suggested above, is "Orientalized" himself or herself in the very process of entering the "Orient" intellectually and sentimentally. Same with the "Oriental," whose very contact with the Orientalist culminates in a distancing from native society, where s/he becomes an object of suspicion, and who in the long run is better able to communicate with the Orientalist than with the society of the Self (remember the quotation from Jiang Tingfu above). In some ways, it is this distancing from the complexities of everyday life in either society that facilitates the metonymic cultural representations that I have described above as a basic feature of Orientalism—whether by the Orientalist, or by the self-Orientalizing "Oriental." Is it very surprising that nationalism in China, which was as much a source of cultural reification as Orientalism, was the production of intellectuals who were themselves products of contact zones, be they Chinese in China, Chinese intellectuals studying abroad, or Chinese overseas?

If locating Orientalism in the contact zone modifies our understanding of the processes whereby Orientalist representations are produced, the same location also reveals different relationships between Orientalism and power. Chen Xiaomei's reminder that Orientalism (or Occidentalism) may have different meanings in different contexts is a valuable one; so long as we relocate the context of which she speaks not in "China," but in the contact zone of "Westernized" Chinese intellectuals. As Chen argues, Occidentalism (the mirror image of Orientalism) serves as a source of critique of an oppressive state ideology. But there is arguably another aspect to such self-Orientalization. However closely Orientalism may be tied in with EuroAmerican power historically, its contemporary manifestations are difficult to explain in terms of a past relationship between Orientalism and EuroAmerican power. The Confucian revival of the past decade, I would like to suggest, is an expression not of powerlessness, but of a newfound sense of power, that has accompanied the economic success of East Asian societies, who now reassert themselves against an earlier EuroAmerican domination. In this sense, the Confucian revival (and other cultural nationalisms) may be viewed as an articulation of native culture (and an indigenous subjectivity) against EuroAmerican cultural hegemony.[45]

The challenge to Eurocentrism in the Confucian revival, within the context of a Global Capitalism, has had reverberations within a EuroAmerican context as well, raising questions about another fundamental premise of Orientalism: the idea of an Occident with a unified culture. Interestingly, even as capitalism has emerged victorious over existing forms of socialism, and global unity under a globalized capitalism seems a real possibility for the first time in nearly a century, new fissures have appeared that are expressed in the affirmation of cultural differences not just in Asia or what used to be the Second and Third Worlds, but within the First World itself. The notion of different "cultures of capitalism," to which I referred above, has been extended by some to differences among EuroAmerican societies themselves, as in a recent work that identifies "seven cultures of capitalism," all but one (Japan) located in Europe and North America.[46] The contradiction may be a contradiction of proliferating "contact zones" under a globalized calitalism, which has been accompanied not by the abolition of but by a simultaneous proliferation of national and ethnic reification of cultures.[47] The idea of a "West" is called into question in a Europe or North America striving for economic and political unification, just as claims to a Confucian zone run aground on claims to national uniqueness in East and Southeast Asia.

The part that self-orientalization may play in the struggle against internal and external hegemony, and its claims to alternative modernities, however, must not be exaggerated. In the long run, self-Orientalization serves to perpetuate, and even to consolidate, 'existing forms of power. Partha Chatterjee has observed that "nationalist thought accepts the same essentialist conception based on a distinction between 'the East' and 'the West,' the same typology created by a transcendent studying subject, and hence the same 'objectifying' procedures of knowledge constructed in the post-Enlightenment age of Western science."[48] Self-essentialization may serve the cause of mobilization against "Western" domination; but in the very process also consolidates "Western" ideological hegemony by internalizing the historical assumptions of Orientalism. At the same time, it contributes to internal hegemony, by suppressing differences within the nation.

Examples of the latter abound in contemporary cultural nationalisms. Most obvious is the use of "culture" to reject calls for "democracy" and "human rights," which is common to a diverse group from Lee Kuan Yew to Mahathir Mohamad to the Government of the People's Republic of China. While there is no denying that "democracy" and "human rights" as they are conceived are EuroAmerican in origin, and are often misused by the latter in the pursuit of power, their denial on the grounds of "cultural imperialism" also justifies oppression at home—and makes little sense when the regimes involved incorporate so much else that is also EuroAmerican in origin.

This "official Occidentalism," as Chen Xiaomei calls it, however, is only part of the problem. "Anti-official Occidentalism" may be just as complicit in oppression in its resort to self-Orientalization as a protest against the oppression of the state. The essentialization and homogenization of the national terrain serves in that case as much as in the case of the state to disguise differences within the nation, including class, gender and ethnic differences. I have suggested above that elites in Asian societies have been complicit all along in the production of Orientalism. This may be more the case than ever in the past, as the idea of the "nation" has become problematic, and the nation difficult to define as a cultural entity, as globalization and diasporic motions of people complicate cultures and challenge state-defined national cultures with localized cultures. Culturalist essentialism, regardless of its origins in the state or with intellectuals, serves to contain and to control the disruptive consequences of globalization. This helps explain the simultaneous appearance of cultural nationalism with calls for economic global-ization. In the works cited above by Harumi Befu, Yoshino Kosaku, Yang Con-grong, and others, the authors all point to the part played by government and business in the production of "cultural nationalism." This has been the case also with the Confucian revival, in which Confucianism appears, on the one hand, as a dynamic ideological force in the development of capitalism, and, on the other hand, as a value-system with which to counteract the disruptive effects of capi-talist development.

While dissident intellectuals may employ Occidentalism or Orientalism to challenge existing hegemonies, internal or external, they often ignore this aspect of the problem. While *He Shang* in Chen Xiaomei's conception may serve the cause of the struggle against oppression at home, it is itself a product of dissident Chinese intellectuals of the "contact zone," who portray Chinese society from a privileged outside (as Chen admits), and render backward not just a reified native tradition but, with it, the people who are carriers of that tradition; thus a ten-dency among Chinese intellectuals in recent years to once again represent the "people" at large, especially the peasantry, not as an oppressed group but merely as carriers of "feudal backwardness."

While as an advocate of the revival of Confucianism someone such as Tu Wei-ming is quite different in his evaluation of China's past, in terms of power rela-tionships his position is revealing of a similar elitism that nourishes off his priv-ileged status as a Westernized Chinese intellectual. In speaking of Cultural China, Tu has suggested that the creation of a Cultural China must proceed from the "periphery" to the "center," from Chinese overseas to Chinese in China (or, in terms of the metaphor used here, from the "contact zone" to China proper). In terms of Chinese societies, the center-periphery distinction suggests that "Cul-tural China" is to be created by the transformation of the centers of power by intellectuals from the margins with little or no power; as this is the configuration of power that the center-periphery model usually suggests. Viewed from a global perspective, however, the power relationship appears quite differently, because in that perspective, the periphery coincides with the centers of global power while the "center" of Chinese society appears as the location of the periphery. "Dias-poric Chinese," to the extent that they are successful in a global economy or cul-ture, then, become the agents of changing China. But their very location suggests that they are no longer "Chinese" in any simple identifiable sense, but the products of the "contact zone," in which the West or the East, or the Occident or the Orient, are no longer identifiable with any measure of clarity. The assertion of "Chineseness" against this uncertainty seeks to contain the very dispersal of a so-called "Chinese culture" into numerous local cultures which more than ever makes it impossible to define a Chinese national culture. This strategy of containment is the other side of the coin to the pursuit of a "Chinese" identity in a global culture. If in the former case it may serve to counter a EuroAmerican hegemony, in the latter case it is itself an expression of establishing a cultural hegemony that denies the diversity of what it means to be Chinese. In this latter case, ironically, it is empowered by the very EuroAmerican hegemony that it seeks to displace.

Aijaz Ahmad in a recent study has criticized Said for ignoring class relations in the emergence of Orientalism.[49] Orientalism is not just a matter of continents or nations representing one another; it also entails class (or, for that matter, gender and ethnic) representations; not only in terms of who is engaged in representation, but how a society is represented. It was the upper-class upper-caste Brahmins who provided British Orientalists with the texts of Hinduism, as well as their assumptions about Hindu spirituality. Jesuits in China, who were initially drawn to Buddhism as a means of entry into China, decided that Confucianism served better than Buddhism in the representation of China because their friends in officialdom pointed them toward the lifestyles of the elite. In our day, Confucianism may be subjected to different evaluations, which also suggest different relations of power within Chinese societies, and between Chinese societies and the outside world. Recent experience also indicates that it is insufficient to conceive of Orientalism simply in terms of Eurocentrism or nationalism. It is its position in the capitalist structuring of the world that ultimately accounts for the changing relationships between Orientalist discourse (Eurocentric or self-Orientalizing) and power. Just as it was the apparent Chinese incapability to make the transition to capitalism that once condemned Confucianism to a defunct past, it is Chinese success in the world of capitalism that now enables its admission to the center of a global modernity as an alternative to EuroAmerican capitalisms—acknowledged as such even by the ideologues of the latter. Intellectuals who themselves have become part of a global elite (not to speak of the managers of capital)play a crucial part in the transformation.

Ironically, the self-assertiveness of "Orientals" under these circumstances would seem to represent not an alternative to, as they claim, but a consolidation of Eurocentric hegemony; or, more accurately, the hegemony of capital globally. As I noted above, Orientalism was a product of capitalist modernization (and colonialism) in Europe; and the very notion of modernization incorporated Orientalist assumptions as an integral premise. Where Orientalism earlier represented the past of modernity, it is now rendered into one of its versions—

but still without history. The cultural nationalisms of recent years, while they make claims to the uniqueness of essentialized national cultures, all share one thing in common: that the unique national culture is a force of modernization, more precisely, capitalist modernization. Rather than question capitalism with Confucian or other Chinese values, for example, the tendency has been to render it into a value-system conducive to capitalist development. While this has dislodged the claim that only Europeans had the value-system appropriate to capitalism, and has asserted the possibility of multiple paths, the multiple paths are all contained within a teleology of capitalism as the end of history.[50]

Said has suggested that the solution to overcoming Orientalism may lie in the cultivation of a "decentered consciousness" that resists totalization and systematization,[51] something, I take it, along the lines of "multiculturalism." If my analysis based on the "contact zone" has any validity, this may not be sufficient, because Orientalism itself may be a product of a consciousness already decentered, if not completely. There is no self-evident reason why a decentered consciousness should not find relief in culturalist fundamentalism, or the reification of ethnicity and culture; the history of Orientalism provides evidence of this strong possibility. Multiculturalism, ironically, may enhance tendencies to Orientalism in its insistence on the cultural definition of ethnicity, which reifies cultural origins at the expense of the historicity of both ethnicity and culture.[52]

It seems to me to be more important to question the assumptions of capitalist modernity (not merely Eurocentrism) of which Orientalism is an integral expression. To the extent that they have assimilated the teleology of capitalism, recent challenges to Eurocentrism (such as with the Confucian revival) have promoted rather than dislodged Orientalism. What is necessary is to repudiate historical teleology in all its manifestations. This would entail the historicization of capitalist modernity itself, and the identification of alternative modernities, not in terms of reified cultures, but in terms of alternative historical trajectories that have been suppressed by the hegemony of capitalist modernity. It also requires questioning not just of continental distinctions (Orient/Occident), but of nations as units of analysis, since the latter also thrive on cultural homogenization and reification. It is necessary, I think, to restore full historicity to our understanding of the past—and the present—historicity not in the sense that Said uses "historicism" (that presupposes organically holistic cultures) but historicity that is informed by the complexity of everyday life, which accounts not only for what unites but, more importantly, for diversity in space and time, which is as undesirable to national power as it is to Eurocentrism. A thoroughgoing historicism subjects culture to the structures of everyday life, rather than erase those structures by recourse to a homogenizing culturalism. This, of course, requires also that we conceive of alternative modernities that take as their point of departure not a reified past legacy, but a present of concrete everyday cultural practices where, as Yang Congrong put it, it is no longer possible to tell what is identifiably Chinese or identifiably Western.

Notes

1. Edward W. Said, *Orientalism* (New York: Vintage Books, 1978).

2. Edward W. Said, "Orientalism Reconsidered," in Francis Barker et al. (eds.), *Literature, Politics and Theory: Papers from the Essex Conference, 1976–84* (London: Methuen, 1986): pp.210–229.

3. Said, "Orientalism Reconsidered," pp.223–224.

4. Ibid., p.215.

5. Said, *Orientalism*, p.118.

6. Johannes Fabian, *Time and the Other: How Anthropology Makes Its Object* (New York: Columbia University Press, 1983).

7. Said, *Orientalism*, pp.116–120.

8. Said, *Orientalism*, p.3.

9. Said, *Orientalism*, p.12.

10. Said, *Orientalism*, p.325.

11. I borrow this subtitle from Yang Congrong, "Dongfang shehuide dongfanglun" ("The Orientalism of Oriental Societies"), *Dangdai* (Contemporary), no. 64 (August 1, 1991):38–53.

12. This argument is developed fully, if somewhat tendentiously, in J.M. Blaut, *The Colonizer's Model of the World: Geographical Diffusionism and Eurocentric History* (New York: The Guilford Press, 1993). For "our contemporary ancestors," see p.16.

13. The inside/outside distinction as a basic feature of Eurocentrism is developed at length in ibid.

14. Kurt Werner Radtke/Tony Saich (eds.), *China's Modernisation: Westernisation and Acculturation* (Stuttgart: Franz Steiner, 1993), p.1.

15. *Orientalism* provides instances of such "Orientalization." Also important for an account of many Orientalists in Europe is Raymond Schwab, *The Oriental Renaissance: Europe's Discovery of India and the East, 1680–1880* (New York: Columbia University Press, 1984), tr. Gene Patterson-Black and Victor Reinking, with a foreword by Edward Said. Jonathan Spence, *To Change China: Western Advisers in China, 1620–1960* (Boston: Little, Brown and Co., 1969), offers insightful portraits of Westerners involved in China whose activities provide insights into the workings of power at the ground level, as does Randall E. Stross, *The Stubborn Earth: American Agriculturalists on Chinese Soil, 1898–1937* (Berkeley: University of California Press, 1986). For a recent work on the Jesuits, see, Charles E. Ronan and Bonnie B.C. Oh (eds), *East Meets West: The Jesuits in China, 1582–1773* (Chicago: Loyola University Press, 1988), which contains a number of articles of great interest. For Lawrence, see his autobiography, T.E. Lawrence, *Seven Pillars of Wisdom* (New York: Dell Publishing Co., 1964), and for William Jones, see, Garland Cannon, *Oriental Jones: A Biography of Sir William Jones (1746–1794)* (New York: Asia Publishing House, 1964).

16. Schwab, *The Oriental Renaissance*, op.cit. What made the veneration condescending was the sense that India contained "the eternal in its present"(p.7). In other words, contemporary India was not truly contemporary, but showed Europe its own past. Nevertheless, the challenge to the earlier "Eurocentric" Renaissance is not to be ignored, and neither is the extension of the boundaries of the "inside" to include Asia.

17. Montesquieu (Charles-Louis de Secondat), *Persian Letters* (New York: Penguin Books, 1993), tr. with an introduction by C.J. Betts; Oliver Goldsmith, *Citizen of the World:*

or Letters from a Chinese Philosopher Residing in London to His Friend in the East, in *Collected Works*, 5 Vols., ed by A. Friedman (Oxford: Oxford Clarendon Press, 1966); Andre Malraux, *The Temptation of the West* (New York: Vintage Books, 1961), tr. with an introduction by Robert Hollander; Edward Friedman and Mark Selden (eds), *America's Asia: Dissenting Essays on US-Asian Relations* (New York: Vintage Books, 1971). It is important to underline that, as with the Oriental Renaissance, works such as Montesquieu's and Goldsmith display an "ethnocentric cosmopolitanism," in other words, employ Asia to European ends. They also render Asians into caricatures of sorts. My concern here, however, is with pointing to varieties of Orientalism, and what this variety might imply for the connection between Orientalism and power.

18. Paul Cohen, *Discovering History in China* (New York: Columbia University Press, 1984), and, John Schrecker, *The Chinese Revolution in Historical Perspective* (New York: Praeger, 1991).

19. Jackson Lears, *No Place of Grace: Antimodernism and the Transformation of American Culture, 1880–1920* (New York: Pantheon Books, 1981), pp.175–176. An interesting example of the utopianization of China as a refuge from modernity, written around the turn of the century, also in epistolary form, was Goldsworthy Lowes Dickinson's, *Letters from John Chinaman* (London: R. Brimley Johnson, 1901) (Subsequently published in the U.S. in 1903 as *Letters from a Chinese Official: Being and Eastern View of Western Civilization*). This work spoke of the conflict between Eastern and Western civilizations, and argued for the moral superiority of Chinese to Western civilization. What makes it interesting in this context is that it was one of the works that helped convince one important reader, Rabindranath Tagore (who was unaware of its English authorship) of the superiority of Asian to Western civilization. See, Stephen N. Hay, *Asian Ideas of East and West: Tagore and His Critics in Japan, China, and India* (Cambridge, MA: Harvard University Press, 1970), pp. 34–35. Of Tagore and Orientalism, more below.

20. Tu Wei-ming, "Cultural China: The Periphery as Center," *Daedalus*, Vol.120, no.2 (Spring 1991):1–32, p.13. This was a special issue of *Daedalus*, "The Living Tree: The Changing Meaning of Being Chinese Today." Tu Wei-ming has recently initiated a new journal with the title, "Cultural China" (*Wenhua Zhongguo*).

21. Wang Jiafeng (Wang Jia-fong) and Li Guangzhen (Laura Li), *Dang xifang yujian dongfang: Guoji hanxue yu hanxuezhe* (Taipei: Sinorama Magazine, 1991). This title, revealingly, conveys a sense of "going West to meet with the East." That this is the sense is confirmed by the editors' introduction, "A Sinological 'Journey to the West.'"

22. Ibid., p.5.

23. Schwab, p. 246. For the Bengal Renaissance, see, Atulchandra Gupta (ed), *Studies in the Bengal Renaissance* (Jadavpur, Bengal: The National Council of Education, 1958), and, David Kopf, *British Orientalism and the Bengal Renaissance: The Dynamics of Indian Modernization, 1773–1835* (Berkeley: University of California Press, 1969).

24. Hay, op.cit. It may be worth noting that another Indian intellectual and political leader, who would play an even more important part in asserting the contemporary relevance of ancient Indian values, Gandhi, first discovered the significance of those values and the texts in which they were embedded during his years of education in London. In his case, in addition to the Theosophists, European intellectuals such as John Ruskin and Leo Tolstoy would play a significant role in his reading of these Indian traditions. See, Mohandas K. Gandhi, *Autobiography: The Story of My Experiments with Truth* (New York: Dover Publications, 1983), especially pp. 59–61. In later years, in his critique of capitalist

modernity and his pursuit of an alternative path for India, Gandhi did not hesitate to call upon Orientalist authorities to justify his advocacy. See the appendix to his *Hind Swaraj or Indian Home Rule*, Revised edition (Ahmedabad: Navajivan Press,1921), pp.170–180.

25. Lionel Jensen, "Manufacturing 'Confucianism': Chinese and Western Imaginings in the Making of a Tradition," Ph.D. dissertation, University of California, 1992. It is note-worthy that before they came to realize the importance of Confucianism through acquain-tance with the Chinese scene, the Jesuits first attempted to enter China through Buddhism, no doubt on the basis of everyday encounters. ". . . when they realized the low esteem in which Buddhism was held by the literati and saw the lifestyle and ignorance of some of the Buddhist monks, they adopted at the urging of some of their literati friends, the attire and lifestyle of the literati." See, Joseph Sebes, S.J., "The Precursors of Ricci," in Ronan and Oh, op.cit., pp. 19–61, p.40.

26. Benjamin Elman, *From Philosophy to Philology: Intellectual and Social Aspects of Change in Late Imperial China* (Cambridge, MA: Harvard University Press, 1984), pp. 47, 62–63, 76.

27. John W. Witek, S.J., "Understanding the Chinese: A Comparison of Matteo Ricci and the French Jesuit Mathematicians Sent by Louis XIV," in Ronan and Oh, pp. 62–102.

28. Theodore N. Foss, "A Western Interpretation of China: Jesuit Cartography," in Ronan and Oh, pp. 209–251. See p.223 for the Kangxi Emperor and the Great Wall.

29. Arthur Waldron, *The Great Wall of China: From History to Myth* (Cambridge: Cam-bridge University Press, 1990).

30. Benedict Anderson, *Imagined Communities* (London: Verso Books, 1993), offers a stimulating critique of nationalism that incorporates the spatial and temporal implica-tions of nationalism.

31. To my knowledge, Partha Chatterjee, in his analyses of Indian nationalism, has pro-vided the most astute analyses of the problems presented by Orientalism to national con-sciousness. See, *Nationalist Thought and the Colonial World* (Minneapolis: University of Minnesota Press, 1993), and *The Nation and Its Fragments: Colonial and Postcolonial His-tories* (Princeton: Princeton University Press, 1993).

32. The use of these various traits in representations of China is so commonplace that I will not attempt citation; some of the interpretive trends discussed below may serve as illustrations.

33. Jiang Tingfu, *Zhongguo jindaishi dagang* (Outline of Modern Chinese History) (Taipei: Jingsheng wenwu gongying gongsi, 1968), pp.4–5.

34. For the relationship between Jiang and Fairbank, see, John King Fairbank, *Chinabound: A Fifty Year Memoir* (New York: Harper and Row Publishers, 1982), pp.85–90, and, Paul M. Evans, *John King Fairbank and the American Understanding of Mod-ern China* (New York: Basil Blackwell, 1988), pp. 50–51. What Jiang said in a lecture in England of returned students like himself is revealing: ". . . we read foreign books and are engrossed in things in which the people have no interest . . . [We can be] eloquent in the class room, in the Press in Shanghai and Beiping, even come to Chatham House and make you think we are intelligent, and yet we cannot make ourselves understood to a village crowd in China, far less make ourselves accepted as leaders of the peasants" (Fairbank, p.90). The statement may distinguish the Chinese intellectual from the foreign, even when they hold similar views.

35. See, for an example, Stewart R. Clegg and S. Gordon Redding (eds), *Capitalism in Contrasting Cultures* (Berlin: Walter de Gruyter, 1990).

36. See, Harumi Befu (ed), *Cultural Nationalism in East Asia* (Berkeley: The Center for Chinese Studies, 1993), and, Kosaku Yoshino, *Cultural Nationalism in Contemporary Japan: A Sociological Inquiry* (London and New York: Routledge, 1992).

37. Arif Dirlik, "Confucius in the Borderlands: Global Capitalism and the Reinvention of Confucianism," *boundary 2*, November (1995):29–73.

38. Hung-chao Tai(ed), *Confucianism and Economic Development: An Oriental Alternative?* (Washington, D.C. : The Washington Institute Press, 1989), p.3. Ironically, Tai agrees with Said's thesis on Orientalism, and sees the "Oriental alternative" of Confucianism as a means to counter Eurocentric Orientalism. Not all those who write of Confucianism engage in this kind of reductionism. An example is Yu Ying-shih's *Zhongguo jinshi zongjiao lunli yu shangren jieji* (Modern Chinese Religious Ethic and the Merchant Class) (Taipei: Lianjing chuban shiye gongsi, 1987). While Yu subscribes to Weberian ideas of modernization, he offers a more nuanced analysis of Confucianism, which accounts both for change in Confucianism over time, and for its different appropriation by different classes, in this case the merchants.

39. (New York: Oxford University Press, 1994), introduction. See also her, "Occidentalism as Counterdiscourse: 'He Shang' in Post-Mao China," *Critical Inquiry*, 18 (Summer 1992):686–712.

40. Yang Congrong, op.cit. I may take not here of an important observation that Yang makes: "If we take the situation in Taiwan as a concrete example, it is very difficult in everyday life now to distinguish clearly what is typically Chinese culture from what is typically Western culture; but a clear distinction between Chinese and Western cultures seems to persist in people's minds. If they cannot refer something to a past that is no longer retrievable, then they insist on finding it in an inexhaustible West with an indistinct visage"(p.50). Yang describes the role the Government and the tourist industry have played in the production of "Chinese culture," much to the denial of the complexities of the living culture of the present. A similar argument is offered by Allen Chun, "The Culture Industry as National Enterprise: The Politics of Heritage in Contemporary Taiwan," *Culture and Policy*, vol.6, no.1(1994):69–89. Both authors cite *Sinorama* magazine, cited above in connection with Sinology, as one of the major organs of such "cultural production."

41. The emergence of Eurocentrism, as an autonomous, self-contained development from ancient Greece to modern EuroAmerica, has been examined incisively by Samir Amin, *Eurocentrism* (New York: Monthly Review Press, 1989), and, Martin Bernal, *Black Athena: The AfroAsiatic Roots of Classical Civilization, Vol. I: The Fabrication of Ancient Greece, 1785–1985* (New Brunswick, N.J.: Rutgers University Press, 1987).

42. Blaut, op.cit., describes this as "the myth of emptiness"(p.15), which included the absence of working over the environment in European ways; in other words, living in harmony with nature.

43. Mary Louis Pratt, *Imperial Eyes: Travel Writing and Transculturation* (London and New York: Routledge, 1992), p.6.

44. Ibid.

45. This is very much the case with Tu Wei-ming's advocacy of a "Cultural China." See, "Cultural China," op.cit., p.2.

46. Charles Hampden-Turner and Alfons Trompenaars, *The Seven Cultures of Capitalism: Value Systems for Creating Wealth in the United States, Japan, Germany, France, Britain, Sweden and the Netherlands* (New York: Doubleday, 1993). For an interesting take on this problem from an entirely different perspective, see, J.G.A. Pocock, "Deconstructing Europe," *History of European Ideas,* Vol. 18 no. 3 (1994):329–345.

47. I have addressed this question of "contact zones," or "borderlands," extensively in Arif Dirlik, *After the Revolution: Waking to Global Capitalism* (Hanover, N. H.: University Press of New England for Wesleyan University Press, 1994). The notion of "borderlands" is quite pervasive in our day in all manner of cultural criticisms.

48. Chatterjee, *Nationalist Thought and the Colonial World*, p.38.

49. *In Theory: Classes, Nations, Literatures* (London: Verso Books, 1992), especially Chapter 5.

50. Needless to say, this is not accepted universally, and has produced predictions of new kinds of conflict in the world. The foremost example, by an influential U.S. political scientist, may be Samuel P. Huntington, "The Clash of Civilizations?" *Foreign Affairs,* 72.3 (Summer 1993):22–49. An example of a history-less Asia that is nevertheless modern is to be found in *Asian Power and Politics: The Cultural Dimensions of Authority*, by the distinguished political scientist and China specialist, Lucian W. Pye, with Mary W. Pye (Cambridge, MA: Harvard University Press, 1985). Pye argues for differences among Asian societies, but differences on a common site marked by a culture of "paternalism and dependency." Pye's argument is echoed by many an advocate of Confucianism. I noted Yu Ying-shih's study of Chinese merchants above as an example of a different, more historical, approach to the problem of Confucianism and capitalism. It is necessary, in my opinion, to distinguish economic change from capitalist modernization. That Chinese society at different points had flourishing economic change does not imply that it was, therefore, headed for capitalism; just as the absence of capitalism does not imply that it was, therefore, stagnating. Such conclusions follow only from a hindsight application of the teleology of capitalism, as in the "sprouts of capitalism" idea in Chinese Marxist historiography.

51. "Orientalism Reconsidered," p.228.

52. Said himself has recognized these possibilities. See, "Orientalism Reconsidered," p. 216.

6

There Is More in the Rim than Meets the Eye: Thoughts on the "Pacific Idea"

A few years back, a discussion of the current economic status of Pacific islands in *The Economist* began with the line, referring to the Pacific, that "it is not just a piece of geography, it is an idea."[1] Ideas depend on who thinks them, in what context and to what purpose. I reflect below on two different ways of thinking the Pacific, one from within and the other from without, that in their contradictoriness have much to tell us about the historical formation of the Pacific. They are also relevant, I will suggest, to thinking the global future both within and without the Pacific, because their very contradictoriness raises questions concerning the ways in which we think about the past and the present.

The Pacific Rim: EuroAmerican and Asian

The Pacific occupies the prominent place that it does in our consciousness today not because of what is happening within the Pacific, but because of developments on what has come to be called the Pacific Rim. The Rim, especially on the Asian side, has come to serve not only as a frontier of development, but provides a new paradigm for global economic organization and change. But the Rim is ultimately external to the Pacific; at various locations along it are arraigned economic, political and military forces that gaze across an empty Pacific at imagined antagonists somewhere else on the Rim. The Rim in effect erases the spaces within it from which it derives its name. The *Economist* article cited above recognizes this curious situation when it remarks that:

> It is clear that this Pacific does not include Japan or Hong Kong or the west coast of America. These are the rich places in what has come to be called the Pacific Rim, which are convinced they are going to become even richer in the coming "Pacific Century." Neither are Australia and New Zealand part of this Pacific. They are Pacific powers, as are America and the Soviet Union, no-nonsense places concerned with areas of influence and such-like.

> The real Pacific, the proper Pacific, the one in the world's dream-mind, is made up
> of the small Pacific islands, mostly in the South Seas. . . . [Their] reality is that they
> are poor.[2]

Geography tells us little about these spaces; on the contrary, the spaces of
wealth and power inscribe the boundaries of the Pacific. But the "poor" empty
space within the Rim, in its very emptiness, has a part to play as the source of
utopian longings that belies its insignificance in terms of wealth and power:

> The Pacific Idea is important for the mental well-being of the world. There is another
> possibility, it insists. The globe has not become the same all over. The Pacific idea
> stands for a belief in the survival of innocence; the Pacific is not really innocent, but
> something primal lingers there, deeply attractive to the inhabitants of an increasingly
> uniform industrial society that has come to seem, somehow, rather disappointing.[3]

Herein are the two contradictory ideas generated by the Pacific, that have been
integral to the history and, therefore, the formation of the region: the Pacific as a
frontier of capitalist development, and the Pacific as an escape from the ravages
of capitalism. Contradictory as they are, the two ideas are constituent of a single
Pacific discourse; in either case, the Pacific is internalized as a problem in
EuroAmerican well-being.[4]

What is absent from this discourse are the people of the Pacific. What happens to
the discourse when we bring their voices in? Those voices, I would like to suggest
below, are essential to any construction of a Pacific discourse that seeks to break
with the hegemony of the past—actual EuroAmerican hegemony over the people
of the Pacific, and an ideological hegemony of the past over the present in the consciousness of EuroAmericans themselves. In spite of conscious well-intentioned
efforts on the part of many to break with past hegemonies, the latter persists in
Pacific Rim discourse, which is the most recent expression of EuroAmerican hegemony over the Pacific (now joined, however, by Pacific-Asian discourses which are
integral to the discourse of the Rim). Before they may aspire to liberating the Pacific
from hegemony, I will argue, those on the Rim need as a first step to liberate themselves from the hegemony of a past consciousness—for which they may well need
the help of the Pacific peoples, and their conceptions of themselves and of the
world. Before I turn to that question, a few words first about the Pacific discourse
which continues to dominate contemporary consciousness of the Pacific.

The Pacific and EuroAmerican Vision

I reverse the terms in the title of Bernard Smith's seminal work with a purpose; to
draw attention to the ways in which the Pacific altered EuroAmerican ways of seeing the world, which that work documents.[5] Put bluntly, the encounter with the
Pacific was to culminate in an expansion of the EuroAmerican vision of the world
both spatially and temporally. Shortly after the conclusion of Captain James

Cook's third (and to him, fatal) voyage that was to delineate the boundaries of the Pacific as we know it, the Reverend Thomas Haweis, a founder of the London Missionary Society, observed in a sermon:

> A new world hath lately opened to our view, call it Island or Continent, that exceeds Europe in size: New Holland; and now become the receptacles of our outcasts of society—New Zealand, and the innumerable islands, which spot the bosom of the Pacific Ocean, on each side of the Line, from Endeavor Straits to the Coasts of America, many of them full of inhabitants—occupying lands, which seem to generalize the fabled Gardens of the Hesperides—where the fragrant groves, which cover them from the sultry beams of day, afford them food and clothing; whilst the sea offers continual plenty of its inexhaustible stores; and the day passes in ease and affluence, and the night in music and dancing.[6]

The "second new world" revealed by Cook's voyages to a Europe in the midst of a "Pacific Craze" not only expanded the known world by half, but brought into the European consciousness wonders hitherto unknown in the form of new flora and fauna, and new men, to "enlarge the sphere of contemplation"—as John Locke had said with reference to the "first new world."

A contemporary French scholar wrote that for the "philosophical traveller," scrutinizing the peoples of the Pacific showed the way "to the first periods of our own history . . . sailing to the ends of the earth, is in fact travelling in time; he is exploring the past; every step he makes is the passage of an age. Those unknown islands that he reaches are for him the passage of human society."[7] The illusion of panoptical vision engendered by the Pacific was to foster an even more illusory temporal vision that claimed comprehensive historical hindsight. In the guise of noble savage or brutal cannibal both, the Pacific Islanders exemplified even more thoroughly than the indigenous peoples of the Americas the primitivism that Europeans had long left behind. The construction of the primitive was part of the very process of constructing civilized Europe. Writing of European responses to the Americas, J.H. Elliott observes that, "if progress now became a conceivable possibility, this was partly on account of the discoveries themselves . . . the discovery of the New World . . . strengthened the Christian providentialist interpretation of history as a progressive movement which would culminate in the evangelization of all mankind, it equally strengthened the more purely secular interpretation of history as a progressive movement which would culminate in the civilization of all mankind."[8]

Civilization was not necessarily an unqualified blessing and, in the middle of the eighteenth century, the "noble savage" of the Pacific served as the object of nostalgia for those who would escape its ravages. As the faith in European civilization took root, demonstrated by the very global conquest of Europeans, what came to the fore was the image of the uncouth savage, in need of Europeans' civilizing mission, chiefly through the agency of Christianity. Reverend Haweis, having described the enchanted "state of nature" in which the Islanders lived, proceeded immediately to disenchant it by concluding that "amidst these enchanting scenes, savage nature still feasts on the flesh of its prisoners—appeases its Gods with human sacrifices—whole societies of men and women live promiscuously, and murder every infant born amongst them." And as in the Americas earlier, it was unclear whether these savages were genuinely human; civilizing them also implied, therefore, their humanization—even if it meant depriving them of their idyllic existence. Charles de Brosses, the author of the first important and influential work on Pacific voyages in the middle of the eighteenth century, justified the colonization of the Pacific for, while colonization might deprive them of their innocence, it would bring them much benefit, and not just materially: "We must also remember how much they would profit, by adopting our ideas of a regular and well-ordered society; their minds would be opened, and formed, their savage manners softened: In short, those nations would become men, who have just now nothing human but their figure."[9]

The competing notions of the Pacific as idyllic Eden and empty savage land waiting for civilization emerged simultaneously. By the end of the eighteenth century, the latter had won over the former. The image of a Pacific Paradise would survive the progressive physical and cultural destruction of the Pacific over the next century in the nostalgic memories of EuroAmericans; ironically, for part of the destruction entailed the assimilation by the islanders of the EuroAmerican image of them as uncouth primitives.

As Bernard Smith and others have documented, the Pacific was to have a lasting impact on European thinking—from new orientations in the arts to the emergence of the Pacific as a great "laboratory of nature." Perhaps the most significant product of the latter would be the the theories of natural and social evolution. If the evidence of the Pacific played a major part in Charles Darwin's formulation of the theory of evolution, the Pacific peoples would be among the first victims of the colonialism which the theory came to justify. The expansion of EuroAmerican spatial and temporal consciousness by the Pacific was in the end an integral part of the EuroAmerican colonization of the world, of which it was at once a product and an agent.[10]

While colonialism has not disappeared entirely, especially where indigenous peoples are concerned, it is only rarely in our day that we might find a defense of colonialism as a beneficent idea. Rather, since World War II, the diffusion of civilization from EuroAmerica has been transmuted to the idea of modernization. As with earlier notions of civilization, it is still a social order empowered by capitalism that defines modernity, although it is now a capitalism far in advance of its origins in early modern Europe, and no longer confined to Europe or the Americas. Indeed, it is their success with capitalist development that has brought societies of the Pacific Rim to the forefront of our consciousness. Similarly, the inability to assimilate the capitalist order serves as a marker of "backwardness" within the Rim. That capitalist modernity does not serve merely as a measure of welfare, but also of civilization, is implicit in the perverse judgment that *The*

Economist passes on the Pacific Islanders, which differs from the judgments of early Modern Europeans on the islands only in its vocabulary:

> If the Pacific Rim countries do prosper as they expect, investment, large or small, should not be a problem. The main problem may be the islanders themselves. The following paragraphs may offend them. . . . The Pacific islanders have to change their ways. They suffer from, to use a polite word, inertia. The basic needs of life are available with minimum effort. Nobody need go hungry. There are fish in the lagoon and almost anything grows in the climate of perpetual summer. The biggest effort may be deciding what to do with the day. Those who believe that life must offer more find their ambitions stifled by the confines of a small island . . . in a place with a population the size of a small European town, there is not much scope for a clever man.[11]

It is a tribute to the power of the ideology of capitalist modernity that what might appear otherwise as an occasion for celebration appears here as a lack on the part of the islanders. After two centuries of ecological, social and cultural destruction, it may be miraculous that the Pacific islands may still provide the good life. But it is neither human welfare, nor the good life, that is the measure of development; rather, it is the "scope for the ambitious." The paradise may still be a paradise, but only for those suffering from "inertia." They may have full bellies, but they are not civilized. The premises that shape this way of thinking the Pacific still belong in the discourse that was produced by the earlier contact with the Pacific. One solution The *Economist* offers to the dilemma of the Pacific Islanders is tourism; to sell paradise, which will bring to the islands many jobs as restaurant waiters and hotel chambermaids. The other is to import "Indians and Chinese, those bustling, adaptable journeymen of the Pacific, who will bring vitality to the islands." It does not occur to the writer that there may be still another way: to restore a way of life that places human welfare and happiness ahead of development.

With this in mind, let me turn to what some Pacific Islanders may have to say about their own aspirations.

Glimpses from the Inside

If for EuroAmericans the Pacific provided the materials for an expansion and enrichment of their world views, the consequences of the interaction for the Islanders was an impoverishment and contraction (if not the extinction) of the world they had known before European arrival. There, too, cultural restriction and impoverishment were intimately related to material circumstances of existence; the disenchantment of nature went hand-in-hand with the expropriation of material resources in land and sea, which in their case had shaped not only spatial location but the very notions of temporality.

In his comparative examination of Native-White relations in Australia, New Guinea and North America, Wilbur Jacobs wrote:

In a sense, the real test of survival was possession of the land. Next to outright exter-
mination the best technique for destroying natives was dispossessing them of their
land. Land for the aborigines was all important because it was a spiritual ingredient
of their culture; it determined their social groupings and status; and, finally, it was
the source of their livelihood. Thus, if there is a real test for the survival of a native
people it is found in the answer to the question: how much of their land have they
retained after the alien invasion?[12]

Not much, is the evident answer, and when natives retained land, it was totally
reconfigured in settlements that broke with the past spatially, also reconfiguring
social relations and cultural orientations. Ward Churchill writes that for the
American Indian, even "engineering was and is permissible, but only insofar as
it does not permanently alter the earth itself."[13] The White attitude toward the
land was the opposite: if land was not "permanently altered" by human activity,
it was empty land. Thus, White settlers in New Zealand viewed Maori use of the
land to be "undirected and, at worst, wasteful to the point of disallowing indigenous claims to ownership." One English official, himself relatively sympathetic
to the Maori, nevertheless could not refrain from carrying "the imagination to
another century—when this now desert country will no doubt be peopled—
when the plains will be grazed by numerous flocks of sheep, and the streams,
now flowing idly through remote valleys, will be compelled to perform their
share of labour in manufacturing of wool."[14] Maori notions of ownership, based
on a complex interplay of kinship, residence and utilization, were perceived by
the British to lie at the root of this wastefulness, which also accounted for their
"backwardness." Dispossessing them of their land, by substituting private property relations for native notions of ownership, was a benign act of civilization
which would launch the Maori on the way to progress. A report on land division
in 1862 stated that:

> Communism in land is admitted to be the great obstacle to the social and material
> advancement of the Maori people. It is very certain that, under the present system of
> land tenure, the Natives will never be induced to give up their low Maori habits and
> adapt themselves to the requirements of a superior civilization . . . nothing would
> tend to do more to call forth their industrial energies and to promote a desire for
> worldly improvement than the possession, in severalty, of an exclusive title to a piece
> of land, *however small in extent.*[15]

The dispossession of the natives of their land, in remapping their world, would
transform radically their social world, as well as the spatial and temporal configuration of their spirituality, which was bound up with the land and, for the Pacific
peoples, the sea as well. From two ends of the Pacific, we have examples of the contraction of native worlds, which eloquently express the tragic disenchantment of
nature that accompanied their forced entry into the world of progress.

The Australian aborigines believed that at the origins of creation in the Dreamtime, the world had been sung into existence by ancient ancestors, "who had wan-

dered over the continent . . . singing out the name of everything that crossed their path—birds, animals, plants, rocks, waterholes—and so singing the world into existence."[16] The songs then became the legacies of the clans that claimed descent from the various ancestors. The Songlines served as maps as well as direction-finders: "providing you knew the song, you could always find your way across country."[17] It was the song that also served as the basis for property:

> Before the whites came . . . no one in Australia was landless, since everyone inherited, as his or her private property, a stretch of the Ancestor's song and the stretch of country over which the song passed. A man's verses were his title deeds to territory. He could lend them to others. He could borrow other verses in return. The one thing he couldn't do was sell or get rid of them.[18]

The songs did not just map out space, but also contained time. "Aboriginals could not believe the country existed until they could see and sing it." The world must be called into existence again and again through the song. And each time the song was sung, the Dreamtime of the Ancestors was recalled as well.[19] The past and the present were part of the same song, as creation was immanent within it.

At another end of the Pacific, the native peoples sang their way through the seas. In her account, *The Daughters of Copper Woman*, Anne Cameron recalls the words of her grandmother:

> Everythin' we ever knew about the movement of the sea was preserved in the verses of a song. For thousands of years we went where we wanted and came home safe, because of the song. On clear nights we had the stars to guide us, and in the fog we had the streams and creeks of the sea, the streams and creeks that flow into and become Klin Otto. . . . There was a song for goin' to China and a song for goin' to Japan, a song for the big island and a song for the smaller one. All she had to know was the song and she knew where she was. To get back, she just sang the song in reverse.[20]

Here, too, the songs were the legacies of the families who inherited them from their lineages.

"The sickness killed off the songs," Cameron's grandmother tells her, recounting the fate of the tribe with the arrival of the white people, "so many people died. So many songs and stories and sea routes and histories."[21] As the lineages died out, so did the songs, and with them were gone the spaces that the songs had marked—and the temporalities contained within the songs.

The Songlines, and the consequences of their extinction or transformation (as with railroads in Australia), stand as poetic metaphors for the ways in which Pacific spatialities and temporalities were transformed in the course of the invasion of the Pacific by the technologies, property relations, and moral assumptions of a new civilization of progress. In Hawaii, where the great land redistribution of 1848 created private property relations, and led to a large scale transfer of land from native Hawaiians to the white settlers, the result for the Hawaiians was "cultural debasement, economic destitution, and a third-rate status in their own homeland."[22] In this case, Christian missionaries played a central role both in the institution of new property relations, and the direct "deculturation" of the native population. In the words of Haunani-Kay Trask,

> Hymns that told of a suffering Jesus and a sinful humanity replaced chants of the origins of the universe, the evolution of life forms, and the genealogy of an entire people. No longer was an ancient history recited, no longer were new chants composed. A repressive sexual morality reduced the fecund, sensual imagery of the Hawaiians to concepts of evil and filth. For example, where Hawaiians once eroticized their environment with sexual names, they were, under Christian influence, to rename their natural world, as their children, with safe English language referents. . . . Native history and native culture were all but lost along the way.[23]

The respatialization that is implicit in the names, not to speak of the new property relations, served also to distance the Hawaiian present from the Hawaiian past which, when not "forgotten" actively, lived on as a cause for embarrassment. The British sociologist Peter Worsley, writing of the conceptions of time of hunting and gathering peoples, has observed that they were not "dedicated to the accumulation of material wealth. Hence their conception of time was not lineal. If we deny them any importance in history, they denied history as a category of the understanding."[24] The peoples of the Pacific, as they were compelled into history, were also historicized as primitives. As their spaces were renamed to render them into foreigners in their land, so was their temporality transformed from mythic to linear time; in many cases beginning with their entry into "civilization" with their Christianization. The distinguished Samoan writer Albert Wendt observes:

> I said earlier that a society is what it remembers, we are what we remember.
> If we look at written Pacific history, we find that most of it is the work of papalagi/outsiders, and that most of it is based on records kept by papalagi explorers/missionaries/clerks/etc. So we can say that that history is a papalagi history of themselves and their activities in our region; it is an embodiment of their memories/perceptions/and interpretations of the Pacific. And when we teach that history in our schools we are transmitting their memories to our children, and consequently reordering our children's memories.[25]

Adds Malama Meleisea, "The division of time into Before Christ (B.C.) and the Year of Our Lord (A.D.) began for us in 1830 with the arrival of the Gospel. We divide our history into the *pouliuli*, the time of darkness, and the *malamalama*, the time of enlightenment."[26]

Given the colonial erasure of indigenous memory, "re-learning" (in Trask's terminology) or "singing into existence" native spatiality and temporality is an utmost concern for Pacific peoples in search of liberation from colonialism and its legacy—which may account for the prominence of literature and poetry in Pacific writing; or, to put it more accurately perhaps, for the denial by prominent

Pacific writers such as Epeli Hau'ofa, Haunani-Kay Trask or Albert Wendt of conventional distinctions between history, poetry or politics. This is not to suggest that struggles in the Pacific are merely literary struggles; "the struggle for the land" is of crucial significance where colonial rule persists, as in Hawaii. But at bottom the struggle in a broader sense is a struggle against ideological hegemony, to rescue from colonial erasure concepts of space and time that may enable the formulation of alternatives to modes of development which from indigenous perspectives are little more than modes of subjugation—of native lands, as well as of native sensibilities.

I would like to look briefly here at a recent essay by Epeli Hau'ofa which is exemplary of these themes, especially the theme of the recapturing of space as a prelude to recapturing an indigenous identity in development. What makes this piece doubly interesting is that Hau'ofa, an anthropologist by training, is a distinguished writer of fiction, and Head of the School of Social and Economic Development at the University of the South Pacific in Fiji. The combination is an unlikely one, and the very poetry of Hau'ofa's writing, aside from its content, offers an indigenous paradigm of Pacific development that contrasts sharply with the prosaic greed that empowers the Pacific Rim discourse of global capital.

Hau'ofa's essay, entitled "OUR SEA OF ISLANDS," sets out to refute the notion of the "smallness" of the Pacific islands, which implies that "even if we improved our approaches to production . . . the absolute size of our islands would still impose such severe limitations that we would be defeated in the end."[27] It was his concerns as a teacher, Hau'ofa tells the reader, that first led him to question this idea: "What kind of teaching is it to stand in front of young people from your region, people you claim as your own, who have come to the university with high hopes for the future, and to tell them that their countries are hopeless? Is this not what neocolonialism is all about? To make people believe that they have no choice but to depend?"[28] Colonial hegemony is very much on Hau'ofa's mind when he states that "such views, which are often derogatory and belittling, are integral to most relationships of dominance and subordination, wherein superiors behave in ways or say things that are accepted by their inferiors who, in turn, behave in ways that serve to perpetuate the relationship."[29]

This head of a school of development acknowledges without apology that the inspiration for the essay came to him during a trip to Hawaii, where he witnessed that "under the aegis of Pele, and before my very eyes, the Big Island was growing, rising from the depths of a mighty sea." "The world of Oceania is not small," he concluded, "it is huge and growing bigger every day."[30] The idea of smallness was created by Europeans and Americans "who drew imaginary lines across the sea, making the colonial boundaries that, for the first time, confined ocean peoples to tiny spaces." But, Hau'ofa states,

> if we look at the myths, legends and oral traditions, and the cosmologies of the peoples of Oceania, it will become evident that they did not conceive of their world in such microscopic proportions. Their universe comprised not only land surfaces, but

the surrounding ocean as far as they could traverse and exploit it, the underworld with its fire-controlling and earth-shaking denizens, and the heavens above with their hierarchies of powerful gods and named stars and constellations that people could count on to guide their ways across the seas. They thought big and recounted their deeds in epic proportions. . . . Islanders today still relish exaggerating things out of all proportions. Smallness is a state of mind.[31]

"There is a gulf of difference," Hau'ofa continues, "between viewing the Pacific as 'islands in a far sea' and as 'a sea of islands." The difference, we might add, is the difference between living with the hegemony of a colonial past, and a reassertion of Pacific identity in search of new alternatives for the present and the future. He concludes:

> Oceania is vast, Oceania is expanding, Oceania is hospitable and generous, Oceania is humanity rising from the depths of brine and regions of fire deeper still, Oceania is us. We are the sea, we are the ocean, we must wake up to this ancient truth and together use it to overturn all hegemonic views that aim ultimately to confine us again, physically and psychologically, in the tiny spaces which we have resisted accepting as our sole appointed place, and from which we have recently liberated ourselves. We must not allow anyone to belittle us again, and take away our freedom.[32]

Indigenous Visions/Pacific Rim Discourse

The hegemony that Hau'ofa seeks "to overturn" is the hegemony of Pacific Rim discourse. This discourse is heir to two centuries of domination of the Pacific by powers from the Rim, or outside of it, that has been accompanied ideologically by the erasure of the subjectivities of Pacific peoples, and the denial to them of a place in modernity. In our day, Pacific Rim discourse articulates the location on the Rim of new frontiers of capital that dynamize capitalism globally, and revitalize a teleology of capitalist modernity. This teleology continues to marginalize those who do not live up to its expectations; among those so marginalized, as *The Economist* article above exemplifies, are the people of the Pacific.

To recognize the voices of Pacific peoples, conversely, has a significance that is greater than rescuing them from historical oblivion, or recognizing that they have experienced modernity not as progress but as domination and cultural extinction. It is to recognize also the challenge to capitalist modernity that is imbedded in their historical experience and, even more importantly, in their efforts to recapture a way of life that presupposes alternative organization of social relationships, and an alternative relationship to nature. It is, in other words, to reconceive modernity so as to allow for alternatives to capitalist modernity, of which indigenous visions are integral premises. "The Pacific Way," which appears in Pacific Rim discourse as an alternative within capitalism, appears in this other perspective as a means to overcome capitalist modernity to serve as a guide in a global search for alternatives to capitalism.[33]

I have suggested in a recent essay that, with the passing of the idea of the Third World as a critique of capitalism, indigenous visions now remain as a source of critique, as well as new conceptualizations of alternative modernities.[34] Indigenous visions are significant in this regard for a variety of reasons. Chief among them is the challenge in the indigenous vision to a fetishism of development as a goal in itself, without consideration of what development may imply in terms of human welfare, social relations and relations to the natural environment. In this sense, the indigenous vision stands in criticism both of capitalist and socialist approaches to the question of modernity. But the indigenous vision is significant in another sense: in its challenge to our ways of thinking about the world. Hegemonic discourses, in both capitalist and socialist approaches to development, are universalizing discourses, that prescribe identical futures for people around the world universally. Indigenous discourses are of necessity local in orientation, and resist hegemonic universalisms that rest epistemologically on the objectification of the world.[35]

Pacific peoples' visions occupy a particularly important place in the contemporary critique of capitalist teleology because Pacific Rim discourse has emerged as the most recent location for a fetishized developmentalism (recall *The Economist* article, and the priority it gives to the ambitious over human welfare). As is the case with all indigenous visions, however, the use of Pacific indigenous visions in the critique of capitalism presents problems of a profoundly political nature. These problems pertain to the relationship between the aspirations of Pacific peoples, and a critique of capitalist modernity in general; or, more concretely, the relationship between Pacific peoples speaking for themselves, and those outside such as the present author, who find in Pacific visions sources for the critique of problems of a global nature, which may or may not be of relevance to the former.

In a recent article, the Pacific historian Klaus Neumann has offered a cogent and sensitive account of such problems where they relate to "first contact" between Pacific Islanders and EuroAmericans. Neumann focuses on the "politics of historical representation"; in other words, who represents whom, and how. Neumann points out correctly that even those non-indigenous historians writing sympathetically about indigenous peoples' experiences may be complicitous in perpetuating a hegemonic relationship because of the "political economics of academic knowledge production." The very location of non-indigenous academic historians in First World institutions implies that they are speaking about the powerless from their own positions of power, assuming the prerogative of representing the powerless, which means that their discourses are shaped by First World concerns, rather than concerns of the indigenous peoples themselves. For the most part, moreover, non-indigenous historians, by the very requirements of their location, are subject to "the myths of a historiographical practice that pretends that history is merely an account of the past and that past and present do

not and must not intrude upon each other."[36] This latter is obviously worlds apart
from the historiographical practices of indigenous peoples, which are immediately political to the extent that they challenge hegemonic conceptions of their
pasts, and profoundly political in asserting different possibilities of conceptualiz-
ing the past against the objectivist historiography of which Neumann speaks. But
they, too, face a dilemma. Indigenous intellectuals, like other colonial or postcolonial intellectuals, themselves must abide by the assumptions of a hegemonic
historiographical practice—or face marginalization, since they have few spaces of
their own from which to voice alternative epistemologies. To be acceptable as
respectable historians or academics, they must continue to represent themselves
in epistemologies presupposed by the hegemonic culture surrounding them. In
Hau'ofa's satire, "The Glorious Pacific Way," a successful player in cultural politics
advises a would-be rebel that "in dealing with foreigners," who control the funds
for cultural work, one should "never appear too smart; it's better that you look
humble and half-primitive, especially while you are learning the ropes. And try to
take off six stone. It's necessary that we're seen to be starved and needy. The reason why Tiko gets very little aid money is that our people are too fat and jolly."[37]
Hau'ofa, as head of a school of development, may get away with his utopian
visions of a Pacific because of his reputation as a writer, which foregrounds the
poetry of his utopia rather than its developmental relevance. It may be for the
same reason that indigenous writers have on the whole chosen "fiction" over "history" in their self-representations.[38]

In addition to the question of "who," the problem of representation also
involves the problem of "how." Again, to cite Neumann: "These days, Papua New
Guineans . . . do not appear overtly interested in being told about the horrors of
colonialism, as such accounts potentially belittle today's descendants of yesterday's victims."[39] Such accounts may be of greater relevance to self-flagellating
non-indigenous historians than to indigenous peoples, seeking to make a life for
themselves in the contemporary world. But I think there is here a deeper issue;
the issue of a modern history for the indigenous peoples. The preoccupation with
the past, either in terms of colonial horrors, or a revival of precolonial social and
cultural formations, may fall into the same ideological trap of an earlier hegemonic history by ignoring the historicity of the indigenous peoples themselves
and, therefore, their contemporaneity. A preoccupation with the past in terms of
the horrors of colonial extinction may not be all that different epistemologically
than the images of timeless paradise imposed on the Pacific by generations of
EuroAmericans. For better or for worse, the indigenous peoples of the present are
not the indigenous peoples of a bygone day; which is a different way of saying
that they are products of a modern historical experience who are internally differentiated, partake of the social, ideological and cultural diversities of the present
and, consequently, hold diverse views of the present, the past and the future.[40]
Epeli Hau'ofa's vision of a "New Oceania" is by no means shared by others in the
islands. And the Pacific Islanders are themselves quite aware of the problems

involved in the reassertion of native identities.[41] Trask, who is an eloquent spokesperson for the revival of native Hawaiian conceptions of nature and society, concedes readily nevertheless that the struggle for Hawaiian sovereignty is a very contemporary struggle, inspired by and similar to the struggles of African-Americans, Africans, and other colonial and indigenous peoples.[42] The point in every case is not to recover a past that is gone, but reasserting its values as the source of new visions for the future against hegemonic conceptions of history that deny all value to native traditions. Unlike the EuroAmerican utopian blueprints that were inspired by a faceless Pacific, the utopian longings expressed in the works of Hau'ofa, Trask and others, are filled with the concreteness and warmth of immediate social and natural relationships.[43] The past in which they find inspiration is a past that has been worked over by a historical experience of modernity, that is animated by the social and political concerns of the present, and points to a future that is not a mere reproduction of itself, but of which it is an integral ingredient.

For a non-indigenous person speaking about the Pacific as a source of a critique of capitalist modernity, or of alternative paradigms of development, therefore, there is the ever-present danger of appropriating Pacific peoples' struggles for liberation and existence for ends that are not theirs. As we have come to recognize in recent decades, this is a danger implicit in all "politics of representation." It seems that, having recognized the problem of hegemony presented by a single discourse in the representations of the world, our generation faces a genuine epistemological dilemma: risk a renewed hegemony by reinventing a common discourse, or resign ourselves to discourses fragmented along ethnicities (that are implicit in the resolution of the problem by so-called "multiculturalism").

It is possible, and perhaps necessary, that ethnicization or indigenization of epistemology is a necessary first step before we can achieve a genuine inter-discursivity, which would seem to be ruled out so long as the structures of hegemony persist that were put in place by centuries of EuroAmerican domination of the world.[44] Only after the formerly colonized and oppressed have recovered their autonomous voices, will it be possible once again to negotiate a common discourse—negotiate not under conditions of an illusory market equality, but under conditions of social and political equality that remain to be achieved. In the meantime, however, there is room for struggle for such equality on many fronts. Where the Pacific is concerned, one such front is that presented by a hegemonic Pacific Rim discourse that subjects us all to the teleology of a Global Capitalism, as it seeks to erase native subjectivities within the Rim. The oppressors are not all on the Rim, just as the oppressed are not only within it. The Pacific itself is one location for oppressions that are global in scope, and in its reification in a contemporary fetishism of development serves in turn to legitimize oppression globally. The ability of Pacific Islanders to chart out autonomous visions for themselves may be contingent on the eradication of the hegemonic discourse of the Rim.

The question for the critical non-indigenous historian is: can we call on these visions in the creation of alternative modernities, without appropriating them, or turning them into contemporary versions of island paradise, in a common struggle to overturn a hegemonic modernity? Maybe, and maybe not. But definitely not, unless we are able to abolish our distinction of what is in the Rim from what is on or without it, for the distinction is increasingly part of an overall mystification of a world in which the motions of capital recognize no boundaries except those that serve it—mainly to divide people from one another by confining them in their little spaces, which rules out all possibility of resistance to those motions, and all possibility of imagining alternative futures except in the most localized ways. The problem of alternative paradigms presently is a problem of how to reconceive the local and the global simultaneously. That calls for new alliances, and new ways of thinking about the world, that is, new languages. The people of the Pacific have long had to learn to speak in languages that were initially not theirs, but are by now indispensable to their existence. The least we can do on the Rim is to recognize the existence of those new languages in the Rim, and in the process modify our ways of speaking about the Pacific. That may be the best we can do for the present, but it seems to me that it alone would represent an enormous step toward a common ground; a common ground contructed not on the basis of uniformity but on the basis of diverse localisms that do not deny but take as their point of departure the common concerns of a globalized world.

Notes

Presented originally as a keynote address at the conference, "Reimagining the Pacific," University of British Columbia, April 24-26, 1995. I would like to thank the organizers (especially John Wilinsky) for the opportunity, and the participants for the reception. Thanks also to Professor Johann Galtung for his comments and support.

1. "The Pacific Idea: There is a better world," *The Economist* (16 March 1991):15–18.

2. Ibid.

3. Ibid.

4. I am using "Pacific discourse" here in a slightly different sense than the "Pacific Rim discourse" suggested by Chris Connery; what is in the Rim is included here to disturb the latter. For "Pacific Rim Discourse, see, Chris Connery, "Pacific Rim Discourse: The U.S. Global Imaginary in the Late Cold War Years," in Rob Wilson and Arif Dirlik (eds), *Asia/Pacific as Space of Cultural Production*, special issue of *boundary 2*, vol. 21, no.1 (Spring 1994):30–56.

5. Bernard Smith, *European Vision and the South Pacific*, second edition (New Haven and London: Yale University Press, 1985). See, also, O.H.K. Spate, *Paradise Found and Lost*, Vol. III of his *The Pacific Since Magellan* (Minneapolis: The University of Minnesota Press,

1988). Spate's volume deals mainly with the eighteenth century, Smith's with the nineteenth.

6. Quoted in Smith, p.144.

7. Joseph-Marie Degerando, quoted in P.J. Marshall and Glyndwr Williams, *The Great Map of Mankind: British Perceptions of the World in the Age of Enlightenment* (London, Melbourne and Toronto: J.M. Dent and Sons Ltd., 1982), p.294.

8. J.H. Elliott, *The Old World and the New, 1492–1650* (Cambridge: Cambridge University Press, 1970), p.52.

9. Quoted in Marshall and Williams, p.262.

10. Bernard Smith argues this at length for the arts and the sciences. See also the essays in Roy MacLeod and Philip F. Rehbock, *Nature in Its Greatest Extent: Western Science in the Pacific* (Honolulu, HI: University of Hawaii Press, 1988).

11. "The Pacific Idea," p.18.

12. Wilbur R. Jacobs, "The Fatal Confrontation: Early Native-White Relations on the Frontiers of Australia, New Guinea, and America—A Comparative Study," *Pacific Historical Review*, 40.3(August 1971):283–309. The most thorough account of the devastation of nature and people in the Pacific is to be found in Alan Moorehead, *The Fatal Impact: The Invasion of the South Pacific, 1767–1840* (New York: Harper and Row Publishers, 1987) (first published, 1966).

13. Ward Churchill, *Struggle for the Land* (Monroe, ME: Common Courage Press, 1993), p.17.

14. Deborah Montgomery, "COMING TO TERMS: Ngai Tahu, Robeson County Indians and the Garden River Band of Ojibwa, 1840–1940: Three Studies of Colonialism in Action," Ph.D. Dissertation, Department of History, Duke University (1993), p.69.

15. Quoted in Ibid., p.128.

16. Bruce Chatwin, *The Songlines* (New York: Penguin Books, 1987), p.2.

17. Ibid., p.13.

18. Ibid., p.57.

19. W.E.H. Stanner, "The Dreaming," in T.A.G. Hungerford(ed), *Australian Signposts* (Melbourne: F.W. Cheshire Publishing Pty. Ltd., 1956), pp. 51–65.

20. Anne Cameron, *Daughters of Copper Woman* (Vancouver, B.C.: Press Gang Publishers, 1985), pp.96–97.

21. Ibid., p. 98.

22. Noel J. Kent, *Hawaii: Islands Under the Influence* (New York: Monthly Review Press, 1983), p.32.

23. Haunani-Kay Trask, "Hawaii: Colonization and Decolonization," in Antony Hooper, et. al. (ed), *Class and Culture in the South Pacific* (Auckland, N.Z. and Suva, Fiji: Centre for Pacific Studies, University of Auckland and Institute of Pacific Studies, University of the South Pacific, 1987):154–174, p.160.

24. Peter Worsley, *The Three Worlds: Culture and Development* (Chicago: The University of Chicago Press, 1984), p.62.

25. Albert Wendt, "Novelists and Historians and the Art of Remembering," in *Class and Culture in the South Pacific*, pp. 78–91.

26. "Ideology in Pacific Studies: A Personal View," in Ibid., pp. 140–152. *Pouliuli*, incidentally, is the title of Wendt's important fiction/history.

27. "OUR SEA OF ISLANDS," in *A New Oceania: Rediscovering Our Sea of Islands*, ed. by Eric Waddell, Vijay Naidu and Epeli Hau'ofa (Suva, Fiji: School of Social and Economic Development, The University of the South Pacific in association with Beake House,

1993):2–16, p.5. The essay is reprinted in Rob Wilson and Arif Dirlik(eds), *Asia/Pacific as Space of Cultural Production* (Durham, N.C.: Duke University Press, 1995).

28. Ibid.

29. Ibid., p.3.

30. Ibid., pp.5–6.

31. Ibid., p.7.

32. Ibid., p.16.

33. This other "Pacific way" has been satirized by Epeli Hau'ofa in his short story, "The Glorious Pacific Way," in Epeli Hau'ofa, *Tales of the Tikongs* (Suva, Fiji: Beake House, University of the South Pacific, 1993): 84–94.

34. Arif Dirlik, "Three Worlds, One or Many: The Reconfiguration of Global Relations Under Contemporary Capitalism," *Nature, Society and Thought*, 7.1(1994):19–42.

35. For a comprehensive collection on indigenous visions of the world, see Roger Moody (ed), *The Indigenous Voice: Visions and Realities* (Utrecht: International Books, 1993), second edition. Indigenous critiques of the fetishism of development, in either bourgeois or Marxist version, are to be found in Ward Churchill (ed), *Marxism and Native Americans* (Boston: South End Press, n.d.). While Pacific writers such as Haunani-Kay Trask use Marxist analysis of the problems of the Pacific, they are wary of socialist solutions to those problems. For critiques of Marxism for ignoring the particularity of Pacific peoples' problems, see the essays by Trask and Meleisea in *Class and Culture in the South Pacific* cited above.

36. Klaus Neumann, "'In Order to Win Their Friendship': Renegotiating First Contact," *The Contamporary Pacific*, Vol.6, no.1(Spring 1994):111–145.

37. Hau'ofa, op.cit., pp.88–89.

38. See the discussion by Albert Wendt, cited above, in *Class and Culture in the South Pacific*. Wendt, needless to say, refuses to recognize to history greater truth value over fiction, which he describes as "an analog of the real world."

39. Neumann, p.122.

40. Neumann's article cites many works, indigenous and otherwise, that address the question of history in the Pacific. Two systematic investigations are noteworthy here: Robert Borofsky, *Making History: Pukapukan and Anthropological Constructions of Knowledge* (Cambridge: Cambridge University Press, 1987), and, Geoffrey M. White, *Identity Through History: Living Stories in a Solomon Islands Society* (Cambridge: Cambridge University Press, 1991). Meleisa's "Ideology in Pacific Studies," cited above, offers an incisive critique, as well an account of the ironies, of stereotyping the aspirations of Pacific peoples.

41. The essays collected in, *A New Oceania: Rediscovering Our Sea of Islands,* offer a wide range of responses to Hau'ofa's ideas. Hau'ofa himself has a complex vision that is anything but escapist. He, in fact, takes his premise as contemporary capitalism in the Pacific, which has enabled Pacific Islanders once again to range over the ocean as in earlier days. Hau'ofa's literary work is distinguished by a skillful use of Island pidgin as its language (which he distinguishes, as the living language of the people, from "World Bank English" that they need to teach their students in the University of the South Pacific in order that they may succeed in the world). For the perspective of literature on this complex problem, see, Mudrooroo Narogin, *Writing from the Fringe: A Study of Modern Aboriginal Literature* (Melbourne: Hyland House, 1990), and Albert Wendt, "Towards a New Oceania," in Guy Amirthanayagam (ed), *Writers in the East-West Encounter: New Cultural Bearings* (London: Macmillan, 1982):202–215.

42. See her essay, "Hawaii: Colonization and Decolonization," cited above, and the collection of her essays, *From A Native Daughter: Colonialism and Sovereignty in Hawaii* (Monroe, ME: Common Courage Press, 1993). It is noteworthy that Trask's first book was a study of feminism, *Eros and Power: The Promise of Feminist Theory* (Philadelphia: University of Pennsylvania Press, 1986), and that her sister Milinani, another distinguished leader in the Hawaiian sovereignty movement, is a lawyer.

43. Trask's passionate poetry that at once mourns and promises is testimonial to her complexity. See the collection, *Light in the Crevice Never Seen* (Corvallis, OR: Calyx Books, 1994).

44. Let me note here a complex problem embedded in my use of "indigenization" and "ethnicization." I do not mean to equate these terms, nor do I view the processes they describe as processes transitional to a new universalism. This is particularly the case with indigenization, which I use both literally (as with indigenous peoples) and metaphorically (in the sense of localization). It is the latter sense that to me is the most intriguing: indigenization as localization cuts across ethnic or indigenous groups (or, stated differently, localizes them in concrete circumstances), pointing to the creation of local languages, that contrast with the universal but also with the separatism that is implicit in the idea of "ethnicization"; in this sense, ethnicization may be conceived of as being transition to indigenization. The distinction between the indigenous and the universal corresponds to what I mean below by the local and the global, interactive, and yet different. It is also in this sense that it is possible to refer to indigenous movements as paradigms for local political movements, which I have suggested in the essay to which I referred above, "Three Worlds or One, or Many."

7

Three Worlds or One, or Many?
The Reconfiguration of Global Relations
Under Contemporary Capitalism

Recent changes in the world situation have called into question concepts such as nationalism, imperialism and the Third World that have been central to the analysis of global relations since World War II. I am interested in this discussion in the question of the Third World concept, which has held a strategic place in this constellation of concepts. The question is, specifically: why does the concept, Third World, persist in academic, journalistic and political discourses when the conditions that produced it have disappeared, and an intellectual sea-change in recent years has brought it under renewed criticism? We have long been aware of the internal incoherence of the concept, and its residual nature. But so long as global divisions were configured by an opposition between capitalism and communism (the First and the Second Worlds), the concept seemed at least to have a referential meaning. With the disappearance of socialist states, the structural conditions that endowed the Third World with meaning also have disappeared. There is at the very least a numerical absurdity to speak of a Third World when there is no longer a Second World. Under the circumstances, can there be any reason other than a failure to face up to a new world situation, intellectual habit or inertia, and even a nostalgia for past configurations of the world, to account for the persistence of the concept?

I approach the question in two stages. I argue, first, that while existing critiques of the concept have revealed fundamental problems in its formulation, they themselves have not offered viable substitutes for it, and have side-stepped important changes in the global situation that have recast the implications of the concept. There are good analytical and political reasons to argue that it may be more problematic to discard the concept than to retain it. For better or worse, the term is still of some utility in invoking locations on a cognitive map of the globe that seem to share common conditions of existence—due not to any inherent identities but to forces that structure global relations. These forces, and the conditions they produce, arguably predated the appearance of the concept itself, and have survived the conditions that produced it. It may not make numerical sense to use the term Third World when there is no longer a Second World, therefore, but it makes some historical sense, which may be a reason that, once it had come into being, the concept Third World could acquire a life of its own, without reference to the conditions that produced it.

Recognition that the concept may represent something more than an ephemeral abstraction, I argue secondly, is enabling of a more radical critique of the concept, that takes into account both recent transformations in global relations, and the way we think about them. I am particularly interested here in the potential of societies encompassed within the Third World concept to serve as autonomous sources of alternative global visions, a question that is integral to the history of the concept, but is ignored in most current critiques. This question is daily forced to the surface of consciousness by a reconfigured global situation; if only in the erasure of the utopian projects once associated with the Third World. To recall the Third is to recover memories of those utopian projects that are essential to imagining radical alternatives to the present. On the other hand, it is necessary also to disassociate those radical alternatives from the Third World which, in its present reconfiguration, may have become an obstacle to the imagination, let alone the realization, of any such radical alternatives.

The Third World in Contemporary Criticism

In his seminal critique of Three Worlds theory, published in 1981, Carl Pletsch offered the following analysis of what he described as "the deep-structure of the Three Worlds concept":

> the division of the planet into three worlds is based on a pair of very abstract and hardly precise binary distinctions. First, the world has been divided into its "traditional" and "modern" parts. Then the modern portion has been subdivided into its "communist" (or "socialist") and "free" parts. These four terms underlying the idea of three worlds may be thought of as an extremely general social semantics. They are terms which derive their meaning from their mutual opposition rather than from any inherent relationship to the things described. . . . The traditional world is more often the Third World or the underdeveloped world, for example. But making explicit the concept of tradition that underlies these other terms permits us to tease out all the other implications contained in the idea of the Third World and locate them in a structural relationship with the implications of the other worlds. The Third World is the world of tradition, culture, religion, irrationality, underdevelopment, overpopulation, political chaos, and so on. The Second World is modern, technologically sophisticated, rational to a degree, but authoritarian (or totalitarian) and repressive, and ultimately inefficient and impoverished by contamination with ideological preconceptions and burdened with an ideologically motivated socialist elite. The First World is purely modern, a haven of science and utilitarian decisionmaking, technological, efficient, democratic, free—in short, a natural society unfettered by religion or ideology.[1]

Pletsch's was the most thoroughgoing critique of the Third World concept, which had come under increasing criticism in the seventies.[2] His critique was valuable, among other reasons, for demonstrating the residual nature of the concept, as well as locating its derivation in a conceptual structure informed by the juxtaposition of tradition and modernity, reconfigured by the Cold War opposition between capitalism and communism. Rather than a representation of an autonomous reality, the concept referred to an imaginary state in development that encompassed a heterogeneous world, identifiable only as a site for the struggle between capitalism and communism, and transitional to one or the other. The whole conceptual structure, finally, was informed by a hegemonic assumption of the ultimate "naturalness" of capitalism, which provided its teleology. This teleology, expressed in the paradigm of modernization, we may note, also suppressed the heterogeneity of the societies encompassed within the First and the Second Worlds.

The decline and fall of socialism in the 1980s on the surface has fulfilled the prediction of the modernization paradigm where the Second World is concerned. Ironically, the much touted victory of capitalism over communism, rather than confirm the teleology of modernization, has brought to the surface globally conjunctures and disjunctures which have ruptured global spatializations along systemic boundaries, drawn according to earlier economic and political criteria, and rendered the future even more problematic. Two criticisms of the Third World concept, informed by antithetical readings of the new world situation, are especially noteworthy.

One is that in postcolonial criticism, which has raised questions about all "foundational" histories. So-called postfoundational history, in its repudiation of essence and structure and simultaneous affirmation of heterogeneity, also repudiates any fixing of the Third World subject and, therefore, of the Third World as a category. As one scholar puts it:

> The rejection of those modes of thinking which configure the Third World in such irreducible essences as religiosity, underdevelopment, poverty, nationhood, [and] non-Westernness . . . unsettle[s] the calm presence that the essentialist categories—east and west, First World and Third World—inhabit in our thought. This disruption makes it possible to treat the Third World as a variety of shifting positions which have been discursively articulated in history. Viewed in this manner, the Orientalist, nationalist, Marxist, and other historiographies become visible as discursive attempts to constitute their objects of knowledge, that is, the Third World. As a result, rather than appearing as a fixed and essential object, the Third World emerges as a series of historical positions, including those that enunciate essentialisms.[3]

What is rejected here, it seems, is not the concept of Third World, but Third World as a fixed category, which also shifts attention from structures and structured conflicts to a politics of "location" and "difference." The Third World as concept in turn appears as a discursive construct, constructed in different ways according to historical contexts and ideological dispositions.

A second criticism has been offered by Aijaz Ahmad in his critique of some of the seminal literature on the Third World. Ahmad advocates the abolition of the Three Worlds division on the grounds that

> we live not in three worlds but one; that this world includes the experience of colonialism and imperialism on both sides of . . . [the] global divide . . . that societies in formations of backward capitalism are as much constituted by the division of classes as societies in the advanced capitalist countries; that socialism is not restricted to something called 'the Second World' but is simply the name of a resistance that saturates the globe today, as capitalism itself does; that the different parts of the capitalist system are to be known not in terms of a binary opposition but as a contradictory unity—with differences, yes, but also with profound overlaps.[4]

Ahmad's repudiation of the Third World stems from a reasoning that is the antithesis of that in postcolonial criticism: the assertion of capitalism as *the* foundational principle that shapes the globe, uniformly if not homogeneously.

In their range, these criticisms of the Third World concept suffice to illustrate the profound analytical and political problems the concept presents. To summarize: (a) the concept is a discursive construct that bears no "inherent" relationship to the reality it represents, but is a product of an ideological structuring of the world into three parts. For Pletsch, the primary responsibility for the construct lies with EuroAmerican social science, with its hegemonic assumptions about the world that are rooted in the teleology of capitalism. In his 1976 essay, Abdel-Malek already had pointed to the complicity of Third World intellectuals in sustaining such hegemony when he wrote that "The 'Third Worldists' . . . the Westernised sector of the intelligentsia and of the political class . . . take on, objectively, the role of 'compradors' on behalf of the different hegemonic powers . . . accepting the vision of themselves as the West's 'Third World.'"[5] Recent criticism has been, if anything, even more insistent on questioning the instrumentality of the Third World concept in nationalism and nationalist historiography, in which Third World status privileges the nation and the national struggle as a means to overcome that status; (b) represented in terms of a residual category, societies included in the Third World have no autonomous existence of their own, and are placed temporally in one or another of available transitions from a backward to an advanced status; (c) the Third World concept erases the heterogeneity of societies so depicted, as well as differences internal to societies. Pletsch's critique was concerned primarily with the former, without any clear specification of where differences are to be located. Postcolonial criticism insists on heterogeneity at both the international and the national levels, bringing a postmodernist sensibility to the question of difference, which ultimately resides in the politics of "location" or "identity." Ahmad's criticism locates the fundamental difference at the level of classes that cut across national boundaries which, ironically, gives primacy to intranational over international differences.

There is little in these propositions that one could quarrel with, especially in our day when, with the structural constraints of the Cold War removed, the Third World would seem to be at war with itself, boundaries between the Three Worlds seem to be abolished daily with the globalization of capital, to be replaced by boundaries within individual societies, and ethnicity has come forward once again to challenge the domination of nation-states. Where class and gender conflicts are concerned, it is more difficult than ever to distinguish the local, the national and the international. Ahmad is certainly right to insist on the primary significance of classes, for with the globalization of capital, it may be possible for the first time to speak of classes that are not just national but global. On the other hand, judging by the localization of political struggles, so are the postcolonial critics who insist on the localization of all categories, and the politics of location. Perhaps most telling is the appearance of "First Worlds" in the capitals of the formerly Second and Third Worlds, and of "Third Worlds" in the capitals of the First.

Two problems immediately stand out, however, that disturb easy compliance in these propositions as they are stated. First, does the recognition of heterogeneity necessitate the repudiation of the existence of structuring forces globally? Conversely, does it suggest a flattening out of global relations, that leaves us even less able to account for global phenomena? Secondly, if the Third World refers to little more than historically conditioned discursive constructs, are all constructs then equally valid? Do we not need to raise the question of the political implications of alternative constructs? For all its contradictions, Ella Shohat has written, "'Third World' usefully evokes structural commonalities of struggles. The invocation of the 'Third World' implies a belief that the shared history of neocolonialism and internal racism form sufficient common ground for alliances among . . . diverse peoples. If one does not believe or envision such commonalities, then indeed the term 'Third World' should be discarded."[6]

The argument based on difference (accompanied by a suspicion of metanarratives and foundational categories) is quite prevalent presently with the popularity of postcolonial criticism. Insistence on heterogeneity is motivated by a critical urge but, unaccompanied by a sense of structural context, culminates in a radical empiricism that undercuts its own call for critical understanding. Pletsch, for example, criticizes the Three Worlds theory because "Only if we can remember that 'the other' is never defined in intrinsic terms, but always in terms of its difference from the observer, will we have the differentiated understanding of the globe's societies." His essay does not offer an alternative analysis (or tell us at what level to understand the term "society"), however, which leaves us with his introductory quotation from deTocqueville that "the Deity does not regard the human race collectively," but "surveys at one glance and severally all the beings of whom mankind is composed; and he discerns in each man the resemblances that assimilate him to all his fellows, and the differences that distinguish him from them."[7] This is not very helpful, because, in its empiricism, it does not even tell us whether we can compare anything beyond the individual, or why we should even stop at the level of the individual human being. Why should the Deity not survey at one glance all the nations in which humankind is organized, and discern in each resemblances and differences that may place them in larger wholes, which is the question pertinent for the issue at hand?

Pletsch's insistence on "intrinsic terms," or the postcolonial preoccupation with "essentialism," on the other hand, focus too exclusively on some approaches to the question of the Third World to the exclusion of others. It is possible to observe that, rather than being inherent in the Third World concept, the association with the concept of some intrinsic or essential quality may have something to do with the scientist and teleological aspirations of social science, including Marxist social science (in search of immanent qualities for the formulation of laws), or with the obliviousness to history of Orientalist and nationalist historiographies. Those approaches associated with what is described broadly as "world-system analysis," for example, approach the question not in terms of essences but in terms of historically changing global relationships. While it may not be free of problems in other ways, world-system analysis could hardly be held accountable in this regard; unless, of course, we are prepared to deny capitalism and nationalism as forces structuring global relations, as is the case with some versions of postcolonial criticism.

Ironically, the insistence on heterogeneity understood without reference to structural context, as in postcolonial criticism, leads also to a homogenization of differences, as if all differences were equally different; in terms both of location and the distribution of power. Different heterogeneities (e.g., differences between genders versus differences between classes), it is possible to suggest, are qualitatively different from one another, and may not be encompassed within the same "politics of difference." Likewise, the recognition of subjectivity to "the Other" does not in fact negate that the self and 'the other' may be placed structurally in very different power positions, which is quite often ignored these days in the application to such situations of the terminology of the market place, chief among them, "negotiation."

Let me hasten to add here that the "flattening" of global relations by the insistence on heterogeneity without structure finds its counterpart in the insistence on structural unity without heterogeneity. This is the case with Ahmad's insistence on a globe under capitalism, differentiated uniformly along class lines, without reference to other differences, be they national, local, ethnic, or gender. With reference to the question of the Third World, it is possible to state here that taken in terms of certain structural relationships (rather than essences), the concept used with a recognition of historicity has been enabling of one set among others of important boundary distinctions in global relations, which have been erased in these recent alternatives, however valid they may be in terms of the criticisms they have directed at the concept. To speak of a "Third World" within the First, with due recognition of context, for instance, is not to equate the Third World in Los Angeles or Farmville, VA, with Somalia; but it does carry a certain significance and is expressive of certain relations within Global Capitalism.

This brings me to the second problem above, the problem of the Third World as a discursive construct. Criticism of the concept, based on its origins in the Cold War conceptual construction of the world, too readily sweeps under the rug the complex history of the realities and the perceptions within the Third World itself that may have endowed it with much appeal and radical significance; as if the term was able to articulate sensibilities that had been long in the making. In these days, when it is common to speak of how the oppressed appropriate the tools of the oppressor, it is somewhat surprising that so little attention has been given to the appropriation of this Cold War term in the struggles against domination and hegemony. The Third World may have been essentialized in terms of poverty, race, religion, whatever; but it also served for a while as a source of utopian longings for the unity of the oppressed, and for the creation of alternative futures. The prominent Afro-American writer Richard Wright, who in 1955 felt compelled to rush to Bandung as soon as he heard of the upcoming conference of non-aligned nations, wrote (almost in spite of himself, for he was also deeply skeptical of what he found):

> As I watched the dark-faced delegates work at the conference, I saw a strange thing happen. Before Bandung, most of these men had been strangers, and on the first day they were constrained with one another, bristling with charge and countercharge against America and/or Russia. But, as the days passed, they slowly cooled off, and another and different mood set in. . . . As they came to know one another better, their fear and distrust evaporated. Living for centuries under Western rule, they had become filled with a deep sense of how greatly they differed from one another. But now, face to face, their ideological defenses dropped. Negative unity, bred by a feeling that they had to stand together against a rapacious West, turned into something that hinted of the positive. . . . Day after day dun-colored Trotskyites consorted with dark Moslems, yellow Indo-Chinese hobnobbed with brown Indonesians, black Africans mingled with swarthy Arabs, tan Burmese associated with dark brown Hindus, dusty nationalists palled around with yellow Communists, and Socialists talked to Buddhists. But they all had the same background of colonial experience, of subjection, of color consciousness, and they found that ideology was not needed to define their relations.[8]

A utopian moment, to be sure, but one for which longing persisted so long as the generation which had come of age during anticolonial struggles prevailed. It was similar longing that underlay the term "Third World Strike" in ethnic student movements in the United States.

It is also arguable that while the term Third World was coined after World War II, once created, it resonated with longings for alternative development that had been around much longer. We sometimes forget that while as a term "Third

World" was a product of the opposition between capitalism and communism, the First and the Second Worlds, the realities to which it referred preceded the existence of a "Second" World. As early as the turn of the century Chinese radicals such as Sun Yat-sen, well aware of the rising conflict between capitalism and socialism, already envisioned an autonomous path, "a third way," that would provide a national alternative to the other two available paths of development. Examples of a similar consciousness may be found elsewhere, from Turkey to India. Perhaps the most clear expression of a desire for a "third way" was expressed by Mao Zedong in 1940, in his advocacy of a Chinese version of socialism that would serve in similarly placed societies (colonial or semicolonial) not as a model for emulation but as a model for inspiration; to find their own "third ways."[9] It is arguable that the political consciousness which strove for alternative paths of development both underlay and informed the Third World appropriations of the term "Third World" once it had been coined. The Third World in this radical appropriation may hardly be attributed, as Abdel-Malek does, to a "comprador" intelligentsia ready to be "Third-Worlded" as the West's "other." Rather than homogenize the societies so described, moreover, in this usage Third World referred to a common experience, while recognizing the diversity of the societies so described. The representation of the Third World concept (to be distinguished from the term) merely as a product of a world structured by the conflict between the First and the Second Worlds overlooks a complex history of the search for potential "Third Worlds" as developmental and utopian projects. It also overlooks how these alternatives were marginalized, if not suppressed, by a Cold War conceptualization of Three Worlds, which discounted such search for alternatives, reducing them into irrelevancies in societies that *had* to be headed toward either capitalism, or socialism as it existed. Rather than dismiss the Third World concept, we need to consider if, with the fall of socialism, some of these alternatives have indeed made a comeback, albeit in a transformed vocabulary, reduced to nationalist alternatives rather than national liberation alternatives conditioned by a sense of belonging in a Third World. Given the present situation, Third Worldism might indeed play a positive role both internationally and nationally.

These reservations suggest the considerations that need to be included in a thoroughgoing critique of the Third World concept presently: (a) a distinction between present and the past in order, first, to avoid projecting upon the past the discontents of the present, and, second, to enable a critical consideration of the sources of contemporary discourses on the Third World. The critiques of the Third World concept to which I have referred above do not specify differences between the present, when the concept may have become irrelevant, and past conceptualizations in which the idea of a Third World, however problematic, may nevertheless have had something to say about global relations; even if the Third World may be little more than a historically limited discursive construct, it is necessary to spell out the implications of alternative constructs—to distinguish, for instance, discourses informed by a market paradigm from those, such as

Ahmad's, that are informed by a Marxist paradigm of class, (b) it follows that a distinction is also necessary concerning the structural contexts implied by different discourses on the Third World, and (c) the same may be said with regard to the critical political agenda embedded in the Third World concept. Though it may have been a product of a particular Cold War configuration of a global capitalism, the idea of the Third World also implied for some time a challenge to a conceptualization of the world in terms of the teleologies of capitalism or socialism. Is it possible presently to speak of alternative Third World visions of global structuring in any meaningful sense? To the extent that Marxism entered the formulation of such critical visions (distinct from its role in socialism), what does this say about Marxism?

The problem of historicity does not require much comment, and may be dealt with in a consideration of the latter two problems, which I will address briefly below.

Global Capitalism and the Question of the Third World

Whether we think of recent global changes as "restructuring" ("the new world order") or "destructuring" ("the new world disorder"), there would appear to be little room in it for what used to be called the Third World. The question is whether or not this means the disappearance of forces reconfiguring global relations in new ways, however unstable such configurations may be, now that they have been deprived of the political forms that earlier gave some coherence to global structures? Is it possible to identify political formations, striving to be born, that may empower new critical agenda that do not serve the new structures of power, if only implicitly, or fall back upon resistance strategies of a bygone day that are no longer relevant? These questions render necessary a reconsideration of both the structural assumptions of the Third World concept, and of the "nation-form," which in the past has been linked inextricably with Third World liberation struggles.[10]

There is no space or need here to elaborate on my understanding of Global Capitalism which I have described at length elsewhere.[11] How it may bear upon the question of the Third World is suggested by my contradictory validation of the two antithetical positions on the Third World represented by Ahmad and postcolonial criticism; the one insisting on the universality of class structures, the other eschewing any global structures in the name of local confrontations. This contradictory assessment reflects my sense that under conditions of Global Capitalism, the problem of structure presents itself at once as a global *and* as a local problem, due to the motions of capital, unrestricted by earlier political forms associated with capitalism and socialism. Capital, having achieved transnationality in all aspects, but especially in production ("the new international division of labor"), cuts across regional *and* national boundaries to create genuinely global classes, as Ahmad claims, that are articulated organizationally in transnational corporations most obviously without being restricted to them. The recent preoccupation with globalism, internationalism, etc., that is visible in all the national contexts with which I am familiar may be viewed as one ideological expression of Global Capitalism, and what Leslie Sklair has described as a "transnational capitalist class," which now serves as a paradigm for grasping other social groups, not excluding intellectuals.[12] A "deterritorialized" capital subjects earlier divisions in global relations (including nations) to disruptive forces from the outside, sort of to speak, creating productive and consumptive social formations empowered by forces that recognize no divisions: hence the possibility of finding First World formations in the formerly Second and Third Worlds, and Third World formations in the formerly First and Second Worlds.

To stop here, however, would be to overlook the localizing forces, at work at a number of levels, that have a multiplicity of origins, but are also promoted ironically by the same transnational capital in search of diverse markets, that in its very search for profits contributes to local diversification by working over existing differences; as in the so-called "micromapping" and "database marketing" of contemporary marketing strategists.[13] As transnational organizations disrupt earlier boundaries from above, "database marketing" reworks local cultures into new localisms to undermine larger unities from below. Localities in competition with one another to place themselves on the pathways of a transnational capital in perpetual motion speak eloquently to the contradictory (but nevertheless comprehensible) forces at work at the present stage of capitalist development.

In other words, while both the universalizing thesis offered by Ahmad and the localizing orientation of postcolonial criticism may be valid, neither is sufficient without the other to offer a portrayal of the complex forces at work in the contemporary world economy. Recent preoccupation with the global and the local suggests the problematic nature of the relationship between the two, and the necessity of accounting for the global in the local, as well as the localism of the global. The situation is further complicated by the fact that while the older boundaries imposed by political formations are under disruption, it would be naive to claim that they are gone. To suggest that there may be "Third Worlds" in the First World is not to suggest that these Third Worlds have the same status in the conditions of existence. Likewise with the "nation-form." Ahmad and postcolonial critics are at one in calling into question the "Third-Worldist" focus on the nation as the unit of analysis, which disguises the fact that the nation itself is a site of struggles among a multiplicity of forces; which may be more the case today than in the past, when localisms generated by global forces have emerged to challenge the "nation-form." To say that the "nation-form" is undergoing a transformation, however, is not to say that the "nation-form" is, therefore, gone out of existence. Rather, globalization and localization work over existing boundaries, creating new consciousnesses, and new political formations, that present new dangers but also new opportunities for resistance.

"Third-Worldism," which I take here to refer to Third World sites as sources of alternative social and political visions, also needs to be reconsidered in light of these global transformations. To recall Shohat's statement above, is it possible any longer to believe or envision possibilities of resistance that had their sources in the "structural commonalities" once evoked by the very term "Third World?"

Only as a memory, I would like to suggest here; and if such memory is important to keeping alive the possibility of resistance to structures of domination that seem more seamless than before, confounded with present realities, it may also blind us to new possibilities of resistance, and even serve to legitimize forms of domination that have their sources in what once seemed to be promises of liberation. I have in mind here the earlier "national liberation" struggles of the Third World, that took as their goals not just the achievement of national independence and sovereignty, but also linked the national struggle to the realization of goals of social and economic justice. So long as national liberation in this sense was a convincing proposition, there seemed to be little that was objectionable in the linking of Third World struggles to national struggles; it was even possible to rationalize oppressions within the nation on the road to the realization of alternative futures.

This promise is no longer sustainable, as the former Third World nations become integrated into Global Capitalism, and the visions of national liberation are transformed into visions of creating not alternative social formations but alternative versions of capitalism; as expressed in the recent preoccupation with the "different cultures of capitalism."[14] National liberation struggles earlier aimed at what Samir Amin has described as "delinking" from the capitalist world-system in order to achieve integrated national development that would bring benefits and justice to all within the nation, a goal that was deemed impossible to achieve if incorporated into capitalism.[15] The goal of most so-called Third World states presently is to promote "export-oriented economies," which may help national development figures, but at the cost of marginalizing or opening to global exploitation significant portions of their populations, something that once was deemed undesirable. Interestingly, the "globalization" or "internationalization" of the national economies, as it undermines earlier notions of national economic sovereignty, or national integration, results in the reconstruction of national cultures in ways that may help counter the global forces that threaten to disrupt national existence as such. Having compromised national integration at the economic, political and social levels, national elites now express themselves in the language of so-called cultural nationalism, which proclaims national or cultural essences of one kind or another to contain the profoundly disruptive forces of Global Capitalism.[16] Neither should it be very surprising to observe that, in many cases, these national essences are constructed to legitimize incorporation into Global Capitalism; in other words, to demonstrate that the national culture in essence is one that is consistent with, if not demanding of, participation in a capitalist economy. Discussions of cultural nationalism in recent years have been inextricably tied in with discussions of national cultures of capitalism. Such essentializations of national cultures in practice, when radical theory repudiates all essentialisms, may be an indication of the gap that separates radical theorizing in our day from the practices of mundane politics. More to the point here, Third-Worldism has abandoned its earlier goals of national liberation in the sense above, to turn into neo-Fascist reifications of national cultures and, rather than provide alternatives to the capitalist structuring of the world, not only legitimize capitalism but also contribute to a resurgence of Fascism globally.

These trends may be illustrated briefly through the example of China. China is especially interesting because under the leadership of Mao Zedong, and well into the post-Mao years, Chinese leaders made claims to both socialist *and* Third World status. During revolutionary years, China was also paradigmatic of a national development strategy premised on delinking from the capitalist world system.

Since the second "opening" of China beginning in the eighties, but especially the nearly reckless opening to capitalism in the early nineties, China has emerged as a, if not the, playground for global capital, with the consequence that national political boundaries have become severely problematic as the coastal areas have become economically linked to a variety of regional economies (Japanese, Korean, Taiwanese, etc.).[17] The boundary problem has been complicated further by the intense involvement in the Chinese economy of "diasporic" Chinese, including other Chinese states of East and Southeast Asia, as well as Chinese overseas.

As the Chinese economy has been globalized, strong localizing forces have also appeared, as the new development strategy has called upon (or permitted) localities to take the initiative in attracting foreign capital. This has resulted not only in the uneven development of the economy, but also has transformed the relationship between the center and the localities (between the national and the local economies), to the point where the central government has repeatedly acknowledged its inability to exert control over localities.

The contradictions created by simultaneous globalization and localization are manifested in the realm of politics and culture in an emerging contest between the global (a society defined by its incorporation in a globalized economy and culture), national (a notion of Chineseness that differentiates Chinese everywhere from others), and local (differences of Chinese from one another, depending on location) cultures. The new localism shows in the reassertion of local identities within territorial China, most notably in the South but elsewhere as well, corresponding it would seem to economic success. It also shows in the claims on Chineseness of diasporic Chinese, some of whom view themselves as guardians of traditional values that have been forgotten in territorial China under Communist rule. As with the economy, national culture no longer is containable within the political boundaries of the nation, which are disrupted from both within and without; as is visible in the appearance of a new idea of a "Cultural China." "Cultural China," a product of the very difficulties of defining "Chineseness," however, represents also a "strategy of containment," the construction of an essentialized identity in terms of remote historical myths, or the ideologies of a bygone day, chief among them Confucianism. Given the Chinese success in capitalist development, these essentialized identities also serve, needless to say, as hallmarks of a Chinese "culture of capitalism."[18]

The Chinese situation shows the irrelevance of analysis based on the Third World concept. That this former promoter of national liberation ideologies has now turned into a promoter of an essentialized national identity, that provides a new legitimation for capital globally, also is revealing of the irrelevance of any notion of the Third World as a source of utopian alternatives to the structuring of the world by capital. Neither implies that there are no longer forces structuring the world; but only that these forces structure societies globally in ways that are no longer containable within a Three Worlds framework.

"Reinventing Revolution"

The awareness of a new structuring of the world has become increasingly apparent over the last decade in the interest, on the one hand, in questions of Global Capitalism and, on the other hand, in the redirection of attention to problems of the relationship between the local and the global. The global, conceived in terms of transnational corporations, commodity chains and flows, human diasporas, cultural flows, whatever, is the realm ultimately of capital, which in its motions sets in motion not just production but cultures and peoples as well. The local as it appears now is incomprehensible without reference to the structuring powers of capital; it may even be suggested that the production and marketing strategies of capital have played a major part in drawing attention to the local, if not in actually manufacturing it. This may also be a reason that the local, rather than any Third World, has now emerged as the site of resistances, struggles, and the generation of alternative conceptualizations of development.[19]

In a recent study, *Reinventing Revolution: New Social Movements and the Socialist Tradition in India*, Gail Omvedt points to women's, peasants', tribal and environmental movements, with women playing central roles in all, as the sources for new visions of development in India.[20] While these movements have been particularly prominent in India, localized struggles for survival and resistance to capital are by no means restricted there, and cut across divisions of First, Second and Third Worlds.[21] What the emphasis on the local as a site of struggle as well as a source of alternative visions seems to suggest is that unlike in an earlier day, when socialist or national liberation programs promised even development across national economies (even if they did not realize the promise), within the structure of Global Capitalism such promises have been abandoned, and localities are left on their own to fend for their survivals. They also have emerged as sites for the negotiation and resolving of inherited exploitations and oppressions along class, gender and ethnic boundaries, as well as in the social relationship to the immediate natural environment. Hence their potential as sources of alternative visions that, unlike in the reified visions of capital, socialist developmentalism, or national schemes of development, are premised on immediate social relationships or relationship to the immediate environmental context. This attention to the immediate social and ecological situation, I should add here, does not imply a localistic parochialism. Those involved in such movements are quite aware of the necessity of overcoming inherited oppressions locally, as well as the necessity of translocal alliances without which local movements must remain at the mercy of global capital.

I would like to underline here one form of such local struggles, that of indigenous peoples (the "Fourth World"), that I think may have a paradigmatic role to play within this new historical situation. Indigenous voices, as with the local, have become more audible in recent years, and indigenous struggles are now an inescapable element in global economic and political landscapes. What makes indigenous struggles pertinent in the present context is the oppression that they have been subjected to, regardless of location in the Three Worlds of a bygone day. My intention in assigning a paradigmatic status to indigenous struggles here is not to erase the particular problems of indigenous peoples by writing them into a text of local struggles. Nor do I wish to imply that there is a single indigenous vision of the world. Finally, I have no desire to get embroiled in controversies over whether or not contemporary indigenous visions are products of invented or reconstructed traditions.[22] That indigenous utopias may be based on reconstructed pasts makes them more relevant as utopian alternatives for the present, because the pasts thus reconstructed account for inherited inequalities and oppressions within indigenous societies. What makes indigenous visions compelling presently I can only summarize here, without excessive distortion or simplification, I hope:[23] (a) The repudiation of developmentalism, in both its capitalist and socialist visions, along with a repudiation of abstract epistemologies (of Enlightenment derivation) that legitimize such developmentalism. As developmentalism is called into question, so are notions of advanced and backward, that are the intellectual products of the ideology of development; (b) The affirmation of the primacy of ties to the land, and to nature, as the source both of subsistence and of community identity; (c) The reenchantment of nature, against the alienation from it, as in Enlightenment epistemologies advocating the conquest of nature, or in the commodification of the human relationship to nature (and, therefore, to one another); and (d) A vision of the world as a federation of communities.

This vision of the world, its relationship to the present and the past, is eloquently expressed in the following lines:

> In our dreams we have seen another world. A true world, a world more just than the one we now walk in. We saw that in this new world armies were not necessary, and

that peace, justice and liberty were not spoken of as distant ideals, but as common, everyday things, named as easily as the other good things of this world: bread, bird, air, water, and even, for some, book and voice. And in this world, government by the many was the will and the reality of the people, and those that commanded were thoughtful people who commanded by obeying. And this new, true world was not a dream from the past; it was not something that came from our ancestors. It came to us from the future; it was the next step that we had to take.

And so it was that we began our journey to have this dream sit at our table, light up our house, grow among our corn, fill the hearts of our children, wipe the sweat from our brow, heal our history—and to win this dream for everyone.[24]

The dream here is of people constituting and reconstituting themselves against capital and the state. If the indigenous vision in most cases also involves a reification of constructed pasts (which is not the case with Subcomandante Marcos, who draws on the future), unlike in the cases of nations and ethnicities, such reification aims at the creation of communities about whose fragileness and, therefore, need for identity, there is little question; the reification here, as it seeks to account for inherited inequalities, aims at liberation from rather than justification for such inequalities and oppressions. It represents, in other words, pasts that have been worked over already by visions of "liberty, justice and democracy" for all.

These dreams of indigenous communities, while they have concrete sources in indigenous histories, may be found in our day in many of the local struggles to which I referred above.[25] Utopian or not, these struggles all take as their premise the need to overcome a fundamental problem of life under Global Capitalism. In his recent book, *Brave Modern World: The Prospects for Survival*, the distinguished French Marxist historian Jean Chesneaux, takes Hong Kong as a paradigm of the new Global Capitalism to describe the current world economy as an "off-ground" economy, which then becomes a characteristic of life in general under Global Capitalism.[26] The solution to this "off-ground" existence seems to be implicit in his metaphor: the economy and, with it, life in general must somehow be regrounded. It is from this urgent need that the indigenous vision, and local visions in general, derive their contemporary significance. It may be for the same reason that we must remember the Three Worlds of yesterday, but also forget them.

Notes

1. Carl E. Pletsch, "The Three Worlds, or the Division of Social Scientific Labor, circa 1950–1975," *Comparative Studies in Society and History* 23 (October 1981): 565–90.

2. For an early example by a "Third World" intellectual, see, Anouar Abdel-Malek, "The Third World and the Orient," in Anouar Abdel-Malek, *Civilisations and Social Theory* (Albany: State University of New York, 1981):130–138. Originally published in French in 1976.

3. Gyan Prakash, "Writing Post-Orientalist Histories of the Third World: Perspectives from Indian Historiography," *Comparative Studies in Society and History* 32 (April 1990), p.384.

4. Aijaz Ahmad, *In Theory: Classes, Nations, Literatures* (London: Verso Books, 1992), p. 103.

5. Abdel-Malek, op.cit., pp.132–33.

6. Ella Shohat, "Notes on the 'Post-colonial,'" *Social Text*, 31/32 (1992), p.111.

7. Pletsch, pp.563, 590.

8. Richard Wright, *The Color Curtain: A Report on the Bandung Conference* (New York: The World Publishing Co., 1956), pp. 175–176.

9. Mao Zedong, "On New Democracy," *Selected Works*, Vol. 2 (Peking: Foreign Languages Press, 1965): 339–394.

10. For "nation-form," see, Etienne Balibar, "The Nation Form: History and Ideology," in Etienne Balibar and Immanuel Wallerstein, *Race, Nation, Class: Ambiguous Identities* (London: Verso Books, 1993):86–106.

11. Arif Dirlik, *After the Revolution: Waking to Global Capitalism* (Hanover: University Press of New England, 1994).

12. Leslie Sklair, *Sociology of the Global System* (Baltimore: The Johns Hopkins University Press, 1991): 52–84.

13. For a recent example, see the cover story, "Database Marketing," in *Business Week*, 5 September 1994: 56–62.

14. For examples of such discussions, see *Capitalism in Contrasting Cultures*, ed. by Stewart R. Clegg and S. Gordon Redding (Berlin: Walter de Gruyter, 1990).

15. Samir Amin, *Delinking: Toward a Polycentric World* (London and New Jersey: ZED Books, 1990), for an example. Needless to say, most world-system practitioners, including Immanuel Wallerstein, subscribe to this view.

16. See, for an example, the essays in *Cultural Nationalism in East Asia*, ed. by Harumi Befu (Berkeley: The Center for Chinese Studies, 1993).

17. For an illuminating discussion, see, Xiangming Chen, "China's Growing Integration with the Asia-Pacific Economy," in Arif Dirlik (ed), *What Is in a Rim? Critical Perspectives on the Pacific Region Idea* (Boulder: Westview Press, 1993): 89–119.

18. For a discussion of regional self-assertion, see Edward Friedman, "Reconstructing China's National Identity: A Southern Alternative to Mao-Era Anti-Imperialist Nationalism," in *The Journal of Asian Studies*, 53, no.1(February 1994):67–91. This article illustrates the point I make here, but is otherwise quite different in premise and thrust from my argument. Friedman's goal seems not to be the analysis of the impact of Global Capitalism on cultural formations, but to validate Southern Chinese capitalism against Maoist notions of the national economy. For the revival of pre-Communist ideologies, see, Arif Dirlik, "Confucius in the Borderlands: Global Capitalism and the Reinvention of Confucianism," *boundary 2* (November 1995):29–73. The Communist state recently decided to call for "a renewal of Confucian values in an effort to fill a moral vacuum which, since the birth of economic reforms 15 years ago, is being replaced by 'money worship,'" *Japan Economic Newswire*, 9 September 1994. I am indebted to Rebecca Karl for bringing this item to my attention.

19. I discuss this problem at length in "The Global in the Local," in Rob Wilson and Wimal Dissayanake (eds), *Global/Local: Cultural Production and the Transnational Imaginary* (Durham: Duke University Press, forthcoming). For another discussion that approaches the problem from the perspective of diasporas," see, Arjun Appadurai, "Global

Ethnoscapes: Notes and Queries for a Transnational Anthropology," in Richard G. Fox (ed), *Recapturing Anthropology: Working in the Present* (Santa Fe, N.M.: School of American Research Press, 1991):191–210. I must note here that diasporas, too, have served as sources of new utopias, as global networks that may promise alternative social and cultural formations, but in the dispersion they imply of peoples, what kind of resistance they may generate is much more problematic. For an eloquent example, see, Epeli Hau'ofa, "OUR SEA OF ISLANDS," in *A New Oceania: Rediscovering Our Sea of Islands*, ed. by Eric Waddell, Vijay Naidu and Epeli Hau'ofa (Suva, Fiji: The University of the South Pacific, 1993):2–16. The volume is a collection of responses to Hau'ofa. For a different take than mine on the problem, see Paul Gilroy, *Small Acts: Thoughts on the Politics of Black Cultures* (London: Serpent's Tail, 1993). Gilroy, too, insists in seeing diasporic cultures in their localizations, rather than in terms of a reified essence that homogenizes diasporic peoples.

20. Gail Omvedt, *Reinventing Revolution: New Social Movements and the Socialist Tradition in INDIA* (Armonk, N.Y.: M.E. Sharpe, 1993). I am grateful to Roxann Prazniak for bringing this book to my attention.

21. For an example from the United States, see, Rachael Kamel, *The Global Factory: Analysis and Action for a New Economic Era* (n.p.: American Friends Service Committee, 1990). Kamel offers an account of efforts, based on localities, to unite labor in the United States, Mexico and the Phillipines.

22. For one such controversy, between anthropologist Jocelyn Linnekin and Hawaiian sovereignty advocate Haunani-Kay Trask, see, Jeffrey Tobin, "Cultural Construction and Native Nationalism: Report from the Hawaiian Front," in Rob Wilson and Arif Dirlik (eds), *Asia/Pacific as Space of Cultural Production*, special issue of *boundary 2*, Volume 21, number 1 (Spring 1994):111–133. Indigenous visions differ not only because of differences among indigenous peoples and their historical experiences, but also because of different relationships to the present global situation. Against the localized nature of most indigenous visions, for instance, is the diasporic vision of Epeli Hau'ofa, to which I referred above, n. 19.

23. The items I note here are derived from the following works by distinguished indigenous leaders and spokespeople: *From A Native Daughter*, by Haunani-Kay Trask (Monroe, ME: Common Courage Press, 1993); *Marxism and Native Americans*, ed. by Ward Churchill (Boston: South End Press, n.d.); *Struggle for the Land*, by Ward Churchill (Monroe, ME: Common Courage Press, 1993); the collection of Zapatista communiques published by the *Anderson Valley Advertiser* (Mendocino County, CA), Vol.42, No.31(August 3, 1994); and works included in *The Indigenous Voice: Visions and Realities*, ed. by Roger Moody, second edition (Utrecht, The Netherlands: International Books, 1993).

24. "Thanks to the NGO's for Their Protection," Subcomandante Marcos (March 1, 1994), in *Anderson Valley Advertiser*, pp.13–14.

25. See, for example, the influential book by Vandana Shiva, *Staying Alive: Women, Ecology and Development*(London: ZED Books, Ltd., 1988).

26. Jean Chesneaux, *Brave Modern World: The Prospects for Survival*, tr. from the French by Diana Johnstone, Karen Bowie and Francisca Garvie (London: Thames and Hudson, 1992).

8

Postcolonial or Postrevolutionary?
The Problem of History
in Postcolonial Criticism

There are diverse perspectives from which to examine problems associated with the so-called postcolonial criticism.[1] The perspective I adopt here is historical, in two related senses: the problem of history as it appears in postcolonial criticism, and the problem of the historicity of postcolonial criticism itself. I choose to focus on the issue of revolution because it brings into dramatic relief the ways in which postcolonialism breaks with the past, and proceeds from that break to reconstitute the past in accordance with its own premises. Contrary to the professions of "postcolonial critics," I argue that this reconstitution of the past is sustained by a teleological erasure of historical alternatives to the claims of postcoloniality, most prominent among them, revolution.

I propose below that "postrevolutionary" in the senses both of "after-" and "anti-" serves better than "postcolonial" in encompassing both the premises and the claims of the postcolonial argument. In a spatial sense, to the extent that the postcolonial argument has global pretensions, and its premises have been embraced globally, even by intellectuals from formerly revolutionary but not formally colonial societies such as Chinese society, postrevolutionary enables a more comprehensive grasp of the intellectual and political implications of a world situation of which the postcolonial idea is a product. That postcolonialism has provided for such intellectuals an intellectual space in which to take refuge from a revolutionary past they yearn to leave behind also indicates the anti-revolutionary stance of the postcolonial argument as a whole.

Temporally, too, postrevolutionary captures more effectively both the condition described by postcoloniality (in other words, the question of periodization), and its stance toward that condition. Even advocates of postcoloniality readily concede the problematic nature of the temporalities encompassed by the term when it is generalized beyond specific situations. There is, however, also a problem that goes beyond the problem of description. In its conceptualization of modern history, the postcolonial argument erases the revolutionary alternatives in recent history by assimilating them to postcoloniality or, more frequently, by simply ignoring them. Even more profoundly, the epistemological premises of postcoloniality are such as to abolish revolutions as meaningful historical events. Indeed, rather than investigate the revolutionary past as a possible condition of its own emergence, the postcolonial argument seeks to project its own utopianized (and, therefore, dehistoricized) self-image upon the past.

Perhaps most tellingly, the emergence of an articulated consciousness of postcoloniality coincides historically not with the end of colonialism (which, after all, has taken place over a broad historical period covering two centuries and is not yet over), but with the apparent emergence of a new world situation over the last decade, of which the repudiation of revolution is a crucial moment. As my observations above suggest, the substitution of postrevolutionary for postcolonial also brings into relief the ways in which the postcolonial idea resonates with the claims concerning the past in contemporary culture, which may account for the almost immediate popularity it has acquired in institutions of cultural production over the last decade. I will say a few words on the latter below, following a brief elaboration of the problem of history in postcolonial criticism.

Finally, a word of caution on the scope of the discussion. What I say below may not apply equally to all those who promote, subscribe to or are in sympathy with postcolonial criticism, and it may apply in some measure to intellectual positions that are not marked explicitly as postcolonial but are associated more generally with "postmodernism." In its rapid ascendancy as an intellectual phenomenon, postcolonial criticism has come to encompass diverse positions, with considerable confusion in the understanding and uses of the term. As the editors of a recently published reader observe, "the increasingly unfocused use of the term 'postcolonial' over the last ten years to describe an astonishing variety of cultural, economic and political practices has meant that there is a danger of its losing its effective meaning altogether. Indeed, the diffusion of the term is now so extreme that it is used to refer to not only vastly different but even opposed activities. In particular the tendency to employ the term 'postcolonial' to refer to any kind of marginality at all runs the risk of denying its basis in the historical process of colonialism."[2] I myself share in some of the positions encompassed under postcolonial criticism, even though I argue below that the term as such disguises more than it reveals; part of my purpose here is to force a clarification of the historical claims of postcolonial criticism. To this end, I focus on those writers who have had something to say explicitly on the problem of history in relationship to postcolonialism. Gurus of postcolonialism, such as Homi Bhabha, enter the discussion only to the extent that their views are pertinent to the discussion here.[3] I also say little about the work of the historians associated with *Subaltern Studies*. While their work has been appropriated for postcolonial criticism, it seems to me that their own claims are much more limited both theoretically and in scope, and in some ways are at odds with those of the postcolonial critics who have found in their work a cause for celebration. I will give an instance of this incongruity below.

Postcolonial Criticism and History

Ella Shohat has drawn a distinction between postmodernism and postcoloniality that is worth quoting at some length for its underlining of the historical claims of the postcolonial argument:

> Echoing "postmodernity," "postcoloniality" marks a contemporary state, situation, condition or epoch. The prefix "post," then, aligns "postcolonialism" with a series of other "posts"—"poststructuralism," "postmodernism," "post-Marxism," "postfeminism," "post-deconstructionism"—all sharing the notion of a movement beyond. Yet while these "posts" refer largely to the supercession of outmoded philosophical, aesthetic and political theories, the "postcolonial" implies both going beyond anti-colonial nationalist theory as well as a movement beyond a specific point in history, that of colonialism and Third World nationalist struggles. In that sense the prefix "post" aligns the "postcolonial" with another genre of "posts"—"postwar," "post-Cold War," "post-independence," "postrevolution"—all of which underline a passage into a new period and a closure of a certain historical event or age, officially stamped with dates. Although periodizations and the relationships between theories of an era and the practices which constitute that era always form contested terrains, it seems to me that the two genres of the "post" are nonetheless distinct in their referential emphasis, the first on disciplinary advances characteristic of intellectual history, and the latter on the strict chronologies of history *tout court*. This unarticulated tension between the philosophical and the historical teleologies in the "postcolonial," I would argue, partially underlies some of the conceptual ambiguities of the term.[4]

The "postmodern" and kindred epistemologies may not be as innocent of temporality as Shohat suggests but she is right, I think, to point out that postcolonial makes much more definitive claims on temporality. More importantly, the analytical distinction that Shohat draws between the two genres of "post-" enables us to grasp postcoloniality as a product of the conjuncture between a EuroAmerican temporality with its own epistemologies, and the temporalities of societies formerly subject to EuroAmerican domination, whose epistemologies are presented in the postcolonial argument in their complicity with EuroAmerican epistemologies. The result, I would like to suggest, is more than ambiguity. It is rather the incorporation of formerly colonial societies into a generalized condition of postmodernity which issues in the rewriting of their presents and their pasts in accordance with a corresponding postmodern epistemology. The ambiguity, such as it is, is a product of the difficulties encountered in this rewriting of the history of colonialism and its aftermath, and may be overcome only by erasing alternative histories. To the extent that the postcolonial succeeds in this erasure of alternative histories, it does so by substituting textuality for history, and privileging certain kinds of texts over others. Conspicuous for their absence from the texts of post-colonialism are the texts of political economy and revolution.

There is no reason why the term postcolonial should be inappropriate in the description of concrete historical situations; its difficulties are rooted in the global pretensions in its usage, which raises immediate questions concerning its references. Leaving aside for the moment the complex question of whether or not EuroAmerican colonialism is already over either as actuality or legacy (on which question postcolonial critics would seem to be divided), it is important to ask for whom colonialism is a thing of the past. The term postcolonial ignores not only the many indigenous peoples scattered around the globe who are still the subjects of the most degraded forms of colonial rule, but also the "internal" colonialisms that are the condition of life for ethnic groups from Tibetans in China to the Kurdish populations of Western Asia. In the face of these colonialisms which are quite contemporary, the assertion of postcoloniality may be sustained only by equating colonialism with Eurocentrism, and challenges to the ideological hegemony of EuroAmerican societies with the end of colonialism.

The term postcolonial is no less problematic when placed in historical perspective. If postcolonialism is to be taken in the immediate sense of "after-colonial," it is appropriate to ask, quoting Shohat once again, "when exactly . . . does the 'postcolonial' begin?"[5] Since the liberation from colonialism in different parts of the globe extends over a two-century period (nearly coinciding with the history of colonialism), how does postcoloniality serve as a marker of historical periodization? Authors sympathetic to the postcolonial idea have acknowledged that the terrain covered by the term "postcolonial" is a "contested terrain." Whether postcolonial refers to a condition "after" colonialism or something much broader is a significant question with serious historical and political consequences. So is the question of whether the postcolonial encompasses only "Third and Fourth World cultures," or should be more inclusive in scope.[6]

Such questions may be irrelevant, however, because in its rapid unfolding, postcolonial criticism seems to have "transcended" its concrete historical connections to create a critical discourse "where nation-based examinations of a variable literary Commonwealth, or a variable literary Third World, give way to specific analyses of the discourse of colonialism (and neocolonialism), and where studies in cultural representativeness and literary mimeticism give way to identifying the kinds of anti-colonialist resistance that can take place in literary writing."[7] We may add that a concern with historicity gives way here to the identification in various textual locations of the manifestations of resistance in keeping with a discourse that transcends the concretely historical to lodge itself in a generalized condition of postcoloniality.

In the process, the historical terrain covered by the term postcolonial has been expanded beyond the immediate sense of post-independence to cover everything from the beginnings of colonialism, with the consequence that an epistemology originally associated with the cultural problematic of independence seeking to come to terms with its colonial legacy, appears now as the appropriate epistemology of a historical period that excludes only the "pre-colonial." According to Ashcroft, Griffiths and Tiffin, three enthusiastic proponents of the postcolonial idea, postcolonial covers

> all the cultures affected by the imperial process from the moment of colonization to the present day. . . . So the literatures of African countries, Australia, Bangladesh, Canada, Caribbean countries, India, Malaysia, Malta, New Zealand, Pakistan, Singapore, South Pacific Island countries, and Sri Lanka are all postcolonial literatures. The literature of the USA should also be placed in this category. Perhaps because of its current position of power, and the neocolonizing role it has played, its postcolonial nature has not been generally recognized. But its relationship with the metropolitan centre as it evolved over the last two centuries has been paradigmatic for postcolonial literatures everywhere. What each of these literatures has in common beyond their special and distinctive regional characteristics is that they emerged in their present form out of the experience of colonization and asserted themselves by foregrounding the tension with the imperial power, and by emphasizing their differences from the assumptions of the imperial centre. It is this which makes them distinctly postcolonial.[8]

It is tempting to quip, without being flippant, "tell that to the Indians—and Frederick Jackson Turner," but that is not the immediate issue here. The immediate issue, or issues, are the implications for history of this classification of literary texts. First, that postcolonialism is coextensive with the history of colonialism and, if we assume that by colonialism the authors have in mind modern colonialism, the history of modernity. Second, that postcoloniality is a generalized condition of this period though subject to local variation. And, third, that postcoloniality is as much a condition for the colonizer as it is for the colonized. We might also note in passing, for the moment, that other societies (such as the Chinese, Japanese, Turkish or Latin American, among many others) which also "foregrounded the tension with the imperial power," if anything more insistently, are not included in the postcolonial, because colonialism must serve as the ultimate referent for the term postcolonial. Neither, to be redundant, are the victims of settler colonies.

This expansion of the historical scope of the postcolonial succeeds by confounding many different colonialisms and suppressing others. Implicit to it is also a confounding of the present and the past. This is quite evident in these same authors' introduction to the recently published *the post-colonial studies reader*, of which they are joint editors:

> European imperialism took various forms in different times and places and proceeded both through conscious planning and contingent occurrences. As a result of this complex development something occurred for which the *plan* of imperial expansion had not bargained: the immensely prestigious and powerful imperial cul-

ture found itself appropriated in projects of counter-colonial resistance which drew upon the many indigenous local and hybrid *processes* of self-determination to defy, erode and sometimes supplant the prodigious power of imperial cultural knowledge. Postcolonial literatures are a result of this interaction between imperial culture and the complex of indigenous cultural practices. As a consequence, 'postcolonial theory' has existed for a long time before that particular name was used to describe it. Once colonised peoples had cause to reflect on and express the tension which ensued from this problematic and contested, but eventually vibrant and powerful mixture of imperial language and local experience, postcolonial 'theory' came into being.⁹

Not only the postcolonial condition but even postcolonial theory is extended here over the whole of modern history, and is rendered into a product of the autonomous reflection of the colonized on their experiences with the powerful language of empire, as if it had nothing to do with the present, and the conjunctural circumstances of its production as suggested above. To explore the implications of this suppression of the distinction between past and present, it is important to dwell on the seemingly innocent observation of the authors that "'postcolonial theory' has existed for a long time before that particular name was used to describe it." Assuming that the diacritical marks around postcolonial theory are not intended for the reader not to take the authors seriously, and that the authors ascribe to "naming" greater significance than merely labelling, where any other label might equally serve their purposes, there is a multiplicity of important, and revealing, questions embedded in that statement. So long as the postcolonial retains its concrete historicity, I noted above, it presents serious questions concerning its applicability as a principle of historical periodization. Expanded in meaning to be rendered co-terminous with colonialism (and modernity), it presents even greater conceptual difficulties.

The obvious question to ask of the statement above, assuming that the term postcolonial is not merely a cavalierly applied label, is why the "postcolonial theory" that had existed for a "long time" was named as such at some point in history and not earlier. The authors do not tell us, and I am in no position to say myself, when the term postcolonial was first used to describe the condition or consciousness to which it is applied. In a recent essay, Aijaz Ahmad notes that in a very concrete political sense, the issue of postcolonial societies (meaning societies *after* independence) was a subject of debate already by the seventies.¹⁰ The attitudes encompassed by the later use of the term may also be traced back—still, however, under the marker of colonialism—to such works as Talal Asad's *Anthropology and the Colonial Encounter* (1973) and, most importantly, Edward Said's *Orientalism* (1979). Origins aside, however, the term "postcolonial" and its ascendancy to a veritable academic craze coincides with the second half of the eighties, drawing direct inspiration from the work of Gayatri Spivak and Homi Bhabha, as well as works of anthropologists such as James Clifford and the work of the *Cultural Studies* group in England (to cite these various authors or groups is neither to imply that they hold identical positions, nor to suggest that they bear an identical relationship to postcolonial criticism). A search for titles containing the term postcolonial reveals that the term acquires currency only by the end of the 1980s, which is confirmed by the inclusions in Ashcroft, Griffiths and Tiffin's *Post-Colonial Studies Reader* which, with only a few exceptions, are drawn almost exclusively from works published in the late eighties and after. For whatever it is worth, "postcolonialism" was named as such sometime in the 1980s; its sudden appearance and academic ascendancy suggests that, rather than the product of an evolutionary accumulation of reflections over a long period of time by colonials meditating on their experiences with imperial languages, it was a product of a concatenation of circumstances that led to a re-reading and re-interpretation of the experience of colonialism, past and present. The christening (no less than the rapid popularity), moreover, took place not on Third World or indigenous sites, but in First World academia.

It may be equally relevant to ask why, if a postcolonial condition has existed going back to the origins of colonialism, it was not named as such earlier? If the first question above demands a self-accounting of postcolonialism, this latter question is necessary to elucidating the differences between the present and the past which, I have suggested, is suppressed in the extension of postcoloniality to the origins of colonialism and modernity. Historical periodization presupposes some correspondence between the content of history, and the marker utilized to delineate a period. In this case, too, the extension of postcoloniality to mark modern history is made possible by a certain understanding of postcoloniality:

> The contemporary art, philosophy, and literature produced by postcolonial societies are in no sense continuations or simple adaptations of European models . . . a much more profound interaction and appropriation has taken place. Indeed, the process of literary decolonization has involved a radical dismantling of the European codes and a postcolonial subversion and appropriation of the dominant European discourses. . . . Postcolonial culture is inevitably a hybridized phenomenon, involving a dialectical relationship between the 'grafted' European cultural systems and an indigenous ontology, with its impulse to create or recreate an independent local identity. Such construction or reconstruction only occurs as a dynamic interaction between European hegemonic systems and 'peripheral' subversions of them.[11]

The postcolonial, then, involves (a) the breaking down of Eurocentric codes, (b) recognizing indigenous voices in the formation of postcolonial culture, and (c) recognizing the latter, therefore, as a hybrid culture that is the product of a dialectic.

All that the above statement tells us is that we should recognize the changes that come with historicity against ahistorical claims to a total European domination (erasing the subjectivities of the colonized) or, its opposite, the possibility of recapturing a precolonial identity uncontaminated by colonialism.[12] For a historian of a society such as the Chinese (or for any contemporary historian, for that matter), these conclusions are neither objectionable nor particularly earth-shaking. If anything, the task involves breaking down not just Eurocentric codes, but also their mirror images in sinocentric codes, which have served to disguise the historical dialectic with a Chinese culturalism.[13] (That such a phrasing of the problem may seem novel may be taken as an indication of the extent to which postcolonial criticism is a product of struggles in literature departments, especially English, although obviously there is more to the problem.)

The problem lies elsewhere, in the conclusions drawn from this historical dialectic. The passage above, revealingly, confounds the two historical senses of "postcolonial"; as "after-" and "beginning with" colonialism. Having foregrounded the breaking down of codes with decolonization, it proceeds to render the same dialectic into a general condition of the interaction between colonizer and colonized, which underlies the authors' extension of the "postcolonial" to the origins of colonialism in the introduction to the same work, as well as the more recent reader that they have edited. Colonialism here appears as a phase within postcolonialism, its epistemology indistinguishable from what came after.

Leaving aside for the moment questions pertinent to the more recent ("after-colonialism") period, it is necessary to query what else prevailed during the colonial period that might have endowed its hybridities with a quite different context and meaning than in the more recent period? Everything that we associate with the modern, would seem to be the obvious answer, since as I noted above, postcolonialism thus conceived coincides with the whole history of modernity. The colonial encounter produced not just "hybridity," "in-betweenness," "marginality," etc., but also Eurocentrism (both spatially and temporally) and racism, nationalism, the Third World, etc; in other words, all those essentializations and reifications that postcolonial criticism seeks to refute were products of the same process of colonial encounter.[14] So were the revolutions that were instigated by, and nourished off, "essentializations" such as Third World, nation, class, gender, ethnicity, etc., and were justified by utopianized Enlightenment ideals of rationality and humanity, as well as, in non-EuroAmerican societies, by a the reconstruction of indigenous identities.

In his recent *Colonialism's Culture*, Nicholas Thomas has criticized "colonial discourse" and "postcolonial" theories for their failure to distinguish different kinds of colonialism (in which sense they resemble crude applications of the notion of imperialism).[15] The issue of hybridity in postcolonial criticism is a case in point. Thanks to the work of Homi Bhabha, hybridity (along with "in-betweenness," etc.) is a keyword of postcolonial criticism. But a concept such as "hybridity" is totally lacking in specificity; hybridity is a characteristic of all encounters between different social and cultural groupings. The question is what it means under different circumstances. Speaking to the issue at hand, if hybridity is a criterion of postcolonialism, then all colonialisms, including pre-modern ones, may be described as "postcolonial." Conversely, modern colonialism itself has produced different hybridities, with different meanings attached to them. A classic case may be the Chinese encounter with Christianity. The first such significant encounter, with the Jesuits, produced "hybridity," among both the Jesuits themselves, and among their Chinese converts (and some non-converts, who nevertheless admired the Jesuits for their learning). This encounter took place under a certain configuration of power between China and the Europeans. When European and American missionaries arrived in China two centuries later, the configuration of power had changed, in favor of Europe. That encounter, too, produced hybridities, but now in association with the imperialist domination of China, which endowed hybridity with a different, less favorable meaning. Much the same could be said of other contexts. "Hybridized" natives were in the nineteenth century objects of scorn and suspicion among both the colonialists, and the native population, for being a poor copy of one and a degenerate version of the other. In our day, "hybridized" natives have become a valuable commodity for the role they have to play in global economic and cultural transactions.

In other words, encounters between (and within) societies may produce "hybridities"; they also produce divisions that are accompanied by essentializations of "self" and "other," more often than not simultaneously. To grasp the specific meaning of hybridity, it is necessary to examine the division also, as well as the structural conditions of which they are at once products and sources; in other words, a broader notion of the dialectical relationships involved than that which focuses merely on the production of hybridity, and is silent on, or explicitly rejects recourse to broader structures on the grounds that they represent essentialized foundational categories. Rather than reject "foundational categories," "essentializations," etc. in the name of a universalized (and, therefore, ideological) notion of hybridity, which renders hybridity into a foundational category even as it formally repudiates such categories, a thoroughgoing and critical historicism requires that we ask why people at a different time and a different place held different attitudes toward questions of hybridity and essentialization? We also need to ask what else is rejected in the process of repudiating "foundational categories," "essentializations," "enlightenment ideologies," and "stable identities."

To return to the question raised by "naming," then, if the "postcolonial condition" was not so named until recently, it was not because of an oversight on the part of those living the past but because other conditions that co-existed with the postcolonial condition of hybridity were more important and urgent. And if postcoloniality is named as such in the present, with an unprecedented elevation and reification of hybridity, we also need to ask what may be different about the present from the past, and why this particular product of colonialism, once scorned and viewed with suspicion, has assumed normative status in some quarters. While there are no ready answers to these questions, it is possible to state at the least that we must go beyond the boundaries established by "postcoloniality," and even the boundaries of the "colonial," to even attempt an answer. Historicizing postcoloniality, against the grain of postcolonial criticism, underlines not the irrelevance but the significance of structuring forces in history; colonialism itself may be a most significant moment of these structuring forces, but it is not the only one, for colonialism, too, has history.

Postcoloniality and Capitalism

How we explain the ascendancy of postcolonialism depends on what we understand by the term in the first place. If postcolonialism is nothing more than a means to revising canons and reading texts in departments of English, it might be viewed merely in terms of changes in the structure and constituencies of universities. But as I have suggested above, the claims of postcolonialism reach much further than curricular matters. Even the question of changing constituencies within universities points to larger forces at work.

Because of its explicit repudiation of these larger forces, in other words, the structuring forces in history, the postcolonial argument does not permit an accounting of its own history. What Ellen Meiksins Wood has written of postmodernism is also the case, I think, with postcolonialism: "despite their insistence on epochal differences and specificities, despite their claim to have exposed the historicity of all values and 'knowledges' (or precisely *because* of their insistence on 'difference' and the fragmented nature of reality and human knowledge), they are remarkably insensitive to history."[16] In light of what I have written above, it may be suggested that the postcolonialist uses or misuses of the past present problems of a more serious nature than postmodernist "insensitivity" to history; for while postmodernism's claims are restricted largely to the present, postcolonialism goes further to make claims on the past as well. The obliviousness to structural conditions enables postcolonialism to claim for itself modernity in its entirety (and, if we follow the logic of the argument, human history as a whole). Despite the insistence that colonialism must serve as a frame of reference for the term "postcolonial," the postcolonial argument strips colonialism of all historical meaning by substituting postcoloniality as a condition for all the phenomena (from imperialism to nationalism to revolution) associated earlier with colonialism.

Not the least important of these structural conditions is capitalism. Thomas's critique that the postcolonial argument does not distinguish different kinds of colonialism stops short of the question of a relationship between modern colonialism and capitalism, as he seems to be suspicious himself of "Marxist theory."[17] It is not necessary to reduce colonialism to a function of capitalism to point out that what is most distinctive about a modern colonialism is precisely its relationship to an expanding capitalist order, which nourished off colonialism and, in turn, rendered it into a global phenomenon. For the same reason, the dialectics of capitalism are implicated inextricably in the dialectics of global relations (from the international to the national and the local), as well as in the relationships between the present and the past. I insisted above that the postcolonial argument, in extending postcoloniality to the past, abolishes distinctions between the conditions of its own emergence and past conditions that informed radically different responses to colonialism. That colonial past and the "postcolonial present," however, are also tied together through the agency of capitalism. The question, then, is to explicate the transformations within capitalism that have rendered colonialism from a necessity of capitalist development to an obstacle to it; so that further development of capitalism requires the integration as subjects of those colonials who appeared earlier as the objects of a EuroAmerican capitalism. In refusing to deal with this question (on the grounds that it renders capitalism into a "foundational" category), and instead extending postcoloniality to the past as if there were no differences between the past and the present, the postcolonial argument provides a cultural and ideological alibi to the teleology of capital.[18]

In a previous discussion of postcolonialism, I suggested a connection between postcoloniality as a condition and intellectual attitude, and social and economic trends associated with the emergence to visibility of Global Capitalism.[19] Without repeating what I said earlier, I would like here to elaborate on some of the questions raised in that discussion. Before I go on, it is necessary to stress that pointing to a connection between postcolonialism and Global Capitalism does not require that we render Global Capitalism into a "cause" of postcolonialism, or to reduce the latter into a simple ideological expression of the former; on the contrary, it may be suggested that postcolonialism itself is a constituent cultural/ideological element of a Global Capitalism that is in the process of formation; which may help us understand not just its emergence, but also the immediacy with which it has acquired intellectual currency. Hence, rather than look for simple causes, the task for the present is to sort out some of the moments in a historical conjuncture of the eighties when both postcolonialism and the idea of a Global Capitalism (among other things) appeared on the intellectual horizon. What my argument does suggest, however, is that postcolonialism as intellectual and cultural phenomenon is incomprehensible without reference to the material circumstances of its emergence. Postcolonialism, after all, is not an abstraction floating around but an expression of an attitudinal shift on the part of intellectuals who have consciously distinguished their way of looking at the world from that of previous generations of intellectuals.

Ideologically speaking, the emergence of postcolonialism obviously coincides with the emergence of all the other "posts" of the first genre to which Shohat referred in the statement quoted above, which we may encompass here under the general term, "postmodernism." There is little need to elaborate on this point, except to point out that postcolonialism was not merely a passive recipient of "postmodernism," but has made a contribution to it by explicitly bringing within its scope the Third and the Fourth Worlds as active ingredients. If postmodernism opened up a new space for criticism by questioning an earlier Eurocentric conceptualization of the world (and all that went with it in the questioning of identities, etc.), postcolonialism was to globalize that space (more by opening up the rest of the world to postmodernist critique than by making postmodernism acceptable in the rest of the world, although that too has happened).

Equally important, I think, was the retreat in the socialist alternative that was quite visible in the eighties, and with it an escape from the radical options that were connected with existing forms of socialism, as well as its revolutionary Third World variants. We need to remember that postcolonial critics do not just claim a new conceptualization of the world, they also hold that in some ways their conceptualization of the world is more thoroughly radical than those represented by existing socialisms. The postmodernist repudiation of metanarratives was to question the narratives of socialism as well as that of capitalism; the scramble in formerly socialist states such as the Soviet Union and the People's Republic of China to break with their pasts by the mid-eighties seemed to confirm that such narratives were no longer sustainable.

Aijaz Ahmad observes that "postcoloniality is . . . like most things, a matter of class."[20] Furthermore, he cites Roman de la Campa to the effect that "'postcoloniality' is postmodernism's wedge to colonise literatures outside Europe and its North American offshoots," which he takes to suggest that "what used to be known as 'Third World literature' gets rechristened as 'postcolonial literature' when the governing theoretical framework shifts from Third World nationalism to postmodernism."[21] The class in question is a class constituted by intellectuals from what used to be called the Third World, and it is these intellectuals who have served as "postmodernism's wedge to colonise literatures outside of Europe and its North American offshoots." The question is how did this come about?

This, I think, is where Global Capitalism comes in. Since I have discussed my understanding of Global Capitalism at length elsewhere, I will not dwell on its details here. What may be relevant is what it implies for our understanding of such terms as colonialism, the Third World, nationalism, etc. It has been argued that what went by the name, Third World, was a post–World War II construct that was a product of the conflict between capitalist and socialist states. While this ignores the way in which the term was appropriated for radical purposes, it does point to an important aspect of the Third World experience: that of a battleground between capitalism and socialism.[22] What was clear by the eighties was that capitalism had won the battle for the Third World. The scramble for capitalism that marked the decade in both socialist and Third World societies might alone justify the term "Global Capitalism," but the scramble itself was organized by transnational institutions (chiefly transnational corporations but with all the supporting cast in the World Bank, etc.) which proceeded to reorganize production on a global scale, tearing across not just the boundaries of the earlier "Three Worlds," but national boundaries as well. Economic nationalism, much like socialism with which it had intimate ideological links, was to turn rapidly from a source of strength into a liability, clearly enunciated in development thought in the scramble for "export-oriented economies," most dramatically illustrated by the People's Republic of China.

Coinciding with the globalization of economies worldwide was a new val-
orization of diasporic populations which, over the last decade, have been reeval-
uated as essential players in the global system. Viewed earlier as outcasts of sorts,
objects of suspicion and discrimination in societies of origin as well as in host
societies, migrant populations, most highly valued among them Chinese and
Indian populations for their success at capitalism, have appeared all of a sudden
as key players in a global system whose "cultures" must be factored into the ideology of global capital.[23] Diasporic populations, we may add, have raised crucial
questions on national boundaries and cultures.

This brief summary, crude as it is, will serve the purposes of the argument here.
Conceptualizations of the world in terms of nations or Three Worlds, which
informed earlier understanding of colonialism, imperialism, etc. need to be
reconsidered. And so must the role of "Third Worlders" in the global economy.
Third Worlders playing in the global economy are no longer just "compradors"
serving EuroAmerican businesses; whatever resemblance they may have to the
latter is mediated by a new configuration of power, as transnational corporations
(and other global institutions) seek to "internationalize" their management and
work force in order to operate more efficiently across the globe.

I have suggested elsewhere that for this reason, it may be possible for the first
time in history to speak of what Leslie Sklair has called a "transnational capitalist class." In the discussion of postcoloniality within the academia, too much attention is focused on "postcolonial critics," which occludes consideration of postcolonial intellectuals as a much larger group, that includes not just radical academics but also CEOs and managers of transnational corporations, engineers and
computer experts, professionals and professional business "go-betweens." I am
not suggesting here that the "postcolonial intellectuals" who are under consideration here are merely mouthpieces for the Third World fractions of a transnational capitalist class but only that, viewed from this broader perspective, much
that seems benignly academic resonates with the broader cultural concerns of this
larger group, and the responses to them in the institutions of capital at large.
Globalism and multiculturalism, which are also crucial to the conjuncture of
which I am speaking here, are not merely intra-academic matters, but are products of interaction between universities, corporations and governments. And if
"hybridity" was at an earlier time a liability, it is now an asset because it enables
Third Worlders to serve, in the words of an Indian businessman, as a "conduit"
between society of origin and foreign investors.[24]

This broader perspective offers some clues to both the emergence of postcoloniality as a condition, and the immensely enthusiastic response with which it has
been received in the institutions of the First World. Deprived of the protective
boundaries provided earlier by Third World, national, class and gender identities,
hybridity emerges as a condition of life for Third World intellectuals who are
unwilling to escape into reified ethnic identities, which seems to be the only alternative option left in our day.[25] In this sense, postcoloniality may be viewed as a

predicament of the age. On the other hand, we may suggest also that postcoloniality is popular not because it expresses a predicament, but because it celebrates this condition. After all, with a global capital devoted to an ongoing scrambling and reconstitution of identities, arguments that presuppose scrambled identities come as good news.

It is for this reason that in my earlier discussion of postcoloniality I suggested a complicity between the postcolonial argument and the ideology of global capital. A major reason for this complicity is the inability or the unwillingness of postcolonial intellectuals to offer a historical account for the phenomenon of postcoloniality, and of its relationship to the broader structures of contemporary life, especially the structures of capital, which is rendered impossible by the repudiation of structures and foundational categories in the postcolonial argument. There is, however, a further, and less invisible, problem. The postcolonial argument takes as its point of departure the representation of culture and politics from the margins, from diasporic situations, and the perspectives of the disenfranchised, to question the homogenizing claims of power (Eurocentric, national, ethnic, class) to culture.[26] What it neglects to confront with any measure of seriousness is the fact that not all marginality is equally marginal, that there is a world of difference between culture written from the perspectives of oppressed groups (some of them terminally), and culture written from the perspectives of diasporic (or settler colonial) intellectuals located in First World institutions of cultural power (or managements of transnational corporations), who may be writing from the peripheries of nations or empires, but are seated in the centers of global power. The difference is, as Ahmad puts it, class. In repudiating structures beyond local interactions, the postcolonial argument also disguises the class position in global social relations of postcolonial intellectuals themselves (or is it the other way around?). It also does something that is even more consequential politically. In dissipating histories, identities, subjectivities, etc., the postcolonial argument does question some discourses of power, while legitimating others. One consequence, however, seems to be inescapable: these same discursive maneuvers render it impossible for the powerless to struggle against oppression and exploitation, which continue to be real, material, and not merely "discursive," problems of the contemporary world.

Complicity, however, does not necessarily imply intentionality. While the postcolonial argument in its consequences may play into the hands of power, in some cases intentionally, what is at fundamental issue here is a historical predicament; a predicament that is a product of a conjuncture between the history of colonial consciousness, and of its context in a global history to which it bears a contradictory (in the sense both of unity and opposition) relationship. Postcolonial consciousness, taken in a literal sense, is an unfolding of colonial consciousness, seeking to liberate itself from its colonial past, to achieve a freedom of cultural choice that is no longer bound either by colonial restriction and hegemony, or by national cultural pasts, which took shape in opposition to colonialism, but remained chained to the premises of the latter in its very self-definition. Forgetting the past, under the circumstances, is one basic condition of such liberation.[27] The question I have posed is, why it is possible now to forget, when it was not much of an option at an earlier time? Is it a coincidence that colonials are enabled to forget the colonial past, just as capital seeks to erase its colonizing past, or at the least, relegate it to a past that is best forgotten? The urge to cultural "transcendence" of the formerly colonized coincides at the present with the imperatives of a transnational capital that, unlike in an earlier day, seeks to liberate itself from national boundaries, sees in multiculturalism the most efficient way to manage a multiethnic work force, and is committed both in its productive and consumptive cultures to rendering subjectivities flexible and contingent.[28] If there are resonances between postcolonialism and the culture of contemporary capital, those resonances are products, as well as constituent moments, of the dialectical transactions between the histories of postcolonials and the history of capital in its globalization. Postcolonialism may be viewed as an expression of the predicament created by the ambiguities of this conjuncture. The predicament may be pregnant with critical possibilities, but to the extent that postcolonialism celebrates this predicament, extending it back to the past as well as forward into the future, it appears in its complicity with the ideology of Global Capitalism. By way of conclusion, I will turn to a consideration of postcoloniality in its relationship to the problem of revolution, which may also enable an identification of the critical insights embedded in the postcolonial idea. In light of what I have said above, it seems to me that the promise of these critical insights may be realized only by a confrontation of postcolonialism's relationship to past and present configurations of power; in particular, capitalism, and the changing patterns of class relationships it continues to produce in its unfolding.[29]

Postcolonialism and Revolution

Postcolonialism, as postmodernism, accommodates a broad spectrum of political positions, which may account for its popularity as it offers something to everyone. Yet, postcolonial intellectuals also make claims on radicalism, seeing in postcolonialism an even more radical stance than that associated with earlier Third World revolutionary epistemologies.[30] How seriously are these claims to be taken?

Quite seriously, I would like to suggest below. The same resonance with the contemporary global situation that raises the predicament of complicity for postcolonialism also validates its radical claims; postcolonialism has much to tell us about a new global situation. Its epistemology also offers a critique of earlier revolutionary positions, which may no longer be sustained in this new situation. Besides, if postcolonialism resonates with the ideology of Global Capitalism, it also does so with new radical movements that have arisen in response to the workings of the same Global Capitalism. The question, then, is how the postcolonial argument may be rephrased in order to foreground its critical over its ideological edges?

Though one of the fundamental failures of postcolonial criticism is its failure to account for its relationship to earlier revolutionary ideologies, it is fair to venture that postcolonials are not likely to be offended by a suggestion that postcolonial criticism is post- and even anti-revolutionary, at least as revolution has been understood in the past.[31] The very epistemological thrust of postcolonial criticism is to transcend the oppositions and identifications that informed earlier revolutionary ideologies.[32] Whether we speak of Marxism, or anarchism, or national liberation movements, revolutionary ideologies of the past have been informed by the possibility of a rational grasp of history, and the construction on that basis of subjectivities and social identities for its transformation; assumptions that are challenged by the postcolonial argument, which sees in such assumptions the promise not of liberation but of new kinds of coercion and oppression. The emphasis on the "constructedness" of the past so that it offers no clear guide to the future, the rejection of "foundational" structures, binary oppositions, essentialized identities, and "humanistic" subjectivities all combine to rule out revolutionary activity, except perhaps as contingent possibility, as with Gayatri Spivak's "strategic essentialization," which allows for contingent collective action.[33]

With such guiding premises, it is not very surprising that, depending on their politics, where postcolonial critics have not rejected revolutionary ideologies such as Marxism with hostility, they have either ignored them or sought to assimilate them to postcoloniality when possible. Revolutions and revolutionaries of the past (or the present) find little room in postcolonialist discussions of the possibilities of "subaltern" speech, or the appropriation of European ideologies for local, anti-colonial struggles. Where they do, they are assimilated to postcolonialism. Numbers of writers have noted the way in which Homi Bhabha, among others, has appropriated Franz Fanon for his politics of identity, taking the revolution out of the latter's ideas.[34] Nicholas Thomas has noted the way in which Bhabha does the same with the *Subaltern Studies* group, assimilating their arguments to his own "project" which is "entirely different to the historicized critique advanced by the Subaltern Studies group."[35] Gayatri Spivak does the same with the latter group, though much more self-consciously and explicitly, replacing their efforts to write a new kind of history with her own textual concerns.[36]

The problem with such assimilations of earlier revolutionary ideas is that it obviates the need to engage in a dialogue with the past—which would seem to be ruled out *prima facie* with the assumption that the past is little more than a construct of the present, without the subjectivities that a dialogue presupposes. As Parry, Thomas and others have noted, there would seem to be a basic contradiction in the postcolonial arguments between anti-essentialism, and what seems to be a longing for essentialized identities.[37] A question such as, "Can the subaltern speak?" ignores the ways in which "subalterns" have never ceased to speak, because what it seems to be searching for are "subalterns" in some pure state, rather than historical actors whose "contaminated" identities are identities nevertheless, conceived historically rather than in terms of some essence. In the case of Bhabha, the utopianization of hybridity rules out by intellectual fiat the ability of even "hybrids" to engage in serious revolutionary action; in a very self-contradictory manner, hybridity is rendered into an essential condition of postcoloniality from which there may be no escape. The "free-wheeling pleasures of commuting between cultures available to the privileged postcolonial," in Parry's words, is not only rendered into a condition of postcoloniality for all concerned, but also silences the counter-evidence of history through textual manouvers.[38]

What is at issue here is that postcolonial critics, in their efforts to escape the past by ignoring or assimilating it, fail to fulfill the critical promise of their own ideas. Hybridity, conceived as a "Third Space of enunciation" (in Bhabha's words), does indeed provide a critical space, so long as it is not utopianized or essentialized, but viewed itself in terms of historical contingency. As Larissa Mac-Farquhar has written of the glorification of hybridity and in-betweenness in another context, "identity does not produce . . . [a] claustrophobic reaction in everyone. . . . Seeing oneself in an identity and becoming part of its concomitant community is for most people not just a means of obtaining rights but a 'human desire' in itself."[39] Essentialized identities may be broken down through the critical perspective of "hybridity," but if it is to go beyond postmodern game-playing to serve as the basis for a new kind of radical politics, it is necessary to approach it not as an end in itself, but as the means to constructing new kinds of identities; which may require shifting attention from "strategic essentialization" to "strategic ambiguity." "Strategic ambiguity" may have a crucial part to play in a new radical politics—because it enables the breaking down both of essentialized identities, and of the categories in terms of which they are conceived—so long as it takes as its goal the articulation of new social relationships that are informed by a vision of the good society, which has not lost its relevance because capitalism and its regime of authority appear in a new guise than earlier.[40] There is nothing wrong with a politics of identity, which has raised extremely significant questions about social relationships. It becomes subversive of radical possibilities only if it is substituted for broader understandings of politics, which must account for the broader relationships of power which provide the context for the working out of identities.

Postcolonial criticism is correct to argue, I think, that the revolutionary ideologies of the past are not sufficient to grasp a contemporary situation. The resructuring of the globe by new economic relationships, new means of communications, and newly arisen social forces do indeed force a rethinking of radical politics, which radicals can ignore only at their own risk. While this is not to say that older structures have therefore lost their relevance overnight, the restructuring at work assigns new meanings to even what remains in place. It is impossible in our day to think of nations without reference to transnational institutions, to think of classes without reference to genders, ethnicities, racisms, and, perhaps most importantly, to think of global processes without attention to local differences; the reverse is also the case. If it may be summarized with some inevitable reductionism, not only the processes of political economy and culture, but politics in general requires far greater attention to contextuality than was presupposed in earlier grand narratives and theories. If postcolonial notions of hybridity may be complicitious with contemporary configurations of power, so may essentialized identities. Culture is no longer simply the product of unarticulated historical processes (if it ever was) but an object of continuous, and quite conscious, reworking in accordance with the demands of political and economic power. What meaning to be attached to any element of culture, and what political significance it may carry, is contextual and contingent, impossible to predict from abstract theoretical positions. Critical intellectuals may utilize the notion of the "constructedness of history" to struggle against oppression; so may Disney to sell Pocahontas, or the abortive U.S. History theme park in Virginia. Essentialism may be necessary to the struggles from colonialism of indigenous peoples; but it also lends itself to the contruction of transnational ethnic identities to help out with the operations of capital, as in the case, for example, of the diasporic Chinese and Indian populations to which I referred above.

Contextuality and contingency, however necessary in the appreciation of the complexities of contemporary politics and political economy, are also insufficient to the construction of meaningful politics because the only activity that they permit is localized activity without clear direction. If local needs call for localized strategies, which is a very product of uneven development, the very success of localized action is still contingent on translocal consciousness and practice, as unevenness is impossible to grasp without reference to totalities. As contemporary radical activists have realized, if an older kind of radical activity based on grand narratives is no longer sufficient to deal with the problems presented by a new situation, neither is localism which ignores the role of the global in shaping the local.[41]

The postcolonial argument has stressed the former while ignoring and consciously repudiating the latter. As with its ideological opposition to "essentialized" identities, its suspicion of structuring forces which are part of its own historicity results in an erasure of possibilities for radical action, while at the same time playing up the contingencies of a history without structure or agents; that can claim only the coherence of incoherence. Whatever the intentions of postcolonial intellectuals, this surely must come as welcome news to the holders of economic and political power who may have no qualms about their identities or what they want of the world, but are always needful of alibi for their class interests, especially in a situation where more than anytime in the past, structures of power nourish off the scrambling of everyday life, and the marginalization of those who cannot keep up with the scramble. The scramble includes the scrambling of the histories that until recently called forth revolutions to create alternatives to the hegemony of capital—as well as the scrambling of the very idea of revolution, which since the 1980s has been appropriated by the political right. In this new situation, the assumptions and practices of past revolutions may no longer be appropriate, but their memories are more necessary than ever in countering the structures of power; the nature of the struggle may be different, but the circumstances that called forth the struggle are still with us. And that requires a recognition that the past may have something to tell us beyond our inventions.

Notes

This essay was written originally for the Conference, "Reconsidering Postcolonialism," organized by the Committee on Comparative Literature at Washington University, St. Louis, September 15–16, 1995. For their comments and encouragement, I would like to thank the participants in the Conference, especially Professor Randolph Pope, Chair of the Committee and organizer.

1. For the sake of economy, I forego the hyphen that often marks the term "postcolonial." I have also resisted the temptation to place the term in the quotation marks that it deserves.
2. Bill Ashcroft, Gareth Griffiths and Helen Tiffin (eds), *the post-colonial studies reader* (London and New York: Routledge, 1995), p.2.
3. A thorough critique of Bhabha's work is to be found Benita Parry's "Signs of Our Times: Discussion of Homi Bhabha's *The Location of Culture*," *Third Text* 28/29 (Autumn/Winter 1994):3–24. I would have little to add to Parry's thoroughgoing critique.
4. Ella Shohat, "Notes on the 'Post-Colonial,'" *Social Text* 31/32 (1992):99–113, pp.101–102..
5. Ibid., p.103.
6. Stephen Slemon, "Unsettling the Empire: Resistance Theory for the Second World," in *the post-colonial studies reader*, pp.104–110. Reprinted in abridged form from *World Literature Written in English* (30)2, 1990.
7. Slemon, ibid.
8. *The Empire Writes Back: Theory and Practice in Post-Colonial Literatures* (London and New York: Routledge, 1989), p.2.
9. *The post-colonial studies reader*, p.1.
10. "The Politics of Literary Postcoloniality," *Race and Class* 36:3(1995):1–20, p.1.
11. *The Empire Writes Back*, p.195.
12. The statement seems indeed to be intended less for "Eurocentrics" than for indigenous claims within the context of a settler society. It is preceded by the lines, "this dismantling [of European codes] has been frequently accompanied by the demand for an entirely new or wholly recovered pre-colonial 'reality.'" For more on this question, see below, n. 26.
13. An anecdotal note may be in order here. In the 1950s, the distinguished historian of China, John King Fairbank, argued that "imperialism" was an inappropriate concept for understanding modern Chinese history, because it ignored the role Chinese had played in shaping that history. As a substitute, he offered the term, "synarchy," which implied joint Chinese-foreign control (perhaps with the weight on the former) in the political formation of late imperial China. This view came under criticism in the 1960s both for downplaying imperialism, and for its reification of Chinese society and culture. The epigones of "post-colonial criticism" in the China field (associated with a new journal, *Positions*), while they have attacked Fairbank and his generation for their reductionist understanding of

"culture," have yet to clarify how their premises differ from those underlying "synarchy," except in the scope of application to realms other than politics.

14. Studies arguing the relationship between colonialism and the phenomena listed here are too numerous to cite, but I would like to comment on one study in particular, Edward Said's *Orientalism* and the more recent *Culture and Imperialism* (New York: Vintage Books, 1993). While Said's work may be said at the origins of the kind of thinking that culminated in "postcolonial criticism," and he himself has shown sympathies to the latter, I think the thrust of his own work is to underline the relationship between colonialism and divisive mappings as part of a European modernity. He has said less about the other side, the reifications produced among colonial peoples in the encounter. I have discussed this latter problem in my "Chinese History and the Question of Orientalism" (forthcoming).

15. *Colonialism's Culture: Anthropology, Travel and Government* (Princeton, N.J.: Princeton University Press, 1994), chapter 1.

16. Ellen Meiksins Wood, "What is the 'Postmodern' Agenda? An Introduction," *Monthly Review*, special issue, "In Defense of History: Marxism and the Postmodern Agenda," Vol.47, no.3 (July/August 1995):1–12.

17. See Thomas, p.43.

18. Some "postcolonial critics," Homi Bhabha most prominent among them, avoid this question by fiat. Thus, for Bhabha, the "'new' internationalism" of the present is marked by a transition from "the material to the metaphoric," which I suppose also relegates to the past all material analysis. Such a move also enables Bhabha to reduce to the "metaphoric" analyses that are quite material to their authors, as in his reference to Fredric Jameson's "brilliant allegory of late capitalism!" See *The Location of Culture* (London and New York: Routledge, 1994), pp.5, 174.

19. Arif Dirlik, "The Postcolonial Aura: Third World Criticism in the Age of Global Capitalism," *Critical Inquiry*, 20:2 (Winter 1994):328–356.

20. Ahmad, op. cit. p.16.

21. Ibid., p.1.

22. I discuss these problems, along with some of the important literature, in "Three Worlds or One, or Many? The Reconfiguration of Global Relations under Contemporary Capitalism," *Nature, Society and Thought*, 7.1 (1994):19–42.

23. For the Chinese, see Arif Dirlik, "Critical Reflections on 'Chinese capitalism' as paradigm," paper presented at the conference on "State and Society in South China in the Twentieth Century," Amsterdam, 22–24 May, 1995. For Indians, see "Passage Back to India," *Business Week* (July 17, 1995):44–46. These diasporic populations have attracted attention not just for the enormous amounts of capital that they command, but also for the important role they have to play between the U.S. economy and the new frontiers of capital in China and India. Unlike the corporate players, who are viewed as crucial to the world economy, however, laborers present a real problem and call for new modes of control.

24. *Business Week* (July 17, 1995), p.46.

25. That this is not just a condition of the Third World, but of "postmodernity" in general is argued by Robert Jay Lifton in his *The Protean Self* (New York: Basic Books, 1993). See below, n. 36, for more on this work.

26. Bhabha, *The Location of Culture*, Introduction, is devoted to the discussion of the postcolonial position.

27. For an interesting discussion of this problem for the Pacific islands, see Klaus Neumann, "In Order to Win Their Friendship: Renegotiating First Contact," *The Contempo-*

rary Pacific, Vol.6, no.1 (Spring 1994):111–145. Neumann discusses why, in contrast to First World historians, the formerly oppressed do not wish to dwell on the history of their oppression, which interferes with their ability to live in the present.

28. As Stuart Hall writes, the hegemony of global capital is sustained by recognizing "that it can only, to use a metaphor, rule through other local capitals, rule alongside and in partnership with other economic and political elites. It does not attempt to obliterate them; it operates through them. It has to hold the whole framework of globalization in place and simultaneously police that system: it stage-manages independence within it, so to speak." Hall, "The Local and the Global: Globalization and Ethnicity," in Anthony D. King (ed), *Culture, Globalization and the World-System* (Binghamton: State University of New York, 1991):19–40. How postcolonials are necessary to the operation of this new strategy of capital does not require comment; it suggests, even, that capital must produce postcolonials to sustain itself. Given the periodization I have suggested above for the emergence of "postcolonialism," it is revealing that the decade of the eighties also marked the proliferation of writings on the globalization of capital, and its cultural prerequisites and consequences. For one such study, sponsored by the "Hermes" Corporation (pseudonym for IBM according to one source, named by the author after "the Greek God of Commerce"), see Geert Hofstede, *Culture's Consequences: International Differences in Work-Related Values* (Beverly Hills: Sage Publications, 1980). The surveys on which the study was based were initiated as early as the 1960s. Intended as a social science contribution to "practical policy makers in governments, organizations, and institutions—and to ordinary citizens," the study focuses explicitly on problems of "multiculturalism" long before that term gained currency in academic circles.

29. I have in mind here class position or, more precisely, position on classes. Earlier generations of Third World radicals also came for the most part from elite strata, or were members of that strata by the time of their radicalization; but they held a different position on classes than the postcolonials of our day. While, unlike Aijaz Ahmad (if I understand him correctly), I do not suggest that the question of class be assigned priority under any and all circumstances of capitalism, I think nevertheless that confronting capitalism as structure without also attending to the question of class, may be insufficient for a radical critique of postcoloniality. For a recent example of the celebration of postcolonial positions, that accounts for capitalism while almost completely ignoring class, see Frederick Buell, *National Culture and the New Global System* (Baltimore and London: The Johns Hopkins University Press, 1994). This work also shows the extent to which questions of culture based on nation, ethnicity, etc. have become a means of diverting attention from questions of class and perhaps of gender as well, as when Buell states, drawing on the work of Lisa Lowe, that "present ethnic cultural politics make sure that no aspect of American culture will be free of an ethnic sign"(p.195).

30. The postcolonial argument, too, needs to be contextualized. Some authors have drawn a distinction between "postmodernism" and "postcolonialism," representing the former as a EuroAmerican phenomenon, with new "colonialist" tendencies, and the latter as a more radical response to EuroAmerican hegemony. See, for instance, Stephen Slemon, "Modernism's Last Post," in Ian Adam and Helen Tiffin (eds), *Past the Last Post: Theorizing Post-colonialism and Post-modernism* (Alberta, Canada: University of Calgary Press, 1990):1–11. Readership is also important. Australian and Canadian "postcolonials," for instance, are much more concerned with the relationship between imperialism, settlers and indigenous peoples than are "postcolonial critics" from India, whose concerns are much

more intimately linked with postmodernism. In the former case, there is also an anxious-
ness to represent the settlers as part of a Third World and, therefore, sharing with the
indigenous peoples the status of being "oppressed." At the same time, these same authors
are quite preoccupied with indigenous "self-essentialization," that draws a line between the
settlers and the indigenous peoples. See Diana Brydon, "The White Inuit Speaks: Contamination as Literary Strategy," in ibid., pp.191–204, and, Gareth Griffiths, "The Myth of
Authenticity," in Chris Tiffin and Alan Lawson (eds), *De-Scribing Empire: Post-colonialism
and Textuality* (London and New York: Routledge, 1994):70–85. For a critique of the claims
for settlers, see Linda Hutcheon, "'Circling the Downspout of Empire,'" in *Past the Last Post*,
pp.167–189. As for "diasporic" intellectuals, including those from India, it is evident that
their concerns to problematize national cultures has something with the denial to diasporic
cultures of cultural authenticity conceived in national terms.

31. The significant part played by the disillusionment with earlier national-revolution-
ary movements in the turn to postcolonialism, among other things, is discussed at length
in Buell, *National Culture and the New Global System*. Buell goes too far, I think, in identifying revolution with violence, and placing the burden for the latter on revolutionaries. I
take revolution to mean a striving for systemic alternatives; the violence that followed was
more often than not perpetrated by efforts to preserve the status quo. Revolution has been
repudiated presently, except by the right-wing, but the violence continues. Buell also fails
to note that disillusionment may be confounded easily with self-serving celebrations of
postcoloniality, as in the statement he quotes from Lisa Lowe, that "the most powerful
practices may not always be the explicitly oppositional ones, may not be understood by
contemporaries, and may be less overt and recognizable than others" (p.162). By this reck-
oning, Amy Tan's soapy *Joy Luck Club*, with its "heterogeneity, hybridity, multiplicity," may
be more "powerful" as a radicalism than *The Wretched of the Earth*, with its Manichaean
oppositions. More expressive of a contemporary cultural situation that needs to be
addressed, yes; more powerful as a radicalism, no comment!

32. Homi Bhabha may be the best representative of this position, that seeks to overcome
oppositions such as "colonialism" and "anti-colonialism," since each is necessarily contaminated by the other. For a discussion, see Parry, "Signs of Our Times," op. cit., pp.12–19.

33. See her introduction to *Selected Subaltern Studies*, ed. by Ranajit Guha and Gayatri
Chakravorty Spivak (New York: Oxford University Press), pp.10–21. A similar idea is to be
found in Bhabha in his notion of "contingent agency." See, "The Postcolonial and the Postmodern: The Question of Agency," *The Location of Culture*, pp.171–197.

34. Parry, "Signs of Our Times," p.13. For a recent critique, see F. Shelley, "Africa, Franz
Fanon and the postcolonial world," *News and Letters*, 40:5 (June 1995), p.8. In criticizing
Bhabha's interpretation of Fanon, JanMohamed makes the important observation that the
encounter between colonizer and colonized was not just an encounter between individuals, but a confrontation between different modes of production, in which one mode of
production was ultimately destroyed by another. See Abdul R. JanMohamed, "The Economy of Manichaean Allegory: The Function of Racial Difference in Colonialist Literature,"
Critical Inquiry, 12.1 (Autumn 1985):59–87.

35. Thomas, op. cit., p.47.

36. See "Introduction," *Selected Subaltern Studies*, op. cit. Aijaz Ahmad has chided me
for giving too much credit to the Subaltern Studies group in an earlier essay. See Ahmad,
op. cit., p.20. As he notes gently, I am indeed "uncertain" about Indian history. But then,
my earlier remark was not intended to pass judgment on the issue of Indian history. I have

been particularly intrigued by the politics of the Subaltern Studies group which would seem to have ties to earlier revolutionary ideas in a way that "postcolonial criticism" does not. For a historian of China, it is impossible not to be intrigued by Ranajit Guha's reference in his inaugural essay to *Subaltern Studies* to the idea of "new democracy," which is not only of Maoist origin but is also used by Guha in a very Maoist sense. See Guha, "Historiography of Colonial India," *Selected Subaltern Studies*: 37–44. As I also noted in my earlier essay, the case of Mao and the Chinese revolution is particularly interesting because of the articulation in the course of revolution of many of the problems that are associated with "postcoloniality," including the problem of language. For a further discussion, see Dirlik, "Mao Zedong and 'Chinese Marxism,'" *The Encyclopedia of Asian Philosophy*, ed. by Indira Mahalingam and Bryan Carr (London: Routledge). Mao, of course, articulated those problems in the course of efforts to create a revolutionary identity, and not just in the celebration of "subalternity." In that sense, among others, he was much closer than "postcolonial critics" to Antonio Gramsci's concept of "subalternity," which was not a goal, but a condition to be overcome in the process of revolution.

37. Parry, op. cit., p.19; Thomas, op. cit., pp.48–50.

38. Parry, op. cit., p.21.

39. "Poster Child of Pomosex," *The Nation* (July 17/24,1995):102–104. A review of *Vice Versa: Bisexuality and the Eroticism of Everyday Life*, by Marjorie Garber.

40. For a compelling argument for the significance of ambiguity not only for tolerance but also for human survival in the contemporary world, see Robert Jay Lifton, *The Protean Self: Human Resilience in an Age of Fragmentation* (New York: Basic Books, 1993). Lifton, who as a psychologist has spent a lifetime with the human predicament under extreme conditions, acknowledges that "proteanism is consistent with what is called the 'contingency, multiplicity and polyvocality' of postmodernism in the arts and with its 'playful, self-ironizing' patterns," but goes on to draw a distinction that leaves no question about the thrust of his own argument: "I must separate myself, however, from those observers, postmodern or otherwise, who equate multiplicity and fluidity with disappearance of the self, with a complete absence of coherence among its various elements. I would claim the opposite: proteanism involves a quest for authenticity and meaning, a form-seeking assertion of self . . . .The protean self seeks to be both fluid and grounded, however tenuous that combination."

41. For recent examples, see Jeremy Brecher and Tim Costello, *Global Village or Global Pillage: Economic Reconstruction from the Bottom Up* (Boston: South End Press, 1994), and Arturo Escobar, *Encountering Development: The Making and Unmaking of the Third World* (Princeton, N.J.: Princeton University Press, 1995). Escobar's study is especially interesting, as it relies strategically on the notion of "hybridity," for which he acknowledges Bhabha's inspiration. Escobar sees in "cultural hybridity" a means to dislodge the domination of the discourse of development. What makes his argument effective, however, is his recognition of the crucial importance of the global in the local.

9

The Postmodernization of Production and Its Organization: Flexible Production, Work and Culture

In the discussion below I take up a question that has received little attention in cultural studies: the relationship between culture as a moment in the management of contemporary capitalism, and those epistemological stances associated generally with the term postmodernism. I have two goals in doing so.

First is simply to draw attention to the deployment of culture in locations which, while remote from the disciplinary concerns of cultural studies, are of strategic importance in shaping everyday life and its cultures, of which cultural studies are one expression; a critical appreciation of culture in contemporary life that aspires to any measure of thoroughness can ill afford to overlook the problematic of culture as it appears in a realm of society that may well be part of its own social and intellectual condition. Given the centrality of management to the operations of capitalism, moreover, its confrontations with the problem of culture and the manner in which it deploys culture to resolve structural problems may give us a more concrete understanding of the more general, and controversial, question of the relationship between culture and political economy in the contemporary world.

I approach this question through a consideration of the emergence of culture as a problem in studies of management and work organization. Unlike in discussions of cultural production where it relates to literature, art and architecture, or even everyday forms of cultural life, there is little question in this literature on the existence of an intimate relationship between culture and political economy; not just with reference to consumption, which has received considerable attention in cultural studies, but more importantly with reference to production, which has suffered marginalization under the sign of the postmodern.[1] Discussions of management reveal that the emergence of culture as a problem, and an essential object of management activity, was intimately tied in with the structural and cultural problems presented by an emergent Global Capitalism, and the technologies that made it a possibility, which were to "revolutionize" conceptions both of management and work. The very nakedness in which this relationship is presented in this literature in turn may enable us to grasp the relationship in that other realm of cultural production, where it is easily mystified by assertions of the autonomy of the cultural. It needs hardly to be emphasized here that work, and its organization, impinge on daily life and its culture; new conceptions of work and the corporate reorganization necessary to their realization shape not only communities of people but also our notions of individual and collective identity.[2] While this does not necessarily deny the possibility of the autonomy of culture, any claims to autonomy must account for the structural forces beyond the personal and the local that intrude on efforts to realize such autonomy—very often through conscious effort on the part of the managers of capital.

The very materiality of the problems that give rise to the question of culture in management, and culture in turn is deployed to resolve, also permits a critical evaluation of postmodernist epistemologies in their relationship to contemporary reconfigurations of power, which is my second goal in the discussion. Cultural studies are not to be identified with postmodernism; on the other hand, however vague and complicated the notion of postmodernism may be, it has infiltrated many aspects of cultural analysis, not least in the assertion in the first place of the autonomy of the cultural. The representational turn in postmodernism—that our understanding of the world is not immediate but is mediated by our representations of it, which may be all that is available to understanding—has presented a challenge to an earlier materialist affirmation of reality that few cultural critics can ignore; Fredric Jameson, whose work has been seminal in pointing to postmodernism as ideology, feels constrained nevertheless to acknowledge (in the preface to a collection of his writings on postmodernism) that "I would not want to have to decide whether the following chapters are inquiries into the nature of . . . 'postmodernist theory,' or mere examples of it."[3]

Still, the suspicion lingers that the representationalist reductionism of so much of postmodernist epistemology, and its self-referential denial of the knowability of any reality outside of representation (and, therefore, of its own "determinedness"), may mark it as profoundly ideological; as indeed "the cultural logic of late capitalism" which, in the absence of social and political alternatives to it, seeks also to abolish any conception of an "outside" from which it may be evaluated. The rendering of all problems into problems of language or representation may open up new critical possibilities, but without reference to a world beyond language, where some are better placed than others by virtue of structures of power to utilize language to their ends, it also limits criticism within a world of discursive economy with its own internal rules, substituting this world for the world of political economy of which it serves as a simulacrum.[4] In its problematization of the question of agency, its scrambling of positivistic categories, its insistence on the constructedness of culture, and its revelations concerning the diffusion of power in social and institutional discourses, postmodernism has opened up new possibilities in the understanding and analysis of power. At the same time, the celebration of "deconstruction" in so much of postmodern theorizing confounds deconstruction at the level of theory or representation with the abolition of power in everyday life, with sometimes bizarre consequences, representing the operations of power as problems of textuality, while denying the possibility of subjectivities that may be essential to the struggle against power. Postmodernism's own metanarratives of contingency and de-subjectivization may render it not just into the "cultural logic of late capitalism," but a mystification of contemporary configurations of power.

The uses of postmodernism in organizational theory, which I examine below, provide egregious illustration of such mystification. In the realm of organizations, unlike under diffuse circumstances of everyday life and culture, the configurations of power and their relationship to broader structures of political economy are more readily visible; especially to those who are engaged in the management of such organizations. It is instructive here to contrast the ways in which such managers perceive and deploy culture with the way postmodern cultural theory represents organizations.

To anticipate what I will argue in greater detail below, the intensified concern with culture in management studies has coincided with the so-called re-engineering of U.S. corporations over the last decade. The consequences are well-known. "Re-engineering" has resulted in a massive shift of economic, political and social power to the corporate ruling class, leading even defenders of the status quo to complain of a "class struggle of the rich against the poor." Within corporations, "re-engineering" has increased the power of top management over the white and blue collar work force alike, while rolling back labor rights acquired during a century of struggle. The redefinition of work made possible by new technologies has made contingency and uncertainty into a way of life for workers, at the same time intensifying demands on the laborer and managerial controls over the labor process.

Ideologues of capital are at pains to identify the silver lining behind which to conceal the cloud that casts a shadow over the lives of large numbers of working people. Nevertheless, even fervent gurus of the new management practices are quick to acknowledge serious problems produced by "re-engineering." Coercion is never far behind to back up the demands of the new corporate culture. Discussions of corporate culture in managerial literature, moreover, are infused with the language of manipulation. Cultural indoctrination has become essential to "re-engineering" to make the work force feel good and positive about changes in the nature of work that have created new forms of deprivation and degradation, both physical and psychic.

Postmodernist organizational analysis resonates with the ideological claims of "re-engineering," while it is quite silent about the power relations that inform it. Such analysis is putatively critical in intention in challenging the claims to organizational and managerial rationality in modernist approaches to organizations. On the other hand, it fails to note that the power relations that were legitimized earlier by recourse to managerial rationality persist, and are even intensified, under new managerial practices which have discovered in the abandonment of formal managerial prerogatives even more efficient ways of maximizing corporate power over the work force. Unlike management texts which are quite explicit about the power relations involved, postmodernist analysis renders corporations into discourses without any structural referents in class, gender or race relations, makes management into authorless texts, and represents the operation of corporations as interpretive activities open to participation by all members of the corporation—as well as the communities that surround corporations. Intentionally or not, this substitution of the metaphor of literary texts for the operations of social power end up providing an alibi for contemporary corporate practices.

To spell out the premises of my argument briefly, over the last few decades, capitalism has been undergoing an organizational transformation that is comparable in scope to the transformations at the end of the nineteenth century when, in response to the demands of mass production, the massive bureaucratic corporations were created that are now identified with "modernist" organizations. The move toward flexible organizational forms at the present are likewise a response to changed patterns of production that demand attention to horizontal sprawl (cutting across vast spaces, transgressing national and continental boundaries) against vertical integration.[5] While the change has presented capital with problems, it also offers new possibilities in the maximization of the power of capital over labor. Likewise, as earlier organizational forms required the acculturation of labor in the culture of mass industrial production, the new organizational forms dictate a new culture of flexible production.

Postmodernist social and political analysis is plausible to the extent that it resonates with these changes. This is also its predicament. To the extent that it fails to account for the relationship of postmodernity to the power relations that inform these transformations, postmodernism as culture and epistemology serves not as a critique but as an ideological expression and legitimation—or, at best, avoidance—of the structures of power that earlier found their expression in modernism. As much as the modernism it rejects, postmodernism is bound by its conditions within a capitalist mode of production. Capitalism has history; it has undergone transformations in the past, and it is in the midst of another historic transformation at the present. But the dismantling of modern economic, social and political organizational forms—themselves products of an earlier phase of capitalist development—is intended not to dissolve capitalism, but to allow the further reconstitution of societies globally in accordance with capitalist relations of production, a motive force of capitalism historically to which those forms have become hindrances as new techniques and technologies have opened up new possibilities of its realization. Postmodernism's claims to surpassing modernity are convincing because it carries out in the realms of culture and epistemology the tasks set to it already by the "re-engineering" of the organization of production to further consolidate the social relations of capitalism. So long as it fails to challenge these social relations that bind it to the modernity it claims to replace, post-modernism serves only as the witting or unwitting accomplice of the teleology of capital, which depends for its sustenance not on any historically specific organizational or ideological forms, but on the class relations in which it is an inextricably implicated.[6]

Management and Culture: Transnationalism and the Production of Postmodernity

In their influential best-seller published in 1982, *In Search of Excellence*, Tom Peters and Robert Waterman pointed to the lack of attention to "culture" as a weakness of management studies.[7] That work itself was devoted to demonstrating that in the best managed companies, the culture of the company was of the utmost concern to the management. The authors observed, citing a British management analyst, that in such companies, "the [leader] not only creates the rational and tangible aspects of organizations such as structure and technology, but also is the creator of symbols, ideologies, language, beliefs, rituals and myths."[8]

Since the early 1980s, the question of "culture" has received such attention in management studies that one management analyst, Stewart Clegg, caustically quips, with a pun, that "culture is good for business." Clegg also attributes the new interest in culture in management studies to the Japanese challenge to U.S. business.[9]

There seems to be little question that the Japanese, and East Asian economic success, apparently based on behavioral norms different than those of U.S. companies, played an important part in provoking the new interest in culture. But even a cursory examination of the literature reveals that it was not the only reason. *In Search of Excellence* was itself a symptom of an interest in the question of culture in organization that had been in the making for some time. In late summer 1980, *Business Week* ran a cover study on culture, and the first serious studies of the problem of culture in management preceded *In Search of Excellence*, although that work may have played a seminal role in popularizing the issue. These studies reveal that it was problems thrown up by new developments in capitalist production and competition—namely, transnationalization—that were at the source of the new interest in the issue of culture. In the course of the decade of the eighties, the interest in the issue of culture intensified as a Global or Transnational Capitalism emerged fully into the consciousness of management analysts. By the late eighties, about the same time as it emerged to the forefront of cultural studies, postmodernism was to appear in management studies as a new approach to the understanding of organization and management as cultural entities.

Studies of management that appeared from the late seventies offer clues to the factors that went into the making of the new interest in culture in corporate organization. I offer below an overview of the development of the new interest on the basis of a selected number of works that articulated important aspects of the issue of culture. The list is by no means comprehensive; and I utilize these works merely as important signposts to the new interest, without attributing to them seminal status. I hope the suggestions I make below concerning the problem of culture in organization are provocative enough to stimulate more comprehensive and thorough studies of the subject, which may be crucial to the intellectual and ideological history of our times.

Transnationalism, and the management of transnational production, were very much in evidence in management studies by the late seventies. *Managing Cultural Differences* was the revealing title of a management text published in 1979, that addressed questions of "multiculturalism" or "polyculturalism" that managers faced with regard to organizational behavior, production and marketing in an age of multinationalism. The text argued for a new kind of training for managers that would enable them to operate more effectively in this new situation that demanded cultural flexibility. Such training would not only minimize the effects of "culture shock" as they moved from one cultural realm to another, but would also prepare them for the newly required tasks of creating a "corporate culture" that was to be constituted "synergistically" out of a multiplicity of cultures. The book not only proposed strategies for the training of managers, but also provided in its appendices rather detailed descriptions of selected "cultures" (which, in addition to England, Ireland, China, Japan, and the Middle East, included groups within the United States such as the Puerto Ricans). Most interesting was the authors' explicit renunciation of Eurocentrism in management:

> Only in the last few decades has the one-way Western flow begun to reverse and accept renewed contributions from Eastern thought, whether it be religion, philosophy, health services, or technological achievements. Although many revitalization movements have been spawned as a defense against Western ethnocentrism and dominance, Eastern values and influences offer vital contributions to emerging world culture, which can only benefit by the convergence of East-West thought and perspectives. Today, the People's Republic of China is especially the key crossroad for this interchange.[10]

Even more revealing of the part transnationalism played in the new emphasis on culture was the publication in 1980 of the landmark study, *Culture's Consequences*, by Geert Hofstede.[11] What makes Hofstede's study important is its impressive empirical basis, as well as the sources of its data. The study was based on 120,000 questionnaires from two surveys conducted internationally in 1968 and 1972 among the employees of a "Hermes" Corporation (which, it was to turn out, was a pseudonym for IBM). The purpose of the survey was to understand, so as to manage, Hermes Corporation's sprawling multinational workforce, and to "create" out of this cultural diversity "the organization's own subculture."[12] Hofstede's analysis, premised on an understanding of culture as "mental program," examined the questionnaires with regard to values of "power distance," "uncertainty avoidance," "individualism," and "masculinity" held by a workforce that represented around forty nationalities. Where management was concerned, the study recommended against assumptions that there could be a universal management practice based on a universally shared rationality; while different nationalities might be coming closer in some shared values, significant differences remained, which required an emphasis on "relationism," and circumstantial understanding between the leaders and the led. The concern for "multiculturalism" was in evidence in this study as well in Hofstede's references to "multicultural organization."

The source of Hofstede's data shows the importance of multinationalism in the new concern with culture, but also that the managers of multinational corporations were considerably ahead of management analysts in their appreciation as early as the sixties of the problems of multiculturalism presented by developments within capitalism. By the seventies, however, new developments were at work in the world economy, that would reinforce these early concerns, and help bring the question of culture to the forefront of analysis. The emergence of Japan, and shortly thereafter, of other East Asian "miracle" economies such as Taiwan and South Korea, were to play a significant part, as Clegg suggests, in provoking speculation on the role of culture in economic development. It is necessary also not to overlook the immediate hopes for enormous economic potentialities created in the late seventies by the turn away from revolution toward capitalist development in the People's Republic of China—"the key crossroad" for cultural interchange, as Harris and Moran put it in the quotation above.

A work that was to play a seminal part in drawing attention to an "East Asian" (or "Confucian," or "neo-Confucian") culture as a force for economic development was the futurologist Herman Kahn's 1979 publication, *World Economic Development: 1979 and Beyond*. The anticipation of Kahn's book in some quarters was such that it was rushed into print for pre-publication distribution at the 1978 meeting of the World Chambers of Commerce. It was to be a forerunner of a proliferation of specialized and popular works on East Asian cultures—from the most abstruse philosophical works to books on military strategy and management—over the next decade. It was also cited frequently as a seminal work by promoters of a Confucian revival in the eighties, which was itself empowered by the successful "modernization" of East and Southeast Asian societies of the Chinese sphere.[13]

Describing himself as a "neoculturist," Kahn observed that "Neo-Confucian societies" registered "higher growth rates than other cultures" because of two characteristics embedded in the "Confucian ethic": "the creation of dedicated, motivated, responsible and educated individuals and the enhanced sense of commitment, organizational identity, and loyalty to various institutions [be it 'the family, business firm, or a bureau in the government']."[14] Reversing Max Weber's verdict on the adverse impact of Confucian values on capitalist development, which long had guided scholarly analyses of East Asian modernization,

Kahn went on to declare that "societies based upon the Confucian ethic may in many ways be superior to the West in the pursuit of industrialization, affluence and modernization."[15] Kahn's work was intended explicitly to reaffirm faith in capitalist development at a time when the original capitalist societies seemed to be suffering from a "malaise."[16] "Neo-Confucian cultures," with an unquestioning commitment to development and technological advance, provided him with the help he needed. In Kahn's case, it was not "multiculturalism," but those cultures that discouraged conflict and cultivated the virtues of willing discipline and obedience that were best for business. Nevertheless, his work, and the many works that were to follow in his tracks, also contributed significantly to the elevation of culture over structural factors in the successful management of work. As in the case of Harris and Moran's work, moreover, Kahn challenged Eurocentrism in management and, unencumbered by multiculturalism, even more explicitly pointed to East Asian culture as the foremost candidate for a new culture of capitalism.[17]

Two general observations may be useful here in explicating the use of "culture" in these studies. First, culture appears in these works in various modes of reification, that is almost a necessity of the underlying intention of "managing cultural difference," or utilizing culture for corporate goals. Thus, Harris and Moran, in their appendix offering characterizations of different cultures, represent these cultures in a laundry list of traits that supposedly characterize the behavior of individuals from those cultures. Hofstede, while he understands culture as "mental program" and, therefore subject to re-programming and change (indeed he finds some changes even over the four-year interval between the two surveys he employs), has no qualms about projecting onto nations the survey responses of IBM employees who, we might suggest, might have been atypical culturally by virtue of being IBM employees (not to speak of all the differences internal to any "nation"). The crudest employment of culture may be that of Herman Kahn who encompasses in his "neo-Confucian" cultures not only widely different societies, but also renders into "neo-Confucianism" anything that may have its origins in East Asia.[18] In the case of Kahn, as well as of Harris and Moran with their "East-West cultural interchanges," the challenge to Eurocentrism is informed nevertheless by a highly Eurocentric, Orientalist, notion of the cultures that are now to be included in the new culture of capitalism. It may be interesting to note here that these works coincided almost to the year in their publication with Edward Said's *Orientalism*, which was to provoke intensive questioning in cultural studies of the reified notions of culture that guide these works. The coincidence is a reminder that for all their claims to departures from "Eurocentrism," the mode in which they represented other cultures is still very much the categorical mode of modernity, that eschews considerations of cultural complexity that may not be contained within simplistic equations of nations and cultures, or even more simplistic East-West distinctions.

On the other hand, secondly, these works already point to something beyond modernity in their repudiation of Eurocentrism, as with Harris and Moran and Herman Kahn, and their acknowledgment that organization may not be containable within a single universal rationality, but is subject to cultural complexity both within and without. More significantly, perhaps, discussions of culture in these works is blended almost imperceptibly with discussions of novel organizational techniques that are subsumed within discussions of cultural difference, but are suggestive of those innovations in organizational technique that, contemporaneously, become associated with what David Harvey would later call "the condition of postmodernity." Stewart Clegg points to an emerging interest in management studies around this time in quality circles, team work, closer management-worker cooperation, consumer oriented research and development, just-in-time production, etc., all of them associated with Japanese management techniques, that would come to characterize a postmodern or post-Fordist approach to management, signalling not just a transformation of approach to management but, more fundamentally, a transformation of management practices.[19] As Peters and Waterman were to argue in their *In Search of Excellence* in 1982, such practices were not culturally bound, but already characterized the management of the "best run" companies. Especially precocious in this regard was the work by Harris and Moran, which blended with ease the discussion of "managing cultural differences" with "change in organization cultures." The two authors perceived a change in organization from "bureaucracy" to "adhocracy": the former characterized by "permanence, hierarchy and division of labor," the latter representing the "fast-moving, information-rich, kinetic organization of the future." These organizational cultures also called forth new personality types: the new "associative" person against the "old organization men."[20]

What is of interest here is that transformations in management, required by changes in capitalism that were already under way, were blended with discussions of culture called forth by the need to manage a "multicultural" work force, and reinforced the importance of culture in management. In either case, it was the transnationalization of capitalist production and consumption that rendered culture into a significant issue: culture, rather than being seen as something that would disappear once rationality took root, appeared now as an autonomous force that might qualify the universal assumptions of rationality. If the problems of managing a "multicultural" work force were one source of this realization, the other was the emergence of a competition that seemed to operate according to different practices, and do the job better.[21]

Not surprisingly, in hindsight, the works above coincided in their publication with the appearance of a new interest in political economy in changes within capitalism; described variously as a transition from Fordism to post-Fordism, the emergence of Global Capitalism, of "disorganized capitalism," of a regime of flexible production, etc. *The New International Division of Labor*, by F. Frobel, J. Heinrichs and O. Kreye, was published in 1980 (Cambridge: Cambridge University Press); Michael J. Piore and C.F. Sabel published their *The Second Industrial Divide: Possibilities for Prosperity* in 1984 (New York: Basic Books); Claus Offe's *Disorganized Capitalism* (Cambridge, MA: The MIT Press) followed in 1985, about the same time as Scott Lash and John Urry, *The End of Organized Capitalism* (1987). David Harvey's *The Condition of Postmodernity* was published in 1989 Cambridge, MA: Basil Blackwell), followed by Robert J.S. Ross and Kent C. Trachte, *Global Capitalism: The New Leviathan* in 1990 (Albany: SUNY Press). The list could go on, even without the aid of periodical literature. The 1980s were to be the decade of the Reagan/Thatcher "revolution," when political backing brought forth to the surface of consciousness the forces that had been at work already for two decades in the world economy.

The Reagan/Thatcher "revolution" was made possible by revolutionary changes in production that were already in the process of restructuring the organization of capital. What is important is the message in all these works: that capitalism had entered a new phase of development when, in response to the pressures of multinationalism (in both of the senses above: multinationalism in operation and multinational competition), and with the aid of new technologies, the earlier, multinational organization of capital had given way to a new organization that is better captured by the term "transnational."

Transnationalism may be conceived along multiple dimensions. If we leave aside finances, which long had been transnational, most important may be the proliferation of commodity (or, more appropriately, production) chains; or, the spatial spread of the production of commodities, where the production of one commodity from raw material to finished product was extended over vast spaces, cutting across national boundaries. This "new international division of labor" was made possible in turn, by new information technologies that, in speeding up communications, made it possible to separate the location for design from the location(s) of production, as well as the economics of container transportation, which made it possible to take advantage of lower labor costs elsewhere while minimizing the costs of marketing. The revolution in automation, a byproduct of World War II military technologies, enabled not just standardization but a new flexibility in meeting market demands, without dependence on a skilled labor force.[22] On the marketing side, competition which increased uncertainty of markets led to new practices that go under the names of "niche marketing" or "guerilla marketing," which promoted efforts to capture smaller market shares with greater flexibility, which was made possible once again by the flexibility in production. Pertinent to the discussion here are the new possibilities (and necessities) in production and marketing, which called for smaller and flexible units of production and marketing that could respond to contingent demand with the maximum speed and efficiency (expressed in the contrast between the "just-in-time production" of the new economy against the "just-in-case production" of

Fordist economy, the one emphasizing rapid response, the other the rather waste-ful—under present circumstances of market uncertainty—accumulation of inventories). Organizationally, the new mode of operation also necessitated the shifting of decisionmaking from the bureaucratic center to the locality (which also implied, in contrast to earlier practices, the necessity of recruiting local per-sonnel). Multiculturalism was no longer a characteristic of the work force, but a necessity of management.

Transnationalism, and automated production which made it possible, have called forth a radical reevaluation of conceptualizations of both management and work. What this reevaluation might entail could be gleaned from the works above, but I would like to focus on one work here that claims priority because its author is well placed not just to analyze new developments in the capitalist world economy, but to shape them. Robert Reich's *The Work of Nations* (in its ambitious title, no less than the author's subsequent appointment as the Secre-tary of Labor in the U.S. government) lends clues to the reconceptualization of work in accordance with the new demands of a transnational capitalism. It is also interesting that an academic Democrat should be in a position to articulate with clarity a "revolution" in the world economy that had been engineered by Republican administrations. What Reich has to say in the book provides a cogent summary of earlier trends; in offering insights into the thinking of U.S. admin-istrative circles, it also gives hints of the future.

Summarizing the emergent thinking on the capitalist world economy of the 1980s, Reich wrote in *The Work of Nations*:

> In the emerging international economy, few American companies and industries compete against foreign companies and industries—if by *American* we mean where the work is done and the value is added. Becoming more typical is the global web, perhaps headquartered in and receiving much of its financial capital from the U.S., but with research, design and production facilities spread over Japan, Europe, and North America; additional production facilities in Southeast Asia and Latin Amer-ica; marketing and distribution centers on every continent; and lenders and investors in Taiwan, Japan, and West Germany as well as the U.S."[23]

In accordance with his reading of "trends" in the emerging world economy, Reich proceeded in his book to identify different kinds of labor required under the new capitalism: "routine production services" (what used to be called the "proletariat"), "in-person services" (earlier called the service sector, including everything from secretaries to hamburger helpers), and "symbolic-analytic ser-vices," the new emergent sector, paradigmatic of the new age, which was characterized by a high level of education, transferable skills, and flexibility. To Reich, a country's standing in the world political economy depended on the labor resources it commanded in the last kind of labor: it was the "symbolic-ana-lytical sector," with all its research and design capabilities, as well as its flexibility, that determined leadership in the world economy. Hence education to this end was the goal of development.

Reich projected the long-standing mental-manual labor division as a determination of class standing onto a global scene, in a reconceptualization of the older reason-culture division of an earlier age; the mental denoting the First World, the manual the Third. What he overlooked was, very much contrary to his stated assumptions, that mental and manual labor could come from any source, regardless of national origin, because it was corporate rather than national need that would in the long run determine where each kind of labor was to be recruited. Manual labor could be recruited in the United States, increasing pressures to "Third-Worldization" there, just as mental labor could be cultivated elsewhere, creating "First Worlds" within the Third. What determined recruitment was not national origin, but corporate good; in other words, the accumulation of capital. That Reich engaged in this mystification is not very surprising (nor is it very surprising that it made him acceptable to the Wall Street types with which Clinton staffed his economic policy advisory body, much more so than his Republican predecessors); from the beginning of his analysis, he downplayed the significance of cheap and docile labor as an explanation of the motions of capital, attributing the latter instead to the "quality" of the labor force judged in terms of educational level—ignoring totally the highly educated and qualified personnel that were in the midst of being laid off by corporate decisions in favor of cheap educated labor that could be trained and recruited in the Third World. Whatever his motivations, his distinction reveals a self-censorship that, whether it is self-imposed or imposed by others, rationalizes daily devastation that does little good in the First World or the Third.

Reich's distinction, nevertheless, points to another source of the important position that culture has come to hold in the contemporary world economy: the paradigmatic worker in that economy is the symbolic-analyst, who is not just a recipient but a creator of culture and, in the process, of his/her own subjectivity. Unlike the proletariat of capitalist modernity who, even when highly skilled, was subject to the drudgery of mass production and management decisions over which s/he had little control, the new worker modelled after the symbolic-analyst is a closer approximation of the precapitalist artisan who has far greater control over the product, and the process of production.[24] Indeed, with the new controls over the process of production, this worker is more of an entrepreneur than proletarian, responsible for his/her performance. As a recent special report in *Business Week* on "the new world of work" puts it,

Mobility. Empowerment. Teams. Cross-training. Virtual offices. Telecommuting. Reengineering. Restructuring. Delayering. Outsourcing. Contingency. If the buzzwords don't sound familar, they should: They are changing your life. The last decade, perhaps more than any other time since the advent of mass production, has witnessed a profound redefinition of the way we work. . . . The new compact between

company and worker dismisses paternalism and embraces self-reliance. Bid farewell
to unconditional lifetime employment.[25]

Or, as Robert Reich, by then Secretary of Labor, was to put it at the Job Conference in Detroit, workers should stress "flexible skills," rather than enduring
relations with employers; job security depended less on "enduring relations" with
employers and more on "portable skills," whereby workers were "equipped to
handle the next job."[26] *INC* magazine, which is a promoter of small business, has
played an important part in portraying the worker as entrepreneur, while promoting an image of management not as the controller of the worker but as a part-
ner in the enterprise (in what is described as "open-book management," where
management shares all the information with the workers). This new conceptualization of work and management, according to one editorial in the journal,
promises to put an end to "the Hundred Years' War" between labor and capital.[27]

The exigencies created by new forms of globalized production as well as intense
competition in sprawling markets, where the numbers of competitors have multi-
plied, have led in recent years to intensive and constant experimentation with
management practices. While the nature of this experimentation is beyond the
scope of the discussion here, the underlying considerations that motivate it are
simple enough to lend themselves to summarization. On the one hand, the new
corporation needs to cope with efficient speed with ever changing situations,
which means that structural and bureaucratic obstacles to constant change must
be removed, as a "de-structured" (or "de-differentiated," as Scott Lash has called it)
organization is better capable of dealing with "chaos" than one that is hierarchi-
cally controlled from the center. On the other hand, the ability of the company to
act as a unit is more important than ever under circumstances of such contingency. Against earlier assumptions that unity was best achieved through bureaucratic controls, which need to be abolished anyway in the name of efficiency, the
new attitude is to achieve willing compliance on the part of the "workers" by allowing them greater initiative, and giving them a sense of partnership in the organization. Only those workers are to be trusted with such initiative, however, who
show themselves capable of flexibility and multiple skills—that is, "educated"
workers, a fundamental marker of "educatedness" being the ability and willingness
to "reinvent" the self in response to organizational needs and demands. The two
basic concerns yield a third conclusion: that the organization works best which is
open, and which brings top management and workers closer together.

Under circumstances of potential or engineered destabilization, and the
absence of formal rules, culture (and ideology) have assumed central significance in enabling the corporation to act as a unit. It is essential to create a corporate culture that enables the corporation to cope with an unpredictable, and
often hostile, environment. Second, it is essential to prevent the emergence of
"subcultures" within the organization, for which the potential is greatest in sec-

tional interests in middle level management. Where these levels are not "down-sized," it is important to move personnel around so as to forestall factionalism.[28]

The undertanding of, and the emphasis placed on, "culture" in management and work literature has undergone a shift over the last decade and a half: from a problem to be confronted as a necessity of transnationalism, to a source of cohesion that is essential to organizational success (and survival). This transformation has corresponded to fundamental structural changes within capitalism. Whether or not an ideology of culture, such as an emergent belief in the necessity of "corporate culture," itself was an autonomous determinant of these structural transformations is more difficult to gauge, but not unlikely, especially as the new "corporate culture" serves purposes of control that are barely disguised in the literature, though it is not often described explicitly as control. More on that question below. I would like to turn here to a discussion of new postmodernist organizational analyses which, emerging in the course of these transformations, have sought to recast organizational analysis in new conceptualizations.

It is arguable that the new developments in capitalism have served as generators of postmodernity in a very strict sense: by condemning older organizational forms associated with capitalist modernity, and calling forth organizational experimentation and destructuring that both contribute to, and partake of, the destabilization that seems to characterize postmodern life against the "certitudes" of modernity.[29] Whether these same developments also generated postmodernism as an attitude and epistemology is more problematic. It should be evident from the discussion above that many of the intellectual orientations associated with postmodernism (and its various offshoots such as postcolonialism) resonate at the level of vocabulary at least with emerging orientations in the literature on management and work: the challenge to universal rationality in the name of local rationalities, the stress on culture over instrumental reason, the repudiation of Eurocentrism in the name of multiculturalism, the elevation of the contingent over the teleological, the search for instabilities, the repudiation of essences and subjectivities implicit in the promotion of flexibility and ongoing reinvention of work (and, therefore, the subjectivity of manager and worker alike), insistence on management as negotiation between company and worker, and, of course, the very important autonomous role assigned to culture in the shaping of organization and subjectivity alike. The ideas and the vocabulary together lend a postmodern ring to these discussions. Referring to the relationship between the emergence of postmodernism and new developments in organizational theory and practice, Kenneth Gergen has observed that "organization theory has hardly been immune to these various developments within the intellectual world. Indeed, the organizational community has made an active and important contribution to many of the issues at stake." Gergen does not specify what he means by "organizational community," but he goes on to cite a number of works on organization theory going back to the early eighties which moved "importantly in the postmodern direction" or adopted "a postmodern stance."[30]

Still, when a full-fledged postmodernism appeared in organization studies, it acknowledged its debt to postmodernism in cultural studies. A landmark article (frequently cited later) by Robert Cooper and Gibson Burrell, published in 1988, introduced to organization studies "the current debate in the human sciences between the opposing conceptual positions of 'modernism' and 'postmodernism' . . . and its implications for organizational analysis."[31] The article outlined basic ideas of postmodernism, with particular emphasis on its indebtedness to Nietzsche, with reference to the work of Deleuze and Guattari, Derrida, Foucault, Lyotard, etc. Subsequent discussions of postmodernism by other authors would add to the list the names of Bakhtin, Baudrillard as well as of anthropologists Geertz and Clifford (considering the seminal theoretical importance of his work, one important name missing, interestingly, is that of Fredric Jameson).[32]

The modernist/postmodernist distinction enabled Cooper and Burrell to reclassify the existing alternatives in organization theory:

> (1) a 'control' model which is referential, instructional and conceived as the expression of human rationality;(2) an 'autonomy' model which is self-referential, processual (i.e., without fixed location) and which acts automatically, i.e., independently of external (human) control. The 'control' model approximates the modernist view of the world, especially in the idea of the ultimate rational subject who can 'meta-organize.' In contrast, the 'autonomy' model approximates the arguments of postmodernism, especially the rejection of the omniscient, rational subject.[33]

Organizational postmodernists challenge the Weberian assumption of bureaucratic rationality that has informed the modernist view of organization.[34] Postmodernism, they believe, enables a radical critique of modernist views of organization. It shifts attention from the "organization of production" to the "production of organization," which reveals that far from expressing a natural rationality, the organization itself is a "self-referential" product of unnamed and unarticulated desires, including the desire for power: "organized rationality, far from originating in *beau*-ideals and consummate logics of efficiency, is founded on sleight-of-hand, vicious agonisms and *pudenda origo* ('shameful origins'). This is the revisionary lesson that postmodernism brings to organizational analysis."[35] Postmodernism also undercuts claims to rationality, by challenging the possibility of the rational subject or a single universal rationality, and instead revealing the contingency and local character of organizational decisions. Organization then appears as a process of many local decisions and conflicts, rather than a structural embodiment of rationality. "Functional" categories in organization such as manager and worker are likewise dissolved into the products of these processes, rather than referring to anything positive. The same processes undercut legitimations of power in the organization with claims to superior rationality. Finally, the modernist conception of organization, rather than represent any reality outside of itself, appears in postmodernist perspective as a discourse of power; indeed, all models of organization represent at best discourses or "metaphors" rather than positive realities. As Gergen puts it,

> our theories of organizations are, first and foremost, forms of language. They are guided by existing rules of grammar, and constructed out of the pool of nouns and verbs, the metaphors, the narrative plots, and the like found within the linguistic context.[36]

Without suggesting that all postmodernist organization theorists hold the same view of what a postmodern conception of organization might be, the following statement is indicative of the postmodernist representation of organization as "text":

> Organizations, as texts, are therefore partially constitutive of the subjectivity of those who are involved in their production. Similarly, they seek to constitute the subjectivity of this readership, their style, strategy and context 'interpellating' them, inviting participation in a certain way. Nevertheless, 'readers' bring their awareness of other texts, other cultural forms, other evocations and explosions of meaning to their reading of any text, and enter into the text, changing its nature and reproducing it as they consume it. As differance illuminates, consumption is an inseparable part of production; as supplementarity confirms, the author is de-centered by the reader. Both authors and readers, creators and consumers, are inseparably bound together in, and are constituted by, the continual process of the emergence of meaning. So it is with organizations as members, be they managers, professionals, superiors, subordinates or amenable to any other taxonomy, are immersed in this unselfconscious negotiation and emergence of their own identities within and without the organization.[37]

Kenneth Gergen, who has emphasized the importance of postmodernism for practice ("theory and practice are inseparable"), is even more emphatic on the production of organization through the inter-discursive activity of its members, as well as "inter-discourse" between the organization and its environment. Gergen describes representation itself as a "communal artifact"; hence, "I do not express myself in relationships through language; relationships express themselves through me."[38] Applying this idea to management, he observes,

> Managers may reframe their sayings over time, colleagues may re-interpret. Rationalities are never written in stone. Further, as a given saying proliferates across different social settings, its meanings may undergo further change. Each attempt to decode the original is a further encoding. And these encodings are open-ended, undecidable until constrained by listeners. A manager's words, then, are like authorless texts; once words are set in motion, the manager ceases to control their meaning. They are possessions of the community.[39]

Gergen's views on organization are shaped by a distrust of "power," which he believes divides the organization internally into power domains, disenabling its operations, and externally erects barriers between the organization and its environment, undermining its ability to grasp external realities and to respond to them effectively. He finds in M. Bakhtin's concept of "heteroglossia" the key to the dynamics of effective organization:

> let us reconstitute Bakhtin's concept of heteroglossia as a dimension. That is, we can view organizations (or their sub-units) as varying in the degree to which they incorporate the discursive forms of surrounding cultures (or other organizational units). Following the argument that the constitution of power is ultimately self-destructive, it follows that organizations acting to increase internal heteroglossia, up to a point, are those most capable of surviving in postmodern society. That is, an active emphasis must be placed on (1) sharing organizational realities acoss sub-units within a firm, (2) exporting organizational realities into the outside culture, and (3) enabling external realities to enter freely into organizational life.[40]

I have quoted from these works in length to convey an idea of the way in which postmodern concepts and vocabulary appear in the literature on organization. While this literature does not, so far as I can tell, refer to the emergent management practices discussed above, its postmodernist stance toward problems of organization resonates, in spite of differences in vocabulary, with central themes in recent managerial practices. This is the case especially with relations of power within organizations (among managers, and between managers and workers), but also in the relationship of the organization to the outside world. Especially noteworthy is the coincidence of the critique in both literatures of formal rules, and formalities in general, in interfering with efficient organization. So is the conception of organization as a product of ongoing experimentation and negotiation, in contrast to earlier views of organization as stable structure.

What is surprising is that while this postmodernist organizational literature is quite explicit in its critique of earlier ("modernist") forms of organization, it has little to say about the realities of contemporary organizations. Gergen, for example, refers to the works by Lash and Urry and Piore and Sabel (see above), but is content to observe that "theories of emerging heterogeneity, disorganization and information dependency in contemporary society all suggest that postmodern shifts in organization theory and practices may be essential to the continuing viability of organization," without pursuing further the relationship between postmodern organizational theorizing and the material conditions of postmodernity. What is also remarkable in almost all of these writings is their silence on contemporary capitalism, even when they are evidently speaking not just about organizations, but capitalist organizations.[41] What these silences might imply is best considered against the issues of culture and control in contemporary management to which I referred above.

Postmodernism: With and Without Capitalism

In a critical evaluation of postmodernism in organizational theory, Jeff Hearn and Wendy Parkin have drawn a distinction between postmodernism with and without oppression. Postmodernism with oppression, they argue, has been quite important in introducing new critical perspectives to organizational theory, as it has revealed the complexities of oppression beyond an exclusive emphasis earlier on class oppression; especially important has been postmodernism's revelations concerning gender and ethnic oppression in organizations. Postmodernism without oppression, on the other hand, has ended up celebrating postmodernity, disguising problems of inequality and oppression that persist in contemporary society.[42]

I would like to carry Hearn and Parkin's distinction on the basis of oppression to a distinction of postmodernism with and without capitalism. This is not to suggest that postmodernists explicitly reject the relevance of capitalism; while on occasion one hears of reference to "postcapitalist" society, such references are rather rare. The issue, rather, is the silence of postmodernism on its context in capitalism. While postmodernists may not explicitly reject problems presented by capitalism, their repudiation of "metanarratives," totalities and structures obviates the need for analysis to account for a structural context in the shaping of which capitalism may be crucial, as the very suggestion of determination by forces emanating from global structurations goes against the grain of postmodernism's emphasis on the local and the contingent. Hence, while postmodern organizational theorizing may nourish off ideas of "disorganized capitalism," it does not dwell long on the senses in which "disorganized capitalism" may be disorganized, and whether or not disorganization implies the absence of any purpose to it. Neither is it overly concerned with the conditions of its own emergence, or plausibility: If the initial moves toward postmodernism appeared from the early eighties, as Gergen suggests, is it possible that postmodern organizational theory itself is a response to conditions created by "disorganized capitalism," and derives its plausibility from its resonance with those conditions? The question is especially pertinent for a mode of theorizing that repudiates both recourse to a universal rationality in judgments of validity, and the possibility of reference to an empirical reality that is independent of linguistic representation. Yet, postmodern organizational theorists not only have few qualms about rejecting "modernist" conceptions of organizations, but also go on to portray "postmodernist" theorizing in such a manner that its relevance is extended beyond the present to the past and the future; in other words, as another "metanarrative" of organizations.[43] History, and historical context, become quite irrelevant under the circumstances to the evaluation of either modernist or postmodernist conceptions of organization.

The refusal to engage questions of historicity, and the structures that enable the demarcation of different periods in history, makes for a deep ambiguity in postmodernist analysis. Postmodernist organizational theorizing is frustratingly vague in its relationship to capitalist modernity: whether what it seeks to negate is capitalist modernity per se, or the modernist institutional structures and their legitimation by an ideology of universal rationality that have stood in the way of realizing the goals of capitalist modernity? This, of course, makes for an ambiguity in the status of postmodernism itself; whether it seeks to break with, and overcome, capitalist modernity, or fulfill its promise. What is at issue here is the complicity of postmodernism with a contemporary capitalism, that is not to be grasped, let alone resolved, without reference to the historical structures of capitalism.

The silence of postmodern theorizing on the conditions of its own emergence and plausibility is an ideological silence. For all its critique of capitalist modernity, organizational postmodernity suppresses its own origins in a postmodernity that is not so much a negation of capitalist modernity as it is a condition for realizing a teleology of capital that assumed "modernist" forms in response to problems of modernity, but can now "liberate" itself from the constraints of those forms, because the conditions have changed, and the problems of modernity have been eliminated. I am not suggesting here that there are no longer any problems in the self-realization of capital, only that the problems of the past are no longer the problems of the present; especially important being the apparent demise of socialist alternatives, and the decline of oppositional labor practices. Capital creates its own problems as it moves along, however, and the managerial experiments of our day have their source not in some outside challenge, now that there is no longer an outside, but in the very dynamics of capitalism.

Postmodern organization theorizing is plausible only to the extent that it resonates with the actual operations of capital in practice. While the examples cited above do not pretend to descriptiveness, and are quite abstract in statement, they are quite consistent with managerial practices that have become evident over the last decade, as a command economy has been replaced by one that achieves its goals by negotiation rather than hierarchical prerogatives, both in internal relationships and in the relationship of the organization to its environment (as customers, consumers, labor source or ecology, in both a social and a natural sense). Managerial literature shows a greater sensitivity to both sets of these relationships. The "authorial" status of management has indeed been transformed by the participation of workers in decision making. Customer service has been forced to speed up its response, as well as to transform its manner of service. Management literature stresses the importance of managing external, as well as internal, relations. And "open-book" management confirms postmodernist analysis by utilizing itself a textual metaphor for management practices. Cultural sensitivity, internal and external, has replaced recourse to abstract reason as a moment in managerial behavior. An earlier monopolistic arrogance in relation to both employee and customer has been disciplined, as it were, by the greater prevalence of corporate competition which, needless to say, has disorganized a Fordist monopoly capitalism. But has the transformation changed the nature of the forces at work, or has it shifted the burden from claims to reality to the manipulation of the representations of reality, from reality to illusion,[44] and from coercion to cultural engineering? Is a capitalism "disorganized" by forces of globalism a capitalism, therefore, without goals? And does "disorganization" imply the absence of structuring forces that are embedded in inequalities of power, that work to intensify rather than correct for inequalities? It is this latter kind of questioning that is missing from postmodernist theorizing, whereas it is quite readily visible in the literature on management.

Gergen's conception of organization as a "polyglot" language community cited above, for example, has little to say about the conditions of power under which such a community is to be realized. Gergen follows up his discussion of "heteroglossia" with an outline of its "practical" consequences:

> Attention is invited to the ways in which members of various organizational sub-units can shift from one locale to another within the firm, incorporating diverse viewpoints, values and modes of action. Such shifting should be undertaken in such a way that consensus within any unit is constantly contested. The emphasis is removed from developing and implementing strong and rational leadership. . . . Centrality is displaced by heterogeneity and an *ad hocing* through the complexities of an ever shifting sea of meaning and action. Rationality becomes situated . . . means must be sought for opening organizational doors to alien realities. For example, minority voices, voices of dissensus within the organization, must be invited to speak out; and, although unsettling the fluid operation of the organization, their messages must be made intelligible, absorbed and integrated. Organizational members should also be encouraged in alternative pursuits—to master alternative argots, from various fields of study, politics, sports, the arts, foreign cultures, specialty clubs and the like. . . . The result of this constant challenge to naturally occurring tendencies toward consensus will be, from the present standpoint, the prevention of hegemonic tendencies of various sub-units (including high-level management) within the firm and the more complete integration of the organization into the surrounding environment. . . . The misleading distinction between *inside* and *outside* the organization blur . . . as organizations join with their surrounding cultures for purposes of mutual empowerment, and the circle of interdependence is ever widened, we may become aware of the world as a total system.[45]

The difference between this utopian conception of organization, and the manner in which organizational culture is approached in management literature, and the practices of management, is not so much one of content as it is of presentation. The organization is subject to constant disorganization and reorganization, and yet there is seemingly no goal or subject to the activity. Rather than the maximization of profit which is the acknowledged goal of any capitalist firm, the goal appears here as if it were the creation of a global awareness. The absence of agency is especially significant since Gergen, in good postmodernist fashion, eschews established rules and regulations, and also concedes "natural" tendencies to stability. Contrast his statement with the following one from a textbook on managing cultures:

> Before they can manage the cultures in their organizations effectively, managers need to become culturally aware; they need to know and understand their organization's cultures. They must also recognize and use various levers they have available to influ-

ence their cultures and resolve the ethical dilemmas involved. In all of these efforts, they need to recognize and learn to accept that some degree of ambivalence, confusion, and contradiction is inevitable. Finally, they must decide whether they should try to maintain, change, or create a culture. Given the multiculturalism of most large organizations, managers in them may find they want to do some of all three.[46]

How these ideas appear in practice is exemplified in an ethnography of a "high-tech" company conducted by Gideon Kunda. The "workers" of this company are highly trained engineers, "symbolic-analysts." This successful company's practice incorporates everything that appears in the two quotations above, including encouraging its employees to learn different "argots." Kunda's description of the ways in which these practices appear may be illustrated by the following passage depicting the beginning of the work day:

> Tom O'Brien has been around the company for a while; like many others, he has definite ideas about "Tech culture" and what it takes to get things done in Engineering. But, as he is constantly reminded, so does the company. When he arrives at work each morning, he encounters evidence of the company point of view at every turn. First are the bumperstickers adorning many of the cars in the Lyndsville parking lot, "I LOVE TECH!" they declare, somewhat unoriginally, the words underscored by the ubiquitous little red heart designed into the company logo. "This shit is everywhere," he says, "I got it on my own car." . . . Inside the building, just beyond the security desk, a large television monitor is playing a videotape of a recent speech by Sam Miller [the company president]. As he walks by, he hears the familiar voice discuss "our goals, our values, and the way we do things." "It's the 'We are One' speech," he notes as he walks by, "nothing new." He has read the speech in a company newsletter, and excerpts are posted everywhere. Turning a corner, he stops by a large bulletin board. . . . On one side is a permanent display including the well-known statement of the "Company philosophy" ("It's the bible—the Ten Commandments for the Techie: make a buck and do it right.") . . . Close by, piles of brochures are stacked on a table in front of the personnel office. Tom takes one, headed, "If you are experiencing signs of stress, perhaps you should give us a call." Inside it offers some words of wisdom: "Everyone experiences stress at some point. . . . Stress isn't necessarily a bad thing." . . . Cultural commentary.finds him in the relative seclusion of his own space. . . . On his technet mail he notices among the many communications another announcement of the afternoon events; a memo entitled, "How Others See Our Values," reviewing excerpts on Tech Culture from recent managerial bestsellers. . . . In his mail ("the hardcopy"), he finds Techknowledge, one of a large number of company newsletters. On the cover is a big picture of Sam Miller against the background of a giant slogan—"We Are One." . . . His bookshelf has mostly technical material, but also a copy of *In Search of Excellence*, distributed to all professional and managerial employees.[47]

So much for heteroglossia! Lest Kunda's account be taken to be that of a jaundiced observer, as early as 1982, Peters and Waterman wrote of the employees of one of the chaotically organized but well managed companies in their study [Minnesota Mining and Manufacturing–3M] that "the members of an extremist political sect are no more conformist in their central beliefs."[48]

In the conclusion to the book, the authors also observed of the companies they had discussed:

> We have mentioned clubby, campus-like environments, flexible organizational struc-
> tures (hiring of new divisions, temporary habit-breaking devices, regular reorgani-
> zations), volunteers, zealous champions, maximized autonomy for individuals,
> teams and divisions, regular and extensive experimentation, feedback emphasizing
> the positive, and strong social networks. All of these traits are positive, the excitement
> of trying things out in a slightly disorderly (loose) fashion.
>
> But at the same time, a remarkably tight—culturally driven/controlled—set of
> properties marks the excellent companies. Most have rigidly shared values. The
> action focus, including experimentation itself, emphasizes extremely regular com-
> munication and very quick feedback; nothing gets very far out of line.[49]

As the "Tech" example shows, these practices have been internalized by management over the last decade. Management consulting literature provides abun-
dant examples of the new "revolutionary" thinking, as does management practice. "Change agent" is a new management title, promoted among others by
Pritchett Associates, a Texas based management consulting firm that lists among
its clients such firms as IBM and McDonalds. The pamphlets of the firm preach
management creation of disorganization and stress, and employee effort to live
up to it, as keys to the operations of a good company; they also recommend
takeover of universities, as all "revolutionaries" have understood the importance
of education to their success.[50]

This management "revolution" has coincided with the enormous redistribution of wealth and power in the United States; last year alone, corporate profits
went up a "sizzling" (*Business Week* description) forty percent, while labor's wages
went up only 2.7 percent, the lowest in recorded history, according to the *New
York Times*.[51] The "management revolution" may or may not be responsible for
the increasing concentration of wealth in the hands of the top twenty percent of
the U.S. population, but especially in the top one percent; there are other factors
in the concentration of wealth, including political ones. But successful American
companies, according to a recent *Business Week* report, have replaced Japanese
companies as "management Meccas."[52] The new management practices have also
rendered "stress" into the most common of job related ailments.[53] Kunda classi-
fies the subjectivities of the employees at HighTech Corporation into "ironic
selves" and "minimal selves." The latter refer to the subjectivities of the service
workers, temporaries, etc., who are of little concern to the culture of the company,
the former to the subjectivities of the "symbolic-analysts" who are crucial. Bom-
barded by company cultural propaganda, the latter cope with stress by distancing

themselves from the company psychologically, expressing themselves in ironic detachment while living with stress.[54] Needless to say, the new management practices also promise to end "the Hundred Years' War between labor and capital," by binding the worker to the company, by undermining the subjectivities of the work force, and by breaking down the conditions for workers solidarity—which is the reverse side of the coin to closer relationships between managers and workers.

Whether or not these changes make for organizational practices that are superior to earlier organizational practices may be a moot question; what is important is that they represent responses to "the modern scourges of globalization, downsizing, and technological change."[55] On the other hand, their effects are felt differently in accordance with position in that global economy, and the corporations through which that economy is organized, or "disorganized," as the case may be. Those positions continue to be determined by the goals and structures of capitalism: "the bottom line" ("make a buck and do it right," as the HighTech slogan has it). The goals or assumptions of capitalist modernity have hardly undergone a transformation, although the means whereby those goals are to be achieved have changed in response to changing conditions—not just of consumption but also of production.

The immense transfer of wealth from the majority population to the owners and managers of capital made possible by these organizational changes is very important, but it may still not be the most significant aspect of the new organizational practices. These practices are also in the process of transforming the relationship between capital and labor in a direction that is consistent with longstanding aspirations of capital. For all the talk of "self-reliance," or the revival of a neo-artisan approach to work, the new practices have enormously enhanced the power of management by increasing the flexibility of capital vis-à-vis labor. Flexibility of access to labor around the world has as its concomitant an increased flexibility at home; turning regular labor into temporary or contract labor, and, where regular labor is retained, increasing the demands on laborers in hours worked (according to company need) or the kinds of work expected of them. Flexible production represents an expansion of the flexibility of the corporation; judging by the pathological "stress" corporate strategies seem to induce in laborers, the laborer (including the "symbolic-analysts," in many cases) experiences "flexibility" as a further loss of control over his/her labor—and life.

Karl Marx, whose sociology presupposed an intrinsic connection between labor and human "species-being," saw in commodity production—and its concomitant, the commodification of labor which rendered the laborer into abstract "labor-power"—the key to understanding alienation in capitalist society. The alienation of the laborer, Marx argued, consisted of four related aspects: alienation from the products of labor, from the process of labor (laboring activity), from the laborer's own "species-being," and, therefore, from other laborers (human beings). He observed,

The worker therefore only feels himself outside his work, and in his work feels outside himself. He is at home when he is not working, and when he is working he is not at home. His labour is therefore not voluntary but coerced; it is *forced labour*. It is therefore not the satisfaction of a need; it is merely a *means* to satisfy needs external to it.[56]

A sociology based exclusively on work may be insufficient at a time when the "workerless factory" may have appeared on the horizon as a possibility, but neither can it be ignored by an evaluation of contemporary capitalism that pretends to any measure of criticalness. If production does not seem to occupy a major place in our consciousness presently, it may be because, as I suggested above, it has been moved elsewhere. Come every Christmas, and many other occasions as well, Americans are urged to consume commodities that have been produced all over the world. A cursory look at labels should be reminder of the relationship between consumption and production; presently that means that Americans are being urged to consume goods the production of which once provided them with jobs, but which has now been moved elsewhere, leaving them as consumers pure and simple (for as long as credit will permit them). It is easy under the circumstances to blame the Japanese or Chinese or whomever, and to overlook that it is the same corporations or companies that are doing the urging for greater consumption that have moved the production; which have few complaints about "slave labor" when it means labor kept cheap by a collusion between corporations and authoritarian Third World governments. Production at home, while it seeks to create the illusion of ever greater corporate openness, subjects the laborer to unprecedented supervision, depriving him/her not only of external but also of internal spaces, which is what "cultural engineering" is about. Whether or not we see production as an important aspect of contemporary life depends on how much of the capitalist totality we wish to see. To keep the totality blurred has been a function of ideology all along. That cultural engineering has assumed such a central part in the functioning of capital in our day may point not to the irrelevance of production but to the extent to which the operations of capital have come to rest on alienated labor. Hence a president of the United States may enjoin American workers, without any hint of irony, "to embrace productivity gains that may lead to a loss of jobs." And "symbolic-analytical workers" continue with unabated enthusiasm to "confer life" on the machines that, more than ever before, confront them—and the rest of us—as something "hostile and alien"; if I may apply Marx's terminology to the new technologies that not only rob people of their livelihood, but also provide the wherewithal to make increasingly engineered lives appear as the epitome of empowerment.

To the extent that postmodernist organizational analysis ignores these conditions, it serves not critical purposes, but purposes of mystification, by re-presenting as linguistic operations activities that are very, for lack of a better word, real. That the organization is a text in the production of which both authors (managers) and readers (employees) participate may have a plausibility at one level of analysis, but in ignoring the origination and the goals of the text, the analysis is seduced by its own metaphor to cover up the differential power relations which are the point of departure for managerial activity, and which also constitute the goals of that activity. The "change agent" may no longer claim legitimacy by recourse to universal reason, but has likely enhanced rather than compromised corporate power. The older bureaucratic organizations with their functional differentiation may have used the appeal to rationality to legitimize the power of the organization, but as management analysts have realized, the same organizations also bred "factionalisms" that impeded total organizational control. The new "cultural management," for all its chaotic appearance, is premised on a tighter organic conceptualization of the corporation than was available with the mechanical rationality models earlier.[57]

Disguising the "subject" in the operations of the "polyglot" firm, a description of corporate operations such as Gergen's above, in its very utopianism, serves to legitimize management practices that are grounded in assumptions of power and inequality that have been the assumptions of capitalist modernity all along. This utopianism also infuses his vision of "heteroglossia" as the means to an awareness "of the world as a total system." Heteroglossia, and the opening up of subjectivities, may indeed be necessary to the realization of global consciousness, but only when it accounts for its conditions of power and inequality. Otherwise, it has about as much plausibility as the promise of a "Global Village" that identifies the global village with the information network and leaves outside of its scope the majority of the world's people who live in real villages, or the "virtual communities" of e-mail that provide escapes from the necessity of confronting problems of living in real communities. Corporations that disorganize communities in managing them are obviously not part of Gergen's analysis. Here, postmodernism, in its utopianization of the configurations of contemporary capitalism, coincides with the obscurantist promises of a new world offered in Tom Peter's "liberation management," or Alvin and Heidi Toffler's *Politics of the Third Wave*, in which House Speaker Newt Gingrich finds a source of endless inspiration.

Organizational Postmodernism—And Postmodernism

A critic, Paul Thompson, has described postmodernism in organization studies as a "fatal distraction."[58] Postmodernism appears as a "fatal distraction," if not as mystification, so long as it is divorced from its material circumstances, and its context within a global capitalist economy. What may be the case with postmodernism in organization studies is also the case with postmodernism in general as epistemology. It may be suggested that the one does not follow from the other, since there is always the possibility that postmodernism as applied to management and organization represents a (mis)appropriation of postmodernism in cultural studies. While management studies indeed have proven themselves capable of appropriating anything available for their consumption (which may be their strength), including revolutionary guerilla strategies, that is not the issue here. To the extent that postmodernism has been extended beyond the study of texts to society and politics in general, it has been made available for such appropriation, and to the extent that postmodernism has been silent about its own material conditions, and even repudiated the relevance of those conditions as part of its epistemology, it has participated in the mystification of the contemporary situation.

What postmodernist organization analysis reveals concerning postmodernism may be, to paraphrase what Georg Lukacs once observed of Marxism, that postmodernism may best be conceived of as a "self-criticism" of modernity, rather than its negation. But even to fulfill this goal, it needs to acknowledge its common circumstances with modernity in the structuring of life by capitalism. Postmodernism's distraction of attention from earlier forms of social and cultural organization is not necessarily undesirable; as Hearn and Parkin point out, the intellectual and social concerns that have gone into the making of postmodernism have served a very important purpose in revealing the complexities of structures of oppression, and the structuring of life in general. The "distraction," in other words, need not be fatal, as it makes it possible to perceive the problems of contemporary life in new, productive ways.

Postmodernism becomes a "fatal distraction" when it divorces itself from its material conditions, localizing oppressions, rendering them contingent, and metaphorizing them so that the structures of power that condition life are pushed to the background, if not denied altogether. While postmodernism in its social concerns has done great service in bringing to the surface of consciousness oppressions such as gender or ethnic oppressions, it needs also to account for consequences: why the liberation of women and ethnics may end up dividing *them* along new faultlines, which are hardly contingent but follow configurations that correspond to broader structures of power. This does not require a renewed reduction of oppression to an earlier opposition between labor and capital, because the question of class has been problematized inevitably in the accounting for new kinds of oppression; but it does require reference to the ongoing reconfigurations of political economy, which retains its modernist goals, but seeks to achieve them by new means. A postmodernism that repudiates such reference on the grounds of abstract epistemologies engages in a disavowal of its own conditions, and confounds criticism with the legitimation of power.

For postmodernism to insist on the autonomy of culture or discourse against putative determinisms is to scratch where it doesn't itch (except, perhaps, for sections of the "symbolic-analytical" elite). The material determinedness of culture, associated at its worst with a vulgar Marxism, long had been on its way out as an idea before postmodernism came along (and may have prepared the way for the latter). The question in our day is not whether or not culture is determined, or discourse is referential, but rather the systematic engineering of culture in accordance with the demands of power, which also assumes the autonomy of culture and, therefore, its manipulability regardless of material circumstances. And such cultural engineering occurs not just in the realm of consumption, or in the selling of presidents, but in the very organization of production and society, where it touches everyone at the level of everyday livelihood and survival. Rather than engage in a critique of this situation, postmodernists lend it legitimacy by their own insistence on the irrelevance of the material to the cultural.

The problem goes even deeper. Whatever its formulators intended initially, postmodernism as it has acquired currency has also assumed features that may most charitably be described as bizarre. I am referring here to the tendency of postmodernists to respond to every evocation of structural conditions as a reassertion of Eurocentrism, or of "monologic neocolonial narratives," as in the example cited above. Starting off as a critique of subjectivities premised on principles of domination, postmodernism has turned into something of a caricature; a caricature that disguises contemporary oppressions, while it attacks critics of oppression on the grounds that any mention of oppression is a denial of the subjectivities of the oppressed.[59] The "democratic" premises of this postmodernism, ironically, end up in very anti-democratic consequences in its denial of oppression as an ongoing determinant of everyday life. This "pop" postmodernism, partaking as it does of the language of an imagined marketplace in its vocabulary of negotiation, lends an illusory sense of equality to exchanges of the market which have been premised all along on "unequal exchange" under capitalism. Politically, it issues in a libertarianism that negates the possibility of collective action which, by their own acknowledgement, is the desired goal of the managers of capital.

If the sustenance of power in our day depends more than ever on "cultural engineering," and the confounding of illusion and reality, it may be more reason than ever to return critique to its origins in the critique of ideology: to break down the illusions that mask reality. It also requires not just the denial, but also the reconstitution of subjectivity: if the integrated, rational, subject of a Eurocentric humanism must be broken down in order to allow recognition of other subjectivities that an earlier modernity denied—be they women, people of color, or non-EuroAmericans—the goal of breaking down subjectivities is not to abolish subjectivity, but to enrich it. Only such enriched subjectivities may provide the resources for resistance against a capitalism that, as it generates postmodernity, also produces the minimal and ironic selves that make impossible any significant resistance to its power. The reconstitution of such subjectivity in turn calls for its own autonomous spaces that are immune to the intrusions of capital, or if not immune, which may not be possible, at least seek to provide an "outside" from which to view, and to deal with, an engineering of society that is the unchanged goal of capitalist modernity. The necessity of creating an "outside," too, was a component of modernism, that used to go under the name of socialism, that nevertheless proved incapable of providing alternatives to the developmentalism of capital, but mimicked it to seal its own fate. The postmodernist promise of, or resignation to, the dissolution of the barriers between community and corporation, likewise, offers little beyond the consumption of community by corporation, but this time in willing compliance.

The point of resistance is to demarcate the line dividing community and corporate capital, not to abolish or to blur it; in such a demarcation may lie the difference, in the words of Jeremy Brecher and Tim Costello, between a global village, that includes villages of living people, and global pillage, that nourishes off the denial of living people in the name of a "progress without people."[60]

Notes

A rough version of this discussion was presented at a seminar in the Humanities Institute at Stony Brook. I would like to thank the participants in that seminar, especially E. Ann Kaplan, the Director of the Institute, for their encouragement to put it in writing. The final version has benefited from comments by friends and colleagues, especially Russell Jacoby, Rebecca Karl, David Noble, Roxann Prazniak, Epifanio San Juan, Jr., Michael Sprinker, Harry Wels, and Zhang Xudong.

1. The seminal works to insist on a relationship between culture and political economy are Fredric Jameson, "Postmodernism, or the Cultural Logic of Late Capitalism," *New Left Review*, 146 (1984):53–92, and David Harvey, *The Condition of Postmodernity: An Enquiry into the Origins of Cultural Change* (Oxford and Cambridge, MA: Blackwell, 1989). However persuasive and provocative his argument, Jameson established at best an abstract and tenuous relationship between postmodernism and capitalist development, and stressed consumption as the deperminant of cultural forms associated with postmodernism. Hans Bertens, *The Idea of the Postmodern: A History* (London and New York: Routledge, 1995), pp. 158, 173, suggests that Jameson's stress on consumption may be due to the influence of Jean Baudrillard on his thinking. Harvey's book is much more detailed in his account of developments in contemporary capitalism, including production, and their relationship to cultural change. He, however, was interested primarily in postmodern cultural formations, rather than cultures of work and management in contemporary capitalism that mediate material and cultural production. Philip Cooke, *Back to the Future: Modernity, Postmodernity and Locality* (London: Unwil Hyman, 1990), has offered the most concrete delineations of the connections between postmodernism and the reorganization of capitalism.

2. For an early and rather precocious confrontation of this question, see the essays in Edward Shorter (ed), *Work and Community in the West* (New York: Harper and Row, 1973).

3. Jameson, *Postmodernism, or the Cultural Logic of Late Capitalism* (Durham, NC: Duke University Press, 1991), p.x.

4. For this problem of cultural production carrying different meanings under different historical circumstances (which already presupposes the relevance of structural conditions), see, Ulf Hannerz, *Cultural Complexity* (New York: Columbia University Press, 1992). Hannerz's argument pertains to the ways in which culture is "distributed" under different historical and social circumstances. Culture as an object of production and distribution may be characteristic of modernity but especially postmodernity, which has rescued culture from "determinedness" and "functionalism" to render it into a plaything at the hand of local circumstances. Hence, postmodernism combines a libertarian view of culture with a rather contradictory "essentialist" affirmation of the cultures of the marginalized.

5. This is what I have referred to elsewhere as Global Capitalism. See, Arif Dirlik, *After the Revolution: Waking to Global Capitalism* (Hanover, N. H. : University Press of England for Wesleyan University Press, 1994). I capitalize global capitalism when I refer to contemporary capitalism below, in order to distinguish it from capitalism in general, which has always been global in aspiration and, to the extent that circumstances have permitted, in practice as well. For an illuminating discussion of the spatial problems presented by the history of capitalism, see Giovanni Arrighi, *The Long Twentieth Century: Money, Power and the Origins of Our Times* (London and New York: Verso Books, 1994).

6. These comments refer to postmodernism as it acquired prominence in the eighties. I will elaborate further below on postmodernism and its history in the U.S.

7. T. Peters and R. Waterman, *In Search of Excellence* (New York: Warner Books, 1982).

8. Ibid., p.104.

9. Stewart Clegg, *Modern Organizations: Organization Studies in the Postmodern World* (London: Sage, 1990), pp.118, 119. I should note at the outset of the discussion here that while management studies may have ignored culture as a problem in the discussion of work, radical historiography has been quite cognizant of the problem for over two decades. In his *Work, Culture and Society in Industrializing America: Essays in American Working-Class and Social History* (New York: A.A. Knopf, 1976), Herbert Gutman noted the way language teaching was utilized in corporate manuals to instill a "puritan ethic" in an immigrant work force (pp.1–9). Gutman's insights in turn owed much to the work of British labor historians such as E.P. Thompson and E.B. Hobsbawm, as well as to U.S. historians such as Eugene Genovese influenced by the work of the Italian Marxist Antonio Gramsci, and helped stimulate the work of historians such as Stewart Ewen and David Noble. It is noteworthy that during the period discussed by Gutman the purpose of cultural activity was to acculturate the laborer to the discipline of mass production, while presently the discipline required is that of flexible production. As such, the significance of culture in the capitalist organization of production is not new; what is new is an explicit recognition that the deployment of culture serves better than the naked exercise of coercion (when that is impossible, or impracticable) in achieving the goals of labor compliance. There is here, however, also a distinction between generations of historians; a generation that grounded culture in its material origins and consequences, and a generation that has divorced cultural analysis from its grounding in political economy. If comprehensiveness in accounting for circumstances is a criterion of validity in the evaluation of interpretation, these works were way ahead of management studies. In this sense, postmodernism is a setback, which corresponds to its defeatism politically.

10. Philip R. Harris and Robert T. Moran, *Managing Cultural Differences* (Houston: Gulf Publishing Co., 1979), p. 33.

11. Geert Hofstede, *Culture's Consequences* (London: Sage Publications, 1980).

12. Ibid., p.393.

13. Herman Kahn, *World Economic Development: 1979 and Beyond* (New York: Morrow Quill Paperbacks, 1979). See preface for the interest with which it was received at the Chambers of Commerce meeting. For the Confucian revival, see, Arif Dirlik, "Confucius in the Borderlands: Global Capitalism and the Reinvention of Confucianism," *boundary 2* (November 1995):29–73.

14. Kahn, p.128.

15. Ibid., p.121.

16. Ibid., p.3.

17. By the mid-1980s, Japan had become a "management Mecca," and "planeloads of executives, fretting about declining U.S. competitiveness, routinely travelled through factories in Japan in search of ideas." "Management Meccas," *Business Week* (September 18, 1995):122–132, p.123.

18. Thus, some of the sources Kahn draws upon for describing "neo-Confucian" cultural characteristics were in fact works promoting a "discourse on Japaneseness"(*Nihon-jinron*) that stressed the uniqueness of Japan, rather than any kind of commonality between East Asian societies.

19. Clegg provides a very useful description of the contrasts between modernity and postmodernity in management practices in his *Modern Organizations,* op. cit., chaps. 5–6.

20. For a detailed listing of the characteristics of each type, see the table, Harris and Moran, pp.108–109.

21. The distinction I draw here between rationality and culture owes much to the distinction identified by Carl Pletsch in his important article, "The Three Worlds, or the Division of Social Scientific Labor, circa 1950–1975," *Comparative Studies in Society and History,* 23 (October 1981):565–590. Pletsch pointed out in that article an important assumption of "modernization theory" that, according to its mapping of the world, identified rationality with the First (or capitalist), ideology with the Second (or socialist), and culture with the Third (or undeveloped) World.

22. For subcontracting or "global sourcing," see Gary Gereffi, "Global Sourcing and Regional Divisions of Labor in the Pacific Rim," in *What Is in a Rim? Critical Perspectives on the Pacific Region Idea,* ed. by Arif Dirlik (Boulder, CO: Westview Press, 1993). For automation, see, David Noble, *Forces of Production: Social History of Industrial Automation* (New York: Oxford University Press, 1986).

23. Robert Reich, *The Work of Nations* (New York: Alfred A. Knopf, 1991), p.171.

24. This may be an appropriate place to speculate on a question raised by the obliviousness in postmodern theorizing to production in favor of consumption or the regime of "signs." As Reich's re-presentation of First/Third Worlds in terms of mental/manual labor suggests, rightly or wrongly production of the kind associated with an earlier capitalism has now been exported to the "Third World," and the "First World" emerges as the world of the "symbolic-analyst," the producer of signs, as well as the world of the consumers of goods produced "elsewhere." It is not surprising that postmodernism, a product of the First World, should be preoccupied with "signs," and not material production. This obviously underlines the ideology in postmodernism; as with Reich, who renders "symbolic-analysts" into the paradigm of the advanced worker, ignoring those many in the First World who are marginalized and "Third-Worldized" by the export of productive jobs, postmodernism, in denying its own structural conditions, suppresses the very material problems of everyday life by interpellating them into the regime of signs. Mike Featherstone, *Consumer Culture and Postmodernism* (London: Sage, 1991), and, Scott Lash, *Sociology of Postmodernism* (London and New York: Routledge, 1990) have stressed the class basis of postmodernism, albeit from the perspective of consumption.

25. Cover Story, "The New World of Work," *Business Week,* October 17, 1994, pp.76–87.

26. As reported in the *Wall Street Journal* (March 16, 1994). At the same conference, President Clinton urged American workers to "embrace productivity gains that often require job cuts." *WSJ* (March 15, 1994).

27. *INC* (June 1995), p.32. See also the very revealing story in the same issue about an employee who managed to convert from proletarian to the new kind of worker, through a story of fall and redemption.

28. The sources for this summary may be found in any number of places, as these ideas have now entered even popular consciousness with the onset of "downsizing" in the nineties. The *Business Week* article on work, cited above, offers a summary. See, also, the cover story (September 18, 1995) of that journal, "Management Meccas," op. cit. For an extensive "textbook" treatment, see, Harrison M. Trice and Janice M. Berger, *The Cultures of Work Organization* (Englewood Cliffs, N.J.: Prentice Hall, 1993). "Managing chaos" is a favorite theme of management guru Tom Peters, who is also an advocate of "anything goes" management that draws its lessons from any source, anywhere, anytime, including, not surprisingly, the works and example of Mao Zedong. See his recent *Liberation Management: Necessary Disorganization for the Nanosecond Nineties* (New York: Alfred A. Knopf, 1992). See also his *Thriving on Chaos: Handbook for a Management Revolution* (New York: Alfred A. Knopf, 1987). I have noted, elsewhere, that present-day experimentation with management, and the terms in which it is conceptualized, is frequently reminiscent of guerilla warfare. See Arif Dirlik, *After the Revolution: Waking to Global Capitalism* (Hanover and London: Wesleyan University Press, 1994), pp.70–73.

29. I am here merely repeating one of the self-images of the postmodern condition, as the "certitude" of modernity, beyond certain ideological faiths, is very questionable, as M. Berman eloquently demonstrated in his study of modernism, *All That Is Solid Melts Away: The Experience of Modernity* (London: Verso, 1983). That there has been a further destabilization in the organization of politics and economy, however, is plausible. In that regard, it should be noted also that the description of these organizational transformations as a transition from "Fordism" to "post-Fordism" may be valid so long as we remember that "post-Fordism" also includes many practices of "pre-Fordism," and even pre-industrial capitalism. Among other things, the new conception of work that I described above is presented on occasion as a return from proletarian to "artisanal" work, where the worker is more of a craftsperson who has control both over the product and the process of production. For a critique, see Edward Shorter, op. cit., Introduction. See, also, Cooke, *Back to the Future*, op. cit. for the reappearance of earlier forms under contemporary capitalism.

30. Kenneth J. Gergen, "Organization Theory in the Postmodern Era," in Michael Reed and Michael Hughes (eds), *Rethinking Organization: New Directions in Organization Theory and Analysis* (London: Sage, 1992):207–226.

31. Robert Cooper, Gibson Burrell, "Modernism, Postmodernism and Organizational Analysis: An Introduction," *Organization Studies*, 9/1(1988):91–112.

32. See the introduction to and the "pro-postmodernist" essays in John Hassard and Martin Parker (eds), *Postmodernism and Organizations* (London: Sage, 1993). I specify the "pro-" because this interesting collection brought together advocates of postmodernism as well as severe critics of the idea.

33. Cooper, Burrell, p. 104.

34. Cooper and Burrell note to their credit, however, that the assumption of bureaucratic rationality is derivative of a distortion of Max Weber's views, instrumentalizing the latter's analysis of organization while ignoring his critique that "rationality" also implied "rationalization"(pp.92–93).

35. Cooper, Burrell, p. 108.

36. Gergen, p.207.

37. Steve Linstead, "Deconstruction in the Study of Organizations," in Hassard and Parker, pp. 49–69.

38. Gergen, p.214. Gergen uses "inter-discourse" in reference to the relationship between professional theorists and their cultural environment, but his usage is extendable to the relationship between the organization and its environment, as in his use of "dialogics" below.

39. Gergen, p.220.

40. Ibid., p.222.

41. Ibid., p.217. For the reference to corporate organization, see, ibid., p.219.

42. Jeff Hearn and Wendy Parkin, "Organizations, Multiple Oppressions and Postmodernism," in Hassard and Parker, op.cit, pp.148–162.

43. For all their insistence on the interpretive nature of all theorizing, postmodernists are frequently quite intolerant of any interpretation but theirs. Thus one postmodernist, in a rather bizarre turn of phrase, describes "totalizing and modernizing" approaches to organization as "monologic neo-colonial narratives of organizational interpretation." Paul Jeffcut, "From Interpretation to Representation," in Hassard and Parker, op. cit. pp.25–48. Postmodernists of Jeffcut's ilk, in their repudiation of any connection between language and reality, would seem to assume the privilege of abusing language any way they can.

44. The creation of illusions may be gleaned from the uses to which capital has put something like "open-book management," which seems quite straightforward in its "openness": "'Open-book' management has even spread to Zambia, where the world's fifth-largest copper mining company is using Stack's [Jack Stack, CEO of International Harvester and a guru of open-book management] ideas to reduce costs and eke higher productivity out of its 55,000 employees. As largely uneducated [illiterate?] workers march into the front entrance, they can't help but spot a 50-foot-high scoreboard that lists monthly and year-to-date financials, from 'copper revenue' to 'corporate depreciation.'" "Management Meccas," p.128. Stack is the author, apparently, of "game management," which dovetails nicely with postmodernist descriptions of organization, after J.F. Lyotard, as "serious games." In this particular instance, at least, the cynicism of "open-book management" matches Disney's description of its highly controlled management practises as "pixie-dust formula." See, "It's Not Easy Making Pixie Dust," *Business Week* (September 18, 1995), p.134.

45. Gergen, pp.222–224.

46. Trice and Berger, *The Cultures of Work Organizations*, op. cit., p.391.

47. Gideon Kunda, *Engineering Culture: Control and Commitment in a High-Tech Corporation* (Philadelphia: Temple University Press, 1992), pp.50–51.

48. Peters and Waterman, *In Search of Excellence*, op. cit., p.104.

49. Ibid., p.320.

50. See the pamphlets, *Culture Shift: The Employee Handbook for Changing Corporate Culture*, by Price Pritchett and Ron Pound (Dallas, TX: Pritchett Associates, 1993) and *High-Velocity Culture Change: A Handbook for Managers*, by Price Pritchett and Ron Pound (Dallas, TX: Pritchett Associates, 1993). On the functional uses of stress, see, the same authors' *A Survival Guide to the Stress of Organizational Change* (Dallas, TX: Pritchett Associates, 1995). For "change agent," see, also, "Management Meccas," *Business Week* (September 18, 1995):122–132, p.126.

51. *The New York Times* (November 1, 1995). Among the hardest hit in the labor force, according to the report, were machinists, machine inspectors, etc., the skilled work force

of an earlier capitalism, who have now been reclassified as "unskilled." For the latter, see, "The New World of Work," *Business Week,* op.cit. p.80: "What's Losing [in the new world of work]: Crafts and Operators and Laborers, the Domain of Low-skill Union Jobs."

52. "Management Meccas," p.123.

53. Jeremy Rifkin, *The End of Work: The Decline of the Global Labor Force and the Dawn of the Post-Market Era* (New York: Putnam, 1994). See, also, "The New World of Work," p.85.

54. Kunda, Chapter 5, "Self and Organization." Rifkin points to relentless supervision of employees as a major source of stress. A Spanish manager, after a tour of AT&T Universal Card Services, one of the "management Meccas," decided that "Universal Card's measure-and-monitor approach" might not be transplantable in Spain "where workers are likely to rebel against a tightly controlled atmosphere, "Management Meccas," p.126.

55. "Management Meccas," p.122.

56. Karl Marx, *Economic and Philosophic Manuscripts of 1844* (Moscow: Foreign Languages Publishing House, 1959), p.72. See, pp. 67–83 for the discussion of alienated labor.

57. A note may be in order here on a question to which I have referred to implicitly on a number of occasions above. While there is no direct evidence except in occasional references to Mao Zedong in the works of Tom Peters, and uses of such terms as "contradiction" in the language of managers themselves, a historian of the Chinese Revolution (such as myself) cannot help but be struck by parallels between contemporary management practices and the "rectification campaigns" that were a regular part of Chinese Communist practice in the years of revolution. The parallels may not be fortuitous. Communist revolutionaries faced problems similar to those of managers today: how to hold together a sprawling party organization that, under circumstances of guerilla warfare, did not lend itself to day-to-day controls, but instead was subject to the centrifugal forces of local circumstances. The stress on culture and ideology in keeping the organization together in the latter case is parallelled today in efforts of corporate managers to use culture to counteract "chaos," and to balance centralization with the demands of localism. For people in the U.S., it is much easier to accept such "manipulation" on the part of Communists, especially Chinese communists, than on the part of corporate managers, but the parallels are inescapable. The question is not necessarily one of influence, but of parallel responses to comparable structural conditions. Corporations are also likely to be more successful in the use of this strategy as they offer tangible rewards, rather than the promise of an abstract "good society," for compliance.

58. Thompson, "Postmodernism—A Fatal Distraction," in Hassard and Parker, op. cit., pp.183–203, for a trenchant criticism of postmodernism in organization studies.

59. The example of Paul Jeffcut above, with his charge of "neocolonialism" against those who would "totalize" the operations of corporations, is one instance of such perverse reasoning (n 41, above). For an example of a work that universalizes this reasoning, without any hint of awareness of the relationship between the slogans of "globalism" and contemporary capitalism, see, Frederick Buell, *National Culture and the New Global System* (Baltimore, MD: The Johns Hopkins University Press, 1994), where the author attacks critics of imperialism for perpetuating Eurocentrism! For a contrary view of the relationship between globalism and contemporary capitalism, see the editorial, "Economic Nationalism: Disaster Ahead," *Business Week* (September 18, 1995), p.178. Ironically, such examples may prove the postmodernist argument that the author has no control over the interpre-

tation of the text, although not in the sense that they intended—which goes to show that there may not be all that is new about postmodernism!

60. Jeremy Brecher and Tim Costello, *Global Village or Global Pillage: Economic Construction from the Bottom Up* (Boston: South End Press, 1994). "Progress Without People" is the title of David F. Noble's collection of essays on Luddism, *Progress Without People: In Defense of Luddism* (Chicago: C.H. Kerr, 1993). It may be interesting to note here an irony in the unfolding of postmodernism. According to Hans Bertens, *The Idea of the Postmodern*, when the idea of postmodern first appeared in the U.S. in the fifties, it was in order to overcome the "intellectualizations" of modernism to reestablish contact with self and nature; in other words, postmodernism was inspired by antimodernism. Postmodernism took a definite turn away from these origins after it connected with French poststructuralism in the seventies and eighties when, if I may add, it took a drastic turn away from reality. It may not be such a bad idea for postmodernism to reconnect with its origins—which would imply a repudiation of modernism in a sense quite different than that of the postmodernism of the eighties. In this particular sense, postmodernism as a periodizing idea would call for a reasoning quite different than that offered by Fredric Jameson, who is unhappy with postmodernism, and yet cannot subject it to a thorough criticism because he is wedded to ideas of a unilinear historicity; which may be a reason for his own agonizing about how to reject something that appears progressive. There is some circularity of reasoning here, as there is with most postmodernists, who wish to reject modernity, but are wedded nevertheless to the progressiveness of modernity (and capitalism). As Frank Bardacke says in his afterword to the recent collection of Zapatista writings, *Shadows of Tender Fury: The Letters and Communiques of Subcomandante Marcos and the Zapatista Army of National Liberation* (New York: Monthly Review Press, 1995), modernity was bad enough to start with, but now we are saddled with a postmodernity which rejects modernity, but still maps time and space in very modern ways.

10

The Past as Legacy and Project: Postcolonial Criticism in the Perspective of Indigenous Historicism

"Men [and women] make their own history, but they do not make it just as they please; they do not make it under circumstances chosen by themselves, but under circumstances directly encountered, given and transmitted from the past. The tradition of all the dead generations weighs like a nightmare on the brain of the living."[1] After nearly a century and a half, Marx's statement still provides a most cogent affirmation of historicity against both a libertarian obliviousness to the burden of the past, and a determinist denial of the possibility of human agency. But I begin with this statement for still another reason. While Marx's own work lies at the origins of so much of present-day theorizing about society and history, against our theory-crazed times, when the logic of abstraction seems to take precedence over the evidence of the world, the statement is comfortingly common-sensical.

Issues of historicity and common-sense are both pertinent to the problem I take up in this discussion. The problem is derivative of a paradox in contemporary cultural criticism and politics. In academic circles engrossed with post-modernity/postcoloniality as conditions of the present, it is almost a matter of faith these days that nations are "imagined," traditions are "invented," subjectivities are slippery (if they exist at all) and cultural identities are myths. Claims to the contrary are labelled "essentialisms," and dismissed as perpetuations of hegemonic constructions of the world. The denial of authenticity to cultural claims beyond localized constructions is accompanied by the denial to the past of any authority to authenticate the present. In the words of one "postcolonial critic," criticism, if it is to be thoroughly antihegemonic, needs to learn from the experiences of "those who have suffered the sentence of history—subjugation, domination, diaspora, displacement." Recognition of these experiences

> forces us . . . to engage with culture as an uneven, incomplete production of meaning and value, often composed of incommensurable demands and practices, produced in the act of social survival. . . . It becomes crucial to distinguish between the semblance and similitude of the symbols across diverse cultural experiences . . . and

the social specificity of each of these productions of meaning as they circulate as signs within specific contextual locations and social systems of value. The transnational dimension of cultural transformation—migration, diaspora, displacement, relocation—makes the process of cultural translation a complex form of signification. The natural(ized), unifying discourse of "nation, peoples or authentic folk" tradition, those embedded myths of culture's particularity, cannot be readily referenced. The great, though unsettling, advantage of this position is that it makes you increasingly aware of the construction of culture and the invention of tradition.[2]

As if by some devilish design to mock the postcolonial argument, cultural politics in our day exhibits an abundance of such claims to cultural authenticity which, rather than disappear, would seem to be proliferating in proportion to the globalization of postmodernity—with deadly consequences for millions. Cultural nationalism, ethnicism, indigenism have emerged as markers of cultural politics globally; over the last decade ethnicity has moved to the center of politics, overshadowing earlier concerns with class and gender. Claims to cultural authenticity, moreover, have been accompanied by efforts to discover or restore authentic pasts as foundations for contemporary identity; most urgently among those who have suffered "the sentence of history."

The most basic problem presented by this paradoxical situation is the disjuncture between cultural criticism and cultural politics. Even as cultural criticism renders the past into a plaything at the hands of the present, the burden of the past haunts contemporary politics in a reassertion of cultural identities. Postmodern/postcolonial criticism would seem to have little to say on this situation, except to insist even more uncompromisingly on its own validity. Where the postmodern/postcolonial intellectuals themselves are concerned, the repudiation of essentialized identities and authentic pasts seems to culminate in a libertarianism which asserts the possibility of constructing identities and histories almost at will in those "in-between" spaces that are immune to the burden of the past (and the present, in its repudiation of "foundational" structures). Ironically, however, postmodern/postcolonial critics are unwilling to recognize a similar liberty to those who seek to invoke the past in the assertion of cultural identities, labelling all such attempts as misguided (or ideological) essentialisms that ignore the constructedness of the past. That groups which have "suffered the sentence of history" are internally divided and differentiated is not a particularly novel insight; what seems to be new about the current historical situation is the erasure in the name of difference of differences among such groups in their efforts to cope with "the sentence of history," especially those efforts that contradict the new ideology of postmodernism/postcolonialism. "In-betweenness," universalized as a human condition and extended over the past, is thus naturalized in the process, and becomes a new kind of determinism from which there is no escape. At the same time, the label of "essentialism," extended across the board without regard to its sources and goals, obviates the need to distinguish different modes of cultural identity formation that is subversive not only of critical but also of any meaningful political judgment.

It is some questions raised by these different modes of cultural identity formation that I address below. To assert that cultural identity is ambiguous and the historical materials out of which it is constructed are invented is in some ways to state the obvious. The question is what different modes of identity construction imply intellectually and politically, and how we construe the relationships they presuppose between the present and the past. The discussion is organized around three questions that I take to be critical to distinguishing among these identity formations: (a) what is their relationship to power? (b) whether the pasts out of which they are formed are reified pasts, or pasts recognized in their historicity? and (c) what relationship do they establish between the past as legacy, and the past as project? My critique of the discourses on these questions both in legitimations of power, and in postmodern/postcolonial responses to it, is informed strongly by a perspective afforded by indigenism, the ideological articulation of the aspirations to liberation of those native peoples—designated the Fourth World in recent years—that I take to be the terminally marginalized of all the oppressed and marginalized peoples around the world.

Cultural Identity and Power

Leslie Marmon Silko prefaces her novel, *Ceremony*, with a song-poem (also entitled "Ceremony") that tells the reader that the story she is to tell is more than just a story:

> *I will tell you something about stories,*
> *[he said]*
> *They aren't just entertainment,*
> *don't be fooled.*
> *They are all we have, you see,*
> *all we have to fight off*
> *illness and death.*
>
> *You don't have anything*
> *if you don't have the stories.*
>
> *Their evil is mighty*
> *but it can't stand up to our stories.*
> *So they try to destroy the stories*
> *let the stories be confused or forgotten,*
> *they would like that*
> *they would be happy*
> *because we would be defenseless then.*[3]

There may be a postmodern ring to the idea that stories create reality, which drives Silko's narrative, but the intention is anything but postmodern. *Ceremony* is about the recovery of identity destroyed by war and cultural incoherence through a reliving of ancient stories, and as a story itself, seeks to create a reality for native peoples different than the one which is in the process of destroying them. The theme of restoring an indigenous identity by salvaging the native past from its distortions in EuroAmerican historiography is a common one among indigenous peoples from native Americans to the Australian aborigines, from Hawaiians to the Indians of Chiapas. As the Hawaiian sovereignty movement leader Haunani-Kay Trask puts it,

> Burdened by a linear, progressive conception of history and by an assumption that EuroAmerican culture flourishes at the upper end of that progression, Westerners have told the history of Hawai'i as an inevitable if occasionally bitter-sweet triumph of Western ways over "primitive" Hawaiian ways. . . . To know my history, I had to put away my books and return to the land. I had to plant *taro* in the earth before I could understand the inseparable bond between people and '*aina* [land]. I had to feel again the spirits of nature and take gifts of plants and fish to the ancient altars. I had to begin to speak my language with our elders and leave long silences for wisdom to grow. But before anything else, I needed to learn the language like a lover so that I could rock with her and lie at night in her dreaming arms.[4]

"Indigenous peoples," according to the Cree author George Manuel, who is also the founding president of the World Council of Indigenous Peoples, are peoples "descended from a country's aboriginal population and who today are completely or partly deprived of their own territory and its riches."[5] They have been described also as "the Fourth World: the world on the margin, on the periphery."[6] Annette Jaimes describes the various aspects of indigenism as follows:

> In terms of economics, the Native peoples tend to have communal property, subsistence production, barter systems, low impact technologies and collective production. . . . In terms of political relations, Native people have consensual processes, direct "participatory" democracy, and laws embedded in oral traditions. . . . In respect to their social relations, they differ [from modern society], generally, in terms of matrilineality versus patriarchy, extended versus nuclear families, and low versus high population density. . . . Finally, regarding differences in world view, the Native peoples are polytheistic, derive an understanding of the world from the natural order's rhythms and cycles of life, and include animals and plants as well as other natural features in their conceptions of spirituality.[7]

The goal of indigenism, then, is to restore these features of Native life which have been associated in EuroAmerican historiography with "primitivism." Fundamental to indigenism is the recovery of land and, with it, the special relationship to nature which is the hallmark of indigenous identity.

"Indigenous ideology," as its proponents present it, defies all the protocols associated with postmodern/postcolonial criticism—to the point where it could be said fairly that it replicates the colonizers' views of indigenous peoples. Not only does it affirm the possibility of "real" native identity, but it asserts as the basis for such identity a native subjectivity that has survived two centuries of colonialism and cultural disorientation. Not only does it believe in the possibility of recapturing the essence of precolonial indigenous culture, but bases this belief on a spirituality that exists outside of historical time. The very notions of Indian or Hawaiian that are utilized to describe collective identities take for granted categories invented by colonizers, and imposed upon the colonized, in remapping and redefining diverse peoples in a EuroAmerican reconstruction of space in the process of colonization. An articulate spokesman for indigenous ideology such as Ward Churchill not only utilizes this terminology, but also insists that the collectivities thus depicted are "referents" (to recall Bhabha's term in the quotation above) for Indian nationhood, or people-hood.[8] In all these different ways, indigenous ideology would seem to provide a textbook case of "self-Orientalization," that replays the features ascribed to the Others of Eurocentric modernizationism which have been analyzed by Fabian in his *Time and the Other*.[9] What Nicholas Thomas says of "New Age primitivism" in Australia could describe equally well the self-essentialization that is a feature of indigenous ideology in general: "Constructing them as culturally stable since the beginning of humanity does imply an ahistorical existence, an inability to change and an incapacity to survive modernity; this essentialism also entails stipulations about what is and what is not appropriately and truly Aboriginal, which marginalizes not only urban Aboriginal cultures, but any forms not closely associated with traditional bush gathering."[10]

Not surprisingly, indigenous ideology has come under criticism from postcolonial positions, or positions that share certain basic premises with postmodern/postcolonial criticism. A prominent Australian proponent of postcolonial criticism, Gareth Griffiths, wonders of the protests against oppression of "subaltern people" that, "even when the subaltern appears to 'speak,' there is a real concern as to whether what we are listening to is really a subaltern voice, or whether the subaltern is being spoken by the subject position they occupy within the larger discursive economy." Griffiths goes on to state that his goal is not to question

> whether the claim of Aboriginal peoples in Australia and elsewhere to restitution of their traditional lands and sacred places, or to the voices and practices of their traditional cultures, is legitimate. Nor do I question the importance of locality and specificity in resisting the generalizing tendencies and incorporative strategies of white society . . . it is not my business to comment on this. What I am concerned with is the impact of the representation of that claim when it is mediated through a discourse of the authentic adopted and promulgated by the dominant discourse which 'speaks' the indigene within a construction whose legitimacy is grounded not in *their* practice but in *our* desire.[11]

Similarly, but obviously with fewer qualms about offending indigenous sensibilities, a Canadian postcolonial critic writes:

> While postcolonial theorists embrace hybridity and heterogeneity as the characteristic postcolonial mode, some native writers in Canada resist what they see as a violating appropriation to insist on their ownership of their stories and their exclusive

claim to an authenticity that should not be ventriloquized or parodied. When directed against the Western canon, postmodernist techniques of intertextuality, parody, and literary borrowing may appear radical and even potentially revolutionary. When directed against native myths and stories, these same techniques would seem to repeat the imperialist history of plunder and theft. . . . Although I can sympathize with such arguments as tactical strategies in insisting on self-definition and resisting appropriation, even tactically they prove self-defeating because they depend on a view of cultural authenticity that condemns them to a continued marginality and an eventual death. . . . Ironically, such tactics encourage native peoples to isolate themselves from contemporary life and full citizenhood.[12]

Nicholas Thomas has observed that cultural studies in the United States have been largely silent on the question of native Americans: "In U.S. journals that address race, more reference is made to racism and colonial conflicts elsewhere—in South Africa or Britain—than to native American struggles."[13] One noteworthy exception that is pertinent to the discussion here may be the questions raised by the anthropologist Jocelyn S. Linnekin on the claims to cultural authenticity of the Hawaiian independence movement. In an article published in 1983, "Defining Tradition: Variations on the Hawaiian Identity," Linnekin argued not only that Hawaiian society was internally differentiated (and hence not to be homogenized), but that the "traditions" which served as symbols of Hawaiian nationalism—such as Hawaiian seafaring capabilities or the "love of the land"—were invented traditions. Especially damaging were the questions she raised about the traditional sanctity of the island of Kahoolawe, used by the U.S. Navy for bombing practices, which were to be used by the navy as legal evidence to justify continued use of the island as a target against Hawaiian claims to the island's sanctity.[14]

Whether these critiques are based on sufficient readings of indigenous ideology is a question I will take up below. It is necessary here to examine more closely the relationship of indigenous self-assertion to its context in a colonial structure of power. Griffiths' concern that the dominant discourse "speaks" the indigene raises the important question that the reification of indigenous identity not only replicates the assumptions of the dominant discourse, but also opens the way to the "consumption" of indigenism by the dominant society; after all, people who are outside of history are more easily placed in museums and theme parks than those who are part of a living present, and exoticized cultures provide a ready-made fund for the production of cultural commodities.[15] What he overlooks, however, is that it is the power context rather than the reification that may be the more important problem. As the case of Linnekin shows, the denial of reified pasts is equally open to exploitation by power. Disney these days justifies its constructions of the past or of the Other on the grounds that since all pasts are invented or constructed, their constructions are as valid as anyone else's. It is arguable that postmodern/postcolonial denials of historical or cultural truths render the past or other cultures more readily available for commodification and exploitation by abolishing the possibility of distinguishing one invention from another. The premise that all truths are "contingent" truths, without reference to the structures of power that inform them, opens the way to silencing "the subalterns" who cannot even claim authentic custody of their own identities against their "construction" by academic, commercial or political institutions of power.

The importance of accounting for power relations in judgments on identity formation may be illustrated further by placing indigenous ideology within the context of the current proliferation of cultural nationalisms with which it shares much in common in terms of intellectual procedures. There has been a resurgence in recent years of fundamentalistic nationalisms or culturalisms against EuroAmerican ideological domination of the world, that range from Islamic fundamentalism to Pan-Asianism, from assertions in Japan of an ideology of "Japaneseness" to the Confucian revival in Chinese societies. These revivals, while antihegemonic in some respects, are also fueled by newfound power in formerly Third World societies which have achieved success in capitalist development, and all of a sudden find themselves in a position to challenge EuroAmerican models of development. They are also motivated, however, by efforts to contain the disintegrative consequences of such development. The assertion of homogenized cultural identities on the one hand celebrates success in the world economy but also, on the other hand, seeks to contain the disintegrative threat of "Western" commodity culture, the social incoherence brought about by capitalist development, and the cultural confusion brought about by diasporic populations which have called into question the identification of national culture with the space of the nation-state. Thus the Confucian revival among Chinese populations points to Chinese success in capitalist development to argue that the Confucian ethic is equal, if not superior, to the "Protestant ethic" which Max Weber had credited with causative power in the emergence of capitalism in Europe; a "Weberized" Confucianism in turn appears as a marker of Chineseness regardless of time or place. In the idea of a "cultural China" that has been promoted by proponents of a Confucian revival, cultural essence replaces political identity in the definition of Chineseness. At the same time, the idea is one in the promotion of which Chinese states, capital and academic intellectuals (mostly in First World institutions) have played a crucial part. No less important is the fact that non-Chinese academics in the United States closely connected with academic and commercial institutions of power have participated in this revival, and have even played an important part in legitimizing it; Confucianism, reduced to a few ethical principles conducive to social and economic order, has been rendered in the process into an ideology of capitalist development, superior to the individualistic ideology of EuroAmerican capitalism in its emphasis on harmony and social cohesiveness. The latter aspect prompted the government of the People's Republic in China, in 1994, to declare a "Confucian renaissance" on the grounds that with socialism having lost its ethical power to counter undesirable social tendencies, Confucianism might serve as a suitable native substitute.[16] Naturalized as a marker of Chineseness, Confucianism also serves to erase memories of a revolutionary past.

The tendencies toward the proliferation of fundamentalisms and culturalist nationalisms were no doubt on the mind of Samuel Huntington when he wrote in his celebrated 1993 essay:

> World politics is entering a new phase . . . the fundamental source of conflict in this new world will not be primarily ideological or primarily economic. The great divisions among humankind and the dominating source of conflict will be cultural. Nation states will remain the most powerful actors in world affairs, but the principal conflicts of global politics will occur between nations and groups of different civilizations. The clash of civilizations will dominate world politics. . . . With the end of the Cold War, international politics moves out of its Western phase, and its centerpiece becomes the interaction between the West and non-Western civilizations and among non-Western civilizations. . . . Civilization identity will be increasingly important in the future, and the world will be shaped in large measure by the interactions among seven or eight major civilizations. These include Western, Confucian, Japanese, Islamic, Hindu, Slavic-Orthodox, Latin American and possibly African civilization.[17]

A critique of cultural "essentialism" that offers no articulated means to distinguish between the essentialism of indigenous ideology, and the essentialism of a Confucian revival or Huntington's vision of war among civilizations, may be methodologically justifiable; but it is, to say the least, morally irresponsible and politically obscene. Indigenous claims to identity are very much tied in with a desperate concern for survival; not in a "metaphorical" but in a very material sense. Indian lands in the United States, or what is left of them, are not just reminders of a bygone colonial past, but are still the objects of state and corporate destruction in what Churchill describes as "radioactive colonization."[18] In accordance with racist policies established since the nineteenth century, according to Annette Jaimes, Indian identity in the United States is determined either by the recognition of tribal governments or by what has been described as "the blood quantum," the degree of "Indian blood" in any one individual as certified by the Bureau of Indian Affairs (the minimum for qualification set at "quarter blood").[19] Churchill, who describes the implications of the "blood quantum" as "arithmetical genocide," writes,

> The thinking is simple. As the historian Patricia Nelson Limerick frames it: "Set the blood quantum at one-quarter, hold to it as a rigid definition of Indians, let intermarriage proceed as it has for centuries, and eventually Indians will be defined out of existence." Bearing out the validity of Jaimes' and Limerick's observations is the fact that, in 1900, about half of all Indians in this country were "full-bloods." By 1990, the population had shrunk to about twenty percent. . . . A third of all Indians are at the quarter-blood cut-off point. Cherokee demographer Russell Thornton estimates

that, given continued imposition of purely recial definitions, Native America as a whole will have disappeared by the year 2080.[20]

Cultural identity, under such circumstances, is not a matter of "identity politics" but a condition of survival, and its implications may be grasped only by reference to structures of power. There is a world of difference between a "Confucian identity," promoted by states and capital, and intended to carve out a place in a global structure of political and economic power, and an indigenous identity that may be essential to survival as a social and cultural identity against the depredations of power. Postmodern/postcolonial criticism, especially in the United States, has not only been insensitive to such differences in its unqualified affirmation of "hybridity and heterogeneity," but, as the quotation from Brydon above suggests, quite intolerant of any efforts to "construct" the past differently than is allowable to "postcolonial critics"; in fact, it is difficult to see how Brydon's "join up or shut up attitude" differs in any significant sense from that of colonialist attitudes toward indigenous peoples.[21]

What renders indigenous ideology significant, however, is not what it has to reveal about postmodern/postcolonial criticism. Its intellectual and political significance rests elsewhere: in its claims to a different historicity that challenges not just postcolonial denials of collective identity, but the structure of power that contains it. To criticize indigenous ideology for its reification of culture is to give it at best an incomplete reading. It also disguises the complexity of what indigenous authors have to say about the relationship between culture and history, which is considerably more radical ideologically than is suggested by its apparent culturalism.

Cultural Identity/Historical Trajectory

One of the celebrated conflicts in U.S. letters in recent years is that between the Chinese-American writers Frank Chin and Maxine Hong Kingston. Following the publication of Kingston's *Woman Warrior* in 1976, Chin launched an attack on the book for its misrepresentation of Chineseness. The attacks continue to this day, but have been broadened now to include other prominent Chinese-American writers such as Amy Tan and David Hwang. Chin has accused all of these authors of stereotyping Chinese culture and distorting its realities by adopting what he takes to be a "missionary" view of Chinese society.[22]

Chin's attacks on these authors have been ascribed to his misogynistic attitudes, and envy at their success. Whether or not there is any merit to such charges, his own refusal to bring any kind of subtlety to his criticisms has not helped his cause. His insistence that his is the only viable and authentically "Chinese" position has further isolated him, and, unfortunately, obviated the need for elaborating on his critique which, I feel, has much to say about the problem of history in a minority group's construction of its ethnicity.[23]

At the heart of this particular controversy is Kingston's (mis-)use of Chinese legends and the liberties she took with the interpretation of Chinese characters (namely, the association of the character for woman with the character for slave) in *Woman Warrior*. Kingston has conceded the liberties she took, but has explained them in terms of literary license. Chin has refused to accept this excuse. Legends, to him, represent cultural truths that are not to be tampered with; Kingston's distortions of Chinese legends were all the more serious because, at the insistence of the publisher, she consented to having *Woman Warrior* classified as autobiography, rather than fiction as originally intended, which further endowed her distortions with the status of truth. She thus played into the hands of the dominant society's stereotypes of Chineseness.

Kingston herself has expressed regrets that *Woman Warrior* was indeed received as a description of Chinese society, contributing to the image of an exotic China. This may have something to tell us about the plight of minority literature, but it will not do to ascribe it just to the parochialism of the dominant society, as Frederick Buell has suggested recently.[24] The problem with Kingston's representation of Chineseness may lie not in the distortions of Chinese legends or characters (although these are certainly problems), but in the manner in which the relationship to the past is represented in the *Woman Warrior*. A comparison with Chin's representation of this relationship may lend us a clue. Chin's own work engages in a stereotyping of Chineseness by associating it with certain primordial characteristics; indeed it is arguable that Chin's notion of the cultural endowment of Chinese in his formal statements is one-dimensional in contrast to that of Kingston who perceives in Chinese culture the location both for oppression and the struggle against it, as personified in the woman warrior.[25] Nevertheless, in his fiction, Chin presents a relationship to the past that resists appropriation into the image of an exotic China. Why one representation should lend itself to appropriation while the other should resist it is an important question that has been sidestepped in the whole controversy.

The part history plays in mediating the Chinese-American relationship to the Chinese past is crucial, I think, to understanding the difference. While complex, Kingston's representation of the past relegates it to a Chinese space, which then haunts the Chinese-American as burden or promise, but in either case as a legacy from a different time and place ("haunts" in an almost literal sense, as she uses the metaphor of "ghosts" to depict the presence of the past in the present). Chin in his fiction is relatively unconcerned with Chinese culture—except in relationship to the Chinese-American; it may be suggested even that he substitutes the culture of the Chinese-American as he understands it for Chinese culture. The relationship of Chinese-American to Chinese culture in his representation is a relationship both of sameness and difference, mediated by a history that is grounded in a U.S., not a Chinese, temporality. The difference between the two representations is the difference between Chinese culture as a past legacy that continues to haunt the American Chinese, versus Chinese culture as a source of struggle to define a Chinese-American identity that defies "death by assimilation" while reaffirming its irreducible Americanness. In this latter case, the past serves not merely as legacy to be left behind as the ghosts of China themselves eventually recede to invisibility. Rather, it is a fundamental moment in the creation of a Chinese-American history even as that history is distanced from its sources in China. What makes Chin's version resistant to exoticism, as well as to assimilation, I think, is its claim to a Chinese-American historicity that derives its trajectory from the reworking of past legacy within an American topography, that makes it as American as any other history; but at the same time proclaims a historicity that is different from, and challenges, American history as represented in dominant historiography—one that has written the Chinese-American out of history, and has denied the Americanness of the Chinese-American in doing so. Also, in this representation, we might note, there is a shift of emphasis (in spite of Chin's own longings) from cultural legacy that resists history, to a historical legacy that rephrases the question of cultural identity in terms of its historicity.[26]

Despite his insistence on his being the only "real" Chinese around, it is arguable, therefore, that Chin is the most "American" of all the Chinese-American writers, and it is his alternative vision of being American, rather than his insistence on his Chineseness, that endows his work with a radicalism that resists appropriation. The complexity of Chin's notion of Chineseness may be gleaned from the following passage from his novel, *Donald Duk*:

> A hundred years ago, all the Chinatowns in America were Cantonese. They spoke Cantonese. The only Chinese Donald has any ears for is Cantonese. Donald does not like the history teacher, Mr. Meanwright. Mr. Meanwright likes to prove he knows more about Chinese than Donald Duk. Donald doesn't care. He knows nothing about China. He does not speak Mandarin. He does not care a lot about Chinatown either, but when Mr. Meanwright talks about Chinatown, Donald Duk's muscles all tighten up, and he wants Mr. Meanwright to shut up.[27]

It is Chinatown culture that is Chinese-American culture, and while Chin has taken liberties with representing this culture as a metonym for Chinese culture as a whole, it is Chinese-American culture that has been his major preoccupation. Early on in his career, he acknowledged not only that Chinese-Americans were not recognized as "real" Chinese by those from China, but complained about the confusion of Chinese-American with Chinese culture.[28] Interestingly from our present vantage point, the happy "in-between land" of postcolonialism appeared at the time as "no man's land." He and Jeffrey Chan wrote of the concept of "dual personality" (the unblendable "blending of east and west") that pervaded studies of Chinese-Americans at the time:

> The concept of the dual personality successfully deprives the Chinese-American of all authority over language and thus a means of codifying, communicating, and legitimizing his experience. Because he is a foreigner, English is not his native tongue.

Because he was born in the U.S., Chinese is not his native tongue. Chinese from China, "real Chinese," make the Chinese-American aware of his lack of authority over Chinese, and the white American doesn't recognize the Chinese-American's brand of English as a language, even a minority language, but as faulty English, an "accent." The notion of an organic, whole identity, a personality not explicable in either the terms of China or white America . . . has been precluded by the concept of the dual personality . . . the denial of language is the denial of culture.[29]

The realization of just such a personality, that is not a hybrid of two cultures but a product of historical experience, emerges then as the goal (this may be the reason that Chin consistently uses the derogatory term, "Chinaman," to describe his characters, turning the tables on racist usage). The grounds of the experience are very much American, but to resist assimilation the experience must draw upon the Chinese past, the authenticity of which then becomes crucial to the plausibility of a Chinese-American identity. An underlying theme of a novel such as *Donald Duk* (as well as Chin's other writings) is the erasure of Chinese from American history (literally absent from the photograph at Promontory Summit, Utah, where the Union Pacific met the Central Pacific, after Chinese workers had done so much to build the railroad from Sacramento). The goal is to restore that history, but as Chinese, not as shadows of white society:

> "I think Donald Duk may be the very last American-born Chinese-American boy to believe you have to give up being Chinese to be an American," Dad says. "These new immigrants prove that. They were originally Cantonese, and did not want to be Chinese. When China conquered the south, these people went further south, into Vietnam, Laos, Cambodia, Thailand. They learned French. Now they're learning English. They still speak their Cantonese, their Chinese, their Viet or Lao or Cambodian, and French. Instead of giving anything up, they add on. They're including America in everything else they know. And that makes them stronger than any of the American-born, like me, who had folks who worked hard to know absolutely nothing about China, who believed that if all they knew was 100 percent American-made in the USA Yankee know howdy doodle dandy, people would not mistake them for Chinese."[30]

In *Donald Duk*, legendary Chinese heroes appear as railroad foremen, and the hundred-and-eight outlaws of the Chinese novel, *Water Margin*, offer their aid in the semblance of "the ghost riders in the sky."

The historicity of identity does not make it any the less whole, nor does the constructedness of the past make it any the less significant in shaping history. Each generation may rewrite history, but it does so under conditions where it receives as its historical endowment previous generations' constructions of the past. For the marginalized and oppressed in particular, whose histories have been erased by power, it becomes all the more important to recapture or remake the past in their efforts to render themselves visible historically, as the very struggle to become visible presupposes a historical identity. In the face of a "historiographic colonialism" that denies them their historicity, capturing the truth of history, of oppression and the resistance to it, is a fundamental task that for its accomplishment requires constant reference to the precolonial past.[31] But it is also the case that those who are engaged in a struggle for identity can least afford to dehistoricize or reify the past, for the struggle is always the struggle for the present, and must address not just the legacy of the past but also problems of the present. Cultural identity itself, then, is a terrain of the very struggles that it inspires. Whether it is reified, hybridized or historicized, the meaning to be attached to alternative constructions of cultural identity is inseparable from the totality of the struggle that provides its context. The Confucian revival, Kingston's feminist construction of China, and Chin's use of popular religious and literary traditions all construct Chineseness differently, but also with different implications for the relationship between culture and history. They also imply different relationships to social and political power.

Chin's use of the past provides a cogent illustration that cultural construction is not a "zero-sum" process (either Chinese or American) or a matter of hybridity or in-betweenness (neither Chinese nor American), but a historical process of production in which the dialectical interaction between past legacy and present circumstances produces cultural identities that are no less integrated for being historical, that derive their trajectories of change from the accretion of experiences which may be shaped by the legacies of the past but also transform the meaning of the latter, and in which local experience interacts with structural context to produce at once forces of difference and unity. Cultural essentialism does not consist merely of defining cultural essences, but requires the isolation of culture from history, so that those essences come to serve as abstract markers which have little to do with the realities of cultural identity. Notions of cultural purity and hybridity alike, ironically, presuppose a cultural essentialism; from a perspective that recognizes the historicity of culture, the question of essentialism becomes quite irrelevant. In this sense, assertions of hybridity or in-betweenness as well as claims to cultural purity are equally culturalist, the one because it rejects the spatiality and temporality of culture, the other because it renders into spatial differences what are but the temporal complexities of the relationship between the past and the present. The historicization of culture against such culturalism is also quite radical in its consequences, in that it opens the way to an insistence on different histories which, unlike the insistence on different cultural spaces or spaces in between, are not to be contained within a cultural pluralism, let alone assumptions of cultural unity; hence the resistance of a historicized insistence on culture to appropriation.

Historicizing Chinese culture, Chin's account seeks also to indigenize it in the topography of a new location for history, where it challenges the claims of the dominant culture. But its own claims are those of one group of settlers against other settlers; an assertion that the one group of settlers has the same claims on history as another. What, if any, alternative vision of the future is embedded in this alternative history remains unclear.

This is where the radicalism of indigenous ideology comes in. If Chin indigenizes Chineseness in a new historical location, indigenous ideology historicizes indigenism in the face of a new historical situation, but without conceding its topographical claims, and an alternative way of life embedded in that topography. Not only does it insist on a different history, in other words, but it does so through a repudiation of the very idea of history promoted by the settlers as it refuses to distinguish temporality from spatiality. I suggested above that readings of indigenous ideology that ascribe to it a simple cultural essentialism may not be sufficient. Contrary to critics wedded to ideas of "heterogeneity and hybridity," who see in every affirmation of cultural identity an ahistorical cultural essentialism, indigenous voices are quite open to change; what they insist on is not cultural purity or persistence, but the preservation of a particular historical trajectory of their own. In this case, however, the trajectory is one that is grounded in the topography much more intimately. And it is one that is at odds with the notions of temporality that guide the histories of the settlers.[32]

Silko might be echoing Chin when she writes,

> The people nowadays have an idea about the ceremonies. They think the ceremonies must be performed exactly as they have always been done. . . . But long ago when the people were given these ceremonies, the changing began . . . if only in the different voices from generation to generation, singing the chants. You see, in many ways, the ceremonies have always been changing. . . . At one time, the ceremonies as they had been performed were enough for the way the world was then. But after the white people came, elements in this world began to shift; and it became necessary to create new ceremonies. . . . Things which don't shift and grow are dead things. They are things the witchery people want. That's what the witchery is counting on: that we will cling to the ceremonies the way they were, and then their power will triumph, and the people will be no more.[33]

Change is necessary, but it is to be contained within the history of the ceremonies. And, in this case, the ceremonies are inseparable from the land. Silko's narrative is a confirmation of the coexistence of the timeless and the temporal; a sensibility of timeless validity, and the changes that are necessary to sustain that sensibility. The Indian is responsible for both. It was Indian witchcraft that "invented" the whites, who threaten the eternally valid. While the Indian "invention" of the whites points to the Indians' responsibility for their own fate (rather than blaming the whites for it), it also reverses the historiographical relationship by making whites into creatures of a quintessentially Indian history.[34] Only by overcoming witchcraft can the Indian once again restore the sensibility that is necessary to the sustenance of life.

Indigenism thus conceived is both a legacy and a project (as is ethnicity, when viewed in this perspective). Arguing against the "determinism" of culturalism, Jean-Paul Sartre wrote in *Search for a Method* that,

The project, as the subjective surpassing of objectivity toward objectivity, and stretched between the objective conditions of the environment and the objective structures of the field of possibles, represents *in itself* the moving unity of subjectivity and objectivity, those cardinal determinants of activity. The subjective appears then as a necessary moment in the objective process. . . . Only the project, as a mediation between two moments of objectivity, can account for history; that is, for human *creativity*.[35]

The project, Sartre noted, contains a "double simultaneous relationship. In relation to the given, the *praxis* is negativity; but what is always involved is the negation of a negation. In relation to the object aimed at, *praxis* is positivity, but this positivity opens unto the 'non-existent,' to what *has not yet* been."[36]

To an indigenist such as Ward Churchill, indigenism is a "negation of the negation," which also affirms "that which is most alive and promising for the future of the Indian people."[37] By indigenism, Churchill writes,

I mean that I am one who not only takes the rights of indigenous peoples as the highest priority of my political life, but who draws upon the traditions—the bodies of knowledge and corresponding codes of values—evolved over many thousands of years by native peoples the world over. This is the basis upon which I not only advance critiques of, but conceptualize alternatives to the present social, political, economic and philosophical status quo. In turn, this gives shape not only to the sorts of goals and objectives I pursue, but the kinds of strategy and tactics I advocate, the variety of struggles I tend to support, the nature of alliances I'm inclined to enter into, and so on.[38]

The point of departure for this indigenism is the present, and its goal is not to restore a bygone past, but to draw upon the past to create a new future (which also explains why Churchill uses the term, "Indian," fully aware of its colonial origins, as does Frank Chin with "Chinaman" and Trask with "Hawaiian"). In working out the scope of indigenism, moreover, Churchill also strives to account for challenges that are very contemporary, such as problems of class, sexism and homophobia.[39]

Likewise, Annette Jaimes describes indigenism as a "reworking of . . . concepts which are basic to an American Indian identity on the threshold of the twenty-first century," and Trask, like most indigenous writers, links the struggles for Hawaiian independence to the struggles of oppressed people around the world.[40] The same is true of writers of the Pacific, such as Albert Wendt and Epeli Hau'ofa, who have affirmed that the effort to recapture a native identity and history may proceed only by struggles against colonialism that nevertheless recognize the historical transformations wrought by colonialism.[41] The effort to overcome Eurocentrism and colonialism does not require denial of an immediate past of which EuroAmerican colonialism was an integral part but presupposes an identity through a history of which EuroAmerican domination was very much a reality.[42]

What is of fundamental significance here (and distinguishes these arguments from postcolonialism), however, is a recognition that the common history which united the colonizer and the colonized was also a history of division. What the colonizer may have experienced as unification the colonized experienced as an oppressive denial of native identity. The insistence on a separate historicity is driven by this sense of division: to liberate native history from "historiographic colonialism," it is necessary not just to revive memories of a precolonial past, but to write the ways in which the precolonial past was suppressed, as well as the ways in which it informed past struggles against colonialism. As the Australian aboriginal writer Mudrooroo Narogin puts it:

> It is no use declaring, as some Aborigines do declare, that the past is over and should be forgotten, when that past is only of two hundred years duration. It is far too early for the Aboriginal people to put aside that past and the effects of that past. Aboriginal people must come to realise that many of their problems are based on a past which still lives within them. If this is not acknowledged, then the self-destructive and community-destructive acts which continue to occur will be seen as only resulting from unemployment, bad housing, or ill-health, and once these are removed everything will be fine.[43]

Mudrooroo's comments show that the struggle over history is no longer just a struggle between colonizer and colonized, but among the colonized themselves; between those who would forget the immediate past, and those who insist on remembering.[44] Indigenism's insistence on remembering the immediate past distinguishes it from reifications of precolonial cultural markers, and renders it fundamentally threatening to the status quo, even when that status quo is redefined in terms of cultural diversity and difference; as Gillian Cowlishaw writes, "Forty thousand years of history and spiritual links with the land gain a more sympathetic hearing than accusations of past injustices and displaying of old wounds received in the struggle for equality."[45] The reasons are not very complex: the reification of the precolonial past may be accommodated within a cultural pluralism much more easily than the insistence on the construction of alternative futures, that draw not only on primordial traditions but also of the struggles of the immediate past. The difference is the difference between a multiculturalism that enables assimilation without challenge to the social, political and economic status quo, and a multihistoricalism that questions the totality of existing relations, and the future of the history that legitimizes them.

The indigenous historical challenge, moreover, is not "metaphorical" but deeply material. The insistence on a special relationship to the land as the basis for indigenous identity is not merely spiritual, an affirmation of an ecological sensibility, but also calls for a transformation of the spatial arrangements of colonialism or postcolonialism. Indigenism, in other words, challenges not just relations between different ethnicities, but the system of economic relations that provide the ultimate context for social and political relationships: capitalist or state socialist. In this challenge also lies the possibilities for opening up indigenism to other radical advocacies of social change. Instead of a multiculturalism that presupposes coexistence of multiple ethnicities identified by ahistorical cultural markers, which elevates ethnicity to a determining principle of social life without saying much about the political and economic system as a whole, the historicity of the indigenous argument permits the design of open-ended projects that promise a return to a genuinely common history once the legacy of the colonial past has been erased—not just ideologically but materially as well.

Concluding Remarks

In his critique of Jocelyn Linnekin's criticisms of the Hawaiian independence movement, Jeffrey Tobin has called for greater attention to context in evaluating political movements and their constructions of native identity. "It is important," he writes, "to distinguish between discourses that naturalize oppression and discourses that naturalize resistance."[46] Similarly, responding to critiques of "essentialism" by James Clifford and Edward Said, Nicholas Thomas writes that,

> what . . . these critiques pass over is the extent to which humanism and essentialism have different meanings and effects in different contexts. Clifford writes as though the problem were merely intellectual: difference and hybridity are more appropriate analytically to the contemporary scene of global cultural transposition than claims about human sameness or bounded types. I would agree, but this does not bear upon the uses that essentialist discourses may have for people whose projects involve mobilization rather than analysis. Said might be able to argue that nativism as a political programme or government ideology has been largely pernicious, but nativist consciousness cannot be deemed undesirable merely because it is ahistorical and uncritically reproduces colonial stereotypes. The main problem is not that this imposes academic (and arguably ethnocentric) standards on non-academic and non-Western representations, but that it paradoxically essentializes nativism by taking its politics to be uniform.[47]

Thomas also recognizes that "nativist-primitivist idealizations can only be productive . . . if they are complemented by here-and-now concerns, and articulated with histories that do not merely recapitulate the 'imperialist nostalgia' of the fatal-impact narrative."[48]

The insistence of the postcolonial argument on history, ironically, conceals a deeply ahistorical reluctance to distinguish anything but the local, embedded in an ideology of "heterogeneity and hybridity." It is also an argument that undercuts the ability to resist oppression except on the level of "identity politics." It is ironic that the insistence on the inventedness and the constructedness of the past should not be accompanied by a more acute self-awareness of the inventions of postcolonialism itself, but instead should be disguised, as in the case of Linnekin, by claims to a disinterested search for truth. Viewed from these perspectives, postcolonialism itself appears as a project among competing projects, that reifies into the eternal condition of humanity the endowments of a limited group.[49] In this case, however, the project is one without a future, that condemns everyone without distinction to existence in ethnic margins—including those in the margins whose efforts to overcome their marginality are subject to immediate condemnation.

The call for greater attention to political context in evaluations of identity construction is common-sensical to the point of being trivial. Common sense, unfortunately, is never transparent, but is loaded with ideological assumptions. The postmodern/postcolonial questioning of identity is itself quite commonsensical; it is when it is generalized and universalized to the point where it will brook no deviation from its own assumptions that it becomes intellectually counterproductive, and is driven into a political dead-end that extinguishes the possibility of political alternatives. Sharpened awareness of the constructedness of identity or of history may have rendered political and moral choice more complex and difficult; it has not eliminated the necessity of choice. Postmodernism may be an ideology of defeat, as Terry Eagleton suggests, or a "matter of class," as Aijaz Ahmad puts it; in either case, it reifies into a general analytical or political principle what may be but a condition of our times.[50]

In a recent essay, I suggested that indigenism may be of paradigmatic significance in contemporary politics globally.[51] This is not to suggest that indigenism provides a ready-made utopia, as in New Age constructions of indigenism. Indigenous proponents of indigenism are quite aware of the problems of native societies: that they have been disorganized by centuries of colonialism and reorganized in accordance with the political and cultural prerogatives of colonialism, which has led to a social and political disintegration, as well as a nearly total incoherence of native identity, that will take enormous effort to overcome; that their cultures continue to be cannibalized by tourist industries and New Age cultural consumerism, often with the complicity of the native peoples themselves; and that the dream of recovering the land, crucial both to material and spiritual existence, may be just that, a dream.[52] It may be out of this deep sense of the historical destruction of their societies that indigenous writers are insistent on recovering the process of history "as it really was"—for them. As indigenous people were written out of history for being "unhistorical," it becomes all the more necessary to document meticulously the process whereby they were erased from history in order to recover historicity.[53]

The insistence on a separate history is itself not without problems, especially these days when tendencies to the ethnicization or even the biologization of knowledge threatens not only a common understanding of the world, but the possibility of common political projects as well. While the cannibalization of indigenous cultures (by tourist or anthropologist) is very real, the fact remains that its very reality divides indigenous from non-indigenous projects; especially when issues of identity are framed around spiritualities that are accessible only to those on the inside.

Nevertheless, it is arguable that indigenism is as much a utopian aspiration that seeks to contain and overcome these problems as it is an expression of native sensibilities. The same utopianism—history as project—also offers possibilities of common struggles and aspirations. Indigenous ideology, while insistent on a separate history, also finds common ground with other histories in the problems it addresses. What makes it particularly pertinent in our day are the questions it raises about the whole project of development, capitalist or socialist; while some indigenous writers have pointed to common features between socialism and indigenism, this is a socialism that is far removed from the state socialisms as we have known them, grounded in the reassertion of community.[54] The indigenous reaffirmation of a special relationship to the land as the basis of a new ecological sensibility obviously resonates with growing ecological consciousness worldwide. The indigenous reassertions of ties to authentic pasts is not as divisive as it may seem, but may contain a lesson that is broadly relevant. If the past is constructed, it is constructed at all times, and ties to the past require an ongoing dialogue between present and past constructions; except in linear conceptions of history where the past, once past, is irrelevant except as abstract moral or political lesson. The repudiation of linear temporality in indigenous ideology suggests that the past is never really past, but offers "stories" that may be required to resolve problems of the present, even as they are changed to answer present needs.[55] The notion of dialogue between past and present also suggests the possibility of dialogue across present-day spaces, among indigenous peoples and with the nonindigenous as well, in which lies the possibility of common understanding as well as common historical projects.

If indigenous ideology claims as its basis an indigenous sensibility, it also opens up to others through problems that cut across any ethnically defined identity, those of class and gender oppression in particular. Just as local political movements in our day have had to reconsider such problems as class, gender and ethnicity in light of ecological and community needs, indigenous ideology has had to reconsider the meaning of indigenism in light of those problems. Surely such movements may learn from, and cross-fertilize, one another while respecting their different identities. If indigenism does have paradigmatic significance, it is because it shares with other political movements in our days both common problems, and the necessity of common action to resolve those problems.

I cannot think of a better way of concluding this discussion, and illustrating what I have just said, than to quote the eloquent words of a leader of a contemporary movement for indigenous self-assertion that has caught the attention of many in these bleak political times:

> Not everyone listens to the voices of hopelessness and resignation. Not everyone has jumped onto the bandwagon of despair. Most people continue on; they cannot hear

the voice of the powerful and the fainthearted as they are deafened by the cry and the blood that death and misery shout in their ears. But in moments of rest, they hear another voice, not the one that comes from above, but rather the one that comes with the wind from below, and is born in the heart of the indigenous people of the mountains, a voice that speaks of justice and liberty, a voice that speaks of socialism, a voice that speaks of hope … the only hope in this earthly world. And the very oldest among the people in the villages tell of a man named Zapata who rose up for his own people and in a voice more like a song than a shout, said, "Land and Liberty!"

And these old folks say that Zapata is not dead, that he is going to return. And the oldest of the old also say that the wind and the rain and the sun tell the campesinos when they should prepare the soil, when they should plant, and when they should harvest. They say that hope also must be planted and harvested. And the old people say that now the wind, the rain, and the sun are talking to the earth in a new way, and that the poor should not continue to harvest death, now it is time to harvest rebellion. So say the old people. The powerful don't listen, the words don't reach them, as they are made deaf by the witchery that the imperialists shout in their ears. "Zapata," repeat the youth of the poor, "Zapata" insists the wind, the wind from below, our wind.[56]

The choices may be complex, but they are ours to make.

Notes

This paper was presented originally as a public lecture and keynote address for the Annual Graduate Student Conference at the Humanities Institute at Stony Brook, November 3, 1995. I would like to thank the Institute for the invitation, and the participants in the lecture for their enthusiastic and stimulating input. I would also like to thank Ward Churchill for his comments and support.

1. Karl Marx, *The 18th Brumaire of Louis Bonaparte* (New York: International Publishers, 1967), p.15.

2. Homi Bhabha, "The Postcolonial and the Postmodern: The Question of Agency," in Bhabha, *The Location of Culture* (London: Routledge, 1994):171–197, p.172.

3. *Ceremony* (New York: Penguin Books, 1977), p.2.

4. "From a Native Daughter," in Haunani-Kay Trask, *From a Native Daughter: Colonialism and Sovereignty in Hawaii* (Monroe, ME: Common Courage Press, 1993):147–159. *The Indigenous Voice: Visions and Realities*, ed. by Roger Moody (Utrecht, The Netherlands: International Books, 1993), offers the most comprehensive selection I am aware of of indigenous problems and perspectives. See also Ward Churchill, "A Little Matter of Genocide: Sam Gill's *Mother Earth*, Colonialism and the Expropriation of Indigenous Spiritual Tradition in Academia," in Ward Churchill, *Fantasies of the Master Race: Literature, Cinema and the Colonization of American Indians*, ed. by M. Annette Jaimes (Monroe, ME: Common Courage Press, 1992):187–213; Albert Wendt, "Novelists, Historians and the Art of Remembering," in Antony Hooper, et. al. (eds), *Class and Culture in the South Pacific* (Auckland, N.Z. and Suva, Fiji: Centre for Pacific Studies of the University of Auckland in collaboration with the Institute of Pacific Studies, The University of the South Pacific,

1987):78–91; Epeli Hau'ofa, "OUR SEA OF ISLANDS," in *A New Oceania: Rediscovering Our Sea of Islands* (Suva, Fiji: School of Social and Economic Development, The University of the South Pacific, 1993):2–16; and Alan Duff, *Once Were Warriors*, (Honolulu: University of Hawaii Press, 1990).

5. Quoted in Ward Churchill, "I Am Indigenist: Notes on the Ideology of the Fourth World," in Ward Churchill, *Struggle for the Land: Indigenous Resistance to Genocide, Ecocide and Expropriation in Contemporary North America* (Monroe, ME: Common Courage Press, 1993):403–451.

6. Quoted in Ibid., p.411.

7. M. Annette Jaimes, "Native American Identity and Survival: Indigenism and Environmental Ethics," in Michael K. Green (ed), *Issues in Native American Identity* (Lang, 1994).

8. "Naming Our Destiny," in Ward Churchill, *Indians Are Us? Culture and Genocide in Native North America* (Monroe, ME: Common Courage Press, 1994):291–357.

9. Johannes Fabian, *Time and the Other: How Anthropology Makes Its Object* (New York: Columbia University Press, 1983).

10. Nicholas Thomas, *Colonialism's Culture: Anthropology, Travel and Government* (Princeton, NJ: Princeton University Press, 1994), p.176.

11. "The Myth of Authenticity," in Chris Tiffin and Alan Lawson (eds), *De-Scribing Empire: Post-Colonialism and Textuality* (London: Routledge, 1994):70–85. The title suggests, in spite of Griffiths' disclaimer, that what he says in this passage would apply to aboriginal claims as well, and not just to the dominant discourse. An earlier work leaves no doubt that, under postcolonial conditions, "the demand for a new or wholly recovered precolonial reality," while "perfectly comprehensible . . . cannot be achieved," because "postcolonial culture is inevitably a hybridized phenomenon involving a dialectical relationship between the 'grafted' European cultural systems and an indigenous ontology, with its impulse to create or recreate an independent local identity." In Bill Ashcroft, Gareth Griffiths and Helen Tiffin (eds), *The Empire Writes Back: Theory and Practice in Post-colonial Literatures* (London: Routledge, 1989), p.195

12. Diana Brydon, "The White Inuit Speaks: Contamination as Literary Strategy," in Bill Ashcroft, Gareth Griffiths and Helen Tiffin (eds), *The post-colonial studies reader* (London: Routledge, 1995):136–142. Originally published in Ian Adam and Helen Tiffin (eds), *Past the Last Post: Theorizing Post-Colonialism and Post-Modernism* (New York: Harvester Wheatsheaf, 1991). Brydon's arguments are largely directed at Linda Hutcheon, who is much more sympathetic toward indigenous claims against the "settlers." See her, "Circling the Downspout of Empire," in *The post-colonial studies reader*, pp.130–135. What Brydon has to say reveals more cogently than Griffiths that what postcolonial critics have to say on the subject of indigenism could be said easily without the aid of a "postcolonial consciousness." Thus, a former Smithsonian historian writes that: "Those who decry the intrusion of the white presence in Indian history are often simply unwilling to recognize that Indian history is, for good or ill, shaped by the white presence, whether physically, in terms of European immigrants, or intellectually, in terms of Western historical or anthropological theories." Wilcomb E. Washburn, "Distinguishing History from Moral Philosophy and Public Advocacy," in Calvin Martin (ed), *The American Indian and the Problem of History* (New York: Oxford University Press, 1987):91–97.

13. Thomas, p.172. This is not to say that such discussions do not exist. Thomas has in mind progressive cultural critics. As noted in the last footnote above, there is no shortage

of criticisms of indigenous ideology, albeit without the marker of "postcoloniality." For a more sympathetic criticism that points out the origin in EuroAmerican power and the EuroAmerican mapping of the world of the concept of "Indianness" itself, see Robert F. Berkhofer, "Cultural Pluralism versus Ethnocentrism in the New Indian History," in *The American Indian and the Problem of History*, pp.35–45.

14. Linnekin, "defining tradition: variations on the Hawaiian identity," *American Ethnologist*, 10 (1983):241–252. For a discussion of the case, and the controversy it provoked between Linnekin and Haunani-Kay Trask, see Jeffrey Tobin, "Cultural Construction and Native Nationalism: Report from the Hawaiian Front," in Rob Wilson and Arif Dirlik (eds), *Asia/Pacific as Space of Cultural Construction*, special issue of *boundary 2*, 21,1(Spring 1994): 111–133.

15. See also Thomas, Chapter 1, for a discussion of this problem. In the United States, the New Age craze drew extensively on "tribal cultures" for its lore.

16. For further discussion, see Arif Dirlik, "Confucius in the Borderlands: Global Capitalism and the Reinvention of Confucianism," *boundary 2*. For the role of the state in this revival, see Allen Chun, "An Oriental Orientalism: The Paradox of Tradition and Modernity in Nationalist Taiwan," *History and Anthropology*, 9,1(1994):1–29.

17. Samuel P. Huntington, "The Clash of Civilizations?" *Foreign Affairs* 72,3 (1993):22–49.

18. Ward Churchill, "Radioactive Colonization: Hidden Holocaust in Native North America," in Churchill, *Struggle for the Land*, pp.261–328. Where Indians refuse the use of reservations as dumping grounds, the state uses its power "to disestablish" the reservations, as is the case most recently with the Yankton Reservation in South Dakota. See *Indian Country Today*, August 3, 1995. "Radioactive colonization" is also an ongoing threat in the South Pacific.

19. M. Annette Jaimes, "Some Kind of Indian: On Race, Eugenics, and Mixed Bloods," in Naomi Zack (ed), *American Mixed Race: The Culture of Microdiversity* (Boston: Rowman and Little, 1993):133–153, p.137.

20. Churchill, "Nobody's Pet Poodle," in Ward Churchill, *Indians Are Us?*, pp.89–113, pp.92–93 for the quotation.

21. In case this seems like an exceptional case, we may take note here of the special issue of *Public Culture* devoted to the critique of Aijaz Ahmad's *In Theory*, which also came under severe attack for its "transgressions" against postmodern/postcolonial criticism. Rather than address the issues raised by *In Theory*, most contributors to that special issue engaged in *ad hominem* attacks on Ahmad. Especially noteworthy are the red-baiting comments by Peter van der Veer and the religious bigotry displayed by Marjorie Levinson. *Public Culture* 6,1 (1993).

22. Frank Chin, "Come All Ye Asian American Writers of the Real and the Fake," Introduction to Jeffrey Paul Chan, Frank Chin, Lawson Fusao Inada and Shawn Wong (eds), *The Big AIIIEEEEE! An Anthology of Chinese American and Japanese American Literature* (New York: Meridian, 1991):1–92. All the above named authors were excluded from this collection.

23. For a discussion of these various issues, see, Edward Iwata, "Word Warriors," *The Los Angeles Times* (June 24, 1990), section E, pp.1, 9.

24. Frederick Buell, *National Culture and the New Global System* (Baltimore: The Johns Hopkins University Press, 1994), pp. 180–181.

25. Chin, "Come All Ye Asian American Writers of the Real and the Fake," *passim*.

26. I do not wish to overlook here the different experiences of oppression that inform the works of the two authors. Chin is concerned almost exclusively with the oppression of Chinese in general, and the "feminization" in the process of Chinese men in particular. Kingston is concerned with the "double" oppression of Chinese women, as Chinese and women, the latter including oppression sanctified by Chinese cultural tradition. While Chin is right to point out that Kingston's portrayal of Chinese tradition as relentlessly oppressive of women plays into the hands of EuroAmerican stereotypes of China, he nevertheless goes overboard in presenting a portrayal himself of idyllic gender relations in Chinese history. All I would like to say on this issue here is that gender relations, too, must be rescued from cultural stereotyping, and placed within historical context, as has been argued by writers on Third World gender relations since the publication of *Woman Warrior*.

27. Frank Chin, *Donald Duk* (Minneapolis, MN: Coffee House Press, 1991), p.34.

28. See the interview in Victor G. Nee and Brett deBary Nee, *Longtime Californ': A Documentary Study of an American Chinatown* (New York: Pantheon, 1973), p.359, for the interview. For the confusion of Chinese-Americans with Chinese, which ignores "the obvious cultural differences," see, Frank Chin and Jeffery Paul Chan, "Racist Love," in Richard Kostelanetz (ed), *Seeing Through Shuck* (New York: Ballantine Books, 1972):65–79. This article, incidentally, should put to rest the notion that Chin's recent criticisms of Chinese-American writers are motivated by envy, because he and Chan raise here all the questions that have been brought up again in recent years. At the time, Chin was the only well-known Chinese-American writer.

29. "Racist Love," p.76.

30. *Donald Duk*, p.41.

31. Calvin Martin, "The Metaphysics of Writing Indian-White History," in *The American Indian and the Problem of History*, pp.27–34.

32. The very notion of "first nations," which is especially common in Canada and Australia, in this sense, represents a compromise, since it makes it possible to speak of a second, third, etc., converting a fundamental difference into an ordinal one. Against this perversion, however, we might note a historicization, as in the case of Annette Jaimes, who proclaims that Indian tribes have been open all along to outsiders, as shown in marriage practices, etc., which skirts around the issue of "openness" while making the quite valid point that racial differences were not the most important criteria of difference.

33. *The Ceremony*, p.126.

34. Ibid., p.135. This appropriation of whites for Indian history seems to have an interesting parallel among Australian aborigines, who have appropriated white social scientists for their own "traditions." Says one, "I am thrilled at the knowledge that has come through archeologists and scientists about the Aborigines. To me, it is as though the ancients are trying to relay a message not only to the Aboriginal race, but to the human race." Quoted in Robert Ariss, "Writing Black: The Construction of an Aboriginal Discourse," in *Past and Present*:131–146.

35. *Search for a Method*, tr. by Hazel E. Barnes (New York: Vintage, 1968), pp.99, 101.

36. Ibid., p.92.

37. "Nobody's Pet Poodle," p.107.

38. "I Am Indigenist," p.403.

39. Ibid., pp.418–420.

40. M. Annette Jaimes, "Native American Identity and Survival," p.276, and Haunani-Kay Trask, "Hawaii: Colonization and Decolonization," in *Class and Culture in the South Pacific*:154–174.

41. Epeli Hau'ofa, "The Future of Our Past," in Robert C. Kiste and Richard A. Herr (eds), *The Pacific Islands in the Year 2000* (Honolulu: Pacific Islands Studies Program Working Paper Series, 1974) L151–170, and, Albert Wendt, "Towards a New Oceania," in Guy Amirthanayagam (ed), *Writers in the East-West Encounter: New Cultural Beginnings* (London: The Macmillan Press, 1982):202–215.

42. I am paraphrasing here Geoffrey M. White, *Identity Through History: Living Stories in a Solomon Islands Society* (Cambridge: Cambridge University Press, 1991).

43. Mudrooroo Narogin (Colin Johnson), *Writing from the Fringe: A Study of Modern Aboriginal Writing* (Melbourne: Hyland House, 1990), p.25.

44. Klaus Neumann writes that, "these days, Papua New Guineans . . . do not appear overtly interested in being told about the horrors of colonialism, as such accounts potentially belittle today's descendants of yesterday's victims," "'In Order to Win Their Friendship': Renegotiating First Contact," *The Contemporary Pacific*, 6, 1(1994):11–145. Likewise, Deirdre Jordan notes the complaints of adult Aboriginal students in Australia about emphasis on white oppression, "which seems designed to call forth in them responses of hostility and racism and which, they believe causes a crisis of identity," "Aboriginal Identity: Uses of the Past, Problems for the Future?" in Jeremy R. Beckett (ed), *Past and Present: The Construction of Aboriginality* (Canberra: Aboriginal Studies Press, 1994): 109–130, p.119. There are others, needless to say, who would suppress the past for reasons of self-interest.

45. "The Materials for Identity Construction," in Beckett, *Past and Present*: 87–107.

46. Tobin, "Cultural Construction and Native Nationalism," p.131.

47. Thomas, pp.187–188.

48. Ibid., p.189.

49. Frederick Buell, *National Culture and the Global System*, provides an example of the fetishism of hybridity. Buell is intolerant of any argument that suggests the possibility of integrated identity, and the main target of his argument are those who would foreground divisions between oppressor and oppressed.

50. Terry Eagleton, "Where Do Postmodernists Come From?" *Monthly Review*, 47, 3 (1995):59–70, and Aijaz Ahmad, " The Politics of Literary Postcoloniality," *Race and Class*, 36,3 (1995):1–20.

51. Arif Dirlik, "Three Worlds or One, or Many? The Reconfiguration of Global Relations Under Contemporary Capitalism," *Nature, Society and Thought*, 7,1 (1994):19–42.

52. Churchill writes of the "go it alone" approach that he advocates: "I must admit that part of my own insistence upon it often has more to do with forcing concession of the right from those who seek to deny it than it does with putting it into practice." "I Am Indigenist," p.432.

53. See, for example, Ward Churchill, "Bringing the Law Back Home: Application of the Genocide Convention in the United States," in Churchill, *Indians Are Us?*, pp.11–63. The necessity of documentation is closely related to legal efforts to recover or protect treaty rights. It is also interesting that in a volume such as *The American Indian and the Problem of History*, while most of the non-indigenous contributors speak of different temporalities and conceptions of history, the distinguished indigenous scholar Vine Deloria, Jr., stands out for his advocacy of old-fashioned historical documentation.

54. Churchill, "I Am Indigenist," p.409.

55. The rewriting of history implied here is not merely a matter of writing indigenous sensibilities into existing history, but rewriting history in accordance with indigenous sen-

sibility. Lenore Coltheart offers a challenging discussion of the distinction between "history about Aborigines" and "Aboriginal history," in "The Moment of Aboriginal History," in Jeremy Beckett (ed), *Past and Present*, pp.179–189.

56. Subcommandante Marcos, quoted in Alexander Cockburn, "Jerry Garcia and El Sup," *The Nation* (August 28/September 4, 1995), p.192.

About the Book and Author

The essays in this volume tackle a range of issues from cultural self-representation in China to more general problems of reconceptualizing global relationships in response to contemporary changes. Although the new era of global capitalism calls for the remapping of global relations, such remapping must be informed both by a grasp of contemporary structures of economic, political, and cultural power and by memories of earlier radical visions of society. Without these two conditions, Arif Dirlik argues, the current preoccupation with Eurocentrism, ethnic diversity, and multiculturalism distracts from issues of power that dominate global relations and that find expression in murderous ethnic conflicts.

In lieu of multiculturalism, Dirlik offers "multi-historicalism," which presupposes a historically grounded conception of cultural difference, seeks in different histories alternative visions of human society, and stresses divergent historical trajectories against a future colonized presently by an ideology of capital. Arguing that the operations of capital have brought the question of the local to the fore, he points to "indigenism" as a source of paradigms of social relations and relationships to nature, to challenge the voracious developmentalism that undermines local welfare globally.

Arif Dirlik is professor of history at Duke University.

Index

Printed in the United States
711000003B